SANCTIONS, BUSINESS AND HUMAN RIGHTS

Sanctions, Business and Human Rights

Prof. Alena F. Douhan

EDITOR

Clarity Press, Inc.

ISBN: 978-1-963892-24-6
EBOOK ISBN: 978-1-963892-25-3

In-house editor: Diana G. Collier
Book design: Becky Luening

Library of Congress Control Number: 2025940119

Clarity Press, Inc.
2625 Piedmont Rd. NE, Ste. 56
Atlanta, GA 30324, USA
https://www.claritypress.com

Table of Contents

v

....

PART III.
Humanitarian Impact of Unilateral Sanctions
and Business Over-Compliance

Introduction

As we approach the 80th Anniversary of the UN Charter, which sets forth as its *objective "to reaffirm faith in fundamental human rights, in the dignity and worth of the human person,"[1] with* due respect to the request of the Universal Declaration of Human Rights to recognize the *"inherent dignity and the equal and inalienable rights of all members of the human family,"* we all need to uphold these human rights principles as *"the foundation of freedom, justice, and peace in the world."[2]*

The use of unilateral sanctions, the means of their enforcement and over-compliance, and the implementation of the UN Security Council resolutions in the face of unilateral sanctions all raise serious concerns from the point of view of international law, including international human rights and humanitarian law, as well as questions around political and economic decision-making.

Despite the existence of multiple publications focusing on UN Security Council sanctions and on unilateral sanctions, the issues of over-compliance, sanctions enforcement, assessment of the legality and impact of various types of unilateral sanctions, and the access to justice and to remedies appear to have been overlooked. The current state of affairs with regards to unilateral sanctions demonstrates a clear need for a comprehensive analysis and assessment, not only from the perspective of human rights law but also by involving other disciplines, such as political science and economics, as well as other areas of international law itself, such as principles of international law, international trade law, including the WTO law, international air law, international law of the sea, international humanitarian law, the sources of international law, the law of international responsibility,

---

1 Charter of the United Nations, Preamble. https://treaties.un.org/doc/publication/ctc/uncharter.pdf

2 Universal Declaration of Human Rights (UDHR), Preamble. https://www.un.org/en/about-us/universal-declaration-of-human-rights.

international commercial arbitration, international private law and many other areas.

Multiple reports demonstrate that access to justice, to remedies, and to mechanisms of accountability and redress universally recognized as the means of promotion and protection of all human rights, as well as of the rule of law in general, cannot be guaranteed in sanctions environments and sometimes cannot be applied at all. Lawyers, who traditionally play an important role in the promotion and protection of human rights, are affected by unilateral sanctions and subjected to higher risks and responsibility for the circumvention or alleged circumvention of unilateral sanctions regimes. All the above demonstrate an urgent need to identify the international legal norms to be applied by UN organs, states, regional organizations, banks, businesses, humanitarian organizations and other non-governmental actors in the unilateral sanctions' environment.

As the Special Rapporteur on the negative impact of unilateral coercive measures on the enjoyment of human rights I undertook a number of consultations, side events and expert meetings with civil society actors, including businesses, legal professionals, scholars, and non-governmental organizations. I also received multiple submissions throughout the period of 2022–2024, that enabled the development of the Guiding Principles on sanctions, business and human rights[3] and a Commentary[4] thereto.

The Guiding Principles intend to clarify basic rules to be applied by all states as well as regional organizations and businesses, to prevent compliance with unilateral sanctions and over-compliance with both unilateral and UN-imposed sanctions by all actors, to minimize the risk of penalties for business communities in the sanctions' environment, to establish clear frameworks and accountability mechanisms to ensure that sanctions do not unduly impact human rights. The Guiding Principles do not create nor do they intend to create new legal norms. They elaborate on the application of existing treaty or customary legal

---

3 Guiding Principles on Sanctions, Business and Human Rights (2025). https://www.ohchr.org/sites/default/files/documents/issues/ucm/events/international-conf-sanctions-business-hr/gps-sanctions-business-hr.pdf

4 Guiding Principles on Sanctions, Business and Human Rights: Commentary (2025). https://www.ohchr.org/sites/default/files/documents/issues/ucm/commentary-gpssbhr-2025.pdf

norms by states, international organizations and other relevant actors operating within a sanctions' environment.

The International Conference on Sanctions, Business and Human Rights took place in Geneva on November 21–22, 2024, to encourage the discussion of the Guiding Principles and the Commentary thereto at the levels of states, UN experts, humanitarian actors, scholars and legal practitioners,[5] and to address the most sensitive issues in the sphere. The present book compiles contributions of participants of the conference and people who contributed actively to the drafting of the Guiding Principles.

As the legal assessment of unilateral sanctions is mostly done from the perspective of the law of international responsibility only, and other spheres of international law as well as the humanitarian impact of unilateral sanctions are nearly ignored, I hope that this volume will encourage sanctioning and sanctioned states, the United Nations Organization, its organs, entities and specialized agencies, corporations, lawyers, humanitarian organizations, scholars and other actors to assess the use of unilateral sanctions, means of their enforcement, derisking policies from the perspective of international law and humanity as enshrined in the Charter of the United Nations in full respect of its norms and fundamental principles, and to pay more attention to the problem and do more research prior to policy enactment.

I am grateful to all actors who have contributed to this volume, the development of the Guiding Principles and the Commentary thereto, and participated in the discussion at the conference.

Prof. Dr. hab. Alena F. Douhan
UN Special Rapporteur on the negative impact of
unilateral coercive measures on human rights

---

5 International Conference on Sanctions, Business and Human Rights, 21–22 November 2024. https://www.ohchr.org/en/events/events/2024/international-conference-sanctions-business-and-human-rights

PART I

....

GENERAL CHALLENGES POSED BY THE USE OF SANCTIONS AND OVER-COMPLIANCE

CHAPTER I

The Evolution of Overreach in U.S. Sanctions Practice
From Extraterritoriality to Over-compliance

Joy Gordon[1]

Abstract

This chapter looks at the development of U.S. sanctions practice, specifically the ways in which it has extended well beyond the legitimate scope of jurisdiction as ordinarily recognized in international law. This chapter focuses on two developments in this regard. First, it considers U.S. sanctions that are explicitly extraterritorial, and the response of the international community to these measures. The chapter monitors and assesses the emergence of over-compliance, which extends the effects of sanctions without directly raising the kinds of concerns seen with regard to extraterritoriality. Over-compliance follows in part from the financial and personnel costs of compliance and due diligence. In addition, the fundamental ambiguity of key regulatory terms is a critical factor, as well as the inconsistency and unpredictability of their interpretation and enforcement. Finally, this chapter looks at the magnitude of the penalties, and the emergence of penalties that cannot be incorporated as a cost of doing business but instead present an existential threat. I will look at these factors specifically in the context of the U.S. Treasury Department's Office of Foreign Assets Control.

---

1 Ignacio Ellacuría, S.J. Professor of Social Ethics in the Department of Philosophy at Loyola University Chicago

Introduction

In the 1990s, the United States introduced a new range and new types of unilateral sanctions that were broadly criticized by the international community as being extraterritorial. While the U.S. imposed unilateral economic measures against Cuba and other countries during the Cold War, the impact of these was blunted, as the target countries sought out trade relations with the Eastern bloc. However, with the dissolution of the Soviet Union, the global economic landscape changed considerably. Unilateral sanctions imposed by the U.S. carried far greater potential for economic harm and for political leverage. In retrospect, it was not surprising that after 1990 the U.S. aggressively developed new and far more extreme forms of economic pressure than had previously been the case. Notably, the 1990s saw the introduction of extraterritorial measures against Cuba, Iran, and Libya that would greatly expand the scope of U.S. economic pressure. However, these measures not only impacted the target countries, but also compelled the compliance of third-country nationals. As such, they came under fire from the international community.

The Torricelli Act[2] was adopted by Congress in 1992, aggressively expanding the scope of the existing measures against Cuba. It was aimed at undermining major sectors of Cuba's economy as well as its major areas of vulnerability; as an island nation, it was heavily dependent on imports and exports. The Torricelli Act targeted Cuba's access to shipping by prohibiting any ship, regardless of nationality, from docking in the U.S. within 180 days of docking in Cuba. The potential penalties are quite severe: in the case of violation, the U.S. may confiscate not only the ship's cargo but may also confiscate the ship itself. Since cargo ships from, say, Europe or Asia, would often have significant trade in the U.S. as well, it becomes commercially unfeasible for them to deliver goods or take on shipments from Cuba. Consequently, to purchase foodstuffs or fuel, Cuba effectively has to pay double: it must pay for the goods to be shipped to Cuba, and then it must pay for the ship to return empty, since it cannot stop in the U.S. to take on cargo. It might be argued that this provision is not "extraterritorial," since the U.S. is asserting power over those entering its ports; but rather is only a "secondary" sanction, affecting third

---

2 Cuban Democracy Act, 22 U.S.C. 69 § 6001–10 (1992).

parties who trade with Cuba.[3] However, in this case, it seems that this is a distinction without a difference: the net effect is that European and other foreign companies are compelled to comply with U.S. measures targeting Cuba.

The Torricelli Act also restricted Cuba's trade with foreign subsidiaries of U.S. companies. Even during the Cold War, the U.S. had not sought to intervene in Cuba's trade with, say, a British subsidiary of a U.S. company. Presumably, this would not have been strategically useful to the U.S., since Cuba had robust trade relations with the Eastern bloc. However, the dissolution of the Soviet Union and loss of trade with the Eastern bloc left Cuba in an extremely precarious moment, with its economy in free fall, and the country scrambling to find new trade partners. Cutting off access to foreign subsidiaries of U.S. companies was a means of restricting the range of possibilities available to Cuba. The impact of this was even greater in the face of the global mergers and acquisitions that took place in the 1980s and 1990s, resulting in U.S. ownership of a broader range of foreign entities, and further limiting the commercial space in which Cuba could operate.

The U.S. administrations had also been reluctant to assert jurisdiction over foreign subsidiaries of U.S. companies because of the political and legal problems that would likely entail. A state properly exercises jurisdiction over persons, property, or conduct found within its territory.[4] "Extraterritorial jurisdiction" may be defined as *"jurisdiction that lacks a territorial nexus between the state and the regulated action."*[5] A state may also legitimately have jurisdiction in other cases, such as asserting jurisdiction over its nationals that are abroad.[6] However, under international law, corporations are generally deemed to be nationals of the place in which they are incorporated, regardless of whether they may be owned, in whole or in part, by a corporation based in another country. Claiming jurisdiction over a subsidiary that is

---

3 See generally Joshua Andreson, "US Secondary Sanctions: Lawful After All?" in *Routledge Handbook of the Political Economy of Economic Sanctions,* ed. Ksenia Kirkham (London: Routledge, 2023), pp. 305–317.

4 Susan Emmenegger, "Extraterritorial Economic Sanctions and their Foundation in International Law," *Arizona Journal of International and Comparative Law* 33, no. 3 (2016), p. 638.

5 Ibid., p. 639.

6 Ibid., p. 649.

thus a foreign national would risk the ire of other countries that would consider this to be extraterritorial, in violation of international law, and an incursion on their sovereignty. This was indeed the response of the international community to the Torricelli Act, as well as the later Helms-Burton Act, which was adopted in 1996.[7]

The Helms-Burton Act introduced an additional set of extraterritorial measures. Among them, it provided that third-country companies could not export goods to the United States that contained materials or components originating in Cuba. Cuba's exports, such as sugar and nickel, are a major part of its economy. Under the terms of the Helms-Burton Act, if a Belgian company were to use Cuban sugar in the production of chocolate, it could not export that chocolate to the U.S. without running afoul of U.S. law. We see the impact of this through to the present. Cuba has significant reserves of nickel and cobalt; nickel is used in producing stainless steel, and cobalt is used in the batteries, among other things, of electric vehicles.[8] Cuba has a joint venture with the Canadian company, Sherritt, to mine and refine these metals. One of Sherritt's customers is Panasonic, which makes batteries for electric cars; and one of Panasonic's customers is Tesla, which manufactures electric vehicles. Because Tesla cannot sell any product in the U.S. containing even small amount of materials from Cuba, in 2018, Panasonic suspended its business with Sherritt.[9] Thus, while the U.S. position is that it is asserting jurisdiction over imports to the U.S., in fact it is also disrupting trade between Cuba and a Canadian company, and also between a Canadian and a Japanese company.

The Helms-Burton Act also introduced another provision that is extraterritorial. Title III of the statute authorizes Cuban nationals who lost their Cuban property after the revolution of 1959 (and are now U.S. nationals) to sue third-country nationals that now use those properties in U.S. courts. So, for example, if a Cuban individual owned property in Cuba prior to the revolution, and that property is now a

---

7 Cuban Liberty And Democratic Solidarity (Libertad), Act 22 U.S.C. 691 § 6021–91 (1996).

8 Pratima Desai and Makiko Yamazaki, "Exclusive: Tesla's battery maker suspends cobalt supplier amid sanctions concern," *Reuters,* July 19, 2018. https://www.reuters.com/article/us-tesla-cuba-cobalt-exclusive-idUSKBN1K92Q9

9 Ibid.

hotel run by a Spanish hotel chain, and the Cuban individual has since acquired U.S. citizenship, he can sue the Spanish hotel company in U.S. courts for "trafficking" in confiscated property. This would be extraterritorial in the sense that the U.S. is extending its jurisdiction to a property dispute involving land in Cuba, a Cuban property owner, and a Spanish hotel company.

The U.S. government as well as some scholars maintain that such measures are not in fact extraterritorial. In regard to foreign subsidiaries of U.S. companies, Andreson maintains that it is fully legitimate to *"hold U.S. persons responsible for the actions of the entities they own or control and instruct U.S. persons either to divest from those entities or ensure that they do not violate U.S. sanctions law."*[10] Similarly, Andresen maintains that it is not illegal for the U.S. to restrict the reexport of goods containing a small amount of U.S.-origin materials[11] or to deny foreign banks and entities access to the U.S. financial system.[12] Such measures, he maintains, are *"perfectly within [the U.S.'] sovereign prerogative."*[13] His argument is that access to a country's market or financial system is a privilege that a country may or may not choose to extend to foreign actors. A foreign nation *"has no right to the privilege of trading with"* the U.S., or any other country; and sanctions simply put *"foreign actors on notice that, if they participate in the specified activities, they will be cut off from certain privileges in the U.S. market."*[14]

However, in many regards the U.S. holds a singular role in the global economy. The U.S. has by far the largest economy in the world; in 2024, U.S. GDP was $25.43 trillion, while China had the second largest economy, at a little more than half of that, $14.72 trillion; Japan was third, with a GDP of $4.25 trillion.[15] At the same time, the U.S. dollar is the dominant global reserve currency, constituting

---

10 Joshua Andresen, "US Secondary Sanctions: Lawful After All?," in *Routledge Handbook of the Political Economy of Sanctions,* ed. Ksenia Kirkham (London: Routledge, 2023), p. 309.

11 Ibid., p. 310.

12 Ibid., p. 311.

13 Ibid., p. 308.

14 Ibid., p. 309.

15 Safeguard Global, "Top 15 Countries by GDP in 2024," accessed February 6, 2025. https://globalpeoservices.com/top-15-countries-by-gdp-in-2024/

nearly 60% of central bank reserves globally.[16] Further, according to SWIFT, the hub for international banking transfers, almost half of all payments were denominated in U.S. dollars, and the large majority of transactions involving trade and finance were dollar-denominated.[17] Thus, it seem disingenuous to frame U.S. sanctions as simply a sovereign right to determine when, and to whom, to grant access to the U.S. market and financial system, as a purely domestic matter.

In addition, the international community has consistently held the view that such sanctions measures are indeed extraterritorial, and that as such, they run afoul of international law.[18] There was considerable protest from the international community regarding the extraterritorial measures found in the two statutes regarding Cuba. In 1992, in response to the Torricelli Act, Cuba introduced a resolution in the UN General Assembly, denouncing the U.S. actions as a violation of international trade law. The resolution passed with fifty-nine votes in favor, with two countries opposed (the U.S. and Israel), and the remainder of the member states abstaining. Each year after that, when the resolution was re-introduced, more countries shifted from abstentions to support. For many years now, it has been the case that nearly every country in the world supports this resolution, including almost all U.S. major allies. The most recent vote, in October 2024, was 187 countries in favor, two opposed (the U.S. and Israel), and one abstention.[19]

In addition to the annual General Assembly resolutions, there were legal actions brought against the U.S., objecting to the extraterritorial nature of the U.S. measures. In the late 1990s, the European Union and the United Kingdom brought an action against the U.S. before the World Trade Organization on the grounds that the U.S. measures against Cuba constituted illegal interference in international trade. The matter was ultimately resolved through negotiation when the Clinton

---

16 International Monetary Fund, "Currency Composition of Official Foreign Exchange Reserves (COFER)," accessed November 16, 2024. https://data.imf.org/?sk=E6A5F467-C14B-4AA8-9F6D-5A09EC4E62A4

17 SWIFT, "RMB Tracker: Monthly Reporting and Statistic on Renminbi (RMB) Progress Towards Becoming an International Currency," October 2024, accessed November 16, 2024. https://www.swift.com/swift-resource/252344/download

18 See, e.g., annual United Nations General Assembly votes denouncng U.S. measures against Cuba as extraterritorial. United Nations, "General Assembly renews long-standing call for end to U.S. embargo against Cuba," UN Press, October 30, 2024. https://press.un.org/en/2024/ga12650.doc.htm

19 Ibid.

Administration agreed to suspend Title III, which many considered to be the most controversial provision.[20] The Clinton Administration did suspend this provision consistently, in consecutive six-month periods, as did all U.S. administrations thereafter, until the Trump Administration of 2017–2021, which reversed this practice, allowing Title III to again take effect. The Biden Administration followed suit, except for a brief reversal in January 2025; and the incoming Trump Administration then re-activated the provision.

There were also retaliatory laws adopted in response to the U.S. measures. Canada,[21] Mexico,[22] and the European Union[23] (EU) passed "clawback" legislation, providing a venue for their nationals to bring countersuits against U.S. nationals who had brought suit in U.S. courts.

In response to extraterritorial measures against Cuba and other countries, some countries also adopted "blocking" legislation, which prohibits their nationals from complying with foreign laws that are extraterritorial. This can be seen in the case of U.S. sanctions against Iran. In response to Iran's nuclear program, the UN as well as the EU, U.S., and other countries imposed collective and unilateral sanctions against Iran.[24] When the Joint Comprehensive Plan of Action (JCPOA) was negotiated in 2015, it was agreed that the sanctions would be lifted once there was confirmation that Iran had complied with demands regarding its nuclear program.[25] This occurred in 2016, and the Security Council, EU, and U.S. lifted significant components of the sanctions on Iran. European companies, such as British Airways and Air France, resumed business with Iran. However, in 2018, the Trump Administration withdrew from the JCPOA, and reimposed secondary sanctions, which would impose penalties on third-country companies doing business with Iran. The EU responded by updating its blocking legislation, which in turn imposed penalties on European

---

20 Secretary of State Madeleine K. Albright, "Statement on U.S.-EU Understanding on Expropriated Property," May 18, 1998.

21 Joaquín Roy, *Cuba, The United States, and the Helms-Burton Doctrine: International Reactions* (Gainesville: University Press of Florida, 2000), p. 88.

22 Ibid., p. 93.

23 Ibid., p. 120.

24 See, e.g., United Nations Security Council Resolutions 1696 (2006), 1737 (2006), 1747 (2007), 1803 (2008), and 1929 (2010); Council Common Position 2007/246/CFSP; "Comprehensive Iran Sanctions, Accountability, and Divestment Act" (2010), Executive Order 13574 (2011), Executive Order 13590 (2011).

25 United Nations Security Council, Resolution 2231 (2015).

companies that complied with extraterritorial measures, such as the U.S. secondary sanctions.[26] Thus, European companies found themselves in an untenable position: if they did business with Iran, which was legal under European law, then they risked penalties from the U.S., including potential exclusion from the U.S. market. On the other hand, if they complied with U.S. law and terminated their business with Iran, they faced penalties from the EU for complying with extraterritorial laws, which were viewed as a violation of the sovereignty of European nations. In the end, some companies resolved their situation by terminating their business with Iran, while giving only vague reasons for doing so.[27]

Thus, while the U.S. continues to employ extraterritorial measures against Cuba, Iran, and other countries, it has done so in the face of significant opposition and public outcry from the international community. At the very least, it is surely embarrassing for the U.S., which regularly denounces Cuba for its human rights violations, to find that nearly every country in the world joins with Cuba in annually denouncing the U.S. extraterritorial sanctions as violations of international law.

In the last decade or so, we have seen the emergence of a second strategy by which the U.S. has magnified the scope of its unilateral measures such that their impact becomes nearly global. This was evident in an obscure incident in 2012, when an Iranian American college student in Alpharetta, Georgia, entered an Apple store to buy an iPad while speaking to her uncle in Farsi. The store refused to sell her the iPad, because of her ostensible ties to Iran. She was not on any U.S. terrorist list. But the sanctions regimes employ a strict liability standard, such that penalties for selling technology that inadvertently

---

26 "Commission Delegated Regulation (EU) 2018/1100 of 6 June 2018, amending the Annex to Council Regulation (EC) No. 2271/96 protecting against the effects of extra-territorial application of legislation adopted by a third country, and actions based thereon or resulting therefrom." https://eur-lex.europa.eu/legal-content/EN/TXT/?uri=CELEX:32018R1100

27 For example, British Airways announced that it was terminating its flight to Iran "as the operation is currently not commercially viable," while Air France said that it would stop flights to Iran because of "the line's weak performance." Sinéad Baker, "British Airways and Air France are stopping all flights to Iran, just before crushing new US sanctions kick in," *Business Insider,* August 23, 2018. https://www.businessinsider.com/british-airways-air-france-suspend-flights-to-tehran-2018-8

and indirectly ends up in Iran are severe.[28] Around the same time, the U.S. Treasury Department's Office of Foreign Assets Control (OFAC) began imposing massive fines on foreign banks and companies for violating U.S. sanctions regimes on Cuba, Iran, and elsewhere. These included a penalty of $619 million imposed on the Dutch bank ING in 2012.[29] Penalties totalling almost $9 billion were imposed on the French bank BNP Paribas in 2014.[30] BNP was also partially and temporarily denied access to the U.S. Federal Reserve, sending a chill through the international banking community. In March 2015, the German bank Commerzbank AG was required to pay a total penalty of $1.45 billion.[31] There were massive fines imposed as well on other financial institutions, including HSBC[32] and Crédit Agricole Corporate.[33] Even before these massive fines, numerous Canadian and European banks severed ties with Cuba, including Barclays, the Bank of Nova Scotia, Credit Suisse, Deutsche Bank, Royal Bank of Canada, and HSBC.[34]

What has now emerged in response is an extensive practice of over-compliance. This is discussed in "Guiding Principles on Sanctions, Business and Human Rights," which calls for businesses

---

28 Joy Gordon, "The Human Costs of the Iran Sanctions," *Foreign Policy,* October 18, 2013. https://foreignpolicy.com/2013/10/18/the-human-costs-of-the-iran-sanctions/

29 U.S. Department of the Treasury, "Settlement Agreement," ING Bank N.V., MUL-565595, June 11, 2012.

30 U.S. Department of the Treasury, "Treasury Reaches Largest Ever Sanctions-Related Settlement with BNP Paribas SA for $963 Million," press release, June 30, 2014.

31 Department of Justice, Office of Public Affairs, "Commerzbank AG Admits to Sanctions and Bank Secrecy Violations, Agrees to Forfeit $563 Million and Pay $79 Million Fine," March 12, 2015. https://www.justice.gov/archives/opa/pr/commerzbank-ag-admits-sanctions-and-bank-secrecy-violations-agrees-forfeit-563-million-and

32 Department of Justice, Office of Public Affairs, "HSBC Holdings Plc. And HSBC Bank USA N.A. Admit to Anti-Money Laundering and Sanctions Violations, Forfeit $1.256 Billion in Deferred Prosecution Agreement," news release, December 11, 2012. https://www.justice.gov/opa/pr/hsbc-holdings-plc-and-hsbc-bank-usa-na-admit-anti-money-laundering-and-sanctions-violations

33 Department of Justice, Office of Public Affairs, "Crédit Agricole Corporate and Investment Bank Admits to Sanctions Violations, Agrees to Forfeit $312 Million," press release, Oct. 20, 2015. http://www.justice.gov/opa/pecr-dit-agricole-corporate-and-investment-bank-admits-sanctions-violations-agrees-forfeit-312

34 U.S. Government Accountability Office, *Economic Sanctions: Agencies Face Competing Priorities in Enforcing the U.S. Embargo on Cuba* (2007), p. 54, fn 110.

"to eliminate and/or minimize over-compliance with unilateral sanctions."[35]

Professor Alena Douhan, the United Nations Special Rapporteur on Unilateral Coercive Measures and their negative effects on human rights, has defined over-compliance as a form of excessive avoidance of risk. It may involve blocking all financial transactions with a sanctioned country, entity or individual even when some transactions are authorized by humanitarian exemptions or fall outside of the sanctions' scope. It may also take the form of deterring authorized transactions by requiring cumbersome, onerous documentation or certification, charging higher rates or additional fees, or imposing discouraging long delays.

Over-compliance also occurs when banks decide to freeze assets that are not targeted by sanctions, or deny individuals the possibility to open or maintain bank accounts or to engage in transactions simply because they are nationals of a sanctioned country, even when the individuals are refugees from that country.[36]

Prof. Douhan has noted that unilateral sanctions regimes:

> create a generalised fear among different stakeholders who constitute key players in the performance of otherwise authorised activities in connection with a sanctioned country, and result in instances of over-compliance and derisking with catastrophic consequences on the general populations, let alone the most vulnerable."[37]

---

35 "Mandate of the Special Rapporteur on the negative impact of unilateral coercive measures on the enjoyment of human rights," p. 8.

36 United Nations Special Rapporteur on Unilateral Coercive Measures, "Guidance Note on over-compliance with Unilateral Sanctions and its Harmful Effects on Human Rights." https://www.ohchr.org/en/special-procedures/sr-unilateral-coercive-measures/resources-unilateral-coercive-measures/guidance-note-over-compliance-unilateral-sanctions-and-its-harmful-effects-human-rights

37 Mandates of the Special Rapporteur on the negative impact of unilateral coercive measures on the enjoyment of human rights; the Special Rapporteur on the situation of human rights in the Democratic People's Republic of Korea; the Special Rapporteur on the right to development; the Special Rapporteur on the right to food and the Independent Expert on human rights and international solidarity, "Letter to Permanent Delegation of the European Union," Ref.: AL OTH 106/2022, October 26, 2022, p. 4.

The practice of over-compliance is not, in a sense, unreasonable. Indeed, it follows directly from the nature of the regulatory regime. Verdier notes that "Over-compliance is a rational response to uncertainty in sanctions rules."[38] He notes also that the problematic results may include the loss of "legally permissible commercial relations with sanctioned countries or persons."[39] For policymakers, "widespread over-compliance may undermine the subtle design choices that inform targeted sanctions programs."[40] Additionally, "over-compliance may exacerbate the humanitarian impact of sanctions, for instance by making it impossible to use humanitarian exceptions embedded in sanctions programs. "[41]

Breen distinguishes between over-compliance in response to primary sanctions, and over-compliance in response to secondary sanctions. Primary sanctions are imposed on those who have a U.S. nexus, such as citizenship, residency, or incorporation.[42] The source of uncertainty in this case may be whether a person or company is a "U.S. person" under the sanctions law, since this term is defined differently under different statutes.[43] Because this is not always clear from the statute or regulations, a foreign individual or a company with no direct ties to the U.S. may nonetheless feel compelled to comply with primary sanctions, rather than risk penalties in the event that a U.S. authority deems it to be a "U.S. person."

Secondary sanctions are imposed on those with no U.S. nexus; there is "no territorial or personal link with the U.S. and would not

---

38 Pierre-Hugues Verdier, "Sanctions Over-compliance: What, Why, and Does It Matter?," *North Carolina Journal of International Law* 48, no. 3 (2023), p. 473.

39 Ibid., p. 472.

40 Ibid.

41 Ibid.

42 Emmanuel Breen, "Corporations and US Economic Sanctions: The dangers of over-compliance," in *Research Handbook on Unilateral and Extraterritorial Sanctions*, ed. Charlotte Beaucillon (Cheltenham, UK: Edward Elgar Publishing Limited, 2021), p. 258.

43 Terms such as "U.S. person" and "person subject to U.S. jurisdiction" are defined in the implementing regulations for a particular sanctions program in 31 CFR chapter V. (*See e.g.,* 31 CFR § 560.314 (Iranian Transactions and Sanctions Regulations (ITSR)); 31 CFR § 598.318 (Foreign Narcotics Kingpin Sanctions Regulations)." U.S. Treasury Department, Office of Foreign Assets Control, Frequently Asked Questions #11, "Who Must Comply with OFAC Sanctions?," accessed February 2, 2025. https://ofac.treasury.gov/faqs/11

normally be subject to U.S. law."[44] These include, for example, the Iran Sanctions Act (1996) and the Comprehensive Iran Sanctions, Accountability, and Divestment Act (2010), which authorize the president to impose sanctions on non-U.S. entities engaging in activities such as investing in the Iranian energy sector. Breen suggests that "[a]ny form of compliance with U.S. secondary sanctions by a non-U.S. entity may in a way be considered an instance of over-compliance, because this entity is not legally obligated to comply with U.S. law."[45]

However, over-compliance is often viewed a bit differently: as terminating business relations, or withdrawing from entire markets, because it is simply unclear what exactly must be done to avoid penalties, or compliance is so costly and burdensome that it is not commercially feasible. This form of over-compliance is driven by three conditions.

First, the terms of the regulations are irreducibly vague. Key terms, such as "U.S. persons," are not made fully clear. The same is true for the due diligence requirements, such as Know Your Customer (KYC). A bank, shipping company, insurer, or other company may be held responsible for the acts of its customer, so it must determine whether its customer may, for example, ultimately send the funds or goods involved to a sanctioned country or an individual listed as a Specially Designated National (SDN), either directly or indirectly.[46] Further, in some contexts, a private actor must not only know its customer but must know its customer's customer[47] (KYCC)—that is, the responsibility of the private actor may expand exponentially. In addition to due diligence, other key terms are also not entirely clear, such as the prohibition on providing "material support" to a terrorist organization.

For example, the U.S. law "Countering America's Adversaries Through Sanctions Act of 2017 (CAATSA)," in part targets those involved in Russia's invasion of Ukraine. The law imposes secondary

---

44 Ibid., p. 260.

45 Ibid.

46 Dow Jones, "Risk and Compliance Glossary: Understanding the Steps of a 'Know Your Customer' Process," accessed February 25, 2025. https://www.dowjones.com/professional/risk/resources/glossary/know-your-customer

47 KYC/AML Guide, "Understanding KYCC: A Comprehensive Guide for Businesses," accessed February 25, 2025. https://kycaml.guide/blog/understanding-kycc-a-comprehensive-guide-for-businesses/

sanctions on individuals and entities, including those that are not U.S. nationals, if they knowingly facilitate "significant transactions" for persons who are listed by the Treasury Department in relation to Russia's aggression against Ukraine.[48] While the Office of Foreign Assets Control offers some guidance on the factors it will use in gauging whether a transaction is "significant" in this context, OFAC noted that the guidance it provided was not exhaustive, and they emphasized that they would take a case-by-case approach. Because OFAC ultimately holds considerable discretion in determining whether there has been a violation, banks and other private actors do not have complete certainty as to how they should interpret and implement the regulations.

Second, the penalties for violations are not just severe; they are potentially catastrophic. Thus, the risk that is at play is not an ordinary one. Commercial actors, whether banks or others, routinely determine that a given risk is acceptable as a cost of doing business, where it is outweighed by the likely revenues. But OFAC penalties are different in nature: they present not just a potential business loss, but rather the possibility of a **catastrophic** loss and an **existential** risk. In the case of BNP Paribas, the penalty was not only a massive fine, but also the temporary and partial suspension of access to the U.S. financial system.[49] For any bank that engages in U.S. dollar transactions—and the majority of the world's financial transactions take place in U.S. dollars—denial of access to the U.S. financial system is known as the "death penalty." While a private actor may conceivably decide that many kinds of risks are still worth taking, a risk such as that, which may effectively spell the end of the enterprise itself, is presumably unaffordable in any circumstances.

Finally, the standard for the imposition of penalties is unforgiving. If penalties were imposed for, say, intentional wrongdoing, then compliance is relatively easy. If penalties were imposed for negligence, then training programs and other measures could be taken to demonstrate that the actor is not negligent. However, the standard is

---

48 "Countering America's Adversaries Through Sanctions Act of 2017 (CAATSA)," Pub.L. 115-44, 84 Stat. 1114 (2017), Section 22827.

49 U. S. Department of the Treasury, "Treasury Reaches Largest Ever Sanctions-Related Settlement with BNP Paribas SA for $963 Million," press release, June 30, 2014.

strict liability, so penalties may be imposed even for violations that are inadvertent, where there is neither intent nor negligence.

OFAC may impose civil penalties for sanctions violations based on strict liability, meaning that a person subject to U.S. jurisdiction may be held civilly liable even if such person did not have knowledge that it was engaging in a transaction that was prohibited under sanctions laws and regulations administered by OFAC.[50]

In the face of these factors, the costs of compliance have skyrocketed, and the consequences of over-compliance include extensive disruption of global trade and finance. It is unsurprising to see banks terminate financial services, including the correspondent relations that are essential for transnational transactions, with countries and regions perceived as high risk, such as Africa and the Arab world. The result is that even for apparently legal transactions such as the transfer of funds by humanitarian aid organizations—that is, transactions with no plausible relation to terrorism or money laundering—it becomes virtually impossible to find a bank that will provide the necessary services.

As these developments have in turn generated criticism and political pressure, we now see a move by the Treasury Department to shift blame to the private actors involved, by criticizing them for their derisking practices. Regarding financial institutions, the Treasury Department issued a report on its "derisking strategy."

For this study, Treasury focuses on "derisking" as the practice of financial institutions terminating or restricting business relationships indiscriminately with broad categories of clients rather than analyzing and managing the risk of clients in a targeted manner. Such a practice is not consistent with the risk-based approach that is the cornerstone of the Anti-Money Laundering/Countering the Financing of Terrorism (AML/CFT) regulatory framework for U.S. financial institutions....[51]

In this report, the Treasury Department, ironically, expresses its concern "with the phenomenon of financial institutions making wholesale, indiscriminate decisions about broad categories of customers, rather than assessing and mitigating risk in a targeted way."[52]

---

50 U.S. Treasury Department, Office of Foreign Assets Control, "Frequently Asked Questions," accessed February 6, 2025. https://ofac.treasury.gov/faqs/65

51 U.S. Treasury Department, "AMLA: The Department of the Treasury's Derisking Strategy," April 2023, p. 1.

52 Ibid., p. 4.

Thus, Treasury Department officials seem to be insisting that the problem is not its regulatory structure. Rather, they maintain, the solution is for banks to engage in ever more granular examination of its customers and their transactions. If the banks prefer to terminate customers or withdraw from entire markets, the argument goes, that is their decision to make. But, I would suggest, that is disingenuous: when the risks created by the Treasury Department and other U.S. government actors are not only high, but rather are catastrophically high; when the costs of compliance are increasingly exorbitant; and when the key regulatory terms are irreducibly vague; then it becomes simply commercially unfeasible to engage in a wide range of even the most ordinary of transactions, with legitimate actors, in situations of great human urgency.

And the pattern that we see regarding banks is then replicated in many other domains as well—shipping, insurance, investment, donor support for aid organizations, and on and on.

Conclusion

I suggest that we can see an evolution, of sorts, in U.S. sanctions practice, as it has moved from one form of overreach to another, specifically from extraterritoriality to over-compliance. During the Cold War, unilateral sanctions were limited in their impact, since any country targeted by the West could turn to the Eastern bloc for trade. Once the Cold War was over, there was quite abruptly the possibility that unilateral sanctions could be vast, even global, in their reach, and devastating in their impact. For the U.S., this marked the beginning of a set of new practices that were not only far more aggressive but were also extraterritorial. In the 1990s, this was notably the case regarding measures imposed on Cuba, as well as Iran and Libya. These measures were challenged in various fora, including the World Trade Organization, as well as triggering retaliatory measures and blocking legislation on the part of the European Union and others. These responses, as well as the nearly unanimous annual votes in the UN General Assembly denouncing the U.S. for its unilateral measures against Cuba, surely caused some political pressure, or in some cases rifts in relationships between the U.S. government and key allies.

I suggest that we can see over-compliance as the successor to the practice of extraterritoriality. They are similar in that both are forms of overreach, whereby a country acting unilaterally, and arguably in violation of international law, nonetheless finds a way to magnify the scope of its actions, in effect transforming the legally questionable practices of a single country into a policy of global reach.

However, the international response to each of these has been quite different. Extraterritoriality triggered broad-based accusations and criticism from the international community. This was only possible because extraterritorial measures are clearly attributable to the sanctioner. But with over-compliance, it is possible for the sanctioner to claim that it bears no responsibility for the decisions of private actors. That is in fact what Treasury Department officials have repeatedly maintained. However devastating, indiscriminate, and disproportionate the consequences of over-compliance may be, the sanctioner can seek to sidestep responsibility in this manner.

But the sanctioner is indeed responsible. While banks and other private sector actors may choose to withdraw from entire countries, or sometimes entire regions, this is driven by the conditions that the Treasury Department and other U.S. government actors have put in place.

So, I would suggest, we may say that over-compliance is the successor of the extraterritoriality that was harshly criticized two decades ago. However, over-compliance seems to be even broader in scope. For example, the U.S. extraterritorial legislation against Cuba in the 1990s prohibited any ship that entered a Cuban port from entering a U.S. port within sixty days. By contrast, the phenomenon of over-compliance will enter into the risk assessment and decision making of every ship owner who may engage with the scores of countries throughout the world that are subject to unilateral coercive measures. But over-compliance as the successor of extraterritorial policies is perhaps even more successful, so to speak, in a different regard: that the sanctioner may, and does, simply say that this is not it doing at all, even though it sets the conditions that ensure that over-compliance will be inevitable.

CHAPTER 2

International Law Double Standards in the Case of Unilateral Coercive Measures

Pouria Askari[1]

Abstract

In the realm of international law, double standards are typically identified when States and international organizations react differently to the same violation, when the actors responsible for those violations vary. This Chapter argues that another form of double standards exists when the same outcomes arise from different behavior, yet international norms are not designed to address these situations equivalently. The Chapter contends that the treatment of unilateral coercive measures, in comparison to the treatment of human rights violations, the illegal use of force, and breaches of international humanitarian law, exemplifies this double standard within international law. Furthermore, it calls upon concerned States and the academic community to leverage the existing norms and structures of international law to address this issue. In this context, it particularly highlights the recent Guiding Principles prepared by the Special Rapporteur on UCMs concerning sanctions, business, and human rights as a crucial example of what is needed.

Introduction

Unilateral Coercive Measures (UCMs) predominantly represent economic sanctions, wielded like a sceptre by powerful States, with the United States at the forefront. These measures target countries that, in the sanctioning State's perspective, deviate from the established norms

---

1 Associate Professor of Public International Law, Allameh Tabataba'i University, Iran (p.askari@atu.ac.ir)

of international relations or exhibit questionable domestic conduct towards their citizens. The ongoing discourse surrounding the legality of UCMs, which remains inconclusive, is a complex interplay of legal and political perspectives. However, considering the profound burden UCMs impose on the common populace and their human rights, it is expected that international law would delineate certain restrictions on the application of these measures. Despite the United Nations (UN) General Assembly and the Human Rights Council adopting some non-binding resolutions,[2] international law's success in this realm remains limited.

In essence, the question concerning limitations on the imposition of UCMs continues to seek a comprehensive resolution. Having said that, it is important to remind that, from a pure legal perspective, as mentioned on many occasions by the UN Special Rapporteur on Human Rights and UCMs, "coercive measures can only be taken by States and international organizations in the course of the implementation of resolutions of the UN Security Council adopted under Chapter VII of the UN Charter, or when such measures do not violate their international obligations (retorsions), or their wrongfulness is precluded under international law when the measures constitute countermeasures in full conformity with the rules of the law of international responsibility. All other unilateral means of pressure [. . .] are illegal under international law."[3]

This chapter acknowledges the possibility of unilateral responses as countermeasures to address threats posed by international wrongful acts, while also highlighting the ambiguity and shortcomings in international legal regulations governing such unilateral activities. This is viewed as an exemplification of double standards in international law from three vantage points. Firstly, the paper references the cases brought forth by the State of Qatar before the International Court

---

2 United Nations Documents on Unilateral Coercive Measures (UCM)s, Organization for Defending Victims of Violence, 2023. https://odvv.org/resources/attachment/1696145996_8c4d9b1bd1db5da73eacd78b50ba88ed.pdf

3 Mandate of the Special Rapporteur on the Negative Impact of Unilateral Coercive Measures on the Enjoyment of Human Rights, Draft Guiding Principles on Sanctions, Business and Human Rights, 2024, para. 17.2. https://indico.un.org/event/1013607/attachments/17742/50871/GPs%20sanctions,%20business%20and%20HR_09-09-2024.pdf

of Justice (ICJ)[4] and the UN Committee on Racial Discrimination (CERD),[5] arguing that while international law proscribes many forms of unjustified discrimination, the discrimination ensuing from the implementation of UCMs remains largely overlooked. Secondly, the chapter scrutinizes the limitations that the Security Council enforces when sanctioning, such as the humanitarian carve-out referred to in the recent resolution 2664,[6] and contends that such limitations are practically non-existent in the face of UCMs' related factors. Thirdly, the paper argues that the hardships engendered by unilateral sanctions in the daily lives of people affected by them often surpass those resulting from armed conflicts. While the law of armed conflict and international humanitarian law (IHL) prohibit belligerents from inflicting suffering on civilians in many ways, the adverse impacts of UCMs, which may manifest as collective punishment, limitations in access to food, medicine, or other essentials, or in some cases famine or starvation, do not encounter clear prohibitions in international law.

Lastly, the chapter examines the 2024 draft Guiding Principles on Sanctions, Business, and Human Rights proposed by the Special Rapporteur on UCMs to assess how these principles address the aforementioned shortcomings.

Two Aspects of Double Standards in International Law

A double standard, in short, means applying different treatments to the same issue. In the realm of international relations, double standards often refer to situations where the world has different reactions to almost similar contexts. For instance, this text is written in October 2024, when many people are questioning why the reaction to atrocities in the Middle East and Africa is not as strong as the response to violations in Europe or other Western regions.[7]

---

4 ICJ, Application of the International Convention on the Elimination of All Forms of Racial Discrimination (*Qatar v. United Arab Emirates*), 2018.

5 CERD Interstate Communication, *Qatar v. Kingdom of Saudi Arabia* and *Qatar v. United Arab Emirates,* 2018.

6 UNSC/RES/2664, December 9, 2022.

7 Khoitil Aswadi, "The Double Standards of International Law: A Comparative Study of the Conflict in Ukraine and Palestine," *Tirtayasa Journal of International Law* 2, no. 1 (2023), pp. 71–81. https://dx.doi.org/10.51825/tjil.v2i1.19694; "Qatar Condemns 'Double Standards' at ICJ hearing on Israeli Occupation," *Al Jazeera*, February 23, 2024. https://www.aljazeera.com/news/2024/2/23/qatar-condemns-

From an international law perspective, double standards refer to the inconsistent legal responses to similar cases or the uneven application of international law to identical issues. This often occurs in the realm of human rights law, where States accused of violating international human rights norms may argue that such accusations are politically motivated, pointing to similar behaviors by other states that go unchallenged.[8] Many other aspects of international law are also undermined by the application of double standards, primarily by major powers seeking to exempt themselves or their allies from accountability. Readers may recall instances of such behavior when considering laws related to the use of force, international humanitarian law, international criminal law, and international disarmament law, among others.[9]

The examples provided above illustrate one aspect of double standards in international law, primarily concerning the inconsistent application of the same norms and rules. However, in my view, another facet of international law double standards that is less frequently discussed in scholarly works is the lack of effective norms to address similar issues that are examined under different spheres of international law for various reasons.

As mentioned in the introduction, this chapter argues that the imposition of unilateral coercive measures serves as a prime example. Despite being discussed by numerous scholars and UN bodies for the significant suffering they can cause to the affected populations, UCMs still lack clear regulation and restrictions within the broader framework of international law. In contrast, in similar scenarios of suffering, we observe clear rules of international law that unequivocally establish that certain behaviors are illegal or subject to significant restrictions. The following section elaborates on this by providing some examples.

---

double-standards-at-icj-hearing-on-israeli-occupation; Evan Dyer, "Angry Claims of 'Double Standards' in International Law Roil the UN," *CBC,* September 26, 2024. https://www.cbc.ca/news/politics/united-nations-israel-gaza-1.7334158

8 Jan Willem Sap, "Double Standards. The Political Character of International Human Rights," *NTKR,* 2020. https://www.uitgeverijparis.nl/nl/reader/208970/1001526229

9 Mag. Michael J. Moffatt, *Double Standards in International Law*, Universitat Wien, May 22, 2018. https://ssc-rechtswissenschaften.univie.ac.at/fileadmin/user_upload/s_rechtswissenschaft/Doktoratsstudium_PhD/Expose1/Voelkerrecht/Understanding_Double_Standards_in_International_Law.pdf

UCMs and the Lack of Certainty in Legal Terms

UCMs and the Prohibition of Discrimination

Modern international law, as noted by many scholars, is primarily recognized as a normative system inspired by human rights and humanity.[10] Therefore, it is not surprising to assert that discrimination of any kind is prohibited within this framework. However, it is unfortunate to note that unilateral coercive measures are not universally regarded as a form of discrimination against those living under sanctions. The UN Special Rapporteur has highlighted that UCMs can create severe distinctions in various areas, such as the treatment of vulnerable populations, including the sick, trade relations, scientific cooperation, and family life.[11] While the discriminatory impacts of unilateral coercive measures are evident in the devastating consequences of their implementation, the double standards in international law regarding the concept of discrimination hinder us from unequivocally asserting the absolute prohibition of discrimination in arguments against the legality of these measures.

A good and recent example is the Case before the International Court of Justice brought by State of Qatar against United Arab Emirates (UAE) on the application of the International Convention on the Elimination of All Forms of Racial Discrimination (ICERD). In the core of its arguments, Qatar argued that because of the imposition of UCMs "the UAE has enacted and implemented a series of discriminatory measures directed at Qataris based expressly on their national origin."[12] Moreover, the Applicant stated that UAE actions ". . . targeting Qatar and Qataris (collectively, 'discriminatory measures')

---

10 Theodor Meron, *The Humanization of International Law* (Brill, 2006).

11 Report of the Special Rapporteur on the Impact of Unilateral Coercive Measures on the Right to Health, A/HRC/54/23, March 28, 2024; Report of the Special Rapporteur on the Secondary Sanctions, Civil and Criminal Penalties for Circumvention of Sanctions Regimes and Over-compliance with Sanctions, A/HRC/51/33, July 15, 2022; UN Press Release, Unilateral Sanctions Threaten Scientific Research and Academic Freedom: UN Experts, July 7, 2022. https://www.ohchr.org/en/press-releases/2022/07/unilateral-sanctions-threaten-scientific-research-and-academic-freedom-un; UN Press Release, UN Expert Concerned at Reported Use of Family Ties as Sole Grounds for Sanctions Designations, October 16, 2024. https://www.ohchr.org/en/press-releases/2024/10/un-expert-concerned-reported-use-family-ties-sole-grounds-sanctions.

12 ICJ, *Qatar v. United Arab Emirates,* Application Instituting Proceedings, June 11, 2018, para. 3.

are unlawful. The UAE imposed them on Qataris across the board, without any justification under international law, and in particular, without exception and without reference to the particular circumstance of the Qataris impacted."[13] Qatar has also argued that: "the majority of the measures were broad and non-targeted, making no distinction between the Government of Qatar and its population. In that sense, they constitute core elements of the definition of unilateral coercive measures."[14] ICERD Article 1(1) defines "racial discrimination" as:

> Any distinction, exclusion, restriction or preference based on race, color, descent, or national or ethnic origin which has the purpose or effect of nullifying or impairing the recognition, enjoyment or exercise, on an equal footing, of human rights and fundamental freedoms in the political, economic, social, cultural or any other field of public life.

Qatar referred to "national origin" in this provision and, on that basis, argued that the respondent State violated several of its obligations under the ICERD.[15] On February 4, 2021, the Court rendered its judgment on the preliminary objections and unfortunately declared that the ICJ does not have jurisdiction *ratione materiae* in this case.[16] The Court reached this conclusion because in its view "the aim of the [ICERD] Convention is ... to eliminate all forms and manifestations of racial discrimination against human beings on the basis of real or perceived characteristics as of their origin, namely at birth."[17] On this basis, the ICJ argued that the ICERD "was clearly not intended to cover every instance of differentiation between persons based on their nationality. Differentiation on the basis of nationality is common and is reflected in the legislation of most States parties."[18] Having said that the Court consequently argued that "the term 'national origin' in Article 1, paragraph 1, of ICERD, in accordance with its ordinary

---

13   Ibid., para. 5.
14   Ibid., para. 7.
15   Ibid., para. 65.
16   ICJ, *Qatar v. United Arab Emirates,* Judgment, February 4, 2021, para. 114.
17   Ibid., para. 86.
18   Ibid., para. 87.

meaning, read in its context and in the light of the object and purpose of the Convention, does not encompass current nationality."[19]

This finding of the Court was surprising specially because the CERD Committee, in its General Recommendation XXX, declared that:

> Differential treatment based on citizenship or immigration status will constitute discrimination if the criteria for such differentiation, judged in the light of the objectives and purposes of the Convention, are not applied pursuant to a legitimate aim, and are not proportional to the achievement of this aim.[20]

With this interpretation in mind, Qatar submitted two interstate communications to the Committee on the Elimination of Racial Discrimination on March 8, 2018, against the United Arab Emirates and the Kingdom of Saudi Arabia. On August 27, 2019, the Committee determined that it had jurisdiction over the communications submitted by Qatar against both countries. However, these two interstate communications did not proceed due to an agreement between the parties to terminate the cases.[21]

The ICJ did not dismiss either the interpretation of the Committee or the fact that the CERD has confirmed its jurisdiction to delve into both cases. However, the Court reminded that in accordance to its previous judgments "[the ICJ] in the exercise of its judicial functions, [is in no way obliged] to model its own interpretation of the [. . .] [Convention] on that of the Committee."[22] Hence, the Court announced that, it will follow its own line of argument in interpreting the scope of the ICERD and exclude the current nationality from the domain of the prohibited discriminations thereto.[23]

---

19 Ibid., para. 88.

20 Committee on the Elimination of Racial Discrimination, General Recommendation XXX on Discrimination Against Non-Citizens, 2005, para. 4.

21 Inter-State Communications under CERD. https://www.ohchr.org/en/treaty-bodies/cerd/inter-state-communications.

22 ICJ, *Qatar v. United Arab Emirates,* Judgment, para. 101.

23 Ibid. It is important to mention here that the court took this decision by eleven votes in favor to six against (Judgment, February 4, 2021, para. 115). The members of the court who did not vote in favor of this Judgment in their separate opinions referred

With this very narrow interpretation of the concept of "national origin," the ICJ deprived international scholars advocating against UCMs of a compelling basis to argue that these measures fundamentally contradict the obligations of State parties to the ICERD. That said, in my opinion, the Court did not completely close the door on further arguments that the imposition of UCMs, while not necessarily violating the prohibition of racial discrimination, may contravene the general prohibition of discrimination as outlined in other international instruments, such as the Universal Declaration of Human Rights and regional human rights treaties. In that respect it is important to remind that Qatar also invoked the jurisprudence of the European Court of Human Rights, the Inter-American Court of Human Rights and the African Commission on Human and Peoples' Rights, which, it contends, have interpreted the term national origin as including nationality.[24] As the Court put forward "[Qatar] refers to this jurisprudence to reiterate that discrimination consists in a difference in treatment

---

to important issues. For example, President Yusuf in its declaration stated that "a measure may amount to de facto racial discrimination when it has a disproportionate effect on a group of people having a common "national or ethnic origin," regardless of whether that measure was intended to target a particular 'nationality'" (para. 16). https://www.icj-cij.org/sites/default/files/press-releases/0/172-20210204-JUD-01-01-EN.pdf; Judge Sebutinde in her dissenting opinion said that: "I am of the considered view that the approach of the majority whereby the jurisdiction ratione materiae of the Court turns on a theoretical definition or analysis of the term 'national origin' without taking into account the facts and evidence adduced by Qatar in support of its claims (paragraphs 75 to 105) is not in the interests of justice" (para. 22). https://www.icj-cij.org/sites/default/files/case-related/172/172-20210204-JUD-01-02-EN.pdf; Judge Bhandari in his dissenting opinion stipulates that "As a general proposition, in my view, the definitions of the two words indicate that 'national origin' refers to a person's belonging to a country or nation. Belonging in this sense may be long standing or historical, and defined by ancestry or descent, or it may be confirmed by the legal status of nationality or national affiliation. Thus, current nationality, even if considered in a purely legal sense to be within the discretion of the State and subject to change over a person's lifetime, is in any event encompassed within the broader term 'national origin'" (para. 10). https://www.icj-cij.org/sites/default/files/case-related/172/172-20210204-JUD-01-03-EN.pdf; Judge Robinson in his dissenting opinion state that: "national origin refers not only to the place from which one's forebears came; it may also refer to the place where one was born. For that reason, it is clear that national origin can encompass nationality because the place where one was born can give rise to both one's nationality as well as one's national origin" (para. 8). https://www.icj-cij.org/sites/default/files/case-related/172/172-20210204-JUD-01-04-EN.pdf

24 ICJ, *Qatar v. United Arab Emirates*, Judgment, para. 102.

without legitimate justification and without a reasonable relationship of proportionality with the aim to be achieved, which in its view is true of the measures at issue in this case."[25] Reacting to the above references, the Court first emphasized that in the present dispute it is for the Court to determine the scope of discrimination in the framework of the ICERD.[26] However, the Court did not stop here and added that:

> The Court notes that the regional human rights instruments on which the jurisprudence of the regional courts is based concern respect for human rights without distinction of any kind among their beneficiaries. The relevant provisions of these conventions are modelled on Article 2 of the Universal Declaration of Human Rights of 10 December 1948 [...].[27]

The Court further stated "while these legal instruments all refer to 'national origin,' their purpose is to ensure a wide scope of protection of human rights and fundamental freedoms."[28]

Does this imply that the Court believes that, beyond the narrow scope of the ICERD, any discrimination based on national origin and/or current nationality, as referenced in the jurisprudence cited by Qatar, is prohibited under international human rights law? In my view, the answer is affirmative. However, the Court's implicit approach to declaring this important point may serve as an obstacle for international law in reducing instances of double standards.

Humanitarian Exceptions in the case of UCMs

Chapter VII of the United Nations Charter authorizes the Security Council (UNSC) to impose sanctions to restore international peace and security. As a matter of law, these enforcement measures decided by the Security Council are legal and, in accordance with the Charter, obligatory for all member States. The Security Council has utilized this option in numerous cases to promote the rule of law within the international community. The counter-terrorism measures implemented by the Security Council serve as notable examples.

---

25 Ibid.
26 Ibid., para. 104.
27 Ibid.
28 Ibid.

Having said that, it is important to remind ourselves that even the Security Council is not permitted to cross the redlines of humanity and proportionality in imposing the sanctions. There is a huge number of scholarly works which indicate that in accordance with international law the Security Council, in the process of imposition of sanctions against States, individuals and other entities, is obliged to be bound by the principles of humanity and proportionality.[29] In this regard, the 2023 factsheet of the Security Council on sanctions regime specifies that: "over the past five decades, sanctions regimes have changed in focus and scale. One of the most significant changes has been the shift away from use of comprehensive sanctions. Since 2004, all new sanctions regimes have been targeted, meaning that they are intended to have limited, strategic focus on certain individuals, entities, groups or undertakings."[30] In other words, the Security Council has tried to decrease the adverse humanitarian impacts of the sanctions.[31] One of the latest developments in this regard is the adoption of Resolution 2664 in 2022. As put by Lewis, Kapur and Modirzadeh:

> The core of the resolution reflected a politically negotiated policy shift with extensive legal implications. In short, the UNSC decided that humanitarian aid and protection should reach affected populations in areas under the de facto or de jure control or authority of actors designated for UNSC-imposed asset freezes, including in relevant counterterrorism contexts, irrespective of whether those designees may benefit in the process.[32]

---

29 Mary Ellen O'Connell, "Debating the Law of Sanctions," *European Journal of International Law* 13, no. 1 (2002), pp. 63–79. https://doi.org/10.1093/ejil/13.1.63.

30 United Nations Security Council, Fact Sheets 2023, p. 4. https://main.un.org/securitycouncil/sites/default/files/subsidiary_organs_series_7sep23_.pdf; Joanna Weschler, "The Evolution of Security Council Innovations in Sanctions," *Canada's Journal of Global Policy Analysis* 65, no. 1 (2010), pp. 31–43. https://doi.org/10.1177/002070201006500103

31 Annalisa Ciampi, "Security Council Targeted Sanctions and Human Rights," in Bardo Fassbender (ed.), *Securing Human Rights? Achievements and Challenges of the UN Security Council, Collected Courses of the Academy of European Law* (Oxford, 2011), pp. 98–140. https://doi.org/10.1093/acprof:oso/9780199641499.003.0005

32 Dustin A. Lewis, Radhika Kapoor, and Naz K. Modirzadeh, *Resolution 2664 (2022) and Counterterrorism Measures: An Analytical Frame for States* (Harvard Law School Program on International Law and Armed Conflict, 2024), p. 2. https://

Further, for the first time, this Resolution considers the importance of "assessing potential humanitarian impacts prior to a Council decision to establish a sanctions regime," a longstanding recommendation in line with the prerogative to design targeted sanctions measures. As noted by Chowdhury and Sarfati "such recommendations to more carefully assess the needs and impacts prior to the adoption of resolutions have increasingly been made in the area of counterterrorism, where a proliferation of resolutions has raised questions about needs and gaps, impacts, and effectiveness."[33] The preambular paragraphs also note that sanctions are "intended to be temporary" and that they may be "adjust[ed] and terminate[d]" depending on the evolving situation on the ground and the need to mitigate humanitarian impacts, opening the way for possible sunset-clauses or criteria development for their adjustment and termination.[34]

Examining the details of the aforementioned restrictions on the work of the Security Council is beyond the scope of this chapter. However, the key takeaway for our discussion is significant: even the most legally justified forms of pressure, aimed at restoring or maintaining international peace and security, must align with the limitations imposed by international law.

In other words, international law norms and regulations also aim to mitigate the humanitarian impacts of UN sanctions. But is this true for unilateral coercive measures as well? Are there clear limitations imposed by established norms of international law regarding UCMs? Are there any humanitarian exemptions or carve-outs? Is there a rule that obligates the sanctioning State to assess the humanitarian impact of UCMs before imposing them and during their implementation? Is there a court to which victims can refer their cases? Is there any due process of law provided in this context? And are there regulations to mitigate or terminate UCMs? In her interview with the International Review of the Red Cross, the Special Rapporteur on UCMs states that:

---

hls.harvard.edu/wp-content/uploads/2024/03/Res.-2664-and-Counterterrorism-Measures.pdf

33 Naureen Chowdhury Fink and Agathe Sarfati, "Milestone in the Security Council: What the New Humanitarian 'Carve-out' Means for UN Sanctions Regimes," *IPI Global Observatory*, December 16, 2022. https://theglobalobservatory.org/2022/12/new-humanitarian-carve-out-un-sanctions-regimes/

34 Ibid.

When I compare this situation with the practice of the UN Security Council, there is quite a bit of difference. [...] the practice of the UN Security Council since the late 1990s and early 2000s reveals that there have been repeated efforts to assess the humanitarian impact of its sanctions. [...] Unfortunately, so far there have been no reports and no assessment of the humanitarian impact of unilateral sanctions. That is why I would say that the aspect of derisking and over-compliance exists to a certain extent when we speak about sanctions of the UN Security Council, but there is a continuous policy to minimize this negative impact and to assess the humanitarian impact of those sanctions. This is absolutely not the case for the application of unilateral sanctions today [...].[35]

In general, the situation is as follows: while legitimate coercive measures authorized by the Security Council are upheld by international law, the legitimacy of unilateral coercive measures is fiercely debated within this legal framework. Furthermore, there are no explicit obligations for the sanctioning State to address the negative consequences of these measures. The existence of illegal secondary sanctions exacerbates this issue, as companies and other stakeholders may adopt a zero-risk policy, leading to excessive compliance with UCMs.[36] Moreover, those designated by the sanctioning State, along with individuals and communities affected by the direct or indirect consequences, lack adequate access to justice to pursue their rights.[37]

---

35 "Unilateral Coercive Measures, IHL and Impartial Humanitarian Action: An Interview with Alena Douhan," *International Review of the Red Cross* 103, nos. 916–917 (2021), pp. 39–40. https://doi.org/10.1017/S1816383121000230; UN Press Release, "Humanitarian Exemptions in Unilateral Sanctions Regimes Ineffective and Inefficient: UN Experts," November 24, 2022. https://www.ohchr.org/en/node/104258.

36 UN Press Release, "Over-Compliance with Secondary Sanctions Adversely Impacts Human Rights of Millions Globally: UN Expert," September 14, 2022. https://www.ohchr.org/en/press-releases/2022/09/over-compliance-secondary-sanctions-adversely-impacts-human-rights-millions.

37 UN Press Release, "Special Rapporteur Concerned by Limited Access to Sanctions-Related Justice," October 29, 2024. https://www.ohchr.org/en/press-releases/2024/10/special-rapporteur-concerned-limited-access-sanctions-related-justice.

This serves as another clear example of the double standards in international law regarding unilateral coercive measures compared to sanctions imposed by the Security Council.

UCMs and Limitations derived from Law of Armed Conflicts

The Law on the Use of Force

As stated in Article 1(1) of the UN Charter, the primary purpose of the UN's founding members was to maintain international peace and security. This is achieved through collective measures to address threats to peace and through the peaceful resolution of disputes based on principles of justice and international law. In this context, Article 2(4) of the Charter prohibits the use of force in international relations. It stipulates that, aside from the use of force against the territorial integrity or political independence of States, any other forms of threat or use of force that are inconsistent with the purposes of the UN are also prohibited.

The formula presented in this provision is difficult to understand without examining the meaning of the term "force." As noted in the Oxford Commentary on the UN Charter, this concept is not universally agreed upon.[38] The Commentary stipulates that "the developing countries and formerly the Eastern bloc countries had repeatedly claimed that the prohibition of the use of force also comprises other forms of force, for instance, political and, in particular, economic coercion."[39] The Commentary admits that "the actual wording of Art. 2(4) does not provide a clear solution to it."[40] Having said that, the Commentary refers to the preamble and Article 44 of the Charter and concludes that "the prevailing view is further corroborated by a teleological interpretation of Art. 2(4): were this provision extend to other forms of force, States would be left with no means of exerting pressure on other States which act in violation of international law."[41] The Commentary also reminds that at the San Francisco Conference a proposal by Brazil to

---

38 Oliver Dörr and Albrecht Randelzhofer, "Article 2 (4)," in Bruno Simma, et al. (eds.), *The Charter of the United Nations: A Commentary*, Vol. I, 3rd Edition (Oxford Commentaries on International Law, 2012), p. 208. https://doi.org/10.1093/law/9780199639762.003.0010, p. 208.

39 Ibid., pp. 208–209.

40 Ibid., p. 209.

41 Ibid.

extend the prohibition of the use of force to economic coercion, was rejected.[42]

However, in the years after the adoption of the UN Charter, as noted by Batinga in his thought provoking paper, countries in the Global South advocated for the United Nations to adopt a broader interpretation of Article 2(4) that encompasses economic coercion as a form of force.[43] This perspective stems from the belief in the Global South that the devastating effects of coercive measures, particularly unilateral coercive measures, can be equivalent to military force. In some cases, these measures can cause even greater harm. For instance, during the eight-year war between Iran and Iraq, the Iranian economy did not suffer as severely as it currently does under the UCMs imposed by the United States.[44]

This reflects anther clear double standard in international law regarding the consequences of unilateral coercive measures. While the Charter and customary international law prohibit States from using force in their international relations, the prevailing interpretation does not allow for a broader understanding of "force" to include all threats to peace and humanity. This narrow interpretation overlooks the fact that non-military forms of force can lead to humanitarian catastrophes that in many cases exceed the devastation caused by wars.

In this context, it is important to recall the point raised by the late Judge Antônio Augusto Cançado Trindade in his insightful separate opinion regarding the Order of October 2018, from the International Court of Justice. This order addressed the provisional measures in the Treaty of Amity case between Iran and the United States, specifically concerning the reimposition of sanctions on Iran following the U.S. withdrawal from the Iran nuclear deal.[45] He said:

---

42 Ibid.

43 Jacob Batinga, "Reconciling the Global North-South Divide on the Use of Force: Economic Coercion and the Evolving Interpretation of Article 2(4)," *Wisconsin International Law Journal* 41, no. 2 (2024), p. 111. https://wilj.law.wisc.edu/wp-content/uploads/sites/1270/2024/01/103-143-Batinga.pdf

44 Report of the Special Rapporteur Visit to the Islamic Republic of Iran, A/HRC/51/33/Add.1, October 4, 2022.

45 ICJ, Alleged Violations of the 1955 Treaty of Amity, Economic Relations, and Consular Rights (*Islamic Republic of Iran v. United States of America*), Order on Provisional Measures, October 3, 2018.

Once again in the present case and always, human beings stand in need, ultimately, of protection against evil, which lies within themselves. [. . .] In such perspective, the raison d'humanité is to prevail over the raison d'Etat.[46]

International Humanitarian Law

Unilateral coercive measures can profoundly affect civilian populations in a variety of ways. Numerous reports document how sanctions contribute to non-development, poverty, humanitarian situations, health complications, food insecurity, educational challenges. etc.[47] As noted earlier, the harmful effects of UCMs often inflict greater suffering on ordinary people than armed conflicts do. Thus, it can be concluded that sanctions represent some of the most violent measures employed in international relations.[48] In a recent article, the authors criticize the effectiveness of the sanctions imposed on Russia following its attack on Ukraine, stating that "sanctions that are enacted after undesirable target State behavior are typically used for the purpose of exacting punishment. [. . .] This is really not much different than carrying out the same punishment through military actions. The ways employed are different, but only slightly so. More important, the intended effects are the same. That is, to exact enough punishment by damaging something of value to the target to get them to change their behavior. Therefore, it is not unreasonable for a target of economic sanctions to view sanctions as an act of war."[49] In another scholarly study the authors found that "when sanctions have a large economic

---

46 Separate opinion of Judge Cançado Trindade on the ICJ Order of October 3, 2018, p. 683. https://www.icj-cij.org/sites/default/files/case-related/175/175-20181003-ORD-01-01-EN.pdf

47 Joy Gordon, "The Brutal Impact of Sanctions on the Global South," *Yale Journal of International Law* Online, June 28, 2023. https://www.yjil.yale.edu/the-brutal-impact-of-sanctions-on-the-global-south/

48 Alexandra Hofer and Mohammad Kanfash, "Sanctions as Violence," *E-International Relations*, June 17, 2024. https://www.e-ir.info/2024/06/17/sanctions-as-violence/; Michael Fakhri, "Situating Unilateral Coercive Measures Within a Broader Understanding of Systemic Violence," *Yale Journal of International Law* Online, June 23, 2023. https://www.yjil.yale.edu/situating-unilateral-coercive-measures-within-a-broader-understanding-of-systemic-violence/

49 Brent Lawniczak, "Questioning the Efficacy of Sanctions on Russia," *Journal of Advanced Military Studies* 14, no. 2 (2023). https://doi.org/10.21140/mcuj.20231402011

effect on the target, they can have severe public health consequences. These consequences are substantively similar to those associated with major military conflicts."[50]

Studies and discussions like those mentioned above demonstrate that the negative impacts of unilateral coercive measures—often referred to as "economic warfare"[51]—on the lives of ordinary people can be likened to acts of war. From this perspective, many scholars argue that the rules and principles of international law governing armed hostilities—such as the principles of neutrality, distinction, necessity, and proportionality in international humanitarian law—should also apply in the context of economic warfare.[52] Though scholars advocating for this perspective also acknowledge that, under the current framework of international law, implementing this idea is impractical. This is primarily because the rules and regulations of IHL apply only in situations of armed conflict. In other words, these provisions serve as the *lex specialis* for armed conflicts, and when a situation of violence does not meet the criteria for an "armed conflict," the applicability of IHL becomes irrelevant. This rationale underscores why Tilahun and Okafor, in their analysis of the applicability of IHL rules to economic sanctions, assert that:

> [...] more systemic conceptualization, perhaps in the form of an international code of conduct, is needed to articulate the humanitarian principles that will govern sanctions praxis. [...] A contextual articulation and reaffirmation of

---

50 Susan Hannah Allen and David J. Lektzian, "Economic Sanctions: A Blunt Instrument?," *Journal of Peace Research* 50, no. 1 (2013), pp. 121–135. https://doi.org/10.1177/0022343312456224

51 See e.g. : Elizabeth Rosenberg, Daniel Drezner, Julia Solomon-Strauss and Zachary K. Goldman, *The New Tools of Economic Warfare; Effects and Effectiveness of Contemporary U.S. Financial Sanctions* (Center for New American Security, 2016). https://www.cnas.org/publications/reports/the-new-tools-of-economic-warfare-effects-and-effectiveness-of-contemporary-u-s-financial-sanctions

52 Nema Milaninia, "Jus Ad Bellum Economicum and Jus In Bello Economico: The Limits of Economic Sanctions Under the Paradigm of International Humanitarian Law," In: Ali Z. Marossi and Marisa R. Bassett (eds.), *Economic Sanctions under International Law* (T.M.C. Asser Press, 2015), pp. 95–124. https://doi.org/10.1007/978-94-6265-051-0_6; Amichai Cohen, "Economic Sanctions in IHL: Suggested Principles," *Israel Law Review* 42, no. 1 (2009), pp. 117–49. https://doi.org/10.1017/S0021223700000479

the fundamental principles of distinction and proportionality could, for example, take the form of an exclusionary rule with respect to critical economic infrastructure, a precautionary obligation (*ex ante* impact assessment), and an obligation to undertake cumulative assessment of harms caused by sanctions over time."[53]

This highlights another stark example of the double standards that exist within international law regarding the humanitarian impacts of economic warfare. When a situation is classified as military conflict, numerous norms are in place to protect the victims. However, when the means of coercion, even if they have more devastating effects, do not qualify as traditional armaments, the victims are left without the protections afforded by international law.

Concluding Remarks

The facts and features discussed in this chapter demonstrate that the current system of international law, in both its normative and structural dimensions, lacks adequate tools to confront the challenges posed by unilateral coercive measures, which have led to catastrophic consequences for individuals and communities, both directly and indirectly. In contrast, this same system has developed sufficient norms and structures to address the similar hardships and suffering resulting from the use of force, armed conflicts, and human rights abuses. These tools include various prohibitions against illegal conduct and provide humanitarian measures aimed at alleviating the suffering of those affected by such violations. The observations presented in this chapter highlight a troubling example of the double standards present in the current international legal system, a disparity that deserves attention in inter-state, civil society, and academic discussions.

From this perspective, any efforts to promote and inspire discussions aimed at strengthening the norms and structures of international law to address the challenges posed by the imposition of UCMs are crucial. This is how one should assess the recent Guiding Principles

---

53 Nathanael Tilahun and Obiora Okafor, "Economic Sanctions and Humanitarian Principles: Lessons from International Humanitarian Law," *Yale Journal of International Law,* June 26, 2023. https://yjil.yale.edu/posts/2023-06-26-economic-sanctions-and-humanitarian-principles-lessons-from-international

developed by the Special Rapporteur on the negative impact of unilateral coercive measures on the enjoyment of human rights, concerning sanctions, business, and human rights: a code of multiple principles which include general principles, principles for States and principles for businesses.

In the Commentary of the Guiding Principles, the Special Rapporteur emphasized that "the guiding principles do not create and do not intend to create new legal norms. They elaborate on the application of existing treaty or customary legal norms by states, international organizations and other relevant actors in a sanctions' environment."[54] In this way, the Special Rapporteur emphasized that the core obligations referred to in this code already exist in the normative domain of international law.

Having this in mind, the Guiding Principles, *inter alia*, declare that: "people in States affected by unilateral sanctions, and in the absence of sanctions of the UN Security Council, shall enjoy humanitarian assistance regimes not less favorable than those proposed for countries under sanctions of the UN Security Council. They shall fully benefit from the principle of humanity and access to humanitarian aid and assistance."[55] This is how the Guiding Principles aim to extend the humanitarian carve-out discussed earlier to unilateral coercive measures. Furthermore, the Guiding Principles declare that "States shall not purport to derogate from their human rights obligations, including their obligation not to discriminate against any person on the basis of race, nationality, gender, political opinion or any other recognized ground [. . .]."[56] With the above discussions in mind, the emphasis on the notion of "nationality" in this paragraph is particularly illustrative.

Moreover, the Guiding Principles state that: "extraterritorial application of unilateral coercive measures is illegal under international law, being a violation of fundamental principles of international law."[57] The Commentary on this guiding principle does not directly reference the principle prohibiting the use of force; nonetheless,

---

54 The Commentary on the Draft Guiding Principles on Sanctions, Business and Human Rights, p. 17. https://indico.un.org/event/1013607/attachments/17742/54787/Commentary(Draft)-UCM%20Mandate.pdf

55 Draft Guiding Principles on Sanctions, Business and Human Rights, para. 11.5.

56 Ibid., para. 14.1.

57 Ibid., para. 19.4.

it states that: "secondary sanctions imposed extraterritorially also contradict international law, firstly because they are based on illegal primary coercive measures, and secondly because of equivalent objections to extraterritorial enforcement. Further, they infringe the sovereignty of other States by violating the legal principles of jurisdiction and non-intervention in the internal affairs of States [...]."[58] This may, to some extent, yield similar results to prohibiting the imposition of unilateral coercive measures based on the prohibition of the use of force in the territory of other states.

The examples presented above from the Guiding Principles, along with their comprehensive and significant commentary, illustrate how the work of the mandate holders of the Human Rights Council can advance discussions in the realm of international law to prohibit illegal forms of coercion and mitigate their adverse effects on the international legal order, which currently suffers from unreasonable double standards in this area. It is anticipated that concerned States and the academic community will actively promote this initiative.

---

58 The Commentary on the Draft Guiding Principles on Sanctions, Business and Human Rights, p. 70. I have already discussed how the principle of non-intervention may lead to satisfactory outcomes in this context; "The Principle of Non-Intervention and the Dilemma of the Legality of the Unilateral Coercive Measures," in: Ksenia Kirkham (ed.), *The Routledge Handbook of the Political Economy of Sanctions* (Routledge, 2023), pp. 318–29.

CHAPTER 3

Sanctions as Economic Warfare

The USA versus China

Robert Walker[1]

Abstract

Whereas China presents international relations as collaborative seeking to foster a global community, the U.S. and its Western allies seem to view them as inherently competitive. Therefore, the unilateral coercive measures—often termed "sanctions"—imposed on China by the U.S. (and more reluctantly by its allies) might be considered as tools, indeed as weapons, employed in an ideological and economic competition for global supremacy. The sanctions against China have been implemented largely under of U.S. domestic law with extraterritorial effect. Their scope, affecting economic entities and named individuals, has been substantial, with attempts to resist them through international dispute settlement proving mostly ineffectual. There are multiple concerns about the operation of unilateral coercive measures appertaining to their scope, the determination of illegal acts warranting sanction, the adherence to process and proportionality, and the legitimate choice of entities targeted. These generic concerns apply with force to U.S. sanctions imposed on China. They are not only incompatible with international law, which is carefully drafted to allow for diversity of cultures and political systems but seek to replace it with a prescriptive world order that presumes a singularity with respect to the rules of trade and seeks to perpetuate existing power relations.

---

1 Jingshi Academy, Beijing Normal University. I am exceedingly grateful for the support of Professors Li Mianguan and He Hailan, although neither is responsible for any of the deficiencies of this chapter.

Economic warfare is not war without casualties for the collateral damage, in terms of truncated lives, lack of economic growth and development, and increased social distress, is real. Suffering and deaths, sometimes on a large scale, occur as documented with respect to economic sanctions imposed on North Korea,[2] Venezuela,[3] Cuba and Iran.[4] Typically a response to deep insecurity, as with the bully in a playground, trade wars result in victimization, fear and often retaliation. The bully's excuses are various and typically without substance, a tissue of lies that serve to enhance their sense of insecurity. While the bully may feel vindicated, they are truly a social pariah condemned to have no true friends, only reluctant henchmen.

When economic competition becomes war is a matter of definition. The European Parliament defines a trade war as "when both parties keep on increasing tariffs or create other barriers, which can make products more expensive and complicate things for companies."[5] The Oxford English Dictionary similarly defines a trade war "as a state of affairs in which countries try to damage each other's trade, typically by the imposition of tariffs or other trade barriers," but notes that the term can be used to describe "a war fought over trade" although this rare. The stricter definition of a trade war employed in this chapter refers to repeated actions undermining trade relations that, taken by one country against another country or international organizations without the permission of regional or multilateral economic organizations or the consent of the entities targeted, would appear, a priori, to be inconsistent with relevant international rules. Such actions are frequently implemented under domestic laws deemed to have extraterritorial

2 *Korea Peace Now: The human costs and gendered impact of sanctions on North Korea* (October 2019). https://koreapeacenow.org/first-comprehensive-assessment-of-the-impact-of-sanctions-against-north-koreashows-adverse-consequences-for-civilians-especially-women/

3 M. Weisbrot and J. Sachs, *Economic Sanctions as Collective Punishment: The Case of Venezuela* (Washington DC: Center for Economic and Policy Research, 2019). https://cepr.net/images/stories/reports/venezuela-sanctions-2019-04.pdf

4 E. Kessler, *How Economic Sanctions are Used in US Foreign Policy,* working paper (Chicago: Chicago Council on Global Affairs, 2022).

5 European Parliament, "Trade Wars: what are the EU's trade defence instruments?" (2023 update). https://www.europarl.europa.eu/topics/en/article/20180308STO99328/trade-wars-what-are-the-eu-s-trade-defence-instruments

scope. Following American usage, the terms sanctions and unilateral coercive measures are used interchangeably.[6]

The argument to be pursued is that the plethora of unilateral coercive measures currently employed by the United States of America (U.S.) against China, ostensibly to counter illicit practices with respect to trade, security and human rights, in actuality constitute a trade war to preserve geopolitical primacy. With U.S. administrations being aware of the dubious legality of the measures employed, their claims to be acting to protect a consensual rules-based world order are undermined.

Geopolitical Context

Scholars give diverse accounts of the fundamental nature of international relations. Some, often labelled realists or neorealists, portray nations as being locked in competition, intent on pursuing their own self-interests with the most powerful seeking primacy and dominance.[7] International law and intergovernmental institutions are coopted by powerful states to be used to further their national interests. An alternative liberal view of international relations emphasizes the importance of global governance; intergovernmental organizations and law are considered necessary to structure the collective behavior of national governments to protect weaker nations and to benefit the common good.

Neorealism is sometimes taught as a set of policy strategies and is promoted in practical terms by thinktanks in the USA such as the Council on Foreign Relations (CFR) and the Atlantic Council and taken into the U.S. federal government by affiliates of these organizations. Since 1992, the United States has sought to further enhance its dominant position by spreading liberal democracy, strengthening military alliances and modifying international institutions to support

---

6 Kessler, *supra* note 3, at 131; Sanctions should be differentiated from retorsions "which are defined as measures which are merely unfriendly, but lawful, taken by one state in response to a prior unfriendly act of another state. Given that the sender of retorsions by endorsing taxation laws, withdrawing voluntary aid, or immigration laws, has not violated any legal obligation owed to the target, it is not in violation of international law." Sanctions imply the violation of an obligation which may or not be unlawful depending on the circumstances.

7 G. Meibauer, "Neorealism, neoclassical realism and the problem(s) of history," *International Relations* 25, no. 1 (2019): 229.

free trade and unfettered capital markets.[8] It has, however, failed in achieving its "first objective," specified in 1992, which was "to prevent the re-emergence of a new rival."[9]

China, increasingly perceived by the United States as an adversary rather than merely a rival, adopts a liberal approach to international relations, certainly in its language and, arguably, in many of its actions, including the Global Development (GDI) and the Belt and Road (BRI) initiatives. The 2023 *Foreign Affairs White Paper* advises: "to build a global community of shared future, countries should advance democracy in international relations to make sure that the future of the world is determined by all, that international rules are written by all, that global affairs are governed by all, and that the fruits of development are shared by all."[10]

International law exists to regulate relationships between nation states and to foster just transactions between them. It variously rests on custom, treaties, judicial decisions, and opinion.[11] International law creates rules that are well defined and have content that can be understood, applied, and enforced, or if contested in specific circumstances, can be further defined through recognized dispute settlement processes. It is also based on consent and is binding only on those nations that do consent through, for example, the signing and ratification of treaties.

Since around 2017, Western countries led by the United States have increasingly begun to refer to "a rules-based world order" and presentationally to legitimize actions, such as the imposition of unilateral coercive measures, as being in "defense" of this order which China, among other countries, is accused of seeking to challenge.[12] In fact, as John Dugard, Judge ad hoc International Court of Justice and

---

8 J. Mearsheimer, "Bound to Fail: The rise and fall of the liberal international order," *International Security* 43, no. 4 (2019): 7.

9 "Excerpts From Pentagon's Plan: 'Prevent the Re-Emergence of a New Rival,'" *New York Times*, March 8, 1992. https://www.nytimes.com/1992/03/08/world/excerpts-from-pentagon-s-plan-prevent-the-re-emergence-of-a-new-rival.html

10 Full Text: *A Global Community of Shared Future: China's Proposals and Actions,* The State Council Information Office, PRC, September 26, 2023. http://english.scio.gov.cn/whitepapers/2023-09/26/content_116710660_4.htm

11 C. Greenwood, *Sources of International Law: An Introduction* (New York: United Nations, 2008).

12 A. Breuer and A. Johnston, "Memes, narratives, and the emergent US-China security dilemma," *Cambridge Review of International Affairs* 32, no. 4 (2019): 429.

former member of International Law Commission, asserts, it is the rules-based order that "threatens international law."[13] It offers merely a statement of values, rather than rules, and is not based on consent: the values and ill-defined rules are presumed to apply universally and in their entirety, irrespective of whether they prove acceptable to individual governments. Dugard concludes that, not being law, it is instead, "an order employed by the West, . . . particularly the United States, to ensure its dominance."[14]

Unilateral Sanctions Recently Imposed on China

For the purposes of exposition, the multiple unilateral coercive measures or sanctions taken against China are organized into three groups roughly according to rationales presented by the U.S.: trade sanctions, technology sanctions and human rights restrictive measures.[15] Attention is focused on measures implemented by the U.S.; only passing mention is made of those initiated by other states. Space also precludes detailed consideration of secondary sanctions that have been imposed on Chinese nationals and entities because of their alleged violation or circumvention of primary sanctions that the U.S. has imposed on third countries, notably the Russian Federation and the Islamic Republic of Iran.[16]

While invariably controversial, sanctions, if taken in response to a prior unlawful act by another state, may be considered legitimate countermeasures. Clearly the illegality of the prior act used to justify countermeasures may be contested, which is grounds for believing that all sanctions should be undertaken under the auspices of the United Nations and/or other intergovernmental organizations

---

13 J. Dugard, "The choice before us: International law or a "rules-based international order"?," *Leiden Journal of International Law* 36, no. 2 (June 2023): 231.

14 Ibid.

15 The types of sanctions commonly used in recent years fall into the following four categories: (a) Persons or entities subject to asset freeze (Blocked Persons); (b) List-based sectoral sanctions; (c) Regional trade embargoes; (d) Other Non-Blocking Sanctions (Other Non-Asset-Freezing Sanctions).

16 *Visit to China: Report of the Special Rapporteur on the negative impact of unilateral coercive measures on the enjoyment of human rights, Alena Douhan*, Geneva: Human Rights Council, UN General Assembly, Fifty-seventh session, A/HRC/57/55/Add.1 (2024).

rather than unilaterally. Either way, sanctions must meet conditions specified by the International Law Commission (*Draft Articles on the Responsibility of States for Internationally Wrongful Acts [ARSIWA]*). They must be justifiable on a case-by-case basis and prescribe the precise conditions under which the target nation or individual can be "de-sanctioned" and the sanctions removed.

The policy objectives of a sanctioning regime are also relevant for determining the legality of its actions. Rowhani opines that "sanctions generally aim to prevent war, protect human rights, hinder the proliferation of nuclear and mass-destructive weapons, restore sovereignty, and free captured citizens."[17] They should not seek regime change or to alter government structures as both would contravene the sovereign rights of states, nor should they be punitive.[18]

Unilateral Trade Sanctions

Between August 2017 and the G20 Osaka Summit in June 2019, the first Trump administration imposed multiple unilateral trade sanctions against China under domestic legislation.[19] The first to be announced, on March 23, 2018, were tariffs of 25% on steel and 10% on aluminium imports from various countries, including China. These were implemented under Section 232 of the Trade Expansion Act of 1962 after investigations had culminated in the Report on the Effect of Imports of Steel and Aluminium on National Security.[20] They were accompanied by restrictions on Chinese investments in specific

---

17 M. Rowhani, Rights-Based Boundaries of Unilateral Sanctions, *Washington International Law Journal* 32, no. 2 (2023): 132. S. Oxman et al., *Certified Global Sanctions Specialists Study Guide* (ACAMS, 2020). https://www.acams.org/en/certifications/certified-global-sanctions-specialist-cgss

18 R. Mohamad, "Unilateral Sanctions in International Law: A Quest for Legality," in A. Ali Marossi and M. Bassett, M. (eds.), *Economic Sanctions Under International Law* (The Hague: Asser Press, 2015), p. 71.

19 H. Zhang, "Legal Review and Response to the unilateral economic sanctions of the United States," *Review of Political Science and Law* 2 (2020): 92; and J. M. Zhang, "'Hegemonic Long Arm': The Purpose and Implementation of US Unilateral Extraterritorial Sanctions," *Pacific Journal* 2, no. 53 (2020).

20 https://www.federalregister.gov/documents/2020/07/06/2020-14359/publication-of-a-report-on-the-effect-of-imports-of-steel-on-the-national-security-an-investigation

technology sectors and litigation under the auspices of the World Trade Organization (WTO), claiming discriminatory licensing practices.[21]

China retaliated on April 2, 2018, by imposing tariffs (ranging between 15 and 25%) on 128 products (worth US$3 billion), including fruit, wine, seamless steel pipes and pork. The next day the U.S. announced tariffs of 25% on more than 1,300 types of Chinese imported goods. These followed the report of an inquiry conducted under Section 301 of the Trade Act of 1974.[22] On April 4, China proposed 25% tariffs to be applied on 106 products (worth US$50 billion) affecting goods such as soybeans, automobiles, and chemicals (list revised on June 16, 2018).[23]

On June 15, 2018, the U.S. announced a second list of potential sanctions and, on July 6, the U.S. Customs and Border Protection (CBP) began collecting a 25 percent tariff on a reduced list of 818 imported Chinese products. On July 11, a third list was published imposing 10% tariffs on over 6,000 commodities totalling US$200 billion, which was to be implemented in phases. The U.S. subsequently increased the 10% tariff to a 25% tariff on $200 billion worth of Chinese goods on May 10, 2019, but, days before the G20 Osaka Summit on June 29, 2019, a truce was reached, leading, on January 15, 2020, Day 565 of the "trade war," to "a phase-one" trade deal that involved China importing US$200 billion more U.S. goods.[24]

The Biden administration retained many of the tariffs imposed. In March 2024, some US$350 billion of the initial US$550 billion worth of tariffs remained intact although with the provision for individual parties to apply for exclusions. (By comparison, China had responded with tariffs of just US$185 billion as of August 2020).[25] In May 2024, Biden announced new tariffs on US$18 billion worth of Chinese goods which, implemented in September 2024, imposed

---

21 D. Wong and A. Koty, "The US-China Trade War: A Timeline," *China Briefing*, August 25, 2020. https://www.china-briefing.com/news/the-us-china-trade-war-a-timeline/

22 Office of the United States Trade Representative, *Investigation Report on China's Acts, Policies, and Practices Related to Technology Transfer, Intellectual Property, and Innovation under Section 301 of the Trade Act of 1974*. March 22, 2018. https://ustr.gov/sites/default/files/Section%20301%20FINAL.PDF

23 Ibid

24 Ibid.

25 "No end to US trade war with China, Biden administration pledges in policy document," *South China Morning Post*, March 2, 2024.

tariffs of 100% on electric vehicles, 50% on solar cells and 25% on electrical vehicle batteries, critical minerals, steel, aluminum, face masks and ship-to-shore cranes.[26]

Donald Trump had long favored tariffs, proposing them against Japan in the 1980s with some commentators linking this to personality: "His obsession with winning ... appearing tough ... and ... with executive power."[27] However, the official account of U.S. reasoning behind the initial imposition and continuation of unilateral tariffs is explained in the 2022 Report to Congress on China's WTO Compliance by the U.S. Trade Representative,[28] which stated that the United States cannot accept "China's state-led, non-market approach to the economy and trade" and sought "solutions independent of the WTO." Referring to actions taken in 2018, the report explained that the United States had launched an investigation into China's acts, policies and practices relating to technology transfer, intellectual property and innovation under Section 301 of the Trade Act of 1974. The findings made in this investigation led to substantial U.S. tariffs on imports from China as well as corresponding retaliation by China.[29]

The reference to "solutions independent of the WTO" is crucial since it indicates that the administration was aware that its actions likely contravened WTO rules. It may or may not be a coincidence that in 2017 the Trump administration started refusing to approve new members of the WTO Appellate Body, claiming that its overreach undermined its fairness and intended function—code for U.S. complaints that it lost too many disputes.[30] By December 2019, the size of the appellate body had fallen below its three-person quorum and was thus unable to hear appeals or pass judgement on U.S. sanctions against China. Moreover, the report of the U.S. Trade Representative

---

26 K. Lobosco, "Biden finalizes increases to some of Trump's China tariffs," *CNN Politics,* September 13, 2024. https://edition.cnn.com/2024/09/13/politics/china-tariffs-biden-trump/index.html

27 Jennifer M. Miller, cited in J. Tankersley and M. Landler, "Trump's Love for Tariffs Began in Japan's '80s Boom," *New York Times,* May 15, 2019. https://www.nytimes.com/2019/05/15/us/politics/china-trade-donald-trump.html

28 United States Trade Representative, *2022 Report to Congress on China's WTO Compliance,* February 2023.

29 Ibid., p. 4.

30 Ian Allen, "It's Time for the United States to End Its Bipartisan Attack on the WTO," *Just Security,* March 4, 2024. https://www.justsecurity.org/93024/its-time-for-the-united-states-to-end-its-bipartisan-attack-on-the-wto/

to Congress in 2023 implies that the U.S. demands nothing less than a reconstruction of the Chinese state—if not regime change, something very close to it. It deems illicit decisions made by a government in the public interest rather than in the interests of entrepreneurial capital, a proposition consistent with the longstanding U.S. position that governments should not be obliged to offer their citizens a right to development:

> The mere fact that decisions in the marketplace are often made based on the objectives of the state, rather than based on commercial considerations, distorts China's economy and, in turn, the global economy in ways that can damage and weaken the economies of China's trading partners.[31]

The U.S. sanctions have targeted China's key export industries, ostensibly aiming to reduce U.S. imports from China and to lessen the U.S. trade deficit. The U.S. has also sought to target core enterprises and to persuade other countries to do likewise.[32] In pursuit of these objectives, the federal administration has exploited the U.S. Trade Act 1974, the National Emergencies Act 1976 (NES) and the International Emergency Economic Powers Act 1977 (IEEPA) to grant executive power to launch extensive investigations into key Chinese-funded enterprises. For example, citing security concerns, the National Defense Authorization Act for Fiscal Year 2019 was employed in 2018 to ban Huawei and ZTE equipment from being used by the U.S. federal government.

In May 2019, Huawei and its foreign subsidiaries and "affiliates" were added to the Entity List administered by the Department of Commerce; the claim made was that the company had allegedly "knowingly and wilfully" caused "the export, re-export, sale and supply, directly and indirectly, of goods, technology and services (banking and other financial services) from the United States to Iran and the

---

31 United States Trade Representative, *2023 Report to Congress on China's WTO Compliance,* February 2024; J. Mack, Explanation of Vote on a Resolution on Human Rights and Extreme Poverty (New York: U.S. Mission to the United Nations, 2020).   https://usun.usmission.gov/explanation-of-vote-on-a-resolution-on-human-rights-and-extreme-poverty/

32 G. Yang, "International Law in the US-China Trade War," *Wuhan University International Law Review* 3 (2018): 120.

government of Iran without obtaining a license from the Department of Treasury's Office of Foreign Assets Control (OFAC)."[33] This restricted U.S. companies from doing business with Huawei without a government license.

An additional 28 Chinese enterprises were added the Entity List in October 2019, including the high-tech companies Hikvision and iFlytek.[34] As of August 2022, over 600 Chinese companies, institutions and individuals were named on the Entity List, including 110 that had been added under the Biden Administration.[35]

Apart from the Entity List, the Commerce Department also included 37 Chinese companies and research institutions on the so-called "Unverified List" on April 10, 2019, meaning that U.S. exporters could no longer seek license exemptions to engage with the named institutions. By January 2020, a total of 49 Chinese institutions had been added to this unverified list, including renowned research institutions such as the Chinese Academy of Sciences, Tongji University, and Xi'an Jiaotong University.[36]

The first weeks of the second Trump administration in 2025 saw 10% tariffs imposed on all Chinese imports and an attempt made to apply them to low cost packages that had previously been excluded.[37] Tariffs were also imposed or threatened on imports from a range of

---

33 National Archives, Addition of Entities to the Entity List, *Federal Register,* May 21, 2019. https://web.archive.org/web/20190608070718/https://www.federalregister.gov/documents/2019/05/21/2019-10616/addition-of-entities-to-the-entity-list

34 Bureau of Industry and Security, US Department of Commerce, Addition of Certain Entities to the Entity List (Final Rule), May 16, 2019. https://www.bis.doc.gov/index.php/all-articles/17-regulations/1555-addition-of-certain-entities-to-the-entity-list-final-rule-effective-may-16-2019

"US Department of Commerce Adds 28 Chinese Organizations to Its Entity List," Bureau of Industry and Security, US Department of Commerce, October 7, 2019. https://www.commerce.gov/news/press-releases/2019/10/us-department-of-commerce-adds-28-chinese-organizations-to-its-entity-list.

35 "Commerce adds seven Chinese entities to Entity List for supporting China's military modernization efforts," Bureau of Industry and Security, Office of Congressional and Public Affairs, August 23, 2022.

36 *Entity List,* Bureau of Industry and Security, US Department of Commerce, February 2, 2020. https://www.bis.doc.gov/index.php/policy-guidance/lists-of-parties-of-concern/entity-list

37 L. Aratani and agencies, "Trump delays key piece of China tariff plan amid threats to other countries," *The Guardian,* February 7, 2025. https://www.theguardian.com/us-news/2025/feb/07/trump-china-tariffs

other countries, thus generalising economic warfare and using tariffs explicitly as a bargaining chip in pursuit of U.S. geopolitical interests as defined by the new administration.

Unilateral Technology Sanctions

If trade sanctions were imposed on China by the U.S. to protect domestic industries and jobs, as the Trump 2016 election rhetoric foretold, sanctions on advanced technology could be taken to reflect a future orientated agenda of strategic competition for global political and economic hegemony. However, the measures have almost invariably been imposed ostensibly to eliminate threats to national security. It will be recalled that the legitimate objectives for implementing sanctions listed above, though not exhaustive, did not include economic competition. "Preventing war" was included and—liberally interpreted—might accommodate threats to national security, although the severity of any threat could be considered a matter of judgement.

On May 15, 2019, President Trump signed an executive order entitled Securing the Information and Communications Technology and Services Supply Chain, declaring a national emergency so as to prohibit U.S. companies from using telecommunications equipment and services provided by "foreign adversaries."[38] A White House spokesperson subsequently stated:

> This Administration will do what it takes to keep America safe and prosperous, and to protect America from foreign adversaries who are actively and increasingly creating and exploiting vulnerabilities in information and communications technology infrastructure and services in the United States.[39]

---

38 Executive Order on Securing the Information and Communications Technology and Services Supply Chain, The White House, May 15, 2019. https://www.whitehouse.gov/presidential-actions/executive-order-securing-information-communications-technology-services-supply-chain/

39 Statement from the Press Secretary – Infrastructure and Technology, The White House, May 15, 2019. https://trumpwhitehouse.archives.gov/briefings-statements/statement-press-secretary-56/

While the executive order did not mention any country or company by name, the action was undeniably aimed at Huawei.[40]

The Biden administration viewed technological competition as the main axis of the U.S.-China strategic rivalry. In February 2021, Biden emphasized, in a speech at the U.S. Department of Defense, the need to address "risks and opportunities brought by emerging technologies and challenges from China."[41] In April, the U.S. Senate proposed the Strategic Competition Act 2021, urging the Biden administration to engage in comprehensive competition with China in global supply chains and science and technology to protect and promote America's "critical interests and values."

The Biden administration subsequently focussed on prioritizing emerging technological fields, including quantum computing, artificial intelligence, clean energy, and biotechnology, showing a trend of escalating pressure on Chinese technology from specific areas to broad coverage. Its most significant move was probably in October 2022 when it sought to restrict China's access to advanced semi-conductors.[42] It followed the Trump administration in seeking to persuade a reluctant Europe to ban Huawei from their 5G networks and while not all have done so, Google's withdrawal of its licence to use its Android operating system on Huawei phones caused the company considerable transitional difficulties.[43] President Trump had similarly tried, though unsuccessfully, to ban ByteDance's TikTok app on national security grounds in 2020; President Biden signed legislation in April 2024 forcing its sale within nine months but President Trump signed an executive order deferring the sale[44] during the first weeks of his second presidency.

---

40 K. O'Keeffe, J. D. McKinnon, and D. Strumpf, "Trump steps up assault on China's Huawei," *The Wall Street Journal*, May 15, 2019. https://www.wsj.com/articles/trump-telecom-ban-takes-aim-at-china-huawei-11557953363

41 J. Biden, Remarks by President Biden to Department of Defense Personnel, The White House, February 10, 2021. https://www.whitehouse.gov/briefing-room/speeches-remarks/2021/02/10/remarks-by-president-biden-to-department-of-defense-personnel/

42 Y. Huang and G. Slosberg, "China's Response to the U.S. Trade War," *China Leadership Monitor*, June 1, 2023. https://www.prcleader.org/post/china-s-response-to-the-u-s-trade-war

43 J. Strand, "Ban Huawei? Not Europe," Center for European Policy Analysis, January 12, 2023. https://cepa.org/article/ban-huawei-not-europe/

44 "Application of Protecting Americans from Foreign Adversary Controlled

The rhetoric of China becoming a "threat" linked both the first Trump administration and that of Biden and was promulgated through its leadership in alliance systems, multilateral cooperation mechanisms, and dialogue platforms, aiming to mobilize European allies to exert technological pressure on China.[45] Jeffrey Sachs[46] has persuasively argued that both administrations pursued a strategy to preserve U.S. primacy in the global system centred on stemming the rise of Chinese power rather than "continuing to assist its ascendancy" as an influential Council for Foreign Relations special report in 2015 claimed had previously been the case.[47] Apart from seeking to "consciously exclude China" from new preferential trading arrangements, the strategy included a "technology-control regime" to deny China access to high-tech and an investment, notably under the 2022 Inflation Reduction Act, in "disruptive innovations that bestowed on the United States asymmetric economic advantages over others."[48]

The first Trump administration's "China Initiative" announced in November 2018 represented a crackdown on Chinese scientists who supposedly funnelled economic and military research to China. At the height of its implementation, some 5,000 investigators were employed and, while leading to very few prosecutions, drastically reduced both collaborative working and trust.[49] Although the China Initiative is now abandoned, the May 29, 2020, Presidential Proclamation 10043,

---

Applications Act to TikTok," The White House, January 2025. https://www. whitehouse.gov/presidential-actions/2025/01/application-of-protecting-americans-from-foreign-adversary-controlled-applications-act-to-tiktok/

45 A. Ali, "Why Biden's chip war on China is straining US alliances," *Al Jazeera*, January 20, 2023. https://www.aljazeera.com/opinions/2023/1/20/bidens-chip-war-on-china-is-straining-us-alliances

46 J. Sachs "China's economic success in face of growing US, EU protectionism," *Xinhua*, April 4, 2024. https://english.news.cn/20240404/3c9664cd50bb47ffb43cabd105056109/c.html

47 R. Blackwill and A. Tellis, *Revising US Grand Strategy Toward China*. Washington DC: Council on Foreign Relations, Special Report No. 72 (2015). https://cdn.cfr.org/sites/default/files/pdf/2015/04/China_CSR72.pdf

48 Sachs, *supra* note 43, his citations from Blackwill and Tellis. The $891 billion of State-directed investment in technological development facilitated by the Inflation Reduction Act seems remarkably similar to the State-led approach to the economy of which China is accused by the U.S.

49 N. Greenfield, "Study shows drastic decline in U.S.-China scientific exchange," *University World News*, July 11, 2024. https://www.universityworldnews.com/post.php?story=20240711122935490

which imposed an arbitrary ban on Chinese postgraduates seeking to enter the U.S. with an F or J visa for the purpose of study or research, is still in force. While the preamble to the proclamation refers to students bolstering the modernization and capability of the People's Liberation Army (PLA), decisions appear not to need justification with reference to judiciable evidence but are at the "sole discretion" of the Secretary of State or their designee.

Moreover, while the Creating Helpful Incentives to Produce Semiconductors (CHIPS) and Science Act that President Biden signed into law in September 2022 as an indirect descendant of the Strategic Competition Act 2021, was primarily to stimulate strategic investment in innovation, it also imposes restrictions on Confucius Institutes that teach about Chinese culture and language. The Act additionally introduced a "malign foreign talent" recruitment program that effectively prohibits U.S. persons' participation in research funded by China.[50]

Despite improved diplomatic relations, as indicated by the summit between Presidents Xi and Biden in November 2023 and a more "candid" telephone conversation in April 2024, the U.S. has continued to sanction Chinese firms.[51] Six Chinese companies were added to the Entities List on April 11, 2024, for various reasons, including allegedly trading with Iran, acquiring items to support China's military modernization, and purchasing military equipment for Russia.[52] An Executive Order was made on February 21, 2024 to bolster the security of U.S. ports, including an investment of U.S. $20 billion, ostensibly in response security concerns that 90% of port cranes are Chinese.[53]

---

50 M. Bernardini, *US Innovation and Competition Act: A Year On* (London: Kings College, 2022). https://www.kcl.ac.uk/u.s.-innovation-and-competition-act-a-year-on

51 "President Xi Jinping Speaks with U.S. President Joe Biden on the Phone," Embassy of the People's Republic of China in the United States of America, Washington DC, April 2, 2024. http://us.china-embassy.gov.cn/eng/zmgx/zxxx/202404/t20240403_11275451.htm 2024/04/02

52 Federal Register, "Addition of Entities to the Entity List," National Archives, April 11, 2024. https://www.federalregister.gov/documents/2024/04/11/2024-07760/addition-of-entities-to-and-revision-of-entry-on-the-entity-list

53 I. Kardon, "Washington Tackles a New National Security Threat: Chinese-Made Cranes," Carnegie Endowment for International Peace, February 28, 2024. https://carnegieendowment.org/2024/02/28/washington-tackles-new-national-security-threat-chinese-made-cranes-pub-91843

On February 28, 2024, President Biden ordered an investigation into whether imported Chinese electric cars posed a security risk to Americans, albeit the likely reason was fear of the vulnerability of U.S. car manufacturers in the transition away from the internal combustion engine.[54] Treasury Secretary Janet Yellen, visiting Beijing in April 2024, alleged overcapacity in green energy industries, including solar panels, electric vehicles and lithium-ion batteries and refused to rule out further sanctions; these were subsequently announced in May 2024. The U.S. aim, she stated publicly, was to secure "some shifts in [China's] macroeconomic policy, and a reduction in the amount of, particularly local government subsidies, to firms."[55]

However, research cited in the White House announcement of the sanctions demonstrated that previous sanctions had failed to force China to alter its macroeconomic policy or to "liberalize" its socialist market economy.[56] Instead, sanctions cost the U.S. billions of dollars in lost exports and required tens of billions of dollars in subsidies to compensate farmers affected by China's retaliation. With tariffs adding to prices, the policy had hurt American consumers and companies buying imported inputs and harmed American competitiveness through reduced employment and sales. Admitting to knowing this, the true aim of the new sanctions must have been different from that articulated by Yellen. One possibility is that the Biden administration intended to counter Donald Trump's campaign rhetoric of 100% across the board tariffs on Chinese goods. Another is that the true goal was to undermine China's competitive advantage and to destroy its export economy. Neither of these reasons is likely to be compatible with WTO criteria for the imposition of countermeasures or International Law Commission guidance on the implementation of coercive measures.

54　D. Sevastopulo and J. Leahy, "Joe Biden says Chinese smart cars could pose US security threat," *Financial Times,* February 29, 2024.

55　K. Gilchrist and R. Iordache, "Yellen says she won't rule out possible tariffs on China's green exports," *CNBC,* April 9, 2024. https://www.cnbc.com/2024/04/08/yellen-says-she-wont-rule-out-possible-tariffs-on-chinas-green-exports.html

56　FACT SHEET: "President Biden Takes Action to Protect American Workers and Businesses from China's Unfair Trade Practices," The White House, May 14, 2024.　https://www.whitehouse.gov/briefing-room/statements-releases/2024/05/14/fact-sheet-president-biden-takes-action-to-protect-american-workers-and-businesses-from-chinas-unfair-trade-practices/; C. Bown, "China bought none of the extra $200 billion of US exports in Trump's trade deal," Peterson Institute for International Economics, July 19, 2022.

Unilateral Human Rights Restrictive Measures

The U.S. has imposed further restrictive measures on China, citing the rationale of alleged human rights violations in Hong Kong and Xinjiang. Both areas are of strategic importance to China.[57] According to GFCI 36 data, the Hong Kong Special Administrative Region ranks third as a global financial centre behind only New York and London.[58] Xinjiang Autonomous Region, often considered to be the gateway to China's Belt and Road global development initiative, is endowed with China's largest energy reserves, supplies 130 minerals and accounts for 20 per cent of the world's cotton production.

While the UN Charter encourages international cooperation in promoting and encouraging respect for human rights, it arguably does not impose any binding obligation on member states to act in the event of their violation by another state. However, it is widely recognised, as Rowhani explains, that "based on *erga omnes* obligations and in response to human rights violations, in enumerated situations, states are obligated to impose sanctions."[59]

Although the UN Charter equally does not mention democracy, the Vienna World Conference on Human Rights in Vienna in 1993 concluded that "democracy, development and respect for human rights and fundamental freedoms are interdependent and mutually reinforcing." This has arguably led some mistakenly to believe that the absence of a liberal-style democracy is itself an infringement of human rights.[60] This misunderstanding could conceivably explain the U.S. imposition of restrictive measures appertaining to Hong Kong, assuming that U.S. legislators were acting in good faith rather than merely engaging in trade warfare.

---

57 X. Wei, "The Domestic Mechanism of US Unilateral Human Rights Sanctions and China's Legal Countermeasures," *Journal of Shanghai University of Political Science and Law* (Legal Studies Series) 3 (2021): 72.

58 GFCI 36 Rank, *Z/Yen* (2024). https://www.longfinance.net/programmes/financial-centre-futures/global-financial-centres-index/gfci-36-explore-the-data/gfci-36-rank/

59 Rowhani, *supra* note 17, at 168.

60 L. Maizland and C. Fong, *Hong Kong's Freedoms: What China Promised and How It's Cracking Down* (backgrounder), Council on Foreign Affairs, March 19, 2024. https://www.cfr.org/backgrounder/hong-kong-freedoms-democracy-protests-china-crackdown

Motivation aside, for measures to be legitimate they should make clear the "precise conditions for the target to act in order to be de-sanctioned and give the assurance that the sanctions will be thoroughly removed after the target's compliance."[61]

Hong Kong

In the context of social unrest in Hong Kong, understood in the West to be the product of unfair repression of a pro-democracy campaign, the U.S. Congress in 2019 passed the Hong Kong Human Rights and Democracy Act.[62] In May 2020, U.S. Secretary of State Mike Pompeo took powers under the Act to cancel the "differential and special treatment" that the U.S. government had granted to Hong Kong, thereby tightening export controls on Hong Kong and sanctioning specific enterprises and senior executives operating there. In July 2020, the U.S. Congress unanimously passed the "Hong Kong Autonomy Act" and, in October 2020, the U.S. State Department submitted the first report under this Act to Congress, sanctioning 10 officials from mainland China and Hong Kong, and planning to propose a sanction list for certain Hong Kong financial institutions (USEC, 2020).[63] As of November 9, 2023, the U.S. government had imposed financial sanctions on 42 PRC and Hong Kong officials for "undermining Hong Kong's autonomy."

It is unclear how the individuals affected can bring about an end of "sanctioning"; which seems counter to natural justice. Are they expected to prove in U.S. courts that they did not act in the way alleged or, if they had, their actions would likely have been legal in Hong Kong, a special administrative region of the People's Republic of China, where they took place. Moreover, in practice, the sanctions are likely to have affected the Hong Kong economy and not necessarily or exclusively those sanctioned. While it is difficult to precisely assess the economic impact, Vera Yuen (2024) has concluded that the measures have "driven down trade shares" between the U.S. and Hong Kong and led to a situation where " more goods are now rerouted

---

61 Rowhani, *supra* note 15, at 132.

62 Maizland and Fong, *supra* note 57

63 "Release of the Hong Kong Autonomy Act Report," US Embassy in China, Beijing, November 23, 2020. https://china.usembassy-china.org.cn/zh/release-of-the-hong-kong-autonomy-act-report/

around Hong Kong through third countries such as Vietnam and Mexico."[64] Furthermore, it might be argued, given the titles of the U.S. legislation, that the objective of the measures was regime change and, therefore, be in conflict with the principle of state sovereignty.

Xinjiang

The Uyghur Human Rights Policy Act 2019, proposed by U.S. Republican Senator Rubio, received overwhelming bipartisan support in both houses of Congress and was signed into effect by President Trump in June 2020. The face of the Act refers to "gross human rights violations of ethnic Turkic Muslims" and calls for "an end to [their] arbitrary detention, torture, and harassment," allegations which the Chinese government refutes.[65] The Act authorizes the U.S. President to take restrictive measures and impose sanctions on relevant foreign individuals and institutions under the International Emergency Economic Powers Act. Additionally, it requires U.S. companies and individuals to take measures to exclude relevant Chinese companies from their supply and industrial chains, alleging "human rights violations" and "forced labor."

In 2016, Congress enacted the Global Magnitsky Human Rights Accountability Act, a domestic law to address "serious human rights violations," allows for targeting foreign governments, businesses, and individuals with measures including restrictions on entry and asset freezing; they can be implemented with no need for judicial review. This act was subsequently incorporated into the pre-existing Magnitsky Act. Once initiated by Congress members and approved by the President, these measures can be implemented immediately and are not restricted by foreign sovereign immunity, giving U.S. executive authorities much operational freedom. To date, no subject sanctioned under this law has secured the lifting of sanctions through litigation in the U.S. The Xinjiang Production and Construction Corps (XPCC) and the Xinjiang Public Security Bureau (XPSB) are both subject to sanctions under the Global Magnitsky Act as are 12 individuals.

---

64 V. Yuen, "Hong Kong's economy struggles to get back on its feet," *East Asia Forum*, January 3, 2024. https://eastasiaforum.org/2024/01/03/hong-kongs-economy-struggles-to-get-back-on-its-feet/

65 Permanent Mission of the People's Republic of China to the United Nations Office at Geneva GJ/56/2022.

Since 2019, the U.S. Customs and Border Protection has issued multiple hold-release orders for products originating from China's Xinjiang region. The U.S. Tariff Act 1930 merely requires that "there is suspicion that imported or potentially imported products to the U.S. involve forced labor," no substantial evidence is required before the Commissioner of U.S. Customs and Border Protection can sign a hold-release order. The very low requirement for evidence suggests that release orders serve primarily as an administrative tool for sanctioning Chinese companies.

In August 2020, four U.S. government departments jointly issued the so-called Xinjiang Supply Chain Business Advisory. While not having legal force, the advisory still claimed that U.S. companies associated with entities accused of "forced labor" or "mass detention of Uighurs and other human rights abuses" in China's Xinjiang region would face "legal and reputational risks."[66] On March 22, 2022, a formal statement was issued by Secretary of State Anthony Blinken asserting, without evidence, that "the PRC continues to commit genocide and crimes against humanity in Xinjiang." On June 21, 2022, the Uyghur Forced Labor Prevention Act was implemented, banning the import of products allegedly made with Uyghur forced labor and as of March 2024, 117 punitive sanctions were enforced against 60 companies and 35 officials and government agencies, including export bans affecting 53 companies located in Xinjiang and import bans applying to 12 enterprises. The cumulative effect of the U.S. sanctions, which give the impression that Xinjiang is a dangerous place in which to do business, is over-compliance, less because of the contested human rights abuses and more because of the risk of apparently arbitrary sanction by the U.S.[67] In 2021, the European Union followed the U.S. lead in sanctioning four public officials and the Xinjiang Production and Construction Corps Public Security Bureau.

There is little doubt that many of sanctions imposed on China are of dubious legality. However, with the U.S. deliberately acting outside

---

66 W. Ross, Remarks by Commerce Secretary Wilbur L. Ross at the 2020 Meeting of the President's Interagency Task Force to Monitor and Combat Trafficking in Persons, US Department of Commerce, Virtual Meeting, December 9, 2020, para. 4.   https://www.commerce.gov/news/speeches/2020/10/remarks-by-commerce-secretary-wilbur-l-ross-2020-meeting-presidents-interagency

67 Visit to China, *supra* note 16.

the codes of the WTO, and with the WTO's appellate body unable to function, the legitimacy of the sanctions cannot be subjected to public scrutiny. Nevertheless, many of the sanctions appear to be arbitrary, not clearly justifiable case by case, and lacking transparent and affordable modes of redress. Whatever the stated reasons, there is suspicion, albeit supported primarily by circumstantial evidence, that the true motivation of the sanctions is to perpetuate U.S. economic hegemony and to bring about either system or regime change in China.

China's Response: Anti-Unilateral Coercion Legislation and Measures

As already noted, China responded virtually blow by blow during the height of the first Trump trade offensive, although typically with tariffs impacting a smaller volume of imports. The responses were carefully choreographed, directed at products that might negatively affect politically important U.S. producers and reflecting the fact that the volume of U.S. exports to China was less than China's exports, a trade imbalance that had long irritated President Trump. (Ironically, China's trade imbalance with the world was at a historic low point when U.S. tariffs were imposed, 0.2% of GDP compared with a high of 10% in 2007.[68])

To facilitate its response to U.S. trade actions, China introduced an Anti-Foreign Sanctions Law in 2021 and approved mirrors of several U.S. regulations creating a complex legislative framework. Aside from the sanctions law, reference has been made to the Export Control Law of the People's Republic of China and the Foreign Trade Law of the People's Republic of China together with numerous departmental regulations, including the Provisional Regulations on Unjustified Application of Foreign Laws and Measures, and the Blocking Measures for External Legal Application. All contribute to a complex regulatory landscape.

To date, the Chinese Ministry of Foreign Affairs has principally announced sanctions against approximately 41 individuals and nine entities in the United States and Europe, citing their involvement in issues pertaining to Xinjiang, Hong Kong and also Taiwan between 2021 and 2022. The primary targets currently sanctioned by China

---

68 Huang and Slosberg, *supra* note 40.

encompass foreign legislators, senior officials, human rights scholars, human rights committees, law firms, research centres, and foundations in Western countries. The measures include restricted entry of sanctioned individuals and their family members, curtailed exchanges, and the freezing of assets and properties held in China. In practice, many sanctioned individuals lack assets in China that are amenable to execution, nor do they harbour intentions of visiting the country.

The limited scope of targets announced by China for countermeasures, predominantly excluding foreign entities engaged in routine commercial activities, underscores their circumscribed impact on international trade. Its response to the measures announced by the U.S. in May 2024 was similarly low-key but included an anti-dumping investigation into chemical imports from the U.S., EU, Japan, and Taiwan announced on May 19 and, in July, export restrictions on dual use aviation and aerospace technologies, including drones. China has also requested the WTO to establish an expert group to investigate measures, subsidies and local content requirements in Biden administration's flagship Inflation Reduction Act.[69] With the WTO's formal appellate system made defunct by the U.S. refusal to appoint new members, this last action would seem to be symbolic.

However, China has been consistent in responding to U.S. criticisms of its trading practices in suggesting continued dialogue and multilateral solutions while calling attention to changes made to address the stated concerns. In terms of the "phase-one" trade agreement reached in 2020 that entailed China importing another US$200 billion worth of Chinese goods, imports registered a 58% increase. However, the target was unreasonable since governments cannot instruct enterprises to import specific volumes of goods. Moreover, attaining such as target was made more difficult by the COVID-19 pandemic and the previous trade war, which had broken commercial links and encouraged some U.S. manufacturers to move production out of the U.S., thus enabling them to continue trading with China.[70]

---

69 "US-China Relations in the Biden Era: A Timeline," *China Briefing*, October 10, 2024. https://www.china-briefing.com/news/us-china-relations-in-the-biden-era-a-timeline/

70 Bown, *supra* note 53; Huang and Slosberg, *supra* note 40.

The Impact of Unilateral Sanctions Imposed by the United States on China

Irrespective of their stated objectives, the unilateral coercive measures imposed on China by the U.S. (and its allies) are likely to serve primarily to weaken the Chinese economy, curtail its rate of economic growth and development, and thereby necessarily inhibit improvements in the well-being of its citizens. These negative implications are unlikely to be confined to the Chinese economy and population. To the extent that such measures slow global economic growth, they reduce the collective ability to attain the UN Sustainable Development Goals, the failure of which impacts the well-being of people globally. Moreover, to the extent that China's trade and development initiatives are disproportionately concentrated within the developing world, which compared to Western nations they are, the negative consequences are likely to be most felt—especially longer term—by the most disadvantaged populations among the world's least developed countries.

It must be stressed that it is currently impossible to evidence any substantial negative impact of unilateral coercive measures on the enjoyment of human rights in China.[71] China is an extremely large and heterogeneous country that in the last half-century has witnessed probably the most rapid change in world history, affecting all aspects of economic and social life. It boasts the world's second largest economy—on some measures, the largest—which is characterized by great regional and social inequality. Based on previous research, we can presume that the most severe effects of sanctions are being experienced by the already most disadvantaged members of society.[72] However, the enormous complexity of the economy, the under-researched nature of Chinese society and the relatively recent imposition of coercive measures prevent tracking the causal consequences with confidence.

71 Alena Douhan, "Visit to China: Report of the Special Rapporteur on the negative impact of unilateral coercive measures on the enjoyment of human rights," Human Rights Council, UN General Assembly, Fifty-seventh session, A/HRC/57/55/Add.1 (2024).

72 M. Pinna Pintor, M. Suhrcke, and C. Hamelmann, "The impact of economic sanctions on health and health systems in low-income and middle-income countries: a systematic review and narrative synthesis," *BMJ Global Health* 8, no. 2 (2023):e010968. doi: 10.1136/bmjgh-2022-010968.

As noted above, the objective of the sanctions imposed with respect to Hong Kong is opaque, given that the facilitating legislation focused on democracy. It is unlikely that the U.S. expected to achieve regime change and, while it might have liked to encourage street protests to continue, it is unclear how the targeted nature of the "smart" sanctions would have had that effect. Perhaps, instead, the U.S. administration hoped that its sanctions might have prompted China to change its economic policies to be more compatible with the Western interpretation of a "rules-based world order." However, in Kessler's terms, these were unreasonable and unjustifiable goals[73] that the U.S. administration acknowledges have not been achieved.[74] Neither China's leadership, nor most of its population, is dissatisfied with the management of the economy that has dramatically transformed living standards over the last four decades.[75] The population is correspondingly more than content with the Chinese political system and its leadership.

The goal of imposing targeted sanctions on Xinjiang is equally unclear, given that the Chinese government rejects U.S. accusations of abuses against the Uyghur community. Moreover, it would be difficult ever to conclude that change had been achieved given that the baseline evidence of human rights abuses is very fragmented and shaky, based often on hearsay and speculative inference.[76]

An alternative reading of U.S. intent is that it is primarily to degrade the Chinese economy, either to achieve geopolitical advantage or to punish China for not acquiescing to Western hegemonic control. However, account needs also to be taken of political domestic considerations. Certainly, statements and actions taken by the Biden administration in 2024 cannot be divorced from the presidential election campaign during which Donald Trump threatened to impose 60% tariffs on all Chinese imports. Taking the longer view, as Kessler has noted, "sanctions are favored by Congress because members of

---

73 Kessler, *supra* note 3

74 Fact Sheet, *supra* note 55

75 R. Walker, "Open to Chinese democracy," *China Today* 73, no. 3 (March 2024): 46–48. http://www.cnfocus.com/open-to-chinese-democracy/

76 R. Li, *Reproducing the Orient: A Critical Examination of Western Media Representations of China's Uyghur Policies between 2014 and 2021* (Masters Thesis) (New York: CUNY, 2022).

Congress can then tell their constituents and lobbies that they are doing something, even if that something is not likely to deliver results."[77]

U.S. sanctions intended to degrade the Chinese economy or are punitive or have punitive intent would not seem to be justiciable under international law.[78] Such sanctions also have humanitarian consequences through lower economic growth, lay-offs and unemployment. They directly infringe upon the legitimate rights and interests of Chinese enterprises and citizens, while damaging China's overseas interests. The sanctions are likely to create operational difficulties and economic losses for Chinese enterprises, forcing some Chinese companies to close or exit the U.S. market and damaging the compliance image of Chinese enterprises overseas. They may well additionally slow rates of development and technological advance by forcing Chinese high-tech enterprises to cease cooperation with U.S. firms, reducing the scope for technology transfer and limiting access to technologically advanced components that are difficult to replace in the short term. This, in turn, is likely to create unnecessary obstacles to cooperation, disrupt supply chains and inhibit, for example, digital infrastructure construction under the Belt and Road initiative.

To the extent that sanctions are targeted on cutting edge industries, they are likely to slow rates of recruitment of highly skilled personnel, adding to unemployment among recent graduates and reducing wage growth. The concentration of high-tech industries in more densely populated urban areas will have localized negative impacts, not only affecting component manufacturers, but also curtailing the growth of local retail sectors that service the consumption needs of high-tech employees. This, in turn, will impact on migrant workers, cutting remittances, and placing a brake on the revitalization of rural areas. These spatial multiplier effects, though difficult to measure, are likely to be real.

The centrality of Xinjiang to China's leadership of green technology, and its position as a gateway to the Belt and Road corridors, strengthens the suspicion that the human rights sanctions imposed on local entities has more to do with geoeconomics than with the protection of human rights.[79] Xinjiang is the world's leading production

---

77 Kessler, *supra* note 3, at 21.

78 Mohamad, *supra* note 16.

79 "Unilateral US sanctions disrupt global industrial and supply chain stability,"

base for polycrystalline silicon, the basic material of the photovoltaic industry, and it is home to China's largest wind turbine manufacturer, accounting for 13% of global production. Companies included on U.S. sanctions lists account for almost half the global supply of polycrystalline silicon while the U.S. has additionally banned most cotton and tomato products from Xinjiang, agricultural sectors that both account for 20% of global production.[80]

Despite the U.S. sanctions, Xinjiang's overseas trade has continued to increase (it reached a record US$409 billion in the first 10 months of 2023.[81]) However, with no counterfactual (that is, a measure of the level of trade in the absence of sanctions), it remains difficult to assess the true impact of sanctions. Likewise, while the impact on Xinjiang Production and Construction Corps, an enterprise specifically subject to U.S. sanctions, has had no measurable effect on the firm's financial performance, the cost to the Chinese government of shielding the company from direct impact is estimated at US$2 billion.[82]

No econometric modelling is known that has successfully estimated the extent to which the recent relative slowdown in China's GDP growth is attributable to the effect of U.S. sanctions, as opposed to the COVID-19 pandemic, the maturity of the economy, domestic policy decisions, or other factors.[83] While in 2022, U.S. trade with China grew in nominal terms for the third year in row, with 16.5% of total U.S. imports being sourced from China, Mexico replaced China as the top exporter to the U.S. in 2023. U.S. imports from China fell by 20% between 2022 and 2023, falling further in the first three months of 2024.[84]

China Daily, August 2, 2022. www.xinhuanet.com/world/2022-08/02/c_1128884153.htm

80 Visit to China, *supra* note 16.

81 P. Yiu, "Xinjiang foreign trade hits record despite Western sanctions," *Nikkei Asia,* November 20, 2023.

82 J-F. Maystadt, et al., "The impact of humanitarian sanctions: Evidence from US sanctions on Chinese firms," *VoxEU,* April 11, 2024. https://cepr.org/voxeu/columns/impact-humanitarian-sanctions-evidence-us-sanctions-chinese-firms

83 H. Bo, "Implications of the Ukraine war for China: Can China survive secondary sanctions?," *Journal of Chinese Economic and Business Studies* (2022). DOI: 10.1080/14765284.2022.2136933

84 US Census Bureau, *Trade in Goods with China.* https://www.census.gov/foreign-trade/balance/c5700.html

Set against the full range of China's global trade, this decline in U.S. trade is relatively small and may not entirely be the result of sanctions or be sustained. Any substantive or humanitarian effects, even if disproportionately concentrated on Xinjiang, are likely to be difficult directly to detect and thinly spread, albeit with more substantial impact in particular localities, as explained above. Longer term, China will be able to further diversity its markets, innovate and progress cutting-edge technologies from its own resources. Moreover, the scale and dynamism of the Chinese economy and its potential for growth—it is not yet classified as a high-income country—means that China is likely to remain a very attractive trading partner. The reticence with which the European Union has responded to U.S. pressures to disengage economically from China is testament to this fact.[85]

In the short term, the costs of transition from an economy closely interconnected with the U.S. are likely to be borne by those most weakly attached to the economy. These are likely to include persons in insecure noncontracted employment, those in the new private sector less covered by social protection, older workers with fewer skills or productive capacity and those yet to enter employment. The last group will comprise some young and exceedingly well-educated persons, together with others who are disadvantaged by low educational attainment, disability or geographic location.

If China's economic growth continues to be slowed, it may be less able to invest in development programs abroad—the more than US$1 trillion investment in the Belt and Road Initiative (BRI) far exceeds the development assistance provided by the OECD. If so, this may cause a slow-down economic development in the 154 countries formally associated with the initiative. Again, the negative humanitarian implications of lower growth are likely to be concentrated among those already economically disadvantaged even if they are not directly affected. However, it is difficult to speculate about China's overseas investment decisions. China's State Council recently announced that, while participating countries owed more than US$3 million to the Export-Import Bank of China (Eximbank), the BRI has generated

85 M. Schüller, "Disengagement from China: United States and European Union Policies Compared," *GIGA Focus Asia* 1 (2023). https://www.giga-hamburg.de/en/publications/giga-focus/disengagement-from-china-united-states-european-union-policies-compared

US$2 trillion worth of contracts, a sum equivalent in scale to the entire Canadian economy.[86]

Conclusion

To a lay person, unilateral coercive measures—sanctions—appear aggressive, while the evidence presented above indicates that they are largely ineffectual in resolving trade disputes but are potentially economically and perhaps socially destructive. Their imposition points to differences in ideology, political regimes and the logics of international relations that serve as impediments to diplomatic co-operation and dispute resolution. Indeed, to the extent that the U.S. and China trade war initiated under President Trump's first administration was an attempt to maintain U.S. global economic and political primacy, as Sachs surmises, co-operation and compromise were never goals. The goal was, and remains under the second Trump administration, continued dominance with lower global economic growth being viewed as acceptable collateral damage, including higher costs and reduced living standards for U.S. citizens.[87] International law has been another casualty, with the WTO appellate system crippled and many of the actions taken against China neither conforming with international law nor meeting the criteria for collective countermeasures.[88]

Conversations with acquaintances from the Chinese business community indicate that the sanctions imposed on China have seriously undermined trust. The U.S. government is no longer trusted. U.S. companies can no longer be trusted since their actions are severely constrained by the largely unpredictable decisions of U.S. politicians that invariably seem irrational in business terms. Partnership has been replaced by suspicion. Strategic decisions and alliances are becoming more difficult. Global politics are increasingly perceived

---

86 O. Hotham, "China's Belt and Road generated over $2 trillion in contracts," *Barrons*, October 10, 2023. https://www.barrons.com/news/china-s-belt-and-road-generated-over-2-trillion-in-contracts-beijing-f0aca2c0

87 J. Boak and the Associated Press, "Trump admits Americans could feel 'some pain' from his tariffs, but it will be 'worth the price,'" *Fortune*, February 3, 2025. https://fortune.com/2025/02/02/trump-tariffs-americans-some-pain-price-hikes-inflation/

88 Visit to China, *supra* note 16, at 15–16.

to be unpredictable and inherently dangerous. Business is becoming increasingly risk averse.

To the extent that these impressions accurately reflect the views of the business community in China, they point to a continuing influence of sanctions that is likely to extend beyond their immediate impact. They point to a weakening of the beneficial aspects of globalization that have fostered collective learning, technological advance, cultural awareness and humanitarian understanding. Globalization and a more open trading environment have also stimulated faster, albeit unequal and questionably sustainable economic growth that has improved the living standards and enhanced the well-being of a significant proportion of the world's people. China's own economic growth, which itself has reduced global poverty by 65% since 1990, demonstrates the advantages and potential of an interconnected world. To the extent that the U.S. unilateral sanctions have undermined confidence in the global economy, they have reduced the life-chances of every person on the planet.

From the perspective of some U.S. strategists, the decline in trust will be read as a success, weakening a competitor, perhaps isolating China and denying it access to the U.S. knowhow that is thought to have propelled Chinese economic growth. It could encourage the implementation of additional sanctions to further weaken the adversary. This appeared to be the strategy pursued by the U.S. during the first weeks of the second Trump administration. Such sanctions may continue to be justified under the guise of safeguarding national interests, using them as political capital to garner domestic support. To the extent that sanctions are enacted purportedly in the name of protecting rights, they could perversely create or exacerbate the very repressive measures they claim to address. A government threatened, economically weakened and less able to meet the financial needs of its citizens, could seek to exploit the situation by stoking nationalist sentiments, a task made easier in a world with less cross-cultural contact.

A polarized world thus created, becomes an unstable and dangerous world in which strategists place local interests above global ones and ill-informed individuals and nations readily see others as enemies. Neorealist international relations, nations competing to the point of fighting in an anarchic world, afford power to the classroom bully while denying it to the global majority and drive out the possibility of a world community with a shared future. It becomes imperative, therefore, to scrutinize whether nations sanctioning others genuinely prioritizes the welfare of their populations, and whether the measures undertaken truly serve their nations' interests. They serve no-one else's.

Seemingly small actions, limited sanctions, can have global impacts—the "butterfly effect." It is essential, therefore, to revisit the issue of the legitimacy as much as the value of unilateral coercive measures. Resolution 27/21 adopted by the Human Rights Council in 2014:

> Calls upon all States to stop adopting, maintaining or imple-menting unilateral coercive measures not in accordance with international law, international humanitarian law, the Charter of the United Nations and the norms and principles governing peaceful relations among States, in particular those of a coercive nature with extraterritorial effects, which create obstacles to trade relations among States, thus imped-ing the full realization of the rights set forth in the Universal Declaration of Human Rights and other international human rights instruments, in particular the right of individuals and peoples to development.

Rowhani opines that, while resolutions such as the above con-demn the use of unilateral sanctions, "they are still far from creating norms prohibiting their use."[89] This is "due to the voting patterns of these resolutions, as well as the presence of persistent objectors, which are not required to follow the CIL [customary international law]." However, he also argues that to be lawful, coercive "measures should be executed by targeted sanctions that precisely identify the subjective wrongdoer person." It is self-evident that this condition does not apply to the measures described above imposed on China by the U.S. (and some of its allies). It is surely questionable whether any measure can "precisely identify" a wrongdoer, even presuming that there is one. Sanctions that apply to nations or sections of a nation can never fulfil such a condition.

---

89 Rowhani, *supra* note 15, at 168

Resolution 27/21 was approved by a vote of 31 to 14 with two abstentions. China voted for the resolution; the U.S., the UK and all eligible Member States of the EU voted against. A world divided is a good future lost.

CHAPTER 4.

U.S. Unilateral Coercive Measures on Cuba
Terminology, Enforcement and Over-compliance

Raúl Rodríguez Rodriguez[1]

Abstract

For over six decades, unilateral coercive economic measures have been at the core of U.S. policy toward Cuba. The system that stands out for its longevity and comprehensiveness has evolved to become a formidable obstacle for the island's sovereign right to conduct its international economic relations. Blockade, embargo, sanctions, unilateral coercive measures or economic measures, are some of the terms used to define the hostile and punitive policy of the United States government against Cuba for more than six decades. The truth is, many of these terms are used interchangeably, when in reality each of them have different legal implications. It is necessary to emphasize that the most used term to define this policy is the "bloqueo." While the term "blockade" in English implies an actual naval blockade, the Cuban view is that the U.S. measures function in a manner that to a great extent achieves the same effect, given their economic, political and humanitarian impact, and also their extraterritorial implications. In view of the ideological, political and even linguistic differences between the U.S. sender and the target, Cuba, it is important to define the most appropriate terminology for the Cuban case as well as to assess the means and ends of the enforcement and the instances of over-compliance.

---

1 Center for U.S. and Hemispheric Studies, University of Havana

Introduction

The use of unilateral coercive measures in international relations has increased in the past two decades. The dubious legality and legitimacy of unilateral coercive measures generate numerous economic, political and legal conflicts, for which the international order today has no clear solution. The current state of affairs with regards to the use of unilateral coercive measures requires a comprehensive analysis and assessment, not only from the perspective of international law and related areas, but also by involving other disciplines, such as political science and economics.

There is one aspect that stands out when looking at most sender states or groups of states and target states: there is a clear north-south division. The world's major powers have increasingly resorted the application of unilateral coercive measures, replacing the use or threat of use of force as a foreign policy tool in pursuit of geopolitical objectives.

Sanctioning powers often use the protection of human rights, promotion of democracy or the rule of law supposedly intended to promote universal values as legitimizing arguments for the implementation of unilateral coercive policy. However, they often conceal the intention to provoke changes in the economic and political internal affairs of the target state for strategic or ideological purposes. There is obviously no consideration of the political economy of the target states and the humanitarian impact of these unilateral coercive measures. For this reason, mainly developing countries of the south have continually opposed the imposition of these misnamed sanctions, arguing that they imply a hierarchy alien to the international legal order by allowing one State to impose restrictions of its own choosing to put pressure on another sovereign State, thus violating the principle of sovereign equality and overlooking the mandate of the United Nations.[2]

In this context, among other aspects, it is paramount to discuss issues such as terminology, means and consequences of enforcement of unilateral coercive measures that often leads to over-compliance by private and state actors who seek to engage with illegitimately targeted states.

---

2 Principles of Sovereign Equality, Charter of the United Nations, Chapter I — Purposes and Principles, Article 2(1)–(5). https://legal.un.org/repertory/art2.shtml

Terminology discourse is very important, as the use of appropriate terms and a set of concepts accepted and understood in the same way by all members of the international community from north to south is vital for the dialogue.

Another important aspect that will be addressed in this chapter is the means and consequences of enforcement of unilateral coercive measures, which involves the principle of sovereign equality of states and issues of extraterritoriality. It is advocated here that the application of extraterritorial jurisdiction constitutes a violation of the principles of sovereign integrity and non-intervention.

Many western states, and quite notably the United States, are increasingly using economic coercion to pursue geopolitical and geo-economic objectives that result in an aggressive enforcement akin to a culture of punishment. The means of enforcement do not usually rest on legitimacy, but rather on geoeconomic power that in many ways results in over-compliance by banks, state and private enterprises.

Sanctions, Embargo, Blockade and Economic Warfare

Most experts agree on the fact that the current terminology of sanctions is ambiguous and uncertain, and that makes it very difficult to identify a legal framework and the applicable standard; this undermines the rule of law, world order and the authority of the United Nations.[3] By briefly analysing the terms, one realizes that the term "sanction" usually refers to measures that are applied under Articles 41 and 42 of the Charter of the United Nations. It is well established that the United Nations Security Council has unique power to deal with threats to international peace and security. The Security Council can deal with such threats by imposing sanctions against the source of the threat. However, the term has been interchangeably used to refer to both unilateral and multilateral coercion[4] and this is highly questionable.

---

3 Expert consultation on "The Notion, Characteristics, Legal Status and Targets of Unilateral Sanctions" convened by the Special Rapporteur on the negative impact of unilateral coercive measures on the enjoyment of human rights. United Nations Human Rights Special Procedures. Special Rapporteurs, Independent Experts and Working Groups, Geneva, Switzerland, May 14, 2021.

4 Economic coercion as "measures of an economic—as contrasted with diplomatic or military—character taken to induce [a target State] to change some

Currently, we observe an increasing advancement of Eurocentric ideas, manipulating background beliefs that have prevailed for over 500 years, to fend off contrary evidence. Alfred de Zayas writes, "it seems that we west find ourselves in the midst of an epistemology trap, caught in our own indoctrination, propaganda and narcissism."[5] It does seem that the so called "rules based international order" is very often used loosely instead of international law in an inconsistent way to criticize the behavior of non-western and Global South states. Usually targeting "wrongdoers," both individuals and organizations, implies that the sender of the coercive measures has the legal capacity to pass judgment and punish a variety of actions of the target state.

Blockade, embargo, sanctions, unilateral coercive measures and economic measures are some of the terms that have been used to define the hostile and punitive policy of the United States government against Cuba for more than six decades. As a matter of fact, many of these terms are used interchangeably, although in reality each of these has its specific meaning and legal implications.

In the case of the U.S. unilateral coercive measures imposed on Cuba, it is rather a "semantic trap" that must be avoided. The official position of the United States Government, the sender, has been to call the policy of unilateral coercive measures against Cuba an "embargo," as the 1962 original executive order by then President John F Kennedy called it.[6] By using the term "embargo" the U.S. government intentionally, and by extension the western corporate media and even some well-intentioned persons, promote the idea that the U.S. system of unilateral coercive measures is a bilateral issue between Cuba and the United States, consequently, U.S. actions in that sense are legal.

As to the legality of the unilateral coercive measures by using the term "embargo" it is safe to point out that this not only obscures the fact that they are not approved by the UN Security Council under

---

policies or practices or even its governmental structure," Andreas F. Lowenfeld, *International Economic Law* (Oxford University Press, 2008), p. 698.

5 Alfred de Zayas "The Epistemology Trap," *Counterpunch*, March 15, 2014. https://www.counterpunch.org/2024/03/15/the-epistemology-trap/

6 President John F. Kennedy Executive Proclamation 3447, based on the Foreign Assistance Act of 1961, section 620a; provisions of the Trading with the Enemy Act of 1917, section 5b; Cuban Assets Controls Regulations in 1963 (Department of the Treasury). This legal framework has primarily been enforced by the Treasury Department's Office of Foreign Assets Control (OFAC).

article 41 of the UN Charter, but also that they have been rejected by the UN General Assembly more than 30 times in recent history.[7]

It also has other implications; it presumes, in particular, that the United States is responding to a hostile and deliberate act by the Cuban Government and that U.S. unilateral coercion is only economic, as the State Department posts in its website.[8] While the U.S. government could perceive the structural changes[9] in Cuba in the years following 1959 as a hostile act because of their huge economic interests in Cuba,[10] these actions of the Cuban government did not violate any norms of international law.

Historical evidence reveals a lot more. Before President Kennedy formally declared the breakup of economic relations with Cuba, a multifaceted regime change policy had been gradually taking shape, President Eisenhower is on record saying, "If they [the Cuban people] are hungry they will throw Castro out." Regime change was anticipated to come from within and bottom-up.[11] By mid-1960 economic

---

7 "General Assembly Overwhelmingly Adopts Resolution Calling on United States to End Economic, Commercial, Financial Embargo against Cuba," United Nations Meetings Coverage and Press Releases, October 30 and 31, 2024. https://press.un.org/en/2024/ga12650.doc.htm

8 The United States maintains a comprehensive economic embargo on the Republic of Cuba. In February 1962, President John F. Kennedy proclaimed an embargo on trade between the United States and Cuba, in response to certain actions taken by the Cuban Government and directed the Departments of Commerce and the Treasury to implement the embargo, which remains in place today. https://www.state.gov/cuba-sanctions/

9 A new Cuban government after January 1, 1959, took the first steps toward the implementation of a program that involved a strong and swift structural transformation that began incorporating new property and class relations. These policies, in turn, limited the possibilities for private capital accumulation. The main objective was achieving economic sovereignty and social justice by both overcoming economic dependence on the United States and pursuing an alternative model of development.

10 In 1958, the United States accounted for 71 percent of Cuba's exports and 64 percent of her imports. Total U.S. direct private investment in Cuba was close to $2 billion, controlling over 30 percent of the sugar industry, one-third of public utilities, and major shares of the mining and manufacturing sectors. The sales by U.S.-owned companies amounted for over a quarter of Cuba's GNP. A. Zimbalist , "The Prospects for U.S.-Cuba Trade," *Challenge* 20, no. 6 (Jan/Feb 1978): 51–54.

11 Memorandum of a Conference with the President, White House, Washington, DC, January 25, 1960, 11:15–11:55 a.m. Eisenhower Library, Whitman File, DDE Diaries. Secret. Drafted by Goodpaster on January 26. The time of the meeting is taken from the President's Appointment Book. (Ibid.) Also published in *Declassified Documents, 1981,* 123 C. https://history.state.gov/historicaldocuments/frus1958-60v06/d436#fn:1.7.4.4.40.40.8.2

coercion had already become a tool of choice for the U.S.´ policymakers, as is documented extensively in official policy papers.

The oft-quoted Mallory memorandum of April 6, 1960, admitted that the new Cuban government had popular support and that "the only foreseeable means of alienating internal support is through disenchantment and disaffection based on economic dissatisfaction and hardship." It goes on to suggest, "If the above are accepted or cannot be successfully countered, it follows that every possible means should be undertaken promptly to weaken the economic life of Cuba."[12] Unilateral economic measures were designed to produce economic havoc as a way to promote popular discontent, to inflict adversity as a permanent condition of daily life. They were meant to exert a serious pressure on the Cuban economy and contribute to the growth of dissatisfaction and unrest in the country

Economic coercive measures were not launched as an end in themselves, but as a mean to compel Cuba to change its form of government, its socio-economic configuration, and its behavior in the international system. These three are also means to the end of retaking control on the island and thus closing the breach the Cuban revolution had opened in the regional power structure.[13]

The unilateral economic measures against Cuba began to take shape when the Cuban government, after signing a trade agreement with the Soviet Union in February 1960, asked western oil companies—which, according to Rich Kaplowitz, "enjoyed an oligopolistic position" in Cuba by owning the only refineries existing in the Island—to refine up to 2 million barrels Russian petroleum a year.[14]

The oil companies were inclined to comply in view of a pre-1959 law that requested them to do so at the risk of being nationalized. Moreover, the Cuban Government would dedicate part of the refined

---

12 The Decline and Fall of Castro, Secret, April 6, 1960, Memorandum from the Deputy Assistant Secretary of State for Inter-American Affairs (Mallory) to the Assistant Secretary of State for Inter-American Affairs (Rubottom). *Foreign Relations of the United States, 1958–1960, Cuba, Volume VI.* https://history.state.gov/historicaldocuments/frus1958-60v06/d499

13 E. Dominguez Lopez and R. Rodriguez Rodriguez, "There and Back Again: United States policy toward Cuba in the 21st century," *International Journal of Cuban Studies* 14, no. 2 (2022): 309–342.

14 Donna Rich Kaplowitz, *Anatomy of a Failed Embargo: U.S. Sanctions Against Cuba,* (Boulder, CO: Lynne Rienner Publishers, 1998), p. 34.

oil to pay an outstanding debt with the three oil companies: Texaco, Standard Oil and Shell. However, the State Department, at the exigency of Treasury Secretary Robert Anderson, a very influential oil tycoon in the Administration, ordered the companies not to submit to the Cuban Government's request.

Recounting a meeting held in New York on this issue on June 1, 1960, between Anderson, the executives of the three companies and himself, Roy Rubottom, Assistant Secretary of State for Inter-American Affairs, informed the Secretary of State that Mr Anderson had made it clear that it would be in accordance with this government's policy toward Cuba if the companies decided to reject the Cuban demand. He furthermore instructed the companies "to act in unison" and promised the support of the U.S. government.[15]

When Havana responded by legitimately nationalizing the oil refineries, Washington retaliated by suspending the Cuban sugar quota in the U.S. market, thereby attempting to cut the country's lifeline. Thereafter a process of escalation took place resulting in the nationalization of all U.S. property in Cuba and the cutting of all exports to the United States. When the Eisenhower administration cut the Cuban sugar quota in the U.S. market in July 1960,[16] it was easy to anticipate what kind of impact a measure like that would have on a small, underdeveloped country, whose main export was precisely sugar and was heavily dependent on the United States' market for its exports and imports.[17]

---

15 "A Program of Covert Action Against the Castro Regimen," Washington, March 16, 1960, in United States Department of State, *Foreign Relations of the United States, 1958–1960, Volume VI, Cuba,* (Washington, DC: United States Printing Office, 1991), pp. 850–851. This Program, drafted by the Central Intelligence Agency, was approved at a session of the National Security Council of the United States, chaired by President Dwight D. Eisenhower, on that date. Quoted in Carlos Alzugaray, "The U.S. blockade and the development of self-reliance in Cuba," in Ramesh Ramsaran (editor), *Size, Power & Development in the Emerging World Order: Caribbean Perspectives* (San Juan, Trinidad & Tobago: Lexicon Trinidad Ltd., 2006), pp. 131–157.

16 Dwight D. Eisenhower, "Statement by the President Upon Signing Bill and Proclamation Relating to the Cuban Sugar Quota," July 6, 1960, *The American Presidency Project.* https://www.presidency.ucsb.edu/node/235042

17 Raul Rodriguez, "The Political Economy of Sanctions: The Case of Cuba," in Ksenia Kirkham (ed.), *The Routledge Book of the Political Economy of Sanctions* (London: Routledge, 2024).

The U.S. system of unilateral coercive measures has evolved into a combination of statutes and regulations that have been modified over time. Every major method of economic coercion has been employed by the sender state: trade control; suspension of aid and technical assistance; freezing of financial assets;[18] and particularly since the 1990s, the blacklisting of foreign companies that do business with Cuba; individuals, (Cuban and foreign nationals), entire categories of individuals;[19] and entities in Cuba and vessels.

Furthermore, that it is not a simple "embargo," as the U.S. Government claims, can be demonstrated by the fact that it is much more than a refusal to trade with Cuba; it is an all-encompassing policy, which includes elements of extraterritoriality and coercion in order to compel other state and private actors in third countries into compliance with U.S. policy and legislation.

Finally, it must be added that the U.S. "embargo" of Cuba includes not only commercial, but also economic and financial aspects, and is part of a larger, comprehensive set of policies (diplomatic isolation, political subversion and destabilization, covert actions, prohibition of delivery to/from the country). If the United States simply adopted a policy of bilateral suspension of trade, investment and aid, it would be less detrimental to Cuba's business environment and the Cuban economy as a whole.

The other term frequently used is blockade. While the term "blockade" in the English language implies an actual naval blockade, the prevalent view from Cuba is that the U.S. unilateral coercive measures function in a manner that to a great extent achieves the same effect as a blockade, given their economic, social and humanitarian effect, and also its extraterritorial implications.[20] Under international law the term "blockade" has a specialized meaning, which signifies a belligerent measure taken by a nation at war to prevent an enemy from receiving aid.[21] Usually, a blockade involves a physical interference

18 Margaret P. Doxey, *Economic Sanctions and International Enforcement*, 2nd ed. (New York: Oxford University Press, 1980), pp. 14–15.

19 For example, members of the Council of Ministries and employees of the Ministry of the Interior, that is, officials and non-officials.

20 Morris H. Morley, "The United States and the Global Economic Blockade of Cuba: A Study in Political Pressures on America Allies," *Canadian Journal of Political Science* 17, no. 1 (March 1984): 25–48.

21 Since the London naval conference of 1908–1909 international law stipulates

and a blocking of ships or other transport from reaching the target state. Though the U.S. quarantine of Cuba in 1962 during the Missile Crisis has been also called "blockade," some scholars argue that that was not even a full blockade.[22] Finally, if implemented by a nation not at war with another, a blockade has been considered by some authors to be an act of economic war.[23] Nevertheless, as of January 2024,[24] Cuba was the only country sanctioned—unilaterally—under the U.S. Trading with the Enemy Act of 1917, which was enacted as a wartime measure.

Given the ideological, political and even linguistic differences between the sender—the U.S. and the target—Cuba, it is important to define the most appropriate terminology for the Cuban case as well as to assess the means and ends of the enforcement and the instances of over-compliance.

The Cuban Government has insisted in calling the policy a "blockade." It seems obvious that any impartial observer would agree that United States policy toward Cuba is closer to the definition of a blockade than an embargo, since obviously coercion and the threat of force are used to stop the movement of people and goods into and out of Cuba. In his book *Treasury's War*, Juan Zarate asserts that the Office of Foreign Assets Control (OFAC) has been the hub for administering sanctions on Cuba, "restrictions [which] were placed on what

---

that a blockade can be used only in wartime between belligerents. International legal norms do not recognize a blockade in peacetime. *ICRC Declaration Concerning the Laws of Naval War,* London February 26, 1909. https://ihl-databases.icrc.org/es/ihl-treaties/london-decl-1909

22 Nigel D. White, *The Cuba Embargo Under International Law: El Bloqueo* (London: Routledge, Taylor and Francis, 2015).

23 Graeme Bannerman, "'Blockade' and 'Embargo' Have Different Meanings," The Middle East Institute, July 7, 2010. https://www.mei.edu/content/blockade-and-embargo-have-different-meanings; Salim Lamrani, *The Economic War Against Cuba: A Historical and Legal Perspective* (New York: NYU Press, 2013); Andres Zaldivar, *Bloqueo: El asedio más prolongado de la historia* (La Habana: Editorial Capitán San Luis, 2003).

24 I hereby determine that the continuation of the exercise of those authorities with respect to Cuba for one year is in the national interest of the United States. Under section 101(b) of Public Law 95-223 (91 Stat. 1625; 50 U.S.C. 4305 note), and a previous determination on September 7, 2021 (86 FR 50831, September 10, 2021), the exercise of certain authorities under the Trading with the Enemy Act is scheduled to expire on September 14, 2022.

and who could enter Cuba in an attempt to strangle the Castro regime economically."[25]

Morris Morley also uses the term "blockade" as he described the early reactions of the United States as it began the use of its economic hard power unilaterally and extraterritorially from the outset. A Treasure Department internal memo describes the actions that the United States had to take to promote the overthrow of the Cuban government and also stressed the importance of limiting Cuba's economic relations with the rest of the capitalist world.[26]

Therefore, when Cuban officials refer to "el bloqueo"[27] (the blockade) in the majority of cases they are talking about the whole panoply of courses of action taken to produce the avowed "regime change" in the Island.[28] The system of unilateral coercive measures on Cuba by the United States has been also been defined by other authors as a true economic war.[29]

Secondary Sanctions and Extraterritoriality

When a State holds a monopoly on a critical market or, in some other regard, holds a singular role in the global economy, unilateral coercive measures imposed by that state may in effect function as though they were global in reach. In that case extraterritorial as well as secondary sanctions have the consequence of expanding the scope of the sanction's regime well beyond the sender's own nationals.[30] Making use of the centrality of the U.S. in the global economy, it has

---

25 Juan Zarate, *Treasury's War: The Unleashing of a New Era of Financial Warfare* (New York: Public Affairs, a member of the Perseus Books Group, 2013), p. 24.

26 Morris Morley, "The United States and the Global Economic Blockade of Cuba: A Study in Political Pressures on American Allies," *Canadian Journal of Political Science* 17, no. 1 (1984): 27.

27 In this respect, a language difference must be pointed out. In Spanish, the term "bloqueo" is not restricted to a military use, so there is no full equivalence between "bloqueo" in Spanish and blockade in English.

28 Unilateral Coercive Measures against Cuba are not only economic measures.

29 Salim Lamrani, *The Economic War against Cuba: A Historical and Legal Perspective on the U.S. Blockade* (New York: NYU Press, 2013).

Andrés Zaldívar Diéguez, *Bloqueo, El asedio más prolongado de la historia,* (La (Habana: Editorial Capitán San Luis, 2003).

30 Gordon Joy, "Creating Chaos at Bargain Rates," in Surya Subedi (ed.), *Unilateral Sanctions in International Law* (London: Bloomsbury Publishing, 2021), pp. 107–137.

imposed "secondary sanctions" on foreign firms, which are forced to choose between not trading with U.S. unilateral coercive measures targets or forfeiting access to the lucrative U.S. market.[31]

In 2016, then U.S. Secretary of Treasure Jack Lew presented the U.S. view on secondary sanctions and extraterritoriality at the Carnegie Endowment for International Peace "Secondary sanctions prompt particular concerns. Unlike primary sanctions, these measures threaten to cut off foreign individuals or companies from the U.S. financial system if they engage in certain conduct with a sanctioned entity, even if none of that activity touches the United States directly. As a result, they are viewed, even by some of our closest allies as extraterritorial attempts to apply U.S. foreign policy to the rest of the world."[32]

Indeed, what some scholars and politicians call secondary sanctions constitute an exercise of extending domestic jurisdiction on an extraterritorial basis; they raise concerns from the viewpoint of international law, as they may violate the principle of non-intervention in the domestic affairs of other states and state sovereignty.

In the case of Cuba, the United States Government policy of economic coercion had shown instances of extraterritoriality for several decades.[33] Notwithstanding, the 1990s was a significant period. Two pieces of legislation were passed by the United States Congress: the Torricelli Act of 1992 and the Helms-Burton Act of 1996, which codified the already intricate system of unilateral coercive measures in a way that stripped the president of the right to lift or modify major parts of the system. At present, only a vote by Congress can revoke these Acts.

The Cuban Democracy Act (the Torricelli Act), was introduced by New Jersey Democrat Robert Torricelli in 1992.[34] The stated

---

31 Tom Ruys and Cedric Ryngaert, "Secondary Sanctions: A weapon out of control? The international legality of, and European responses to, US secondary sanctions," *The British Yearbook of International Law* (Oxford University Press, 2020), p. 1. https://www.bybil.oxfordjournals.org (accessed Nov. 15, 2024)

32 U.S. Treasury Secretary Jacob J. Lew on the Evolution of Sanctions and Lessons for the Future, Carnegie Endowment for International Peace, Washington, DC, March 30, 2016. https://carnegieendowment.org/events/2016/03/us-treasury-secretary-jacob-j-lew-on-the-evolution-of-sanctions-and-lessons-for-the-future?lang=en

33 Morris Morley, *supra.*

34 Cuban Democracy Act of 1992, Pub. L. No. 102-484, 106 Stat. 2575 (1992), codified at 22 U.S.C.S. §§6001–6010 (1993).

purpose of this bill was to "promote a peaceful transition to democracy in Cuba through the application of appropriate pressures on the Cuban government."[35] The Torricelli Act incorporated extraterritorial measures, affecting third party relations with Cuba by making clear that the U.S. Government would "seek the cooperation of other democratic countries in this policy" and making "clear to other countries that, in determining its relations with them, the United States will take into account their willingness to cooperate in such a policy;[36] Torricelli claimed his bill would "wreak havoc on that island."[37] Indeed, the law affects Cuba's access to shipping; its major exports, such as sugar nickel; and its global trade with companies that are subsidiaries of U.S. companies located outside the United States.

One of the most damaging provisions was the elimination of licenses to foreign subsidiaries of U.S. companies in third countries that were exporting to Cuba. In 1991, prior to the adoption of this legislation, Cuba imported $719 million worth of goods from U.S. subsidiary companies; 90% of this amount was used for food and medicine. But from 1992 to 1995, in response to Cuban government requests to purchase hundreds of millions of dollars' worth food and medicine, a total of only $0.3 million in goods was licensed for sale by the Treasury Department.[38]

The Helms-Burton law of 1996 is as far reaching as the Torricelli Act. Title I of the Act affects Cuba's access to international financial institutions (IFIs), such as the World Bank: the statute mandates the U.S. representative in the IFIs to oppose the admission of Cuba, and

---

35 U.S. Congress, House of Representatives, Mr. Alexander, Mr. Bereuter, Mr. Broomfield, Mr. Burton of Indiana, Mr. Fascell, Mr. Gilma, Mr. Goss, Mrs. Johnson of Connecticut, Mr. Lagomarsino, Mr. Ramstad, Mr. Rangel, Mr. Ros-Lehtinen, Mr. Serrano, Mr. Smith of Florida, and Mr. Torricelli speaking on the Cuban Democracy Act of 1992, H 9084, 102nd Cong., 2nd sess. Congressional Record (September 22, 1992), vol. 138, no. 130, pt. 2. Quoted in Joanna R. Cameron, "The Cuban Democracy Act of 1992: The international implications," *The Fletcher Forum* (Winter/Spring 1996): 137.

36 Cuban Democracy Act of 1992, Pub. L. No. 102-484, 106 Stat. 2575 (1992), codified at 22 U.S.C.S. §§6001–6010 (1993), Sec. 6002. Statement of policy, p. 2

37 Jane Franklin, "The politics behind Clinton's Cuba policy," *The Baltimore Sun*, August 30, 1994.

38 Richard Garfield, DrPH, RN, and Sarah Santana, "The Impact of the Economic Crisis and the US Embargo on Health in Cuba," *American Journal of Public Health* 87, no. 1 (January 1997).

to withhold U. S. payments to the IFIs, should they approve assistance to Cuba over U. S. opposition.[39]

Title III of Helms Burton is deeply consequential for Cuba, and among coercive measures regimes, it is also unique. Under Title III, all expropriated and nationalized Cuban property is considered to be "stolen" and consequently, trading with goods manufactured on or by this property or investing in a "stolen property" is deemed illegal by the U.S., regardless of the nationality of the "perpetrator." Under this statute, it is possible for U.S. citizens and Cuban (naturalized U.S. citizens) individuals and companies to bring civil action for damages before U.S. courts against any person that is doing business with products nationalized after 1959. Thus, in effect, the statute authorizes suit by a (former) foreign national, against a foreign company or person, for an action that took place in a foreign country. This is considered to be "extraterritorial" in violation of international commercial law and has consistently been broadly condemned by the international community.

If the United States simply adopted a policy of bilateral suspension of trade and aid, it would be less detrimental to Cuba's possibilities to develop trading and investment relation with third actors. The United States' economic sanctions regime is structured to constrict Cuba's trade with private and state companies in third countries, in part by generating a chilling effect and over-compliance. In the particular case of Cuba, the term to use extraterritorial unilateral coercive measures.

Unilateral Coercive Measures

The coercive measures that are imposed by member states of the United Nations with the approval of the Security Council would be multilateral as the sender would be a multilateral organization not an individual state. However, in the absence of an effective international

---

39 There are technical avenues for Cuba to have a limited engagement with leading IFIs. However, political considerations within the U.S. government are not favorable. U.S. attitudes weigh heavily because while legally only a majority of (weighted) votes is required for IMF membership, in practice the Fund's executive board hesitates to act counter to strong objections by its major shareholder. Richard E. Feinberg, "Reaching out: Cuba's New Economy and the International Response," Latin American initiatives at Brookings, November 17, 2011, p. 68. https://www.brookings.edu/research/reaching-out-cubas-new-economy-and-the-international-response/

system for conflict resolution and effective means of enforcement by multilateral organizations, powerful states have taken unilateral decisions to impose coercive measures unilaterally.

Therefore, unilateral coercive measures are punitive actions implemented by a sender state or coalition of states with the objective of forcing the target state to modify its behavior according to the preference of the sender state.[40] Unilateral coercive measures violate state sovereignty, one of the oldest concepts in modern international law; they affect states' rights like self-determination and the right to development and they usually entail an illegal extraterritorial application of the sender's domestic legislation.

Apart from the clear objections of the majority of states to the use of unilateral coercive measures, the United States continues imposing coercive measures with unlawful domestic and extra-territorial effects, enforces them and imposes penalties on states that allegedly circumvent them, and thereby usurps the functions of the United Nations and undermines its authority and credibility.

In the case of the U.S./Cuba conflict unilateral coercive measures are understood as a U.S. foreign policy tool used only by the sender without any mandate or prior authorization from the United Nations or other multilateral organization in order to intervene in the internal affairs of Cuba and promote regime change. The punishing coercive strategy goes beyond the economic sphere into the political, diplomatic and security spheres affecting Cuba's right to self-determination.

There are also other measures such as designating Cuba as a state sponsor of terrorism. This unilateral designation also makes Cuba a target for additional disruption, especially in the financial sector, and promotes increased scrutiny for private companies worldwide if they engage in commercial dealings with Cuba.

Even for transactions that are clearly permitted under U.S. law, companies and banks can expect inquiries from the Office of Global Security Risk within the U.S. Government's Securities and Exchange

---

40 United Nations Guiding Principles on Sanctions, Business and Human Rights, Commentary (Draft), United Nations Human Rights Special Procedures, Special Rapporteurs, Independent Experts and Working Groups. Mandate of the Special Rappotteur on the negative impact of unilateral coercive measures on the enjoyment of human rights, p. 27.

Commission for any Cuba transactions.[41] Between August 2021 and February 2022, a total of 100 foreign banks were involved in 261 enforcement actions that included "closing bank accounts and [terminating] established banking contracts, returning transactions, refusing to create accounts, [and] cancelling passwords for the exchange of financial information through the Society for Worldwide Interbank Financial Telecommunication (SWIFT)."[42]

Sanctions Enforcement and Over-compliance

The intensive use of geoeconomics[43] as a strategic weapon by the U.S. and other western states has increased in the last two decades as they have tried to promote a coercion-based international order. In this context, U.S. actions to enforce their unilateral coercive measures regimes rest basically on the prominent hegemonic position that the Northern superpower has enjoyed since the end of the Second World War. The United States has maintained an overwhelming hegemony in the global economy which has been grounded in large measure in its dominant role in the world financial system. Such external projection by the U.S. is more relevant in its geopolitical sphere of influence, as defined by the Monroe doctrine more than 200 years ago.

When the Security Council takes action in the case of the breach or threat to the international peace and security, it usually requests a

---

41 U.S. Embassy Havana, "U.S. Announces Designation of Cuba as State sponsor of Terrorism," January 11, 2021. https://cu.usembassy.gov/u-s-announces-designation-of-cuba-as-a-state-sponsor-of-terrorism/

42 Update to the Report of Cuba on resolution 75/289 of the United Nations General Assembly entitled "Necessity of ending the economic, commercial and financial embargo imposed by the United States of America against Cuba" (August 2021–February 2022), p. 9.

43 Geoeconomics entered the lexicon in 1990 with an article by Edward Luttwak, which argued that following the Cold War, the importance of military power was giving way to geoeconomic power. Edward Luttwak, "From Geopolitics to Geo-Economics: Logic of Conflict, Grammar of Commerce," *The National Interest* (Summer 1990): 17–23. Geoeconomics has been defined as the use of economic instruments to promote national interests and produce geopolitical results. Robert Blackwill and Jennifer Harris explore today's leading geoeconomic instruments— trade policy, investment policy, economic and financial sanctions, financial and monetary policy, energy and commodities, aid and cyber—in Robert D. Blackwill and Jennifer M. Harris, *War by other means: Geoeconomics and Statecraft* (Cambrige, Massachussets: Harvard University Press, 2016).

certain behavior from the targeted state.[44] The Charter of the United Nations provides that all member states are obliged to comply with and implement UN Security Council resolutions and to observe international law in order to eliminate threats to the international peace and security.[45] Consequently the means of enforcement of UN Security Council sanctions rests on this multilateral entity mandated with unique powers.

The means and consequences of enforcement of unilateral coercive measures imposed by one state like the United States is quite different. The United States is not only the world's most active user of unilateral economic sanctions. In particular, the U.S. government's use of unilateral sanctions as a foreign policy tool has increased 933% in the last two decades.[46] The U.S. is also a major enforcer by imposing penalties on alleged violators. U.S unilateral coercive measures impose pressure and punishment on foreign legal and natural persons who do not comply with the U.S. extraterritorial legislation via a variety of limitations, including access restrictions, fines and penalties. Thereby they not only put pressure on operators worldwide but also interfere with the sovereign foreign policy choices of states and international organizations such as the European Union (EU) which supports legitimate trade.[47]

An overview of U.S. unilateral coercive measures in 2023, including the public enforcement actions issued by the U.S. Department of the Treasury's Office of Foreign Assets Control (OFAC) demonstrates that 2023 was a record year for U.S. unilateral coercive measures enforcement, with OFAC assessing over $1.5 billion in penalties across 17 resolutions, dwarfing the total penalty amounts assessed

---

44 The Security Council has used its Article 41 powers under the UN Charter to impose sanctions 30 times since it first established a mandatory sanctions regime on Southern Rhodesia in resolution 232 (1966). Currently, 15 sanctions regimes are in force, with the 751 Somalia regime dating back to resolutions 733 (1992) and 751 (1992), while the 2140 Yemen regime established in resolution 2140 (2014) is the most recent. https://www.securitycouncilreport.org/images/homepage/security_council_sanctions_regimes.pdf

45 Charter of the United Nations Chapter V, Security Council, Article 25. https://legal.un.org/repertory/art25.shtml

46 Treasury Sanctions Review. https://home.treasury.gov/system/files/136/Treasury-2021-sanctions-review.pdf

47 J. Schmidt, "The Legality of Unilateral Extra-territorial Sanctions under International Law," *Journal of Conflict & Security Law* 27, no. 1 (2022): 53–81.

in recent years and representing the highest volume of penalties ever assessed by OFAC in a single calendar year.[48] Enforcement and implementation are shared across the executive branch, primarily among the Department of State, Treasury (through OFAC), the Department of Commerce, and the Department of Justice (DOJ). The U.S. Department of the Treasury's Office of Foreign Assets Control (OFAC) administers and enforces most economic and trade unilateral coercive measures. Specifically, OFAC is responsible for civil enforcement of U.S. laws, and its regulations are enforced on a strict liability basis, meaning that OFAC does not need to prove fault or intent to enter an enforcement action and issue a civil penalty.[49]

The aggressive enforcement of unilateral coercive measures results in over-compliance. That will be defined broadly as a situation in which a market participant refrains from an otherwise desirable transaction or activity involving some connection with a sanctioned country or person—beyond what is legally mandated by the relevant regime.[50]

For Alena Douhan, over-compliance consists of "self-imposed restraints that go beyond the restrictions mandated by sanctions regimes, either as part of a derisking process, to minimize the potential for inadvertent violations or to avoid reputational or other business risks, or as a means to limit compliance costs."[51]

As Joy Gordon aptly points out, in the Cuban case, there are two main factors that drive over compliance with U.S. unilateral coercive measures: the ambiguity of the regulations, and the severity of the penalties. The U.S. Treasury Department's Office of Foreign Assets Control (OFAC) requires banks and other private actors not only to abide by the explicit language of the regulations regarding their own

---

48 Morrison-Foerster, "U.S. Sanctions Enforcement: 2023 Trends and Lessons Learned," March 4, 2024. https://www.mofo.com/resources/insights/240304-us-sanctions-enforcement-2023-trends

49 *Federal Register* 74, no. 215 (November 9, 2009): 57593, Rules and Regulations. https://ofac.treasury.gov/media/7566/download?inline

50 Pierre-Hugues Verdier, "Sanctions Over-compliance: What, Why, and Does It Matter?" *North Carolina Journal of International Law* 48 (2023): 471.

51 Alena F. Douhan (Special Rapporteur on the Negative Impact of Unilateral Coercive Measures on the Enjoyment of Human Rights*), Secondary Sanctions, Civil and Criminal Penalties for Circumvention of Sanctions Regimes and Over-compliance with Sanctions*, No. U.N. Doc. A/HRC/51/33 (July 15, 2022), para. 17.

acts, but also to exercise "due diligence" in regard to what their customers or trade partners might do.[52]

> In terms of the severity of the penalties Cubatrade.org, a U.S. based organization, explains that despite the presentation by the sender or recipient of authorizations and opinions from the Office of Foreign Assets Control (OFAC) of the United States Department of the Treasury, Bureau of Industry and Security (BIS) of the United States Department of Commerce, and Office of the Legal Adviser (OLA) at the United States Department of State, the fear of the cost for an unintentional violation of OFAC transaction compliance regulations and the amount of the fine an increasing number of financial institutions located in third countries are refusing to process transactions which include a sender located in the Republic of Cuba or a recipient located in Cuba.

Treasury Department's Office of Foreign Assets Control, in settlement agreements with financial institutions and companies, includes both the value of the agreed upon financial settlement and the statutory maximum civil monetary penalty. The statutory maximum monetary penalties in recent Republic of Cuba-connected OFAC violations were 35, 89, 266, and 1,473 times the actual imposed monetary penalty. So, the value of the agreed upon financial settlement and the statutory maximum civil monetary penalty is very problematic threat. A Monaco-based financial institution, a subsidiary of a France-based financial institution, was fined US$401,039.00 for a violation that was self-disclosed and constituted a non-egregious case. According to the OFAC, the statutory maximum civil monetary penalty applicable in this matter is US$106,853,346.00, which is 1473 times the actual imposed monetary penalty. It is those multipliers which serve as a financial Sword of Damocles, a disincentive to deter an increasing number of financial institutions from willingness to engage with Cuba-related transactions and overly comply regardless of assurances from the United States government.[53]

---

52 Joy Gordon, "Cuba's economic crisis: U.S. Sanctions and the problem of over-compliance," *Le Monde Diplomatic,* October 7, 2024.

53 "Facing Extinction Like Javan Rhino? Non-U.S. Banks Engaging With U.S.

In the case of Cuba, U.S. officials act with strictness and tenacity in enforcing statutes and regulations whose frequently enactment or modifications add to the uncertainty and aforementioned ambiguity, generating more over-compliance by state and private companies and banks.

The duration in time of the unilateral coercive measures system as well as the ever-changing modifications implemented over more than 60 years also contribute to over-compliance in the Cuban case. For example, in 2016 OFAC authorized U.S. banking institutions to process "U-turn" transactions in which Cuba or a Cuban national has an interest. It allowed Cuban funds originating from a non-U.S. bank to be cleared through U.S. banks and transferred back to a non-U.S. bank. Under this authorization, neither the originator nor the beneficiary of the transaction could be a person subject to U.S. jurisdiction, unless otherwise authorized or exempt under the regulations.[54] In 2019, the next administration would reverse that and other decisions.[55] Subsequently, on May 28, 2024, the acting administration reinstated an authorization for so-called "U-turn" payments, which allowed U.S. banks to process certain U.S. dollar payments in relation to Cuba.[56]

One other factor is the wide scope of the unilateral coercive measures and the lack of legal remedies to avoid them imposition of hefty fines. In his 2006 study entitled Targeted Sanctions and Due

---

And Non-U.S. Entities For Authorized Transactions Involving Cuba Due To Risk Of OFAC Penalties. Since 2015, Only Two U.S. Banks," *Cuba Trade,* October 17, 2022. https://www.cubatrade.org/blog/2022/10/17/ztijoaz9m3hky8hdnb8n6ilvl0h7ee

54 Wynn H. Segall and Jonathan C. Poling, Nnedinma C. Ifudu Nweke, and Christian C. Davis, "Obama Administration Further Eases Sanctions in Advance of Cuba Visit," *Akin,* March 17, 2016. https://www.akingump.com/en/insights/alerts/obama-administration-further-eases-sanctions-in-advance-of-cuba,

55 On September 9, 2019, the U.S. Department of the Treasury's Office of Foreign Assets Control (OFAC) published amendments to the Cuban Assets Control Regulations (CACR) to further implement President Trump's June 2017 National Security Presidential Memorandum Strengthening the Policy of the United States Towards Cuba (NSPM). The amendments, which appear in the *Federal Register* as a final rule that becomes effective October 9, 2019, prohibit "U-turn" financial transactions related to Cuba and impose limitations on remittances to Cuban nationals. https://www.lexology.com/library/detail.aspx?g=2135907d-e0b3-4e66-bd88-d9832c8262c2

56 "Cuba Sanctions: US Government Authorizes 'U-Turn' Financial Transactions," Watson Farley and Williams, June 11, 2024. https://www.wfw.com/articles/cuba-sanctions-us-government-authorizes-u-turn-financial-transactions/

Process,[57] Bardo Fassbender addressed the responsibility of the UN Security Council to ensure that fair and clear procedures are made available to individuals and entities targeted with sanctions under Chapter VII of the UN Charter through which they could challenge measures taken against them. The same applies to unilateral coercive measures imposed by states on other states.

The targets of U.S. unilateral coercive measures are not informed prior to their being listed and accordingly do not have an opportunity to prevent their inclusion in a list by demonstrating that such an inclusion is unjustified.

Dated April 2, 2025, Treasury's OFAC provides a 2435-page list of Specially Designated Nationals and Blocked Persons List that is defined as "a reference tool providing actual notice of actions by OFAC with respect to Specially Designated Nationals and other persons (which term includes both individuals and entities) whose property is blocked, to assist the public in complying with the various sanctions programs administered by OFAC."[58]

There is reference to compliance, which is also not clear and would likely lead to enhanced due diligence and ultimately to over-compliance on the part of third parties who up to the moment of publication of the list or listing may have commercial or financial links to the listed entity or person.

In all cases, there is no reference to "legal remedies" for persons and entities listed; they are not informed, they just learn by press releases, cannot prevent being listed and have no way to appeal. It has been argued by leading scholars of international law that the present situation is a "denial of legal remedies" for the individuals and entities concerned, and is a violation of the principles of international human rights law: "Everyone must be free to show that he or she has been unjustifiably placed under suspicion and that therefore [for instance] the freezing of his or her assets has no valid foundation."[59]

---

57 Bardo Fassbender, "Targeted Sanctions and Due Process," a study commissioned by the United Nations Office of Legal Affairs, Office of the Legal Counsel, March 20, 2006. https://www.un.org/law/counsel/Fassbender_study.pdf

58 U.S. Department of the Treasury, *Specially Designated Nationals and Blocked Persons List (SDN List)*. https://www.treasury.gov/ofac/downloads/sdnlist.pdf

59 See Christian Tomuschat, *Human Rights: Between Idealism and Realism* (Oxford: Oxford University Press, 2003), p. 90. Quoted in Bardo Fassbender, op. cit.

Also, as is the case of Cuba, inclusion on the "blacklist" is mostly politically motivated. Cuba is one of the targets of these types of economic coercion and an important case study for a better understanding of this instrument in real conditions.

Much of the blacklisting against Cuban nationals and Cuba-related entities has taken place through OFAC's Specially Designated Nationals and Blocked Persons List. It includes natural persons, ships, specially designated nationals, specially designated terrorists, specially designated global terrorists, foreign terrorist organizations and specially designated drug dealers. It also includes listings in which all properties and interests of the sanctioned person are blocked, and in which all kinds of transactions with U.S. nationals are forbidden. Third country parties that deal with those listed can be fined or blacklisted.[60]

In this context, European companies have preferred to cancel contracts with Cuban before having to fight potential lawsuits in court or pay hefty fines, even with the protection of the European Union. Such is the case of the French-Italian company Avions de Transport Régional, which had signed a contract with the Cuban government for the sale of two ATR 72-600 turboprop aircraft.[61]

In other cases, companies refrain from advertising promoting business activities with Cuba such as Türkiye's Global Ports Holding that has a management agreement in Cuba to advise and consult on cruise port management best practice the cruise terminal is in the Sierra Maestra complex, in San Francisco pier, with a current capacity for two ships. Recently, the company has removed almost all references to the Cuba to from its website.[62]

---

60 U.S. Department of the Treasury, "Specially Designated Nationals and Blocked Persons List (SDN) Human Readable Lists." https://home.treasury.gov/policy-issues/financial-sanctions/specially-designated-nationals-and-blocked-persons-list-sdn-human-readable-lists

61 "Helms-Burton Law Crushed Investment in Cuba," *The Havana Consulting Group*, May 21, 2020. http://www.thehavanaconsultinggroup.com/enUS/Articles/Article/82

62 "Türkiye's Global Ports Holding Signed 15-Year Management Contract for Cuba's Passenger Ship Operations. Company Has Removed Almost All References From Its Internet Site." *Cuba Trade*, August 29, 2024. https://www.cubatrade.org/blog/2024/8/29/23d9b9rp2q30c5f7gtkgg8w23fp95a

Conclusion

The use of coercive measures by one state versus another is very controversial in contemporary international law and so is the theoretical and political debate. It is paramount to address the issue of terminology because the use of appropriate terms and a set of concepts accepted and understood in the same way by all members of the international community from north to south is vital for the dialogue with observance of international law. In a context of increased geoeconomic confrontation, the use of unilateral coercive measures with extraterritorial reach has increased. It is then paramount to establish the terms to use to define these actions under international law and prevent any group of states based on an economic advantage to impose a coercion-based international order that serves their interests over the rest over of the international system. It is often claimed that the "embargo" of Cuba is a bilateral issue, in which the U.S. restricts only the actions of its own nationals. On the contrary, the sanctions regime has a strong extraterritorial character, deeply impacting Cuba's trade with third countries. In addition, the unilateral coercive measures on Cuba do not include provisions for any periodic assessment of its impact on Cuba's most vulnerable populations. By almost any standard, the unilateral coercive measures on Cuba run counter to human rights concerns.

At the same time, the U.S. system of unilateral coercive measures holds a distinction for both longevity and breadth. The intricate, everchanging web of statutes, rules, regulations and blacklists generates a significant chilling effect affecting potential foreign investors. It forces both states and private actors of third countries into excessive due diligence and over-compliance.

PART II

....

IMPACT OF UNILATERAL SANCTIONS AND OVER-COMPLIANCE ON BUSINESS ACTIVITY

CHAPTER 5

UN Guiding Principles on Business and Human Rights
in the context of UCMs proliferation

Alfred de Zayas[1]

Abstract

John Ruggie's Guiding Principles on Business and Human Rights[2] (GPs, Guiding Principles) launched the normative process of defining the legal responsibility of business enterprises for the human rights impacts of their actions and omissions. The GPs do not address many issues that require closer attention, including the responsibility of business enterprises for the adverse human rights impacts resulting from their implementation and hyper-implementation of illegal unilateral coercive measures (UCMs).

Notwithstanding the numerous General Assembly and Human Rights Council resolutions condemning UCMs as contrary to the UN Charter and international law, there has been a surge in the imposition of UCMs by States and little or no resistance from business enterprises that have become complicit in the ensuing violations of human rights, including the right to life, the right to food, the right to clean water and sanitation, the right to housing, etc.

Alena Douhan's Guiding Principles on Sanctions, Business and Human Rights provide a necessary addition to the GPs and should be implemented by governments and business leaders.

---

1 U.S. and Switzerland, Professor at the Geneva School of Diplomacy

2 *Guiding Principles on Business and Human Rights: Implementing the United Nations "Protect, Respect and Remedy" Framework,* UN Human Rights, January 1, 2012. https://www.ohchr.org/en/publications/reference-publications/guiding-principles-business-and-human-rights

Introduction

Over the past several decades, the legal analysis of the relationship between UCMs and human rights has demonstrated that UCMs are incompatible with the purposes and principles of the United Nations, that they breach existing international treaties and customary international law, impacting the sovereignty of States and the right of self-determination of peoples. Academics have delivered the rationale for their immediate abolition. The challenge has been how to translate international legal principles into political action, how to ensure that the UN Charter is enforced. We observe a serious implementation gap, which is attributable to the absence of effective enforcement mechanisms in the UN system. This has led to the emergence of a culture of impunity. Powerful states consider themselves above international law and morals. Government lawyers concoct spurious arguments to justify the unjustifiable, they corrupt language, they subvert the spirit of the law and attempt to justify obviously illegal UCMs by invoking human rights considerations. This is tantamount to weaponizing human rights and subverting the letter and spirit of the law. How are business leaders navigating the troubled waters created by UCMs, how are they coping with the *contra legem* situation created by illegal UCMs?

In an effort to minimize the risk of heavy penalties for failure to fully implement UCMs, business enterprises have become instruments in the enforcement of UCMs regimes. At the same time, States are failing in their obligation to give protection to business enterprises registered or operating within their jurisdiction, when businesses suffer penalties because of refusal to implement UCMs. In principle, States have an obligation to exercise diplomatic protection on behalf of their citizens who become victims of extraterritorial acts by foreign entities and should invoke the jurisdiction of the International Court of Justice in contentious cases, request an Advisory Opinion to clarify the violations of international law involved and define the level of compensation due to the victims. Other avenues of redress could be the Permanent Court of Arbitration or other settlement mechanisms including Investor-State-Dispute Settlement.

In 2014 the Human Rights Council established an open-ended intergovernmental working group on transnational corporations and other business enterprises with respect to human rights (Res. 26/9) with a mandate to elaborate an international legally binding instrument to monitor and regulate the human rights impacts of business activities.[3] OHCHR's Accountability and Remedy Project should clearly enumerate the articles of the GPs violated by the implementation of UCMs and emphasize the incompatibility of UCMs with both the UN Guiding Principles and the Treaty *de lege ferenda*.

Resolutions of the General Assembly and Human Rights Council condemning UCMs should be the subject of continuous debate in national parliaments and government agencies, including national human rights institutions. Specific rules should be adopted to define the civil and penal liability of corporations for their complicity in the enforcement of UCMs. Victims must have access to effective remedies.

The Incompatibility of UCMs with the Guiding Principles

The incompatibility of UCMs with the spirit that led to the adoption of the GPs is a theme that could and should have been addressed by the Working Group on Business and Human Rights.[4] It appears, however, that none of the 36 reports issued as of October 2024 explored the interrelationship between business activity and UCMs, as if the problem did not exist. The same applies to the yearly Forum on Business and Human Rights, which has held 12 sessions, each session packed with as many as 60 side events.[5] The concept note for the 13th session of the Forum on Business and Human Rights does not make

---

3 *Open-ended intergovernmental Working Group to elaborate a legally binding instrument on transnational cooperations and other business enterprises with respect to human rights,* United Nations Human Rights, October 2018. https://www.ohchr.org/en/events/sessions/2018/open-ended-intergovernmental-working-group-elaborate-legally-binding

Open-ended intergovernmental working group on transnational corporations and other business enterprises with respect to human rights, United Nations Human Rights Council. https://www.ohchr.org/en/hr-bodies/hrc/wg-trans-corp/igwg-on-tnc

Legally Binding Instrument on Business and Human Rights, United Nations Forum on Business and Human Rights, Geneva, November 2024. https://forumbhr2024.sched.com/event/1gev3/legally-binding-instrument-on-business-and-human-rights?linkback=grid

4 Thematic Reports of the Working Group on Business and Human Rights. https://www.ohchr.org/en/special-procedures/wg-business/thematic-reports

5 United Nations Forum on Business and Human Rights. https://www.ohchr.org/en/hrc-subsidiary-bodies/united-nations-forum-business-and-human-rights

any reference to either sanctions or UCMs.[6] It would be desirable for the FBHR to integrate UCMs into the agenda and during the "informal dialogues" at the beginning of each session.[7]

If the UN Guiding Principles on Business and Human Rights are going to be more than milquetoast, it will be necessary to "put teeth to them." Self-regulation has proven to be unsatisfactory, because business enterprises operate according to their own logic—*Pecunia non olet,* profit, profit *über alles.* There is no generally accepted ethics about generating profit. Ontologically the priority of corporations is to generate profit: business enterprises cannot be seen as part of national human rights institutions. It is for the State to ensure that the activities of business enterprises do not result in violations of human rights.

The General Assembly and the Human Rights Council have endorsed the Guiding Principles, but this has not led to the adoption of concrete measures aimed at making the advancement of human rights one of the parameters for doing business. The problem lies with the capitalist[8] mentality that pervades most economies in the West, including the Bretton Woods institutions. This goes back partly to Adam Smith,[9] John Maynard Keynes and Friedrich Hayek among others; a version of it is reflected in the novels of Ayn Rand, e.g. *The Fountainhead* and *Atlas Shrugged.*[10]

The Guiding Principles do not mention the concept of unilateral coercive measures, not even the UN practice of imposing crippling economic sanctions under Chapter VII of the UN Charter, or the infamous Security Council "sanctions lists" pushed by the United States in the context of the First Gulf War and the "*war against terror*" in the

---

6 13th United Nations Forum on Business and Human Rights. https://www.ohchr.org/en/events/sessions/2024/13th-united-nations-forum-business-and-human-rights

7 CGTN official website. https://www.cgtn.com.

8 *Theory of Capitalism,* The Center on Capitalism and Society, Columbia University. https://capitalism.columbia.edu/content/theory-capitalism

9 *An Inquiry into the Nature and Causes of the Wealth of Nations,* 1776.

10 John Maynard Keynes, *The General Theory of Employment, Interest, and Money* (London: Macmillan, 1936); Friedrich A. Hayek, *Law, Legislation and Liberty, vol. 1, Rules and Order* (Chicago: University of Chicago Press, 1973); Ayn Rand, *The Fountainhead* (New York: Bobbs-Merrill, 1943); Ayn Rand, *Atlas Shrugged* (New York: Random House, 1957).

1990s and 2000s, although these UN sanctions resulted in a million deaths in Iraq and enormous human suffering.[11]

Summit of the Future

On September 20–21, 2024, the General Assembly held a Summit of the Future[12] and adopted a Pact for the Future, which pays tribute to the Guiding Principles on Business and Human Rights. Unfortunately, the Pact neither addresses the international law prohibition of interference in the domestic affairs of states, nor mentions the principle of non-intervention or the scourge of UCMs. The term "sanction" does not even figure in the entire document. The need to solve the problem of double standards by many UN institutions is nowhere acknowledged. It is regrettable that a necessary amendment was rejected, which would have added a paragraph stating that the UN "shall be driven by intergovernmental decision-making process" and "its system shall not intervene in matters which are essentially within the domestic jurisdiction of any State" in line with the UN Charter.[13]

Yet, in the Preamble of the Pact for the Future, the States did commit themselves:

> To live up to our foundational promise to protect succeeding generations from the scourge of war, we must abide by international law, including the Charter, and make full use of all the instruments and mechanisms set out in the Charter, intensifying our use of diplomacy, committing to resolve our disputes peacefully, refraining from the threat or use of force, or acts of aggression, **respecting each other's sovereignty** and territorial integrity, upholding the principles

---

11 "*Sayed v. Belgium,* Human Rights Committee," Chapter 7 in Jakob Möller and Alfred de Zayas, *The United Nations Human Rights Committee Case Law* (Strasbourg: N.P. Engel, 2009).

12 United Nations, "Pact for the Future, Global Digital Compact and Declaration on Future Generations," Summit of the Future Outcome Documents, September 2024. https://www.un.org/en/summit-of-the-future. *Pact for the Future*. https://www.un.org/sites/un2.un.org/files/sotf-pact_for_the_future_adopted.pdf

13 Maziar Motamedi, "What's the UN's New 'Pact for the Future' and Why Did Russia Oppose It?," *Al Jazeera,* September 24, 2024. https://www.aljazeera.com/news/2024/9/24/whats-the-uns-new-pact-for-the-future-and-why-did-russia-oppose-it

of political independence and self-determination, as well as strengthening accountability and ending impunity.
Action 5 very gingerly touches on unilateralism:

We are committed to a rules-based, non-discriminatory, open, fair, inclusive, equitable and transparent multilateral trading system, with the World Trade Organization at its core. We underscore the importance of the multilateral trading system contributing to the achievement of the Sustainable Development Goals. We reiterate that States are strongly **urged to refrain from promulgating and applying unilateral economic measures** not in accordance with international law and the Charter of the United Nations that impede the full achievement of economic and social development, particularly in developing countries.[14]

With regard to digital industries, Objective 3 maintains the illusion of self-regulation and stipulates:

We commit to respect, protect and promote human rights in the digital space. We will uphold international human rights law throughout the life cycle of digital and emerging technologies so that users can safely benefit from digital technologies and are protected from violations, abuses and all forms of discrimination. **We recognize the responsibilities of all stakeholders in this endeavour and also call on the private sector to apply the United Nations Guiding Principles on Business and Human Rights**.

It further calls on digital enterprises:

Digital technology companies, developers and social media platforms to respect human rights online, be accountable for and take measures to mitigate and prevent abuses, and to provide access to effective remedy in line with the United

---

14 *Pact for the Future* Objective 3, p. 42 et seq.; p. 6, para. 24. https://www.un.org/sites/un2.un.org/files/sotf-pact_for_the_future_adopted.pdf

Nations Guiding Principles on Business and Human Rights and other relevant frameworks (SDGs 5, 10 and 16).

As with so many UN declarations, the Pact for the Future enunciates big goals but fails to lay down specifics on how to achieve them. It is essentially a "cut and paste" job from old UN resolutions and does not provide fresh ideas or a plan of action to tackle the many challenges facing the present, let alone the future. In view of the suffering caused by ongoing wars and mounting evidence on the adverse impacts of UCMs, including famine, disease, mass emigration, it would have been more sensible to convene a Summit of the Present and adopt an urgent Program for the Present. In any event, the Pact, which is not legally binding, will be largely ignored by States, as they also ignored the 1993 Vienna Declaration and Programme of Action and the 2005 Outcome Document of the World Summit.

Foundational Principles on Business and Human Rights

Like the Pact for the Future, the Guiding Principles on Business and Human Rights fails to make any reference to sanctions or UCMs as direct causes of gross violations of human rights. Yet, many of its provisions are relevant and should be understood as extending to UCMs. Indeed, the three preambular standards can be so interpreted:

(a) States' existing obligations to respect, protect and fulfil human rights and fundamental freedoms; (b) The role of business enterprises as specialized organs of society performing specialized functions, required to comply with all applicable laws and to respect human rights; (c) The need for rights and obligations to be matched to appropriate and effective remedies when breached.[15]

As to the State duty to protect human rights, principles 1 and 2 of the GPs should ensure that business enterprises do not cause human rights violations, including by implementing illegal UCMs. States

---

15 *Guiding Principles on Business and Human Rights*, p. 2. https://www.ohchr.org/sites/default/files/Documents/Publications/GuidingPrinciplesBusinessHR_EN.pdf

should ensure that business enterprises do not become instruments of foreign powers by implementing extraterritorial legislation that has impacts on the territory of the State(s) where they operate. Business enterprises should be held accountable for not incorporating into their business strategies and decisions the clear message of the yearly GA Resolutions that condemn UCMs as contrary to the UN Charter and international law. There is even a pending case before the International Criminal Court on the issue whether UCMs constitute "crimes against humanity" within the meaning of article 7 of the Statute of Rome.[16] Business enterprises are therefore on notice that UCMs are illegal, even criminal. It necessarily follows that by implementing UCMs business enterprises assume both civil and penal liability for the harm caused.

In its operative paragraphs GA Res. 78/202 of December 19, 2023:

> Urges all States to cease adopting or implementing any uni-lateral measures not in accordance with international law, international humanitarian law, the Charter of the United Nations and the norms and principles governing peaceful relations among States, in particular those of a coercive nature, with all their extraterritorial effects, which create obstacles to trade relations among States....[17]

In its operative paragraphs Resolution 78/135 of December 19, 2023:

> Urges the international community to adopt urgent and effective measures to eliminate the use of unilateral eco-nomic, financial or trade measures that are not authorized by relevant organs of the United Nations, that are inconsistent

---

16 ICC, "Statement of the Prosecutor of the International Criminal Court, Mrs Fatou Bensouda, on the Referral by Venezuela regarding the Situation in Its Own Territory," February 17, 2020. www.icc-cpi.int/Pages/item.aspx?name=200217-otp-statement-venezuela; *Report of the Special Rapporteur on International Order on his mission to Venezuela.* https://www.ohchr.org/en/documents/country-reports/ahrc3947add1-report-independent-expert-promotion-democratic-and-equitable

17 UN Document N23/423/58. https://documents.un.org/doc/undoc/gen/n23/423/58/pdf/n2342358.pdf

with the principles of international law or the Charter of the United Nations or that contravene the basic principles of the multilateral trading system and that affect, in particular, but not exclusively, developing countries.[18]

GA Resolution 78/7 of November 2, 2023, was the 31st GA resolution condemning United States UCMs and the financial blockade in Cuba.[19] It was adopted by a vote of 187 in favor and only two against. If nothing else, that proves that the entire world with the notable exception of the U.S. and Israel consider these UCMs contrary to international law and morals, as abundantly demonstrated in the statements delivered by the delegates of country after country.[20] And yet, far from being lifted, the UCMs against Cuba have been intensified, and business enterprises worldwide continue to implement them out of fear of penalties imposed by the U.S. Department of the Treasury.

This entails an affront to international law and the UN Charter. States must therefore demonstrate legal smartness and innovation in their coordination of trade and business policies to render the UCMs ineffective. This also includes adopting measures to make sure that business enterprises registered or operating in their territory do not cooperate with such illegal UCMs, and when they do, they must be subjected to penalties under domestic law. When business enterprises implement UCMs they necessarily violate the United Nations "Protect, Respect and Remedy" Framework. This should have consequences.

The GPs operative principles lay down a general state regulatory and policy function. Principle 3 stipulates: "In meeting their duty to protect, States should: (a) Enforce laws that are aimed at, or have the effect of, requiring business enterprises to respect human rights, and periodically to assess the adequacy of such laws and address any gaps...." It is for States therefore to adopt appropriate legislation that prohibits business enterprises to implement illegal UCMs and ensure their compliance with the domestic law.

---

18 UN Document N23/418/75. https://documents.un.org/doc/undoc/gen/n23/418/75/pdf/n2341875.pdf

19 UN Document N23/336/44. https://documents.un.org/doc/undoc/gen/n23/336/44/pdf/n2333644.pdf

20 General Assembly Document GA/12465. https://press.un.org/en/2022/ga12465.doc.htm

Alas, a serious normative gap exists, because States have not yet adopted specific legislation prohibiting business enterprises from becoming instruments of foreign governments by implementing their illegal UCMs and consenting to the extra-territorial application of foreign legislation, in violation of the State's sovereignty and exclusive jurisdiction. Absent any pertinent legislation, business enterprises tend to take the easy way out and bend under the foreign UCMs. This must be stopped. But then, the State must reciprocate by committing to pro-actively defend its enterprises from penalties eventually levied upon them by the States imposing UCMs. Such protection can take the form of diplomatic protests and could be strengthened by declaring the Ambassador of the country imposing UCMs *persona non grata*, pursuant to article 9 of the Vienna Convention on Diplomatic Relations,[21] by expelling other agents of the State imposing UCMs, and elevating the dispute to the International Court of Justice or the Permanent Court of Arbitration.

For instance, if because of UCMs a private bank refuses to transfer to or receive moneys from a country under UCMs and that failure to perform the normal functions of the bank adversely affects the human rights of the population in the targeted countries, e.g. if money transfers to buy foods or medicines cannot be effected, then the bank is complicit in the famine and death that may ensue. Many countries have "persons in distress" or "duty to rescue" legislation that obligates private persons to assist someone whose life may be in danger. Such legislation entails not only civil tort liability, but also criminal responsibility. Domestic law must oblige banks to perform their functions without discrimination and to reject any effort from a foreign country to interfere in the normal operation of financial transactions. Such interference constitutes a form of intimidation and blackmail that similarly must be prohibited by law as contrary to international *ordre public*.

In civil law countries "duty to rescue" legislation is quite common, e.g. in Belgium, where the obligation was introduced by the law of January 6, 1961, which stipulates that failure to provide assistance is punishable under article 422bis of the Penal Code. The conditions of the duty relate to awareness of the hazard and the possibility of

---

21 *Vienna Convention on Diplomatic Relations* (1961). https://legal.un.org/ilc/texts/instruments/english/conventions/9_1_1961.pdf

helping without putting oneself in physical danger. In the Canadian province of Quebec, the Charter of Rights provides for a general duty to rescue: "Every human being whose life is in peril has a right to assistance.... Every person must come to the aid of anyone whose life is in peril, either personally or calling for aid, by giving him the necessary and immediate physical assistance, unless it involves danger to himself or a third person, or he has another valid reason."[22]

In maritime law there is a rule of customary international law imposing a duty to assist ships in distress.[23] This rule is reflected in article 98 of the United Nations Convention on the Law of the Sea.[24] It is not difficult to understand that when business enterprises refused to sell vaccines, medicine, ventilators to Cuba and Venezuela at the height of the COVID-19 pandemic, they became complicit in the thousands of deaths caused by their failure to assist. These business enterprises gave priority to their profits over the lives of the victims who desperately needed the ventilators.[25] This is not just a matter of ethics and international solidarity; it is a matter of law.

It should be stressed that States are not freed of their international human rights law obligations by merely privatizing the delivery of services that may impact upon the enjoyment of human rights. Principle 5 of the GPs remind States that they must exercise adequate oversight, and this concretely means that they must ensure that financial institutions, banks, insurance providers, etc. do not lend themselves to the implementation of foreign UCMs. Principle 7 provides that public support and services should be denied to business enterprises that are involved with gross human rights abuses, e.g. by cooperating in the implementation of a financial blockade, and that refuse to remedy the situation.

---

22 *Charte des droits et libertés de la personne* (C-12). https://www.legisquebec. gouv.qc.ca/fr/document/lc/C-12

23 Alfred de Zayas, "Ships in Distress," in Rudolf Bernhardt (ed.), *Encyclopedia of Public International Law*, Vol. IV, pp. 397–400 (Amsterdam: North-Holland Publishers, 2000).

24 United Nations Convention on the Law of the Sea (UNCLOS). https://www. un.org/depts/los/convention_agreements/texts/unclos/unclos_e.pdf

25 Raúl Rodríguez, "U.S. Economic Sanctions on Cuba in the Context of the Pandemic COVID-19," Ethics & International Affairs, December 18, 2020. https:// www.ethicsandinternationalaffairs.org/online-exclusives/u-s-economic-sanctions-on-cuba-in-the-context-of-the-pandemic-covid-19

According to the GPs, States should ensure policy coherence. Principle 8 stipulates that "States should ensure that governmental departments, agencies and other State-based institutions that shape business practices are aware of and observe the State's human rights obligations when fulfilling their respective mandates, including by providing them with relevant information, training and support." This could be achieved by issuing administrative instructions to all agencies on a regular basis and ensuring that the agencies monitor the activities of business enterprises with regard to UCMs.

As to the corporate responsibility to respect human rights, it should not be limited to "respecting," but it should be proactive, to ensure oversight and provide adequate remedies. Principle 11 stipulates: "Business enterprises should respect human rights. This means that they should avoid infringing on the human rights of others and should address adverse human rights impacts with which they are involved." This means that business enterprises must refrain from cooperating with illegal UCM regimes. Principle 13 clarifies: "The responsibility to respect human rights requires that business enterprises: (a) Avoid causing or contributing to adverse human rights impacts through their own activities, and address such impacts when they occur...."

Corporate Due Diligence

Principle 15 expounds that "In order to meet their responsibility to respect human rights, business enterprises should have in place policies and processes appropriate to their size and circumstances, including: ... (b) A human rights due diligence process to identify, prevent, mitigate and account for how they address their impacts on human rights...."

Pursuant to this principle every business enterprise is put on notice that it must anticipate and prevent the harm caused by UCMs. The only way to do that is by refusing to implement them and to seek diplomatic protection from one or more States. Principle 17 goes on to exemplify that "the process should include assessing actual and potential human rights impacts, integrating and acting upon the findings." The Commentary to this principle is helpful as it raises the issue of complicity, which "may arise when a business enterprise contributes to, or is seen as contributing to, adverse human rights impacts caused by other parties...."

The Working Group on Business and Human rights issued a report in 2018 concerning corporate due diligence.[26] Again, it does not address the issue that the implementation of UCMs by business enterprises causes enormous harm to millions of innocents throughout the world. The issue has not been addressed by the Working Group, although due diligence would easily discover what those adverse impacts are, their causes and prevention strategies.

Effective Remedy

Principle 22 provides that "Where business enterprises identify that they have caused or contributed to adverse impacts, they should provide for or cooperate in their remediation through legitimate processes." Like with due diligence, what is needed here is good faith and a pro-active mindset. It is not that difficult to identify and quantify the harm caused by UCMs. Professor Jeffrey Sachs and Mark Weisbrot did so with regard to Venezuela in their 2019 Study "Collective Punishment."[27] But hitherto no government or business enterprise has cared to offer any kind of remedy to the victims of UCMs.

Principle 23 makes the sensible recommendation that business enterprises should: "(a) Comply with all applicable laws and respect internationally recognized human rights, wherever they operate; (b) Seek ways to honor the principles of internationally recognized human rights when faced with conflicting requirements; (c) Treat the risk of causing or contributing to gross human rights abuses as a legal compliance issue wherever they operate."

Admittedly, the CEO of a transnational corporation may not have the courage to defy UCMs, because UCMs represent a "conflicting requirement," but like everywhere in life, there must be a balancing of interests, and the universal rule should be that human

---

26 UN Human Rights, *Report of the Working Group on the Issue of Human Rights and Transnational Corporations,* A/73/163, July 16, 2018. https://www.ohchr.org/en/documents/thematic-reports/a73163-report-working-group-issue-human-rights-and-transnational

27 Mark Weisbrot and Jeffrey Sachs, "Economic Sanctions as Collective Punishment: The Case of Venezuela," Center for Economic and Policy Research, April 2019. https://cepr.net/images/stories/reports/venezuela-sanctions-2019-04.pdf

rights requirements take precedence over UCM demands, also bearing in mind that two thirds of humanity yearly condemns UCMs in the General Assembly as illegal and contrary to the UN Charter.

Principle 25 formulates a fundamental norm of international law. *Ubi jus, ibi remedium.* Where there is law, there must be a remedy: "As part of their duty to protect against business-related human rights abuse, States must take appropriate steps to ensure, through judicial, administrative, legislative or other appropriate means, that when such abuses occur within their territory and/or jurisdiction those affected have access to effective remedy."

That is why it is crucial that States legislate on the illegality of UCMs under domestic law and on the unlawfulness for business enterprises to submit to UCMs. Once it is a matter of domestic law, every local court can issue injunctions against business enterprises that would consider bending to UCMs. For instance, when a bank would refuse to make a financial transaction because of fears of having to pay penalties to the State imposing UCMs, this is where the State must step in and guarantee to the business enterprises that they will have all the support needed. This may also entail the necessity of a consortium of States to come together and declare in no uncertain terms that UCMs means economic war and that such illegal measures call for retorsion and countermeasures under articles 49 and 50 of the International Law Commission's Draft Articles on State Responsibility.[28]

There should also be State-based non-judicial grievance mechanisms, as stipulated in Principle 27: "States should provide effective and appropriate non-judicial grievance mechanisms, alongside judicial mechanisms, as part of a comprehensive State-based system for the remedy of business-related human rights abuse." Business enterprises should be involved in the crafting of such mechanisms. Moreover, it is the responsibility of the State and of the business enterprises themselves to make grievance mechanisms well known among potential victims so that they can actually invoke them.

---

28 United Nations Legal, Draft Articles on the Responsibility of States for Internationally Wrongful Acts (2001). https://legal.un.org/ilc/texts/instruments/english/draft_articles/9_6_2001.pdf

Conclusion

By implementing illegal UCMs business enterprises violate numerous provisions of the GPs and should be held accountable for actions and omissions when the foreseeable consequences entail violations of human rights.

The 2011 Guiding Principles on Business and Human Rights are not comprehensive and should be expanded to include the phenomenon of UCMs as a significant source of human rights violations that business enterprises must henceforth avoid. While States have the responsibility to integrate UCM impact assessments into their legislation, business enterprises must also develop a coordinated strategy to push back against UCMs. Surely an isolated business enterprise may not have the courage to defy UCMs, but a consortium of powerful businesses and transnational corporations could agree on a code of ethics that excludes implementation of UCMs as a matter of business policy and *ordre public*.

States should have the courage to formulate pertinent proposals to the Human Rights Council and General Assembly and elevate the issue of the illegality of UCMs to the International Court of Justice requesting an advisory opinion that should also look into the civil and penal liability of business enterprises that implement them. National Action Plans on Business and Human Rights should be crafted and adopted, including a clear prohibition to implement illegal UCMs and a mechanism to provide effective remedies to the victims.

In the light of the clear rejection of UCMs evidenced by yearly resolutions in the General Assembly and Human Rights Council, their proliferation constitutes an affront against the world community, a rebellion against international law and the UN Charter. We are witnessing retrogression in the respect of the "rule of law" and the fundamental rules of civilization.

Nevertheless, it appears that a different wind has started to blow. A gradual shift in the thinking of academics in Western society is taking place, a growing consciousness that unilateral coercive measures are ineffective, that their political justifications are devoid of legitimacy. More and more academics have enunciated the reasons why Western UCMs are conducive to international chaos, sabotage the benefits of globalization, destroy supply chains and result in the deaths of tens of thousands in many countries. Without a doubt, the UN General Assembly and the Human Rights Council will continue issuing resolutions demanding the lifting of UCMs. It is to be hoped that transnational corporations and business leaders will become more aware of the new Guiding Principles on Sanctions, Business and Human Rights,[29] that they take concrete measures to implement the pragmatic recommendations contained therein. Indeed, these principles are not empty rhetoric but constitute a plan of action. They have added value.

---

29 United Nations Human Rights Special Procedures, *Guiding Principles on Sanctions, Business and Human Rights,* Mandate of the Special Rapporteur on the negative impact of unilateral coercive measures on the enjoyment of human rights (2025). https://www.ohchr.org/sites/default/files/documents/issues/ucm/events/international-conf-sanctions-business-hr/gps-sanctions-business-hr.pdf

CHAPTER 6.

The Role of the Individual in Corporate Decision-making about Sanctions

Nicholas Turner[1]

Abstract

   Sanctions—legal rules which threaten heavy penalties against violators—conscript corporate actors into enforcing state policy through the withdrawal of commercial benefits from a sanction's intended target. However, corporations routinely go beyond what is legally required by sanctions and engage in "over-compliance"—the avoidance of legally permissible business. Over-compliance threatens unintended and often harmful consequences for vulnerable populations and economies, as highlighted by the UN Special Rapporteur on the negative impact of unilateral coercive measures on the enjoyment of human rights and other commentators. This chapter considers over-compliance from the perspective of the individual decision-maker within the corporation. Rather than treating corporations as unitary actors, the author proposes that those individuals occupying a variety of roles and perspectives are the ultimate participants in a decision process concerning the interpretation and application of sanctions to business activities. States seek to incentivize individuals to avoid sanctions risk through legal and communication strategies designed to enhance awareness of sanction risks at all levels. Counter strategies must bring attention to and discourage harmful forms of over-compliance in practice. Drawing on the author's observations from advising multinational companies, this chapter offers an inside view of over-compliance and concludes with recommendations for policymakers and practitioners.

---

1 American lawyer residing in Hong Kong

113

Introduction

Sanctions are not self-enforcing. Governments rely on commercial actors to implement sanctions by withdrawing goods and services from their targets. While a government agency may issue regulations imposing sanctions against a foreign adversary, corporations give force to the sanctions by conforming their activities to the regulatory prohibitions.[2] It follows that the effects of sanctions are determined, in large part, by the way corporations interpret and apply sanctions to their activities.

Ideally, regulators and corporations would share a mutual understanding about regulatory expectations. However, as evidenced by the work of the Special Rapporteur on unilateral coercive measures and human rights, and this Collective Monograph, a gap exists between governmental intentions and corporate behavior. While governments claim that their sanctions are increasingly "smart" and "targeted," and that humanitarian exceptions can minimize unintended consequences, the reality is that many companies go beyond what is narrowly legally required of them to engage in "over-compliance": the systematic avoidance of legally permissible business based on risk. There is a growing awareness that this tendency towards over-compliance may harm innocent third parties who are not the stated targets of sanctions.

Studies of sanctions compliance and over-compliance often treat corporations as unitary actors—profit-seeking enterprises motivated by calculations of risk and reward.[3] In reality, corporations, like all groups, are comprised of individuals, each having diverse

---

2 N. Turner et al., "Introduction," in *The Guide to Sanctions* (Global Investigations Review, 2020). https://www.lexology.com/library/detail.aspx?g=cf17e23e-b30b-4fc0-a2ad-d068ef8284a6

3 R. Kagan et al., "Fear, Duty, and Regulatory Compliance: Lessons from Three Research Projects," in C. Parker and V. Lehmann Nielsen (eds), *Explaining Compliance: Business Responses to Regulation* (2011), p. 37, at 39 [describing the "standard economic model" wherein the "regulated business firm is an "amoral calculator," motivated only by economic self interest" (citation omitted)]. G. Gray and S. Silbey, "The Other Side of the Compliance Relationship," in Parker and Nielsen, ibid., 123, at 126. ("In much of the literature, the organization as a set of persons, actions, resources, spaces and times coordinated to achieve a recognized purpose and set of interests, is depicted in terms consistent with the doctrinal fiction of the corporate person: a unitary actor subject to law and legal regulations rather than a network of human transactions.")

perspectives and capabilities.[4] Drawing on the author's experience acting as an advisor to multinational companies, this chapter emphasizes the perspective of the individual within the corporation.[5] Rather than treating the corporation as a unitary actor, this chapter proposes that individuals, occupying a variety of roles, are the ultimate participants in interpreting and applying sanctions to a company's activities. Meanwhile, proponents and enforcers of sanctions, both within and outside the corporation, seek to influence individual decisionmakers by calling attention to perceived risks and threatening consequences for non-compliance. Risk and compliance professionals, as well as legal advisors, play a central role in shaping how organizations understand and respond to these real and perceived risks.

This chapter concludes with several broad recommendations for policymakers and practitioners. In particular, it proposes that government actors forego strict liability enforcement of sanctions in respect of humanitarian activities, except in cases of wilful violations, and that practitioners continue to raise awareness and encourage standards aimed at lessening harmful forms of over-compliance.

Examples of Over-compliance

According to a March 2023 report from the Norwegian Refugee Council (NRC), "a number of key companies and financial institutions . . . have adopted self-imposed bans on any form of trade with Afghanistan."[6] The report attributes the companies' decisions to "[d]iffering interpretations" and "[w]idespread misconceptions" about sanctions, especially from the United States, and a belief that the

---

4 G. Gray and S. Silbey, *supra* note 3, at 126. ("[G]iven the plurality of individuals, actions, resources, spaces, and times that compose an organization, the concept of compliance as a singular conceptualization also breaks down.")

5 This chapter does not consider the broader question of whether the individual is or should be regarded as a subject or object of international law or whether individuals ought to be accountable under international law for the negative effects of over-compliance. Instead, it looks at the individual as an active participant in a process of decision making undertaken on behalf of a business organization in response to efforts to impose and enforce external constraints on their activities. Those constraints may or may not be characterized as international law as such.

6 Norwegian Refugee Council, *Barriers to Afghanistan's Critical Private Sector Recovery* (March 2023), p. 14. https://www.nrc.no/globalassets/pdf/reports/barriers-to-afghanistans-critical-private-sector-recovery/afghanistans-private-sector-recovery_format-.pdf

territory of Afghanistan as a whole was subject to sanctions.[7] The report highlights the negative effects of these practices on the Afghan private sector and economy.

Earlier, in December 2021, the U.S. Treasury Department's Office of Foreign Assets Control (OFAC) published Frequently Asked Question (FAQ) 951, which states in clear terms that Afghanistan is *not* subject to comprehensive or territory-wide sanctions.[8] FAQ 951 further clarifies that "there are no OFAC-administered sanctions that prohibit the export or reexport of goods or services to Afghanistan, moving or sending money into and out of Afghanistan, or activities in Afghanistan, provided that such transactions or activities do not involve sanctioned individuals, entities, or property in which sanctioned individuals and entities have an interest."[9] Additionally, OFAC has issued several "general licenses" that authorize a range of humanitarian activities that would otherwise be prohibited under its terrorism-related sanctions programs.[10] These documents are available on OFAC's website and accessible through search engines. They have been summarized in numerous articles and briefings issued by law firms, consultancies, media outlets, and non-governmental organizations (NGOs).[11]

If OFAC's guidance is clear, why are some financial institutions and companies refusing to facilitate trade with Afghanistan, as the NRC reports?

---

7 Ibid., at 6.

8 Office of Foreign Assets Control, *FAQ 951* (Feb. 25, 2022). https://ofac.treasury.gov/faqs/951

9 Ibid.

10 Office of Foreign Assets Control, "Fact Sheet: Provision of Humanitarian Assistance to Afghanistan and Support for the Afghan People," Apil 13, 2022. https://ofac.treasury.gov/media/922136/download?inline

11 Baker McKenzie, OFAC Issues Additional Authorization and Guidance regarding Humanitarian Activities in Afghanistan (January 4, 2022). https://sanctionsnews.bakermckenzie.com/ofac-issues-additional-authorization-and-guidance-regarding-humanitarian-activities-in-afghanistan/; United States Agency for International Development, New General License 20 Authorizing Certain Afghanistan Transactions (Feb. 25, 2022). https://www.usaid.gov/news-information/press-releases/feb-25-2022-new-general-license-20-authorizing-certain-afghanistan-transactions; Reuters, "U.S. Issues New General License on Afghanistan Financial Transactions – U.S. Officials," *Reuters,* Feb. 25, 2022. https://www.reuters.com/world/asia-pacific/us-issues-new-general-license-afghanistan-financial-transactions-us-officials-2022-02-25/

The Special Rapporteur on unilateral coercive measures defines over-compliance as "a form of excessive avoidance of risk."[12] Examples include "when banks decide to freeze assets that are not targeted by sanctions, or deny individuals the possibility to open or maintain bank accounts or to engage in transactions simply because they are nationals of a sanctioned country, even when the individuals are refugees from that country."[13] Like the example of Afghanistan, these practices are not mandated by law. Yet, they persist in markets around the world. The reasons for this are varied. Sometimes, practitioners are simply confused about the law or uncertain about its application to their work. Other times, companies choose to de-risk from geographies or groups of customers to save costs or avoid external scrutiny. As explained below, over-compliance is often structured into the compliance process, so that individuals are strongly conditioned to avoid sanctions risk.

It must be emphasized that over-compliance with sanctions is not a universal problem. Practitioners, especially in large financial institutions, are broadly aware of the impacts of over-compliance and derisking. Regulators such as OFAC are also aware of the humanitarian impacts of sanctions and have licensed a range of humanitarian activities and issued guidance reinforcing their policies.[14] Humanitarian trade continues to flow, albeit at sub-optimal levels, and many NGOs benefit from the support of private sector partners and generous *pro bono* legal and consulting services. These efforts deserve to be acknowledged and supported. As the use of unilateral sanctions

---

12 Special Rapporteur on unilateral coercive measures, Guidance Note on Over-compliance with Unilateral Sanctions and its Harmful Effects on Human Rights (June 2022). https://www.ohchr.org/en/special-procedures/sr-unilateral-coercive-measures/resources-unilateral-coercive-measures/guidance-note-over-compliance-unilateral-sanctions-and-its-harmful-effects-human-rights.

13 Ibid.

14 U.S. Department of the Treasury, *The Treasury 2021 Sanctions Review* (Oct. 2021). https://home.treasury.gov/system/files/136/Treasury-2021-sanctions-review.pdf. ("... Treasury must address more systematically the challenges associated with conducting humanitarian activities through legitimate channels in heavily sanctioned jurisdictions"); "Trump White House Was Warned Sanctions on Venezuela Could Fuel Migration," *The Washington Post,* July 26, 2024. https://www.washingtonpost.com/business/2024/07/26/venezuela-crisis-immigration-us-sanctions-trump/ (Details U.S. Treasury and State Department officials' concerns about the potential for sanctions on Venezuela's government and state-owned entities to "speed an exodus of millions of migrants to neighboring nations.")

becomes more frequent, the international community's efforts to close the gap between governmental expectations and corporate behavior will become more urgent.

Over-compliance as a Policy and Legal Problem

University of Virginia School of Law Professor Pierre-Hugues Verdier, one of the few scholars to have written specifically about over-compliance and sanctions, describes over-compliance as "situations in which market participants apply sanctions beyond what is legally mandated by the relevant regime."[15] In economic terms, over-compliance is puzzling, as Verdier explains:

> From an economic standpoint, a market participant should engage in all net positive value transactions available to it. …After sanctions are imposed, a market participant should continue to engage in all transactions it would have engaged in absent the sanctions, except those that are prohibited (assuming the expected cost of sanctions is sufficient to make all prohibited transactions unprofitable). In other words, in this simple model, market participants are expected to act as "sanctions optimizers," adjusting their set of activities to track precisely the boundaries set by the sanctions. There should be no over-compliance. … The challenge, then, is to explain why market participants do not "optimize" and instead forgo seemingly profitable transactions that are not prohibited.[16]

Upon further analysis, Verdier concludes that "market participants cannot and should not be expected to "optimize" sanctions compliance" because over-compliance "is a rational response to uncertainty in sanctions rules."[17] Sanctions laws and regulations contain "a wide penumbra of uncertainty in which many market participants may understandably fear to tread."[18] As explained below, individuals facing

---

15 Pierre-Hugues Verdier, "Sanctions Over-compliance: What, Why, and Does It Matter?," *North Carolina Journal of International Law* 48 (2023): 471, 472.
16 Ibid., at 477.
17 Ibid., at 473.
18 Ibid., at 483.

this uncertainty must also consider the risk of enforcement should they judge wrongly. Factoring in the cost of performing due diligence and adopting risk-based compliance controls, sanctions optimization is not an attractive strategy for many firms or individual actors.

In terms of legal rights, the fact that an activity is allowed does not mean that companies are obliged to engage in it. Players in an open market are free to enter into or withdraw from business subject to the terms of their contracts with other players and local market regulations. The reality is, no company engages in *all* of the business it is legally entitled to perform. With finite resources, companies choose to undertake or decline activities based on their own criteria and risk appetites in addition to the law. This discretion is often spelled out in commercial agreements. Take, for example, this market-standard provision from the Terms of Service between a major international bank and its customers:

> We are required to act in accordance with applicable laws, regulations, policies (including our policies), request or guidance of statutory and regulatory authorities or industry bodies or associations operating in various jurisdictions. . . . We may in our absolute discretion take any action as we consider appropriate to comply with all such laws, regulations, policies, requests and guidance. Such action may include but is not limited to . . .
>
> (e) delaying, blocking, suspending or refusing to process any payment or instruction to you or by you in our absolute discretion;
>
> (f) refusing to enter or conclude transactions involving certain persons or entities;
>
> (g) terminating our relationship with you;
>
> (h) reporting suspicious transactions to any authority; and
>
> (i) taking any other actions necessary for us or our affiliates to meet any legal, regulatory or compliance obligations.[19]

---

19 Bank of China (Hong Kong) Limited, Conditions for Services (2024). https://www.bochk.com/en/conditionsforservices.html

While one might assume that profit-seeking enterprises would be willing to engage in all legally permissible "net-positive value" business, in reality, banks and other firms routinely decline transactions based on unpublished, sometimes unwritten, policies and criteria that bear little resemblance to official codes. If their contracts permit it, these practices are relatively unproblematic from a commercial law point of view. Third parties rarely have legal recourse against companies that decline to provide goods or services.[20]

From a policy perspective, over-compliance is also problematic when it leads to any consequences that are contrary to regulators' expectations. As Verdier observes, "widespread over-compliance may undermine the subtle design choices that inform targeted sanctions programs, effectively transforming them into something hard to distinguish from ... comprehensive sanctions."[21] In December 2022, the U.S. Treasury Department announced several measures to implement UN Security Council Resolution 2664, which adopted humanitarian carveouts from UN asset freezes. The Treasury Department press release remarked that "while sanctions remain an essential and effective policy tool, they also must be carefully calibrated to help address their impact on the flow of legitimate humanitarian aid to those in need."[22] A number of these carveouts are relevant to the example of Afghanistan. Their success, like the sanctions themselves, depends on how faithfully companies adhere to them.

Individual Agency in Compliance

Compliance is not simply a matter of applying policies and procedures to business activities. It is a social process through which individuals within a corporate body communicate and enforce a

---

20 Stacy Keen, "Over-compliance with Unilateral Sanctions Can Impact on Legitimate Business," *Pinsent Masons Out-Law News,* August 1, 2022. https://www.pinsentmasons.com/out-law/news/over-compliance-unilateral-sanctions-impact-legitimate-business. ("Firms that have carried out lawful activities in countries to which sanctions are relevant can be left at a loss through no fault of their own when financial institutions are unwilling to process lawful payments based on risk appetite.")

21 Verdier, *supra* note 15, at 472.

22 U.S. Treasury Department, "Treasury Implements Historic Humanitarian Sanctions Exceptions" [press release], December 20, 2022. https://home.treasury.gov/news/press-releases/jy1175

variety of internal and external norms.[23] Yet the experience of the individual as a participant in the compliance process is not well examined. Corporations are worth studying because they are the principal means through which governments' sanctions policies are implemented. To understand over-compliance—and formulate better solutions—it is also necessary to consider how individuals at every level of the organization participate in decision making about sanctions.[24]

As Garry Gray and Susan Silbey comment, research into how companies comply with law "too often downplays the agency of workers and focuses almost exclusively on the relationship between the firm and the state regulatory apparatus."[25] They remark that analyses of corporate compliance typically occur "at the level of the firm," while "frontline workers, whose activities most often produce violations or compliance, have not been systematically incorporated into the literature on regulatory enforcement."[26] Gray and Silbey write: "Rarely if ever do these models adequately take account of the stratification of authority, expertise or ability to comply within organizations. One is hard pressed to find a reference to power, group interests, conflict or inequality within the regulated firm."[27]

Literature on compliance is also limited by its conceptual focus on *non*-compliance. Much scholarship is ultimately concerned with promoting law-abiding behavior.[28] Accordingly, analyses of the

---

23 C. Parker and V. Lehmann Nielsen, "Introduction," in Parker and Nielsen, *supra* note 3, at 6. ("Regulation and responses to regulation are seen as social practices to be understood from different perspectives and in the context of other meaningful social practices."); Ibid., at 7 (contrasting "objectivist research" with explanatory theories "concerned with uncovering the network of social construction processes that create plural understandings of compliance" and "understanding the processes of negotiation and social construction of compliance that are masked by apparently unified, singular and unproblematic social practices and linguistic terms").

24 Gray, *supra* note 3, at 123. ("Attending to the formal agents of law, researchers often miss the most predictable and thus powerful aspects of law and legality: its habitual quotidian enactment, particularly when the formal agents of law may be absent and its coercive force less visible.")

25 Ibid., at 126.

26 Ibid.

27 Ibid., at 124.

28 Veronica Root, "Coordinating Compliance Incentives," *Cornell Law Review* 102, no. 4 (May 2017): 1003; Root "The Compliance Process," *Indiana Law Journal* 94, no. 1 (Winter 2019): 203; Todd Haugh, "Nudging Corporate Compliance," *American Business Law Journal* 54, no. 4 (Winter 2017): 683.

individual are aimed at explaining why individuals may disregard rules to the detriment of their employers or society.[29] Such framing tends to assume that compliance, and more compliance, is desirable as an end in and of itself.[30] The issue of over-compliance complicates this picture by shifting the focus to negative externalities such as harmful effects on the enjoyment of human rights.

With these limitations in mind, a survey of available research strongly suggests that the law is only one factor individuals consider when making decisions about compliance. As Robert Kagan, Neil Gunningham, and Dorothy Thornton write, "Since corporations are staffed by human beings, it should not be surprising that sociological researchers have often found that their responses to regulatory norms are shaped not only by a fear of legal sanctions but also by social pressure and a sense of civic duty."[31] An individual's behavior may be influenced by their status or role within the organization.[32] Other attributes such as education, professional qualifications, and work styles

---

29 Kimberly D. Krawiec, "Organizational Misconduct: Beyond the Principal-Agent Model," *Florida State University Law Review* 32 (2005) 571, 597. ("[C]urrent legal theory largely assumes that misconduct within organizations results from the acts of single, independent agents who disregard the preferences of shareholder principals and their representatives....")

30 Root, "The Compliance Process," *supra* note 28, at 210. ("As a result, misconduct by and within organizations continues to be a topic of significance for courts, regulators, prosecutors, and the individuals affected or harmed, which, in turn, makes the field of compliance of great societal import.")

31 Kagan, *supra* note 3, at 41; Ibid., at 37. ("Sociological explanations of law-abidingness among regulated business enterprises, as well as among individuals, point to three basic motivational factors: fear of detection and legal punishment; concern about the consequences of acquiring a bad reputation; and a sense of duty, that is, the desire to conform to internalized norms or beliefs about right and wrong.")

32 C. Parker and S. Gilad, "Internal Corporate Compliance Management Systems: Structure, Culture and Agency," in Parker & Nielsen, *supra* note 3, at 176. ("The scope of this agency will depend on an individual's place within the formal structure: the agency of senior management includes decisions about adopting formal compliance systems in the first place, the agency of compliance professionals involves strategies regarding its internalization, while lower level employees will generally only have agency to influence its implementation in practice."); David Orozco, "A Systems Theory of Compliance Law," *University of Pennsylvania Journal of Business Law* 22, no. 2 (2020): 244, 284. ("Scholars ... have emphasized that compliance means different things to different people at various levels within the firm, for example, board members, top executives and mid-level executives" [citing Sokol, "Teaching Compliance," *University of Cincinnati Law Review* 84 (2016): 399].)

are also important.[33] Focusing on the role of individuals would allow for a more detailed mapping of the corporate decision process and factors that lead to over-compliance. This in turn would enable more effective strategies to discourage harmful forms of over-compliance.

Over-compliance as an Intended Outcome

As Verdier remarks, companies rarely behave as "sanctions optimizers." Other scholars, such as Sean Griffith, have observed that over-compliance is an expected (even intended) outcome of contemporary governance and enforcement models.[34] Individuals within these environments are incentivized to avoid activities perceived as "high-risk," regardless of their legality. They may even fear personal liability for misjudging sanctions risk.

Sanctions Risk-management in Practice

Compliance has many aims. David Orozco describes compliance as encompassing "the norms, internal company regulations and policies, governance mechanisms, resources and personnel used by a firm to adhere to what the firm interprets is the appropriate response to existing laws and regulations."[35] Griffith refers to compliance as a set of internal processes "by which firms adapt behavior to legal, regulatory, and social norms."[36] In the broadest sense, compliance extends

---

33 Orozco, *supra* note 32, at 259–260. ("As pointed out by scholars, businesses have varying in-house legal capabilities that are used to achieve strategic ends. The same is true of the law-dependent field of compliance. The range of compliance capabilities will vary between complicit compliance officers who look the other way and enable illegal and unethical behavior, to those with a formalistic check-the-box mentality, and those who are forward-looking, preventive and in some cases strategic" [citations omitted]); S. Simpson and M. Rorie, "Motivating Compliance: Economic and Material Motives for Compliance," in Parker and Nielsen, *supra* note 3, at 72. ("[H]ow a person responds to regulation appears to be influenced by personality traits and characteristics. . . . Future research should investigate the ways in which distinct types of personality and individual level differences interact with external controls (both formal and informal) to inhibit or increase the risk of offending [e.g. defiance].")

34 Sean J. Griffith, "Corporate Governance in an Era of Compliance," *William & Mary Law Review* 57 (2016): 2075, 2124–2125.

35 Orozco, *supra* note 32, at 251; Root, "The Compliance Process," *supra* note 28, at 205. ("Compliance refers to a firm's effort to ensure that it and its agents adhere to legal and regulatory requirements, industry practice, and the firm's own internal policies and norms.")

36 Griffith, *supra* note 34, at 2082.

beyond the workplace. Groups outside the corporation not only seek to influence outcomes, but to shape the decision making process itself.[37] To this end, Griffith describes compliance as "an internal governance structure imposed upon the firm from the outside by enforcement agents"[38] and as "a de facto government mandate imposed upon firms by means of ex ante incentives, ex post enforcement tactics, and formal signaling efforts."[39] Griffith observes that "through compliance, the government dictates how firms must comply, imposing specific governance structures expressly designed to change how the firm conducts its business."[40]

Furthermore, Griffith argues that, in a general sense, over-compliance is an intended outcome of governments' growing interest in regulating corporate governance practices. Griffith writes that "governance structures are designed to supply constraints that exceed basic legal commands" and to "inculcate norms of behavior that exceed narrow legal obligations."[41] Griffith writes, "Because the government receives the benefit of the compliance program (in the form of detection and investigation) but does not bear the cost, its incentive is to push firms to overinvest in compliance.... government enforcement agents have structural incentives to mandate excessive compliance."[42] In Griffith's

---

37 Orozco, *supra* note 32, at 267 (describing compliance from the perspective of systems theory as "a dynamic, multi-party and interrelated system"); Ibid., at 269. ("[T]he practice of compliance is impacted by various actors internal and external to the firm. This introduces dynamism and complexity that requires a deep analysis of the various interacting parts that constitute the compliance system."); L. Edelman and S. Talesh, "To Comply Or Not to Comply – That Isn't the Question: How Organizations Construct the Meaning of Compliance," in Parker and Nielsen, *supra* note 3, at 104 (describing the "neo-institutional theory of compliance" emphasizing "the process through which common systems of meaning, values and norms develop among the community of organizations that make up an organizational field"); Sappington, "Incentives in Principal-Agent Relationships," *Journal of Economic Perspectives* 5 (1991): 45, 46. ("In a labor setting, a boss or employer may serve the role of principal, while a subordinate or worker may act as agent. In regulated industries, the regulator might act as principal, designing an incentive scheme for the firm [agent] whose activities are being regulated").

38 Griffith, *supra* note 34, at 2075.

39 Ibid., at 2078.

40 Ibid.

41 Ibid., at 2124–2125.

42 Ibid., note 22, at 2127; Root, "The Compliance Process," *supra* note 28, at 214. ("[G]overnmental actors have a very limited ability to detect misconduct within private organizations and must rely on organizations to police their own members.

view this shift is represented in "the development of policies and procedures that go beyond narrowly applicable rules and regulations ...
to promote a 'culture of compliance.'"[43] This perspective is especially
relevant in the area of sanctions, where the object is to deny as many
services to the sanctions target as possible.[44]

In practice, sanctions compliance involves the adoption of
policies and procedures and controls to identify, escalate, and inter-
dict prohibited activities. Under the widely practiced "three lines
of defense" model, individuals are assigned different roles and
responsibilities depending on their job function.[45] In this model, the
"first line" includes business and operational teams that source and
develop customer relationships and execute transactions. The first
line is understood to "own the risk" associated with customers and
transactions and is responsible for funding the compliance operation.
The second line includes advisory functions such as compliance and
legal who are tasked with understanding, interpreting, and advising on
laws and regulations and guiding the first line in designing controls to
identify and manage risks. The third line includes the audit function

---

Thus, regulators and prosecutors have adopted a range of policies and enforcement
norms that serve as incentives for organizations to monitor their members in an effort
to deter and prevent corporate misconduct."); Orozco, *supra* note 32, at 574. ("[R]
egulators may rationally decide to focus their limited resources on easier-to-win cases
that may be resolved quickly and that provide high-profile victories that maximize
political gains."); Krawiec, *supra* note 29, at 574. ("[I]f the legal regime presumes
that organizational misconduct is simply a principal-agent problem, legal incentives
that induce principals to more carefully police their agents may be a rational response
to that perceived problem.")

43 Griffith, *supra* note 34, at 2093–2094; Orozco, *supra* note 32, at 254. ("As
scholars have pointed out, however, compliance also relies on risk concepts, ethics
and behavioral attributes that extend to individuals internal and external to the firm.
As will be demonstrated by the analysis and generalizations of the systems theory
of compliance, compliance law is a cohesive and broader subject than corporate
governance law" [citations omitted].)

44 Verdier, *supra* note 15, at 472. ("From the government's perspective, this
development has two major advantages: these actors are subject to U.S. jurisdiction,
so that securing their compliance is legally and practically straightforward; and they
possess the capabilities to establish internal compliance procedures under which they
effectively implement sanctions on its behalf.")

45 Institute of Internal Auditors, *The IIA's Three Lines Model: An Update of the
Three Lines of Defense* (Sept. 2024). https://www.theiia.org/globalassets/documents/
resources/the-iias-three-lines-model-an-update-of-the-three-lines-of-defense-
july-2020/three-lines-model-updated-english.pdf

which provides assurance to senior management and the board that the first and second line are adhering to standards.

The three-lines of defense model is reflected in OFAC's *A Framework for OFAC Compliance Commitments* (hereinafter the "OFAC Framework").[46] The OFAC Framework recommends that companies adopt risk-based policies and controls to identify potential sanctions risks and to evaluate the effectiveness of those controls through periodic testing and auditing. As explained in the document's introduction, OFAC may use its enforcement authority to require companies to adopt specific measures as part of a settlement of apparent regulatory violations and would consider the strength of a company's sanctions compliance program among other factors in making penalty determinations.[47] The OFAC Framework not only encourages firms to follow OFAC's regulations; it instructs them on building a "culture of compliance" that revolves around the identification and mitigation of risk, along the lines described by Griffith.

Strict Liability and Individual Liability

As explained by Griffith and other scholars, regulators may encourage over-compliance through the promotion of risk management frameworks that tend to cause corporations to avoid activities that could be legally permissible. These frameworks include procedures to discipline individuals who act contrary to corporate policies or risk tolerances. Sanctions regulators, particularly in the United States and the UK, reinforce this tendency through strict liability enforcement of sanctions and by seeking to impose criminal and civil liability on individuals.

According to the U.S. Department of Justice (DOJ), strict liability enforcement permits the imposition of civil penalties against a defendant "even if such person did not know or have reason to know that it was engaging in a transaction that was prohibited under sanctions laws and regulations."[48] Unlike criminal liability, which requires

---

46 Office of Foreign Assets Control, *A Framework for OFAC Compliance Commitments* (2019). https://ofac.treasury.gov/media/16331/download?inline

47 Ibid., at 1.

48 U.S. Department of Justice, Department of Commerce, Department of the Treasury, and Department of Justice Tri-Seal Compliance Note: Obligations of Foreign-based Persons to Comply with U.S. Sanctions and Export Control Laws (March 2024), at 2. https://www.justice.gov/opa/media/1341411/dl?inline

prosecutors to prove wilfulness on the part of the defendant, strict civil liability allows government agencies to obtain corporate settlements, often involving significant financial penalties, without having to prove that any person within the corporation intended or even knew about the conduct alleged to have violated a regulation.[49] In 2022, the UK Office of Financial Sanctions Implementation was given the authority to impose civil penalties on a strict liability basis pursuant to the Economic Crime (Transparency and Enforcement) Act 2022.[50]

As explained by lawyers from the law firm Gibson Dunn & Crutcher, "the fact that U.S. sanctions can carry significant civil penalties on a strict liability basis . . . is likely a significant contributor in encouraging over-compliance."[51] Similarly, Dr. Justine Walker, Global Head of Sanctions, Compliance and Risk for the Association of Certified Anti-Money Laundering Specialists (ACAMS), writes that the fear of causing "a technical sanctions violation" contributes to a "chilling effect" that may prevent banks and other companies from participating in legally permissible humanitarian trade.[52] Verdier concurs, writing that "conduct that falls close to the line drawn by the sanctions themselves may be exactly that which market participants fear may be interpreted as evasion by enforcers and targeted."[53] The perception of risk is further amplified by law firms and consultancies that (while marketing their services) warn directors and executives of the risk of personal liability for breaches of sanctions regulations.[54]

---

49 Krawiec, *supra* note 29, at 581 (describing "composite regimes" of regulatory enforcement that "assign liability based on a strict liability standard but apportion sanctions based on a negligence standard").

50 Office of Financial Sanctions Implementation, New Enforcement Powers – A Message from Giles Thomson, Director of OFSI (June 2022). https://ofsi.blog.gov. uk/2022/06/08/new-enforcement-powers-a-message-from-giles-thomson-director-of-ofsi/

51 A. Smith et al., "Sanctions Considerations for Non-governmental Organisations," *GIR Guide to Sanctions,* 5th Edition (2024). https:// globalinvestigationsreview.com/guide/the-guide-sanctions/fifth-edition/article/ sanctions-considerations-non-governmental-organisations

52 Justine Walker, "The Public Policy of Sanctions Compliance: A Need for Collective and Coordinated International Action," *International Review of the Red Cross* (Feb. 2022). https://international-review.icrc.org/articles/the-public-policy-of-sanctions-compliance-need-for-collective-action-916

53 Verdier, *supra* note 15, at 483.

54 Brian J. Egan, et al., *Why Directors and Executives Need To Pay Attention to Sanctions, Money Laundering and Export Rules: Skadden's 2023 Insights,* Skadden,

The perception is compounded further by an increasing emphasis on civil and criminal enforcement against individuals involved in sanctions breaches in the workplace. For instance, the DOJ Corporate Enforcement Policy requires a company that wishes to receive credit for voluntarily disclosing violations of U.S. law to disclose "all relevant facts and evidence about all individuals involved in or responsible for the misconduct at issue, including individuals inside and outside of the company regardless of their position, status, or seniority."[55] By its terms, this does not require the company to conclude that the individuals engaged in criminal misconduct. As Deputy U.S. Attorney General Lisa Monaco remarked at a meeting of the American Bar Association in March 2024: "Our first priority has been—and will continue to be—individual accountability. Companies can only act through individuals."[56]

The DOJ's policy was dramatically illustrated in December 2018 when Canadian authorities detained the chief financial officer of Huawei, a Chinese telecommunications company, at the request of the U.S. government, which sought her extradition to face charges of breaching U.S. sanctions against Iran in connection with alleged misrepresentations made to one of the company's commercial banks.[57] Meanwhile, OFAC has entered into civil settlements with individuals, including the executive of a U.S.-based cosmetics company which, in 2023, agreed to pay US$ 175,000 to settle apparent violations of the

---

December 13, 2022. https://www.skadden.com/insights/publications/2022/12/2023-insights/new-regulatory-challenges/why-directors-and-executives-need-to-pay-attention; Schulte Roth + Zabel, *Mitigating OFAC Risks in Mergers and Acquisitions,* 3 February 3, 2020. https://www.srz.com/en/news_and_insights/alerts/mitigating-ofac-risks-in-mergers-and-acquisitions; Treasury Intelligence Solutions, *CFOs in the Firing Line! How to Improve Sanctions Screening and Compliance While Avoiding Personal Liability,* March 13, 2024. https://tispayments.com/resources/cfos-in-the-firing-line/

55 U.S. Department of Justice Criminal Division, Corporate Enforcement Policy, March 2024, at 4. https://www.justice.gov/criminal/criminal-fraud/file/1562831/dl?inline.

56 U.S. Department of Justice, "Deputy Attorney General Lisa Monaco Delivers Keynote Remarks at the American Bar Association's 39th National Institute on White Collar Crime" (7 Mar. 2024). https://www.justice.gov/opa/speech/deputy-attorney-general-lisa-monaco-delivers-keynote-remarks-american-bar-associations

57 U.S. Department of Justice, "Huawei CFO Wanzhou Meng Admits to Misleading Global Financial Institution" (press release), September 24, 2021. https://www.justice.gov/opa/pr/huawei-cfo-wanzhou-meng-admits-misleading-global-financial-institution

Iranian Transactions and Sanctions Regulations (ITSR) "arising from their role as a manager at the [c]ompany."[58] In 2019, OFAC added a Turkish national to the Foreign Sanctions Evaders List, prohibiting him from receiving U.S. financial services, in response to alleged violations of the ITSR that were later disclosed to OFAC as part of a corporate settlement.[59] Companies routinely discipline or fire employees in order to gain mitigation credit as part of OFAC settlements.[60]

To be clear: individuals who violate corporate policies and procedures or the law should be disciplined appropriately. As agents of the corporation, individual employees are accountable for breaches of corporate policy. Companies, which may be held vicariously liable for the actions of their employees, have a strong interest in discouraging misconduct and are justified in doing so. The DOJ is rightly empowered to prosecute criminal violations of sanctions regulations. The point is that it is reasonable to expect that an emphasis on personal liability may cause individuals to over-comply out of a sense of self-preservation, even in the context of legal, humanitarian trade.[61]

---

58 Office of Foreign Assets Control, Settlement Agreements between the U.S. Department of the Treasury's Office of Foreign Assets Control; Murad, LLC, and an Individual, May 17, 2023. https://ofac.treasury.gov/recent-actions/20230517_33

59 Office of Foreign Assets Control, Settlement Agreement between the U.S. Department of the Treasury's Office of Foreign Assets Control and Kollmorgen Corporation; Foreign Sanctions Evaders Determination, February 7, 2021. https://ofac.treasury.gov/recent-actions/20190207

60 Office of Foreign Assets Control, Settlement Agreement between the U.S. Department of the Treasury's Office of Foreign Assets Control and Sojitz (Hong Kong) Limited, January 11, 2022. https://ofac.treasury.gov/recent-actions/20220111_33; Office of Foreign Assets Control, Settlement Agreement between the U.S. Department of the Treasury's Office of Foreign Assets Control and Microsoft Corporation, April 6, 2023. https://ofac.treasury.gov/recent-actions/20230406

61 Parker, *supra* note 32, at 182 (discussing the challenges of compliance professionals in "harmonizing" regulatory expectations with business culture and observing, "Compliance professionals might also seek to amplify the threat of regulatory enforcement in order to raise managers' awareness and investment in compliance against other business goals" [citations omitted]); Krawiec, *supra* note 29, at 574–575. ("In addition, other powerful interest groups have a stake in and benefit from internal compliance-based liability regimes, particularly legal compliance professionals such as lawyers, compliance and ethics consultants, in-house compliance and human resources personnel, and diversity trainers.")

Ways of Over-complying

As proposed above, over-compliance with sanctions is to be expected in an environment where "governance structures ... exceed basic legal commands."[62] Meanwhile, individuals tasked with making decisions about complex sanctions rules must also consider the possibility of strict liability enforcement, even personal liability. Under such circumstances, it is not surprising that individuals would over-comply to protect their professional interests and reputations.[63] Common reasons for over-compliance also include confusion about the law, uncertainty about the application of the law to facts, and deliberate over-compliance to manage costs or reputation.

Confusion about the Law

In the author's experience, over-compliance is often based on a misunderstanding of the law.[64] One example given by the Special Rapporteur is the refusal to provide services to nationals of sanctioned territories who are resident outside of those territories, including refugees. Take, for example, section 542.207 of OFAC's Syrian Sanctions Regulations (SSR), which prohibits "'U.S. persons' from engaging in "the exportation, reexportation, sale, or supply, directly or indirectly ... of any services to Syria."[65] The term "U.S. person" refers to any U.S. citizen or permanent resident alien, any entity organized under U.S. law, or any person in the United States.[66] The SSR do *not* prohibit U.S. persons (including companies and financial institutions) from providing services to Syrian *nationals* provided the benefit of those services are not received in Syria. Furthermore, the SSR do not apply to non-U.S. persons, meaning that non-U.S. companies and financial

---

62 Griffith, *supra* note 34, at 2075.

63 Additionally, in some jurisdictions such as the United Kingdom, senior managers of regulated companies are potentially liable for corporate misconduct "if they did not take reasonable steps to prevent or stop" it; Financial Conduct Authority, Senior Managers Regime, March 30, 2023. https://www.fca.org.uk/firms/senior-managers-and-certification-regime/senior-managers-regime

64 Smith, *supra* note 51 (counting "regulatory misinterpretation" among the reasons that "can often frustrate the ability of parties to engage in legal, non-sanctioned activities in jurisdictions targeted or affected by" sanctions).

65 31 C.F.R. §542.207 (2023). https://www.ecfr.gov/current/title-31/subtitle-B/chapter-V/part-542/subpart-B/section-542.207

66 31 C.F.R. §542.325 (2023). https://www.ecfr.gov/current/title-31/subtitle-B/chapter-V/part-542/subpart-C/section-542.325

institutions have even greater flexibility to accept Syrian nationals as customers. (OFAC's ITSR impose similar restrictions with respect to Iran and Iranian nationals.) Yet, there are numerous media reports of financial institutions in Europe, Asia, and the Middle East, and elsewhere, turning away nationals of "sanctioned territories," ostensibly in order to comply with U.S. restrictions.[67]

Another common error involves UN Security Council sanctions. Many UN sanctions programs are named after a focal territory. These include, for example, the Central African Republic, Democratic Republic of Congo, Somalia, and South Sudan programs.[68] National authorities similarly identify their corresponding sanctions with the name of the relevant territories. The impression given to laypersons is that the sanctions are concerned with the territories as a whole. In reality, the resolutions address specific situations or persons within those territories. Even a cursory review of the underlying UN Security Council resolutions or national regulations would reveal that these

---

67 Gregor Stuart Hunter, "Banks Turn Away Iran and Syria Nationals," *The National,* February 8, 2013. https://www.thenationalnews.com/business/banks-turn-away-iran-and-syria-nationals-1.295594; Peyman Jamali, "Locked Out: Why Are Australian Banks Refusing Customer Transactions with Iran?," *SBS Persian,* May 10, 2022. https://www.sbs.com.au/language/persian/en/article/locked-out-why-are-australian-banks-refusing-customer-transactions-with-iran/zpckrefat; Saeed Kamali Dehghan, "UK Bank Accounts of Iranian Customers Still Being Closed, Says Law Firm," *The Guardian,* April 21, 2017. https://www.theguardian.com/money/iran-blog/2017/apr/21/law-firm-reports-surge-in-iranians-uk-bank-accounts-being-closed-sanctions-iran-nuclear-deal-trump; Massoud Salari, "Italian Banks are Closing Iranian Citizens' Accounts over U.S. Sanctions: Is It Legal?," *Euronews,* February 13, 2020. https://www.euronews.com/2020/02/13/italian-banks-are-closing-iranian-citizens-accounts-over-us-sanctions-is-it-legal; Liz Lee and A. Ananthalakshmi, "Iranians in Malaysia Say Banks Close Their Accounts as U.S. Sanctions Bite," *Reuters,* October 30, 2019. https://www.reuters.com/article/us-malaysia-iran-banks-idUSKBN1X90A9; Saeid Jafari, "U.S. Sanctions Hit Iranian Students Seeking Bank Accounts in Europe," *Al Monitor,* January 11, 2019). https://www.al-monitor.com/originals/2019/01/iran-students-sanctions-impact-banks-europe-us-visa.html#ixzz86UvieLlc; Jess Ma, "Russians Lose Access to Some Banking Services in Hong Kong Due to Western Sanctions over Ukraine," *South China Morning Post,* October 15, 2022. https://www.scmp.com/news/hong-kong/politics/article/3196053/russians-lose-access-some-banking-services-hong-kong-due; Michelle Price and Sumeet Chatterjee, "Focus: Global Banks Eschew Risk as They Navigate Russia Sanctions Quagmire," *Reuters,* March 2, 2022. https://www.reuters.com/business/finance/global-banks-eschew-risk-they-navigate-russia-sanctions-quagmire-2022-03-02/

68 United Nations Security Council, *Sanctions.* https://main.un.org/securitycouncil/en/sanctions/information

programs target a relatively small number of individuals and entities. Yet, in the author's experience, it is not difficult to find examples of companies that treat these territories as "sanctioned" and therefore highly restricted or even off limits. Meanwhile, some companies continue to refer to territories such as Iraq, Libya, and Sudan as "comprehensively sanctioned," even though OFAC has long since terminated those designations.

Even when these errors are pointed out, it is often the case that companies choose to maintain the self-imposed restrictions in the name of risk management. From the company's perspective, it may be better to interpret sanctions too broadly than chance an inadvertent violation.[69]

Uncertainty about the Application of Law

Even where the law is well understood, a company that wishes to undertake a transaction that *might* be prohibited by a sanction must first gather facts to prove their activity falls outside the rule or is permitted under an applicable license or exception. This is not always a straightforward task. Consider OFAC General License (GL) 20, which authorizes U.S. persons to engage in certain transactions involving Afghanistan or governing institutions in Afghanistan. GL 20 states:

> (a) To the extent authorization is required and except as provided in paragraph (b) of this general license, all transactions involving Afghanistan or governing institutions in Afghanistan prohibited by the Global Terrorism Sanctions Regulations...the Foreign Terrorist Organizations Sanctions Regulations ... or Executive Order (E.O.) 13224, as amended, are authorized.
>
> (b) This general license does not authorize:
>
> (1) Financial transfers to the Taliban, the Haqqani Network, any entity in which the Taliban or the Haqqani Network owns, directly or indirectly, individually or in the aggregate, a 50 percent or greater interest, or any blocked individual who is in a leadership role of

---

69 Only rarely are companies challenged to defend their interpretations, usually in response to a court filing from a party seeking to assert a contractual right. *Kuvera Resources Pte Ltd v. JP Morgan Chase Bank,* NA [2023] 2 SLR 389, [2023] SGCA 28.

> a governing institution in Afghanistan, other than for
> the purpose of effecting the payment of taxes, fees, or
> import duties, or the purchase or receipt of permits,
> licenses, or public utility services, provided that such
> payments do not relate to luxury items or services....[70]

On the face of it, GL 20 is meant to give comfort to organizations that their transactions with the government of Afghanistan will not expose them to legal liability. As cited above, FAQ 951 explains that OFAC sanctions do not prohibit most transactions with Afghanistan. GL 20 reinforces this message by removing legal liability from transactions involving the government that otherwise would be prohibited. But this comfort does not extend to transactions described in paragraph (b). In order to be satisfied that GL 20 applies, a company preparing to make a financial transfer to the government would have to decide whether its transfer is for the purpose of "effecting the payment of taxes, fees, or import duties, or the purchase or receipt of permits, licenses, or public utility services," and, if so, that it does not "relate to luxury items or services." Each of these terms is open to some interpretation. If the transfer does not relate to one of the aforementioned categories, the company would have to rule out the involvement of a member of the Taliban, the Haqqani Network, or any other sanctioned person "in a leadership role of a governing institution." If the payment is to a legal entity, the company would have to determine if it is owned 50 percent or more by a sanctioned person or persons.

Suffice it to say, these facts are not always easy to ascertain. Indeed, the NRC cited rising compliance costs associated with due diligence and the need to hire staff and legal advisors as major limiting factors for companies engaging in trade with Afghanistan.[71] As Walker highlights, organizations often face burdensome due diligence

---

70 Office of Foreign Assets Control, General License No. 20, February 25, 2022. https://ofac.treasury.gov/media/918776/download?inline

71 Norwegian Refugee Council, *supra* note 6, at 17; European Parliamentary Research Service, *Impact of Sanctions on the Humanitarian Situation in Syria* (June 2023). ("For instance, humanitarian operators highlight that prohibitions, complex exception frameworks, and extensive export control requirements and associated due diligence, as well as risk management expectations, often require costly legal analysis.")   https://www.europarl.europa.eu/RegData/etudes/BRIE/2023/749765/ EPRS_BRI(2023)749765_EN.pdf

requirements and uncertainty about "what constitutes 'humanitarian assistance' and thus falls within scope of an available permission or license."[72]

Derisking

Derisking refers to the practice of declining to provide services to broad categories of customers based on characteristics such as nationality, location, or industry. Unlike cases involving confusion or uncertainty, derisking involves a conscious decision to withdraw from business or markets, ostensibly in response to sanctions, often with the added justification of reducing costs or avoiding reputational risk. As lawyers with the law firm Gibson Dunn & Crutcher note, "As sanctions proliferate at an unprecedented pace, and where the jurisdictional reach of these restrictions continues to extend, the cost associated with maintaining a programme that can take a more nuanced approach to sanctions compliance may be deemed too high . . . as a matter of profitability or risk appetite."[73] These costs include hiring risk and compliance staff, implementing computerized screening tools to identify high-risk transactions and customers, and undertaking due diligence and investigations of suspected breaches.

Derisking is a common and widely reported on strategy for managing sanctions risk. For instance, a 2021 report from the U.S. Government Accountability Office (GAO) found that U.S. sanctions against Venezuela's government and state-owned entities had impeded the delivery of humanitarian aid to the country. In reviewing the work of the U.S. Agency for International Development (USAID) in Venezuela, the GAO found:

> All nine USAID implementing partners we spoke with reported instances of banks closing their accounts or delaying or rejecting transactions due to concerns over U.S. sanctions . . . Treasury provides licenses to authorize humanitarian-related transactions, but banks may still seek to minimize risk by limiting services for any transactions involving Venezuelan entities, according to Treasury

---

72 Walker, *supra* note 52, at 4.
73 Smith, *supra* note 51.

officials ... Officials noted that such delays occur in all conflict and high-risk jurisdictions, even where there are not U.S. sanctions programs, because banks conduct increased due diligence to comply with their own internal risk-based approaches on money laundering and terrorist financing.[74]

Much of the scholarship on derisking concerns anti-money laundering (AML) regulations and its impact on correspondent banking relationships in underserved markets.[75] The Financial Action Task Force (FATF), a global AML standard setting body, defines derisking as "the phenomenon of ... terminating or restricting business relationships with clients or categories of clients to avoid, rather than manage, risk in line with the FATF's risk-based approach."[76] A 2021 review found that derisking results from a range of "complex and interwoven" factors, chiefly "profitability concerns" and "high compliance costs."[77] The report also cites "fear of supervisory actions, reduced risk appetite in banks, and reputational concerns' as prominent factors."[78] FATF holds that derisking is largely inconsistent with the risk-based approach to compliance.

---

74 U.S. Government Accountability Office, *Additional Tracking Could Aid Treasury's Efforts to Mitigate Any Adverse Effects U.S. Sanctions Might Have on Humanitarian Assistance,* GAO-21-239 (Feb. 2021), at 28. https://www.gao.gov/assets/gao-21-239.pdf

75 Tara Rice, Goetz von Peter, and Codruta Boar, "On the Global Retreat of Correspondent Banks," *BIS Quarterly Review* (March 2020), at 38. https://www.bis.org/publ/qtrpdf/r_qt2003g.pdf; Lea Borchert et al., "The Impact of De-risking by Correspondent Banks on International Trade," VoxEU, September 18, 2024. https://cepr.org/voxeu/columns/impact-derisking-correspondent-banks-international-trade; Eric Moret, *Safeguarding Humanitarian Banking Channels: How, Why and by Whom?,* Norwegian Refugee Council, January 2023. https://www.nrc.no/globalassets/pdf/reports/safeguarding-humanitarian-banking-channels/safeguarding-humanitarian-banking-channels.pdf; Eastern and Southern Africa Anti-Money Laundering Group, *Follow Up Report to Assess the Continued Existence and Impact of De-risking in the ESAAMLG Region,* April 2021. https://www.esaamlg.org/reports/De-risking_FUR_April2021.pdf

76 Financial Action Task Force, *High-level Synopsis of the Stocktake of the Unintended Consequences of the FATF Standards* (27 Oct. 2021), at 2. https://www.fatf-gafi.org/content/dam/fatf-gafi/reports/Unintended-Consequences.pdf

77 Ibid.

78 Ibid.

Recommendations

Since people are ultimately responsible for how companies comply with regulations, solutions to the problem of over-compliance should consider the perspectives and incentives of individuals who help shape their organizations' responses to sanctions.

Firstly, authorities, particularly in the United States and the United Kingdom, should consider foregoing strict liability enforcement in cases involving humanitarian activities, except in cases involving clear, wilful violations of law. To the extent agencies already have informal policies against strict liability in such cases, these practices should be formalized and communicated to the public. For the avoidance of doubt, it should also be made clear that individuals would not be prosecuted for errors in judgment with respect to humanitarian exceptions and licenses. In particular, this approach could help address over-compliance related to uncertainty about difficult to ascertain facts. Removing the threat of strict liability would enable companies to proceed with transactions based on a reasonable, risk-based level of due diligence. There is precedent for this strategy. For example, OFAC provides a "safe harbor" for companies that comply with the limitations and related recordkeeping requirements of its Russia-related oil price-cap sanctions program.[79] According to OFAC, the safe harbor is meant to address concerns that service providers "will be penalized for inadvertently violating" the sanctions.[80] Companies that "comply in good faith ... will not face OFAC penalties."[81]

The safe harbor was adopted to persuade U.S. service providers to continue to transact in relation to Russian-origin oil and petroleum products in accordance with the price-cap policy. A similar approach could be taken to persuade reluctant companies and banks to support legally permissible humanitarian transactions. In this context, OFAC FAQ 1106, which concerns humanitarian carveouts under UN Security Council Resolution 2664, states that "financial institutions may reasonably rely upon the information available to them in the

---

79 Office of Foreign Assets Control, OFAC Guidance on the Implementation of the Price Cap Policy for Crude Oil and Petroleum Products of Russian Federation Origin, December 20, 2023, at 2. https://ofac.treasury.gov/media/931036/download?inline

80 Ibid.

81 Ibid.

ordinary course of business, provided that the financial institution does not know or have reason to know that the transaction is outside the scope of' an applicable general license."[82] While the FAQ is limited to financial institutions, it represents a relaxation of OFAC's strict liability enforcement standard for a subset of humanitarian activities.

Regulatory bodies may also directly discourage over-compliance and derisking by requiring companies to justify certain decisions to decline or terminate lawful business. Such interventions could be taken in response to complaints from affected customers or NGOs. Governments may even proactively scrutinize decisions to engage in certain forms of derisking. For example, the UK Financial Conduct Authority (FCA) has undertaken a review of UK banks' account closure practices that could lead to greater protections for customers' rights to access some banking services.[83] In the EU, the directive on payment accounts gives individuals the right to a basic payment account except in limited circumstances.[84] The People's Republic of China's Anti-Foreign Sanctions Law (AFSL) of 2021 and related measures discourage companies from implementing "discriminatory restrictive measures" such as sanctions targeting Chinese individuals and organizations.[85] (The AFSL is similar to EU and UK statutes prohibiting compliance with certain U.S. sanctions against Cuba and Iran.)[86] None of these initiatives is specific to humanitarian trade. However, they illustrate the potential for governments to intervene to regulate over-compliance practices when called for. To the extent individuals in corporations are motivated by the perception of external

---

82 Office of Foreign Assets Control, FAQ 1106 (20 Dec. 2022). https://ofac. treasury.gov/faqs/1106

83 Financial Conduct Authority, *UK Payment Accounts Access and Closures: Update* (September 2024). https://www.fca.org.uk/publication/corporate/uk-payment-accounts-access-closures-update.pdf; Financial Conduct Authority, *UK Payment Accounts: Access and Closures* (September 2023). https://www.fca.org.uk/publication/corporate/uk-payment-accounts-access-and-closures.pdf

84 Directive 2014/92/EU; OJ 2014 L 257/214.

85 Law of the People's Republic of China on Countering Foreign Sanctions (English translation), June 10, 2021. https://www.chinalawtranslate.com/en/counteringforeignsanctions/

86 European Commission, *Extraterritoriality* (blocking statute). https://finance.ec.europa.eu/eu-and-world/open-strategic-autonomy/extraterritoriality-blocking-statute_en; UK Department for Business and Trade, *Protection of Trading Interests*, June 26, 2023. https://www.gov.uk/guidance/protection-of-trading-interests

risks, the introduction of countermeasures could tip the balance away from over-compliance and toward more careful decision making.

Individual practitioners and professional organizations should continue to pursue and share expertise and educational resources to improve their understanding of sanctions and to identify and correct commonplace errors.[87] To this end, governments should continue to engage with the private sector by providing guidance and clarifications about expectations for compliance. Individuals from all sectors should work to raise awareness of the impacts of over-compliance and to promote professional norms against harmful forms of over-compliance. This is particularly key for individuals in the second line of defense and their legal advisors who exercise the greatest influence within corporate compliance structures.

---

87 Orozco, *supra* note 32, at 280. (."..the quality of personnel can vastly impact the range of legal decision-making options and this also extends to the area of compliance" [citations omitted]); Parker, *supra* note 3, at 181 (discussing the role of professional bodies in the development of "specialized or professional skills, knowledge, commitment and techniques within the organization to respond to regulation"); Ibid., at 181. ("It is also important to understand how compliance professionals' strategies are shaped by their values, perceptions and motivations, and the extent to which these are influenced by their professional membership vis-a-vis local organizational cultures.")

CHAPTER 7

Unilateral Coercive Measures
Financial and Fiscal Implications

Attiya Waris[1]

Abstract

The financial system globally is a patchwork system that is based on actions and reactions and power imbalances where negotiations fail. However, one key area that seems to have been developing predominantly unilaterally due to the absence of any agreed principles and legislation is the area of sanctions and unilateral coercive measures. This paper canvasses the entirety of the fiscal implications and measures that have been developing in the absence of a coherent fiscal and financial architecture with specific refence to the legal effect of recommendations in the absence of a globally agreed legal fiscal system making reference to Financial Action Taskforce process (FATF) and the EU measures on tax.

Introduction and Approach

Historically, even when counties did not have diplomatic relations, economic and trade relations were allowed to continue, albeit through a controlled engagement. One example is the silent barter trade in a fixed geographical location even during times of war between ethnic communities like the Maasai and Kikuyu in Eastern Africa before the colonization of the region by the British.[2] In 2025 we still ask these questions: what is international law, whose international law is being followed and how do we roll out international

---

1 Professor, University of Nairobi, UN Independent expert on Foreign Debt and Human Rights

2 Marie Roué, Nicolas Césard, Yves Constant Adou Yao, and Alfred Oteng-Yeboah (Eds.), *Knowing our Lands and Resources: Indigenous and local knowledge of biodiversity and ecosystem services in Africa*, UNESCO (2017). https://unesdoc.unesco.org/ark:/48223/pf0000247461

law consensually? In the field of cross border financial transactions and the guiding international law, regulation and policy on debt, trade, tax, financial flows we remain without a coherent international fiscal and financial architecture. There are no globally agreed rules of governance, no clear principles of engagement, while there is an absence of institutions to guide engagement across borders as well as a space to resolve disputes. The result not surprisingly is a series of unilateral, bilateral and multilateral agreements and engagements, rules and regulations that are guided by the power and control one state can hold over another, either as a single powerful state or as a group of states depending on the power balance between them.

Sanctions are set out by the United Nations Security Council under the UN Charter. However, over the years, the absence of a financial framework and geopolitical interests have opened up an avenue for compliant and non-compliant states to implement not only official (UN) sanctions, but also unilateral coercive measures (UCMs) not authorized by the UN Security Council.

In fiscal spaces and financial transactions, sanctions and UCMs are rolled out regularly. However, as the financial system has not kept pace in developing global rules and regulations as well as audit monitoring and evaluation, states unilaterally implement at a granular individual and organizational as well as national level, 'sanctions' not authorized by the UN Security Council. These actions implemented and enforced as regards profit making entities and/or citizens of a country result in a rollout where interlocutors find they have no choice but to implement, if they do not want to face fines and penalties, imprisonment and/or expulsion from a country and an inevitable resulting failure of their businesses. It is with this background in mind that this paper will go forward in unpacking 'sanctions' that are regularly rolled out in financial spaces, but which do not actually have the authorization of the UN Security Council and would therefore be deemed as UCMs.

International Financial Obligations from a Human Rights Based Perspective

Understanding Sanctions and UCMs

The UN Security Council can take action to maintain or restore international peace and security under Chapter VII of the United Nations Charter.[3] Sanctions measures, under Article 41, encompass a broad range of enforcement options that do not involve the use of armed forces. Since 1966, the Security Council has established 31 sanctions regimes: in Southern Rhodesia, South Africa, the Former Yugoslavia (2), Haiti (2), Angola, Liberia (3), Eritrea/Ethiopia, Rwanda, Sierra Leone, Côte d'Ivoire, Iran, Somalia/Eritrea, ISIL (Da'esh) and Al-Qaida, Iraq (2), Democratic Republic of the Congo, Sudan, Lebanon, Democratic People's Republic of Korea, Libya (2), the Taliban, Guinea-Bissau, Central African Republic, Yemen, South Sudan and Mali.[4] Security Council sanctions have taken a number of different forms, in pursuit of a variety of goals. The measures have ranged from comprehensive economic and trade sanctions to more targeted measures such as arms embargoes, travel bans, and financial or commodity restrictions.[5] The Security Council has applied sanctions to support peaceful transitions, deter non-constitutional changes, constrain terrorism, protect human rights and promote non-proliferation.[6]

Today, there are 14 ongoing sanctions regimes which focus on supporting political settlement of conflicts, nuclear non-proliferation, and counterterrorism. Each regime is administered by a sanctions

---

3 *Charter of the United Nations,* Chapter VII: Action with Respect to Threats to the Peace, Breaches of the Peace, and Acts of Aggression (1945). https://main.un.org/securitycouncil/sites/default/files/part_vii_final_for_webposting.pdf

4 United Nations Security Council, *Sanctions Committees Overview* (2023). https://main.un.org/securitycouncil/en/content/repertoire/sanctions-and-other-committees

G. C. Hufbauer, J. J. Schott, and K. A. Elliott. *Economic Sanctions Reconsidered,* 3rd Edition (Peterson Institute for International Economics, 2007). https://www.piie.com/bookstore/economic-sanctions-reconsidered-3rd-edition-paper

5 D. Cortright and G. A. Lopez, *The Sanctions Decade: Assessing UN Strategies in the 1990s* (Lynne Rienner Publishers, 2000). Link: https://www.rienner.com/title/The_Sanctions_Decade_Assessing_UN_Strategies_in_the_1990s

6 Thomas J. Biersteker, Sue E. Eckert, and Marcos Tourinho (Eds.), *Targeted Sanctions: The Impacts and Effectiveness of United Nations Action* (United Kingdom: Cambridge University Press, 2016).

committee chaired by a non-permanent member of the Security Council.[7] This paper will proceed on the basis that the word "sanctions" will refer only to the sanctions which are authorized by the UNSC. The list currently includes sanctions regimes with committees set up on: Al-Shabaab; ISIL (Da'esh) & Al-Qaida; Iraq; The Democratic Republic of Congo; Sudan; Lebanon; DPRK; Libya; Guinea-Bissau; Yemen; South Sudan; Haiti and CAR.

At the same time, from a fiscal perspective, fiscal interventions have the same effect regardless of the legal ground (UN Security Council sanctions or unilateral coercive measures); both terms will be used in this chapter interchangeably.

UCMs currently in force include those on Cuba, Iran, Venezuela and Russia, as well as those of sectoral character as well as affecting specific individuals and companies.[8] However, this understanding of UCMs is commonly based on actions by States and does not include guidance from financial and regulatory institutions and entities that create lists of States on whom financial restrictions are placed to coerce them to implement certain rules and regulations, therefore the financial effect might be much broader. In this paper I will also explore the FATF and the EU list of non-cooperative jurisdictions for tax purposes. Whether it is a sanction or a UCM the implications from a fiscal perspective are wide and far-reaching and can have implications on the daily lives and survival of people.

As a result the subsequent discussion will engage with the types of interventions and the implications these fiscal interventions have on the lives of people and as a result, the human rights abuse that one can potentially infer from their implementation.[9] The ensuing discussion will also take stock of how wide reaching these issues are the how

---

7 Kingdom of Belgium, Federal Public Service Foreign Affairs, *Sanctions of the UN Security Council,* 2023. https://diplomatie.belgium.be/en/policy/policy-areas/peace-and-security/sanctions/sanctions-un-security-council

8 Idriss Jazairy, *Negative Impact of Unilateral Coercive Measures on the Enjoyment of Human Rights: Report of the Special Rapporteur on the Negative Impact of Unilateral Coercive Measures on the Enjoyment of Human Rights,* United Nations Human Rights Council, 2019. United Nations General Assembly, *Report of the Special Rapporteur on the Negative Impact of Unilateral Coercive Measures on the Enjoyment of Human Rights,* 2023. https://digitallibrary.un.org/record/3823888?v=pdf

9 Attiya Waris, et al., Letter to IMF Managing Director Kristalina Georgieva, August 26, 2022.

important it remains for them to be implemented rarely and carefully and to be continually monitored to prevent human rights abuses.[10]

The Fiscal and Non-Fiscal Measure Implemented through Sanctions and UCMs

States implementing UCMs and sanctions take the issue into account in economic engagement, foreign policy and development cooperation with a targeted state. Several States and regional blocs have developed a series of rules and regulations that allows them to use the listing of States to guide economic relations with third countries. These measures also extend to a more granular level, involving domestic stakeholders such as bankers, lawyers, accountants and real estate brokers in asset blocking or freezing of States, individuals or corporations, trusts, charities and NGOs.[11] Actions taken include withholding of parts of transactions, market access blocks, currency transaction blocks, debt purchase and acquisition or use as collateral, travel restrictions to trade, the movement of goods and services, ban on equipment/tech software, spending limit per day for citizens travelling to sanctioned State, penalties on a nation trading with a sanctioned State, remittance controls, travel bans for government, party officials, students, scholars, and artists, ban on all trade except for non-subsidized sale of foods and medicine and restrictions on debt investment, collateral, including implementation of high interest.[12] However, the luxury goods and services markets seem to not feature on this list. The rationale that these sanctions and UCMs are put into place, whether because the State in question is undermining democracy or the rule of law or to coerce the handing over of who were responsible for serious human rights violations, becomes shaky. However, the effect of the absence on a floor to these types of interventions is that, indeed, human rights get further undermined.

---

10 Attiya Waris, "Chapter 75: Tax and Development," in *Encyclopedia of Law and Development*, (Cheltenham, UK: Edward Elgar Publishing, 2021), pp. 283–286. https://doi.org/10.4337/9781788117975.00080

11 Michael P. Malloy, "Economic Sanctions and Human A Delicate Balance," Human Rights Brief 3, no. 1 (1995): 12, 14. https://digitalcommons.wcl.american.edu/cgi/viewcontent.cgi?referer=&httpsredir=1&article=1682&context=hrbrief

12 Types of sanctions and their implementation, *OFAC Consolidated Frequently Asked Questions,* U.S. Department of the Treasury, Office of Foreign Assets Control (OFAC), 2023. https://ofac.treasury.gov/faqs/all-faqs

Indirect effects include the collapse of certain industries that rely on risky or even imported raw material as well as those that have patents, like insurance and reinsurance, syringes and even saline bags,[13] and increased risk analysis for investment. The failure to access a government also blocks access to their national data sets, which in turn leads to a failure to adequately measure data. Private investors avoid the State, and the mobile population leave, especially those with globally marketable skills. Businesses will change investment and operational profiles also due to increased risk of audits and reinforced monitoring of transactions. Other legislative measures include non-deductibility of costs incurred in a listed jurisdiction; controlled foreign company (CFC) rules to limit artificial deferral of tax to offshore, low-taxed entities; withholding tax (WHT) measures, to tackle improper exemptions or refunds and limitation of the participation exemption on shareholder dividends.[14]

However, the intended purpose may not be achieved if the funds are not well managed domestically. Such situations are often evidenced by stalled projects worldwide as a result of corruption, poor management and currency fluctuations that make the figures in the domestic currency inadequate. Changes in global and regional economies and violence in neighbouring countries as well as globally have a similar effect. Recent conflicts, such as the conflict in Ukraine, have affected fertilizer and food prices; sanctions on the Islamic Republic of Iran have affected fuel prices; and terrorism in Afghanistan and Pakistan has delayed the achievement of complete global vaccination against polio (A/78/179).

The international fiscal system allows for the secrecy of financial transaction and this embedded principle of secrecy by banking institutions allows UCMs to be more widely taken up with no control and limited oversight.[15] The result can be uncontrolled economic

---

13 Vahid Yazdi-Feyzabadi, et al., "Direct and indirect effects of economic sanctions on health: A systematic narrative literature review," BMC Public Health 24 (August 17, 2024): 2242. https://pmc.ncbi.nlm.nih.gov/articles/PMC11330615/

14 Attiya Waris and Laila Abdul Latif, "Towards Establishing Fiscal Legitimacy Through Settled Fiscal Principles in Global Health Financing," *Health Care Analysis* 23, no. 4 (2015): 376–390.

15 Laila Abdul Latif, "Breaking the Cycle of Domination in Global Tax Governance: Africans Defying Asymmetries and Seizing Opportunities," in I. J. Mosquera Valderrama, F. Heitmüller, J. Chaisse, and A. Christians, A. (Eds.),

contraction; hyperinflation; de facto dollarization and collapse of local currencies; unemployment; increased IFF; growth of a black market and a shift to digital trade.[16] In addition funds cannot be channelled through entities in listed States.[17] Illicit financial flows are not accidental or a by-product of the market; rather they often appear to be the result of State-sanctioned practices and high levels of impunity, insufficient regulations, and the misuse of complex financial vehicles to avoid accountability and traceability. International cooperation and assistance remain crucial to combating illicit financial flows between States and to developing multilateral responses and equitable solutions.[18]

International Finance Related UCMs and Sanctions Regimes Outside the United Nations Security Council

Financial Action Task Force

The Financial Action Task Force (FATF) is an intergovernmental organization established in 1989 with the primary objective of setting global standards and promoting effective measures to combat money laundering, terrorist financing, and the proliferation of weapons of mass destruction. It is not a global body but rather consists of 39-member countries and jurisdictions, along with regional organizations and observers similar to the Security Council membership. This raises questions around decision-making processes, inclusivity and neutrality. It is also unclear whether membership influences the decision-making process and what mechanisms have been put in place to ensure neutrality

The FATF operates under a mandate to develop and promote policies for anti-money laundering (AML) and counter terrorism financing (CTF). It serves as a global standard-setter, providing

Redefining Global Governance. Emerging Globalities and Civilizational Perspectives (Springer, Cham, 2024), pp. 261–284. https://doi.org/10.1007/978-3-031-69793-7_18

16 Volker Türk, Office of the United Nations High Commissioner for Human Rights (OHCHR), *Impact of Sanctions: Statement,* 2023. https://www.ohchr.org/en/statements-and-speeches/2023/09/impact-sanctions

17 "High-Risk Jurisdictions Subject to a Call for Action," Financial Action Task Force (FATF), 2023. https://www.fatf-gafi.org/publications/high-risk-and-other-monitored-jurisdictions/documents/call-for-action-february-2023.html

18 UNIE Foreign Debt Report to the HRC, March 2024.

recommendations and guidance to member countries on effective measures to combat financial crimes. These recommendations, commonly known as the FATF Recommendations, are widely recognized as the international AML and CTF standards. At the same time, these standards do not include poverty alleviation, human well-being or even human rights indicators and there is no floor on when the rollout of recommendations will result in the destruction of a people; what measures FATF would put into place and pull back on through weighing the balance of human life and planetary health. The is no clarity on any existing efforts by FATF to integrate human rights concerns, either.

The list of countries issued by FATF following the plenary is further categorized into two: 'high risk jurisdictions' popularly known as the blacklist[19] and 'jurisdictions under increased monitoring' popularly known as a grey list.[20] The blacklist highlights countries that are uncooperative with FATF's, and by extension the global financial community's, efforts to fight money laundering, terrorism financing and processing of assets from criminal activity (ML/TF/PF) risks. Owing to this non-cooperation, FATF advises that the international financial system applies enhanced due diligence to the named countries, and in some extreme cases, counter measures such as derisking by correspondent banks, targeted financial sanctions etc. There are currently 3 countries on the FATF blacklist: Myanmar, which is recommended for enhanced due diligence, and the Democratic People's Republic of Korea and Iran, both of which are recommended for countermeasures.[21] This choice of countries is not aligned with the Security Council and as a result already gives cause for concern.

The grey list, on the other hand, consists of countries with strategic deficiencies in their ability to counteract ML/FT/PF risks but who have made time-bound political commitments to address these deficiencies.[22] FATF and the regional FATF-style bodies that support it are then involved in undertaking monitoring to ensure that these

---

19 Financial Action Task Force (FATF), High-Risk and Other Monitored Jurisdictions, *"Black and Grey" Lists.* https://www.fatf-gafi.org/en/countries/black-and-grey-lists.html

20 Ibid.

21 FATF, note 19.

22 FATF, note 20.

gaps are closed.[23] In assessing the state of a country's Anti Money Laundering, Combatting Financing of Terrorism and Counter Proliferation Financing (AML/CFT/CPF) regime, FATF relies on regional affiliate bodies known as the FATF-Style Regional Bodies (FSRB) to undertake country assessments and produce what is known as a Mutual Evaluation Report (MER).[24] The MER is therefore an analysis of a country's policy, technical and operational AML/CFT/CPF framework against leading global practices and prevailing risks.[25]

There are 26 countries currently on the FATF grey list subject to increased monitoring.[26] A country feels the effect of grey listing and blacklisting and this listing of countries is far beyond the Security Council's more conservative but none the less globally sanctioned listing, which also continues to also be challenged due concerns of the SCs membership. What also becomes of concern is the racial profile of the listed States, an issue that has been brought up before regarding neutrality in decision making.[27]

The FATF grey list signals to the global financial system to exercise caution in dealings with the country. This raised financial risk profile has far-reaching economic implications, including reduced attractiveness of the country as an investment destination for foreign direct investment, increased cost of doing business for entities domiciled in the country due to the enhanced due diligence applied by counter-parties, restrictions on cross-jurisdictional transactions particularly to/from countries that have stringent measures against grey listed countries, potential derisking by correspondent banks and

---

23 Financial Action Task Force (FATF). (2023). The Role of FATF-Style Regional Bodies (FSRBs), *FATF Global Network.* https://www.fatf-gafi.org/en/countries/global-network.html

24 Financial Action Task Force (FATF), Mutual Evaluation Reports (MERs), *Mutual Evaluations,* 2023. https://www.fatf-gafi.org/en/topics/mutual-evaluations.html

25 Ibid.

26 Financial Action Task Force (FATF), Jurisdictions under Increased Monitoring and High-Risk Jurisdictions Subject to a Call for Action, *"Black and Grey" Lists.* https://www.fatf-gafi.org/en/countries/black-and-grey-lists.html

27 Steven Dean and Attiya Waris, "Ten Truths About Tax Havens: Inclusion and the 'Liberia' Problem," *Emory Law Journal* 70, no. 7 (2021), Brooklyn Law School, Legal Studies Paper No. 670. SSRN: https://ssrn.com/abstract=3822421; Attiya Waris, "Taxation and Multinational Corporations in Africa," *Law, Social Justice & Global Development Journal* 15, no. 1 (2011).

other key relationships, and increased cost of public international debt from finance and development partners, among others. In a sample of 89 emerging and developing countries grey listed between the years 2000 and 2017, a working paper published in 2021 by the International Monetary Fund (IMF) found that capital inflows on average declined by 7.6% of GDP, Foreign Direct Investment by 3% while other investments declined by 3.6% following a country's grey listing.[28] These are markers of vulnerability and the effect on human life and survival needs to be more carefully considered and reflected in these spaces. It has also not been clear if the lists have reduced money laundering or terrorism financing and there is no empirical evidence to support this.

EU List of Non-Cooperative Jurisdictions for Tax Purposes

The EU list of non-cooperative jurisdictions for tax purposes is part of the EU's work on tax evasion and avoidance.[29] It is composed of countries which have failed to fulfil their commitments to comply with tax good governance criteria within a specific timeframe, and countries which have refused to do so. The choice, however, on which States have been added to this list is also quite odd, insofar as they have very small economies and are predominantly island nations. On October 8, 2024, the European Council adopted the EU list of non-cooperative jurisdictions for tax purposes.[30] There are 11 countries on the list: American Samoa; Anguilla; Fiji; Guam; Palau; Panama; Samoa; Trinidad and Tobago; the U.S. Virgin Islands and Vanuatu.[31] As a regional bloc the choice to not include any States internal to the bloc is odd as well as the complete absence of any states listed out by the SC. Historically States that have been on the list in the past included:

---

28 International Monetary Fund, *The Impact of FATF Grey Listing on Capital Flows: Evidence from Emerging and Developing Economies*, IMF Working Paper No. 2021/123.

29 Thomas Rixen, "Tax Competition and Inequality: The Case for Global Tax Governance," *Global Governance* 17, no. 4 (2011): 447–467. https://papers.ssrn.com/sol3/papers.cfm?abstract_id=1488066

30 European Council, *EU List of Non-Cooperative Jurisdictions: Council of the European Union* (2025). https://www.consilium.europa.eu/en/policies/eu-list-of-non-cooperative-jurisdictions/

31 Ibid.

Antigua and Barbuda, Bahamas, Belize, Seychelles and Turks and Caicos Islands, British Virgin Islands, Costa Rica, Marshall Islands.[32]

The criteria have been designed to evolve over time, so that they are aligned with **international tax good governance standards**, developed notably in forums of the Organization for Economic Co-operation and Development (OECD), such as the Global Forum on transparency and exchange of information for tax purposes, the forum on harmful tax practices and the inclusive framework on base erosion and profit shifting, another membership based organization following criteria that is similarly unclear. The lack of clarity is less about which nations are included but rather which ones are excluded and why.

Fiscal and Non-fiscal Effects of Noncompliance

Noncompliance can have severe consequences for financial institutions, including reputational damage, legal penalties, and even exclusion from the global financial system.[33] It is essential for financial institutions to have robust compliance programs in place to identify, assess, and mitigate the risks associated with money laundering and terrorism financing. Noncompliance with regulations can lead to financial penalties, legal repercussions and reputational damage.

Financial penalties for noncompliance can be substantial, often severely affecting a business's bottom line and financial stability. Noncompliance was seriously taken into consideration in 2019. The average fine imposed was 145.33 million U.S. dollars.[34] Penalties can vary depending on the severity of the violation and the industry, with some fines reaching up to 1 million dollars or more. For many organizations, the prospect of such consequences poses a significant challenge, and compliance teams play a crucial role in helping businesses navigate this complex landscape. Maintaining compliance with regulations allows businesses to evade financial penalties and

---

32 Ibid.

33 International Monetary Fund (IMF), *Anti-Money Laundering and Combating the Financing of Terrorism (AML/CFT): Overview,* 2023. https://www.imf.org/en/Topics/Financial-Integrity/amlcft

34 Financial Action Task Force (FATF), *Consequences of Non-Compliance with AML/CFT Standards,* 2023. https://www.fatf-gafi.org/publications/fatfgeneral/documents/consequences-of-non-compliance.html

concentrate on delivering outstanding products and services to their customers.

Legal repercussions of noncompliance can be severe, ranging from litigation and fines to imprisonment, depending on the gravity of the violation. Regulatory authorities have the authority to investigate, levy penalties, and even revoke licenses or permits, depending on the magnitude of the noncompliance. In industries such as healthcare, noncompliance can also directly impact patient safety.

In addition to the above, the legal consequences of noncompliance can extend beyond immediate fines and penalties. Legal proceedings can consume significant amounts of time and resources, diverting businesses away from core business operations. Furthermore, the mere fact of being under investigation can damage a company's reputation, even if the company is eventually found to be compliant. This is particularly true in highly regulated industries, where trust and credibility are paramount. This legal landscape is also continually evolving, with new regulations being introduced and existing ones being updated or reinterpreted. This means that businesses must be proactive in keeping up with the latest regulatory changes to avoid falling afoul of the law. Failing to adhere to contractual obligations can lead to legal liabilities for businesses, while noncompliance with privacy and data protection regulations can result in civil liabilities and even criminal liability. Legal liability risks, such as noncompliance, can lead to dire consequences, including legal fees. This includes third-party claims, such as lawsuits filed by customers, employees, or business partners for compensation due to noncompliance-related issues. Non-compliance with sanctions regulations can result in fines, criminal proceedings, and damaged reputations, affecting businesses' credibility and performance. To avoid these consequences, businesses must prioritize compliance efforts and ensure they are adhering to all relevant sanctions regulations or simply exit a market, and in the current economic climate the easier approach is downsizing. Fines for noncompliance vary depending on the severity of the violation, the industry, and the specific regulation involved. By staying updated on regulatory requirements and investing in necessary resources for compliance, businesses can avoid costly fines and retain a competitive market edge. Examples of companies that have suffered reputational damage due to noncompliance issues include: Danske Bank, 1MDB, Odebrecht, Petrobras and Siemens.

Recommendations and Conclusion

Firstly, it is clear that due to the absence of a coherent financial and fiscal architecture an approach to fiscal implementation is rather blanket done via an *ad hoc* and often unilateral basis without proper monitoring and evaluation.[35]

Secondly, using a principles-based approach is similarly crucial to ensure that the issues are manged in a fiscally legitimate manner, keeping human rights and planetary health at the centre of decisions.[36]

Thirdly, one wonders, in the absence of a global dispute resolution body, whether a case can be made for a class action suit by States affected by these measures to take entities to court for reparations for human rights abuses suffered in consequence.[37]

Fourthly, it would also be important to calculate the accumulated cost of UCMs and ascribe same to individual citizens in the member state implementing the UCM in an effort to encourage public partici-pation and an active and responsible citizenry.

Finally, businesses cannot be holders of human rights, and their transactions should not be allowed to evade scrutiny by falling under the right to privacy and access to information. Ensuring measures are being put into place through a fiscally legitimate process is crucial while also maintaining a clear separation between State, business and diplomacy.[38]

---

35 Attiya Waris, United Nations Human Rights Council (UNHRC), *Fiscal legitimacy through human rights: A principled approach to financial resource collection and allocation for the realization of human rights,* UN Doc A/HRC/55/54, January 16, 2024. https://digitallibrary.un.org/record/4037208?v=pdf

36 Ibid.

37 Attiya Waris, United Nations Human Rights Council (UNHRC), *Taking stock and identifying priority areas: A vision for the future work of the mandate holder,* UN Doc A/HRC/49/47, December 23, 2021. https://documents.un.org/doc/undoc/gen/g21/384/62/pdf/g2138462.pdf

38 Ibid.

CHAPTER 8

Unilateral Sanctions Confronting Technology Companies
Taking a Human Rights–Based Approach

Wei Zhang[1] | *Xiaofan Hu*[2]

Abstract

This paper seeks solutions to the "dilemma" faced by technology companies, namely complying with the unilateral sanction measures that may cause adverse human right effects or refusing to comply at the risk of suffering from civil or criminal penalties. The first part of this paper depicts the "dilemma" embedded in this topic. Technology companies play vital roles in transmitting information, operating online platforms and producing fast updated technological products and services, which have significant impact on individuals' rights. The widespread over-compliance of technology companies with unilateral sanctions, which has been proved to be unlawful and illegitimate in international law, runs afoul of their businesses' duty to respect and protect human rights and may affect basic human rights, including freedom of expression, right to education, right to health and right to access to the internet. The second part of this paper examines the current practices of technology companies in tackling the "dilemma" through the studies of the human rights and sanctions compliance policies of technology companies. Finally, the paper suggests measures for minimizing the negative human rights impact arising from unilateral sanctions, including performing due diligence by assessing the impact of unilateral sanctions on human rights and weighing this

1 Professor Dr. Wei Zhang, Co-Director of Institute for Human Rights, China University of Political Science and Law
2 Xiaofan Hu, PhD Candidate, China University of Political Science and Law

against the risks of penalties of circumventing sanctions requirements. Besides, in accordance with the Guiding Principles on Business and Human Rights (hereinafter referred to as UNGPs), and the Guiding Principles on Sanctions, Business and Human Rights (hereinafter referred to as "Guiding Principles"), the State should enact laws and provide clear and consistent interpretations on the existing policies against over-compliance and zero-risk policies taken by technology companies, and establish an effective supervisory mechanism to prevent human rights violations caused by compliance with unilateral sanctions. Moreover, access to remedy for the victims of human rights violations should be guaranteed.

Introduction

With the development of science and technology, big data and artificial intelligence are booming. More and more States are starting to carry out strategic policies on technology development out of both economic and political concerns, with the imposition of unilateral sanctions being among the most commonly used policies. For example, U.S. has imposed unilateral sanctions against Chinese technological companies since 2017, including export controls and launching administrative and civil charges against designated companies' officials.[3]

Since the enactment of National Defense Authorization Act in 2019,[4] the U.S. has imposed unilateral sanctions against Huawei, ZTE and many other Chinese technology companies, citing national security concerns.[5] Increasingly Chinese technology companies have been put on the Entity List, making them subject to U.S. license requirements for the export or transfer of specific items. In January 2023, more Chinese technology companies were added to the Entity List for

---

3 See United Nations Office of the High Commissioner for Human Rights, "China: UN expert says unilateral sanctions must not be used as foreign policy tool and means of economic coercion" (press release), May 17, 2024. https://www.ohchr.org/en/press-releases/2024/05/china-un-expert-says-unilateral-sanctions-must-not-be-used-foreign-policy

4 See National Defense Authorization Act, H.R. 5515 (2019). https://www.congress.gov/115/bills/hr5515/BILLS-115hr5515enr.pdf

5 Xin Liu and Hongzhang Ni, "Unilateral sanctions against China do not conform with a broad number of international legal norms: UN expert," *Global Times*, May 17, 2024. https://www.globaltimes.cn/page/202405/1312519.shtml

allegedly aiding Russia's military or supplying equipment to countries that were under U.S. sanctions.[6] In May 2024, the U.S. Commerce Department added 37 units of China Electronics Technology Group Corporation (CETC) to the Entity List.[7]

Although the legality of unilateral sanctions is still under debate, abiding by the unilateral sanctions requirements has indeed caused human rights violations. New technologies bring new forms of challenges to traditional human rights.[8] The inalienable right to development, the right to health, the right to education, the right to communication, to freedom of expression may be influenced by technology companies' compliance with the unilateral sanctions.[9] Moreover, technology companies tend to impose self-restriction beyond what is mandated by sanctions and thereby widen the scope of targets to include non-sanctioned individuals and entities. Sometimes their target even includes the entire populations, which results in over-compliance.[10]

Based on the above circumstances, businesses should take a human rights-based approach in conducting activities under unilateral sanctions. The human rights-based approach is firstly proposed in implementing the Sustainable Development Goals. Centered on international human rights law framework, namely binding human rights treaties, the human rights-based approach is a methodology that intends to apply five working principles: human rights for all;

---

6 Iain Marlow and Daniel Flatley, "US Targets Chinese Company in Broader Russia Sanctions Push," *Bloomberg News,* January 26, 2023. https://www.bloomberg.com/news/articles/2023-01-26/us-targets-chinese-company-in-broader-russia-sanctions-push; Karen Freifeld, Susan Heavey, and Alexandra Alper, "U.S. hits Chinese, Russian firms for aiding Russian military," *Reuters,* February 24, 2023. https://www.reuters.com/world/us-commerce-targets-entities-china-other-countries-latest-russia-action-2023-02-24/; Orange Wang, "US sanctions 5 China-based suppliers to Iranian company selling drones to Russia," *South China Morning Post,* March 11, 2023. https://www.scmp.com/news/china/article/3213011/us-sanctions-5-china-based-suppliers-iranian-company-selling-drones-russia

7 Alexandra Alper and Karen Freifeld, Karen, "Chinese companies hit with US trade restrictions over spy balloon incident," *Reuters,* May 10, 2024. https://www.reuters.com/world/us/biden-administration-adds-37-chinese-entities-trade-restriction-list-2024-05-09/

8 Molly K. Land and Jay D. Aronson, "Human Rights and Technology: New Challenges for Justice and Accountability," *Annual Review of Law and Social Science* 16 (2020): 225–226. https://doi.org/10.1146/annurev-lawsocsci-060220-081955

9 United Nations General Assembly, *Secondary sanctions, over-compliance and human rights: Note by the Secretary-General,* para. 58, A/78/196, September 4, 2023.

10 Ibid., para. 7.

meaningful and inclusive participation and access to decision-making; non-discrimination and equality; accountability and rule of law for all; and transparency and access to information supported by disaggregated data.[11] When applied to business activities, the framework of business and human rights (BHR) established by UNGPs provides a clearer guideline. But how this framework prevents human rights violations occasioned by compliance with unilateral sanctions and mitigates the negative human rights impact of sanctions on individuals still remain unclear.[12] This study will examine the current policies and practices of technology companies in addressing human rights violations and negative human rights impact caused by the over-compliance with unilateral sanctions, and propose solutions for eliminating and mitigating human rights impact arising from the unilateral sanctions.

Human Rights Impact of Compliance with Unilateral Sanctions by Technology Companies

In a digital era, technology companies have become much more influential due to their power to control more resources, and their operations may have more profound impact on human rights. This provides a practical basis for technology companies to bear responsibility of human rights protection. Unilateral sanctions are likely to impede the obligation of technology companies, since their illegality may contradict the *erga omnes* obligation of human rights protection, and the over-compliance with sanctions of technology companies will extend the scope of human rights violations.

The Obligations of Technology Companies to Protect Human Rights

As early as 2011, the United Nations issued the UNGPs, which stipulated that corporations should respect human rights and provide

---

11 European Commission Exact External Wiki, "The Human Rights Based Approach (HRBA)," (accessed October 16, 2024). https://wikis.ec.europa.eu/pages/viewpage.action?pageId=50108948

12 Marco Fasciglione, "Unilateral and Extraterritorial Sanctions: Economic Operators and the Rise of the Business and Human Rights International Legal Framework," *OpinioJuris,* February 3, 2022. https://opiniojuris.org/2022/03/02/unilateral-and-extraterritorial-sanctions-symposium-unilateral-and-extraterritorial-sanctions-economic-operators-and-the-rise-of-the-business-and-human-rights-international-legal-framework/

remedies for individuals or groups whose rights have been affected. Although this document is not legally binding, the obligations of corporations to respect human rights has gradually received international consensus and has started to be perceived as an international custom.[13] Private human rights duties have been recognized explicitly and implicitly by various human rights instruments, as well as Human Rights Committee and various UN entities.[14] Specifically, in the digital age, technology companies are the major actors in compliance with unilateral sanctions. They are often in advanced positions to hold more information and data compared to the government and can effectively exercise power in a centralized way to manage the behavior of individuals. Thus, technology companies have, in some ways, "upended the presumptive position of juridical subordinates to the state when considered in light of the authority that they hold within digital spaces to govern and determine individuals' actions, interactions, and transactions."[15]

As the main actor to perform human rights duties, companies acting as data processors have a more profound impact on human rights such as privacy, freedom of speech, and equality. Therefore, companies should perform obligations similar to those imposed on states on the protection of human rights.[16]

Unilateral Sanctions Run Afoul of the Human Right Obligations of Technology Companies

The increasing intensification of unilateral sanctions has put companies in a dilemma when balancing the requirements of unilateral sanctions with human rights standards. On the one hand, one of the reasons why unilateral sanctions themselves lack legitimacy is that they violate human rights including those qualified as *erga omnes* obligations; on the other hand, due to concerns about the large amounts of fines or civil or criminal penalties, the implementation

---

13 David Bilchitz, *The Necessity for a Business and Human Rights Treaty* (November 30, 2014), p. 24. https://ssrn.com/abstract=2562760

14 Jordan J. Paust, "Human Rights Responsibilities of Private Corporations," *Vanderbilt Law Review* 35, no. 3 (May 2002): 817.

15 Kuzi Charamba, "Beyond the Corporate Responsibility to Respect Human Rights in the Dawn of a Metaverse," *University of Miami International and Comparative Law Review* 30, no. 1 (December 19, 2022): 113.

16 Ibid.

of unilateral sanctions is likely to be unreasonably expanded, which causes over-compliance.

The Illegality of Unilateral Sanctions and its Relations with Human Rights Violations

Unilateral sanctions are often deemed to be illegal. The term "unilateral sanctions" could be defined as measures for exercising pressure short of the threat or use of armed force directed against a target state or entity, which are taken by an individual State or a group of States.[17] These restrictive measures may have an economic impact on the entire population of the targeted country, a sector of its economy, a specific company or individual, or even a non-designated individual or company (including those in third countries).[18]

The legality of unilateral sanctions is contested since it is not authorized by the UN Security Council. Unilateral sanctions are also not justified under the doctrine of countermeasures in accordance with the customary international law. The 2001 Draft Articles on Responsibility of States for Internationally Wrongful Acts (hereinafter referred to as the "Draft Articles on State Responsibility") of the United Nations International Law Commission, which codifies customary international law,[19] stipulate that an injured State can only take countermeasures in order to induce the responsible State to cease its unlawful conduct and fulfil its obligations.[20] Additionally, countermeasures must be proportionate to the injury suffered, and shall not affect obligations for the protection of fundamental human rights and obligations prohibiting reprisals against protected persons under international humanitarian law, as well as other obligations under peremptory norms of general international law.[21] It is obvious that the

---

17 Surya P. Subedi, *Unilateral Sanctions in International Law* (Oxford: Hart Publishing, 2021), p. 2.

18 Alena F. Douhan, "Unilateral Coercive Measures: Effects and Legality Issues," *Yale Journal of International Law,* June 20, 2023. https://www.yjil.yale.edu/unilateral-coercive-measures-effects-and-legality-issues/

19 James Crawford, *The International Law Commission's Articles on State Responsibility,* "Introduction, Text and Commentaries" (Cambridge University Press, 2002), p. 309.

20 United Nations International Law Commission, *Draft Articles on Responsibility of States for Internationally Wrongful Acts, with commentaries,* 2001, Articles 49–54. https://legal.un.org/ilc/texts/instruments/english/commentaries/9_6_2001.pdf

21 Ibid., Article 50, 51; commentary of Chapter II, para. 6.

unilateral sanctions clearly do not meet either legitimacy requirement for countermeasures. Moreover, unilateral sanctions are also deemed illegitimate due to their extraterritorial application. There is no clear evidence that the extraterritorial application of foreign laws and unilateral sanctions measures satisfies the basic norms of international law and international relations.[22]

Most importantly, the international obligation of states to ensure the observance of basic rights of the human person, as expressed by the ICJ, is the source of the obligation *erga omnes*.[23] It is this exact fact that unilateral sanctions will violate States' duty to protect human rights that makes them illegal, resulting in their condemnation in multiple resolutions of UN General Assembly.[24] Businesses are required to respect human rights, including human rights *erga omnes,* and to identify, prevent, mitigate or compensate any human rights harm. Therefore, companies should not comply with the sanction requirements due to their illegality.

Over-compliance and Zero-Risk Policies of Technology Companies Resulted from Unilateral Sanctions Exacerbate the Violations of Human Rights

Given the lack of legal authorities to address the legitimacy of unilateral sanctions, States that impose unilateral sanctions always justify

---

22 Marco Fasciglione, "Unilateral and Extraterritorial Sanctions: Economic Operators and the Rise of the Business and Human Rights International Legal Framework," *OpinioJuris,* February 3, 2022. https://opiniojuris.org/2022/03/02/unilateral-and-extraterritorial-sanctions-symposium-unilateral-and-extraterritorial-sanctions-economic-operators-and-the-rise-of-the-business-and-human-rights-international-legal-framework/

23 See ICJ, *Barcelona Traction, Light and Power Company, Limited (Belgium v. Spain)*, 1970, para. 34. https://www.icj-cij.org/sites/default/files/case-related/50/050-19700205-JUD-01-00-EN.pdf. Ragazzi has put forward five criteria for identifying obligations *erga omnes* based on the examples given in the Barcelona Traction case, including that the obligations must be "instrumental to the main political objectives of the present time, namely, the preservation of peace and the promotion of fundamental human rights, which in turn reflect basic goods (or moral values), first and foremost life and human dignity." See Nina H. B. Jørgensen, Chapter 6, "Obligations Erga Omnes" in *The Responsibility of States for International Crimes* (Oxford: Oxford University Press, 2020), p. 96. https://academic.oup.com/book/32480/chapter-abstract/269317514?redirectedFrom=fulltext&login=false,   https://doi.org/10.1093/acprof:oso/9780198298618.003.008

24 See Alena F. Douhan, *supra* note 18.

their decisions with domestic orders or regulations, and technology companies which do not abide by the unilateral sanctions measures usually face penalties and reputational loss. Thus, these companies tend to adopt a business model that seeks to minimize legal, regulatory and financial risks, causing over-compliance with unilateral sanctions. This increases the human rights risks by expanding the negative human rights impact of the sanctions to many additional unintended targets. According to the Special Rapporteur, over-compliance is identified as "self-imposed restraints beyond the restrictions mandated by sanctions, applied as a part of the de-risking process, and therefore the widening of the scope of targets to include non-sanctioned individuals and entities, and sometimes the entire populations."[25]

For technology companies, their role in developing new technologies and making them widely available has become critical in facilitating the enjoyment of human rights around the world. It is well-stated in the report of Special Rapporteur that the right of final consumers to have access to publicly offered software or cyber services, whether free or at a charge, shall not be limited.[26] However, over-compliance by technology companies may negatively affect the right of access to the Internet, freedom of expression, the right to privacy, the right to education, the right to reputation, the right to decent work and the right to health.[27] For example, zero-risk policies and over-compliance by IT companies restrict access to online products and services since the unilateral sanctions imposed by U.S. government expose vulnerable populations in targeted countries to human rights breaches

---

25 See A/78/196, *supra* note 9, para. 7.

26 United Nations General Assembly, *Unilateral sanctions in the cyberworld: Tendencies and challenges – note by the Secretary-General,* August 17, 2022, A/77/296, para. 81.

27 Ibid. Over-compliance which causes the infringement to the right to health exists not only among technology companies, but also in various private sectors. For example, U.S. sanctions against Iran impeded a durable flow of vital medical supplies despite the exemptions that are supposed to allow humanitarian goods to be shipped to the country. Denying or withholding access to health care, which can include obstructing access to a specific medical treatment or causing it to be obstructed, is considered a violation of human rights. Moreover, obstructing or contributing to obstructions of shipments of medical products to Iranian patients violates their right to benefit from the scientific progress that led to the development of these products. See UN Office of the High Commissioner for Human Rights, Communications to the United States of America, USA 19/2022, October 11, 2022. https://spcommreports. ohchr.org/TMResultsBase/DownLoadPublicCommunicationFile?gId=27593

and violate the basic principle of non-discrimination. According to the UN independent experts, "Such restrictions include limitations in accessing software for online communications and web resources, as well as blocking of access to web pages of international organizations from the territory of countries under sanctions, including web pages of UN organs and agencies."[28] Additionally, the Special Rapporteur also notes the existing issues of assessing the legality of the authority of operators of online platforms and their obligations under international law.[29] It requires media platforms, software development companies and businesses providing Internet services to exercise due diligence obligations to guarantee that their activity does not violate fundamental human rights, in particular the freedom of expression.[30]

The reasons for causing over-compliance are multi-faceted. "Confusing and overlapping legislations on unilateral sanctions, threats of secondary sanctions, civil and criminal penalties, maximum pressure campaigns, broad interpretations of sanctions regimes, reputational risks resulting in the growing fear of sanctions, the risk of losing access to the markets of sanctioning countries, and the prospect of fines and imprisonment, are all contributing to the growth of zero-risk policies by private actors."[31] Newer and smaller technology companies in particular are more prone to overly comply with the sanction measures. They lack the internal resources or legal expertise to comply with the myriads of unilateral sanctions regimes around the world and to keep track of evolving lists of sanctioned parties and must rely on outside legal advice to achieve compliance. The costs of this advice can be out of reach. The penalties for violating sanctions

---

28 UNHCHR, "United States: Human rights violated by over-zealous IT companies adhering to U.S. technology sanctions" (press release), May 30, 2024. https://www.ohchr.org/en/press-releases/2024/05/united-states-human-rights-violated-over-zealous-it-companies-adhering-us; See also A/77/296, *supra* note 27, para. 77: "Unilateral sanctions in the cybersphere—preventing access to satellites, the Internet, software, publicly available information and communication platforms and services—target the entire populations of targeted countries, affecting their economic and cultural rights, including rights to the Internet, to information, to education, to health, to life and to development, as well as academic freedoms, and they constitute discrimination on the ground of nationality."

29 See A/77/296, *supra* note 27, para. 73.

30 Ibid., para. 90.

31 See Alena F. Douhan, *supra* note 18.

can be so overwhelming for them that overcomplying with sanctions is considered a reasonable business response.[32]

In the above situations, technology companies can be deemed to breach their responsibilities to respect and protect human rights as mandated by the UN Guiding Principles on Business and Human Rights (hereinafter referred to as UNGPs) together with The Guiding Principles on Sanctions, Business and Human Rights (hereinafter referred to as "Guiding Principles"). The Guiding Principles set forth the minimum standards of human rights precaution and protection during the implementation of sanctions of the UN Security Council, as well as principles and rules of businesses behavior in a sanction compliance strategy. In view of the above principles, technology companies should be invited to seize upon their responsibility of human rights protection to seek to mitigate the over-compliance of unilateral sanctions.

Current Practices by Technology Companies in Dealing with the Human Rights Impact of Unilateral Sanctions

This paper examines publicly available human rights policies and sanctions compliance policies of companies, including Huawei and Microsoft. Specifically, the above statements and policies include Huawei's Commitment to Human Rights 2020,[33] Huawei's Statement of Compliance with Export Control Regulations,[34] Trust Code: Microsoft's Standards of Business Conduct,[35] Microsoft's Commitment to the UN Global Compact,[36] and Microsoft Global

---

32 United Nations Human Rights Council, *Monitoring and assessment of the impact of unilateral sanctions and over-compliance on human rights, Report of the Special Rapporteur on the negative impact of unilateral coercive measures on the enjoyment of human rights, Alena F. Douhan*, A/HRC/57/55, August 9, 2024, para. 17.

33 "Huawei's Commitment to Human Rights 2020." https://www.huawei.com/uk/declarations/huawei%20human%20rights%20commitment, last access October 16, 2024.

34 Huwaei, *Statement of Compliance with Export Control Regulations* (last accessed October 16, 2024). https://www.huawei.com/en/declarations/export-control

35 Microsoft, *Trust Code: Microsoft's Standards of Business Conduct* (last accessed October 16, 2024). https://cdn-dynmedia-1.microsoft.com/is/content/microsoftcorp/microsoft/mscle/documents/presentations/Trust_Code_2022_en-us_2023_0509.pdf

36 Microsoft, *Microsoft's Commitment to the UN Global Compact* (last accessed October 16, 2024). https://s3-us-west-2.amazonaws.com/ungc-production/

Human Rights Statement.[37] However, the human rights impact of their sanctions compliance is not taken into account. Neither company has voluntarily made any commitment on mitigating negative human rights impacts when implementing unilateral sanction measures. On the contrary, they tend to over-compliance. For example, Microsoft has received multi-million dollars in penalties for alleged sanctions violations in 2023.[38] Therefore, it strongly emphasizes that the company takes sanctions compliance very seriously, intended to foster a compliance culture, and would integrate sanctions compliance into an internal communications plan.[39] However, none of the company's documents mention human rights concerns in implementing unilateral sanctions measures. While the companies made no public reference to their own policies regarding over-compliance with sanctions, scattered reports provide anecdotal evidence that over-compliance does occur in the technology sector.[40] After U.S. imposed unilateral sanctions on Huawei, the implementation of zero-risk policies was further exacerbated. After the Trump administration added Huawei to a list of companies that American firms cannot trade with unless they have a license, Google voluntarily restricted Huawei from receiving updates to the Android operating system.[41] ARM, one of Huawei's global partners, also suspended its business with the company.[42] These actions tend to promote technological isolation and hinder smartphone

---

attachments/cop_2020/482288/original/UN_COP_12032019_signed_by_Brad_Smith.pdf?1579061798

37 Microsoft Global Human Rights Statement (last accessed October 16, 2024). https://www.microsoft.com/en-us/corporate-responsibility/human-rights-statement

38 Paul Dixon, *Microsoft's 2023 Sanctions penalties: 5 Key Learning Points,* April 14, 2023. https://www.sanctions.io/blog/microsoft-2023-sanctions-penalties-key-learning-points

39 Ibid.

40 "Input from the Special Rapporteur on the negative impact of unilateral coercive measures on the enjoyment of human rights to the expert consultation to discuss the practical application of the United Nations Guiding Principles on Business and Human Rights to the activities of technology companies" (last accessed on February 28, 2025). https://www.ohchr.org/sites/default/files/2022-03/Special-Rapporteur-on-toxics-and-human-rights.pdf

41 See "Huawei's use of Android restricted by Google," *BBC News,* May 20, 2019. https://www.bbc.com/news/business-48330310

42 See Dave Lee, "Huawei: ARM memo tells staff to stop working with China's tech giant," *BBC News,* May 23, 2019. https://www.bbc.com/news/technology-48363772

users' access to related products and services. The zero-risk policies may inflict significant losses and operational pressures on numerous companies within the semiconductor and telecommunications sectors, as well as companies on their supply chains, further putting their employees at risk of unemployment.

Microsoft serves as another example of the application of penalties. Faced with civil penalties imposed by the Bureau of Industry and Security (BIS) and the Office of Foreign Assets Control (OFAC) due to violations of U.S. export controls and sanctions laws, Microsoft terminated the accounts of the sanctioned persons and updated internal procedures for disabling access to its products and/or services upon identifying a sanctioned party.[43] However, since sanctioned persons can be identified at the discretion of the U.S. government, the above mitigation measures may lead to over-compliance, adversely affecting the work, study and daily life of sanctioned persons. Other persons related to the sanctions may also be potentially impacted by the mitigation measures.

Some external obstacles also impede technology companies from performing their human rights obligations during the imposition of sanctions. For example, due to the lack of clarity around applications and their lengthy and arduous process, as well as potential additional costs, technology companies are likely to be discouraged from seeking licenses to provide basic communications equipment to sanctioned states and individuals, even necessities related to humanitarian requirements. For example, the United States Department of the Treasury's Office of Foreign Assets Control decides on a case-by-case basis whether offering specific services violates United States sanctions. It has been reported that, thus far, GitHub is the only high-profile technology company to have acquired a license to offer previously restricted services to Iranians—an onerous process that took two years.[44] Additionally, legal uncertainty around the scope and legal status of the sanction regulations often frames incompatible

---

43 See Foley Hoag, *The Voluntary Disclosure Landscape After Microsoft's Settlements with BIS and OFAC and the Issuance of the Axelrod Memorandum,* May 2, 2023. https://foleyhoag.com/news-and-insights/publications/alerts-and-updates/2023/may/the-voluntary-disclosure-landscape-after-microsoft%E2%80%99s-settlements-with-bis-and-ofac-and-the-issuance/

44 See A/77/296, *supra* note 27, para. 30.

conduct with vague wording and restrictive terms, causing fear for the companies and encouraging more zero-risk policies that may violate human rights.[45]

Paths Forward for Technology Companies to Eliminate or Minimize Negative Human Rights Impacts Arising from Unilateral Sanctions

In order to eliminate or mitigate the negative impact of unilateral sanctions on human rights and ensure that companies fulfil their obligations, protection mechanisms should be established together by companies, their host states and international organizations. The three parties should coordinate with each other to ensure that companies always adopt a human rights-based approach when facing unilateral sanctions. This paper proposes the following practical methods for implementing the Guiding Principles and establishing the protection mechanisms.

Performing Due Diligence by Assessing the Impact of Unilateral Sanctions on Human Rights

Technology companies shall abide by Article 10.5 of the Guiding Principles on the issuance of corporate policy, and Article 14.2 of the Guiding Principles addressing businesses' duty to elaborate, monitor and implement the compliance policy on a non-discriminatory basis.[46] On the one hand, companies shall find connections between the existing policies on business and human rights and the requirements in the Guiding Principles to combat over-compliance, for example embedding responsible anti-over-compliance business conduct in accordance with the OECD Due Diligence Guidance for Responsible Business Conduct (2018) into their policies and management systems in all sectors of economy.[47] When making operational plans, the business

---

45 United Nations Human Rights Special Procedures, Mandate of the Special Rapporteur on the negative impact of unilateral coercive measures on the enjoyment of human rights, Guiding Principles on Sanctions, Business and Human Rights, Article 10.5 (stating the issuance of corporate policy on avoiding over-compliance and negative human rights impact).

46 Ibid., Article 10.5 and Article 14.2.

47 Ibid., Article 23.2.

enterprises shall be committed to build a system that eliminates or minimizes negative impacts on human right.

On the other hand, companies need to carry out human rights due diligence (HRDD) with the purpose of "identifying, preventing, mitigating and accounting for" how they address their adverse human rights impact. Media platforms, software development companies and businesses providing internet services shall fully exercise due diligence obligations to guarantee that their activities do not violate fundamental human rights. One of the important steps in HRDD is to implement human rights impact assessments (HRIA). When technology companies have to make decisions in compliance with the unilateral sanctions' regime, they shall establish expert panel groups to assess the negative impact of unilateral sanctions on human rights protection and weigh the negative impact against the risks of penalties of circumventing sanctions. The human rights impact assessment shall identify and categorize the human rights risks, and the companies shall refrain from taking actions that may cause severe negative human rights impacts based on the results. This can effectively avoid over-compliance caused by negligent business decision-makings. Additionally, companies can appoint human rights compliance officials, whose responsibility includes the design of anti-sanction and blocking policies to prevent compliance when it negatively affects human rights. When implementing unilateral sanction requirements, companies shall proceed in a clear, transparent and accessible manner in accordance with Article 26.2 of the Guiding Principles and take all reasonable measures to guarantee transparency of the relevant rules and procedures.[48]

Business enterprises can also resort to the laws and regulations in their registered countries to justify their non-compliance of measures that may cause human rights violations. For example, companies can actively use the reporting, exemption, guidance and supporting systems stipulated in the blocking regulations enacted in many countries and regions,[49] which can effectively protect the rights and interests of the business enterprises.

---

48 Ibid., Article 26.2.

49 Council Regulation (EC) No. 2271/96, November 22, 1996. "protecting against the effects of the extra-territorial application of legislation adopted by a third country, and actions based thereon or resulting therefrom," [1996] OJ L309/1.

Enacting Laws and Providing Clear and Consistent Interpretations by States on Over-compliance and Zero-Risk Policies

As for the States where the technology company is registered, it is clearly stipulated in Article 17.4 of the Guiding Principles that they are under the obligation to refrain from implementing unilateral sanctions imposed by other States and are obliged to ensure that businesses under their jurisdiction and/or control do not comply or overly comply with such unilateral sanctions.[50] Otherwise, the State may violate its obligation to promote and protect human rights.[51]

Therefore, States should further improve the current legislations and policies, imposing binding powers to prevent human rights violations resulting from the compliance with unilateral sanctions. For example, the current blocking regulations in EU and China stipulate that a person whose rights are being harmed by unilateral sanctions shall be entitled to remedies.[52] If a business entity breaches the blocking regulations, a State can determine the penalties imposed on the entity. By stipulating the rules on punishment and providing the victims with remedies, the laws and regulations become mandatory and legally binding on the private business entity. Some States and regions also enact their global human rights sanctions regimes in fighting against sanctions on human rights grounds or against sanctions that may negatively affect human rights.[53] The above legislation may assist technology companies to break through the constraints of sanctions and blockades while protecting national interests and basic

---

https://eur-lex.europa.eu/legal-content/EN/TXT/PDF/?uri=CELEX:31996R2271; Order of the Ministry of Commerce of the People's Republic of China, *Rules on Counteracting Unjustified Extra-territorial Application of Foreign Legislation and Other Measures,* January 9, 2021. http://english.mofcom.gov.cn/article/policyrelease/announcement/202101/20210103029708.shtml

50 See Guiding Principles on Sanctions, Business and Human Rights, *supra* note 48, Article 17.4.

51 See Guiding Principles on Sanctions, Business and Human Rights, *supra* note 48, Article 30.2.

52 Council Regulation (EC) No. 2271/96, November 22, 1996, Article 6, 9. https://eur-lex.europa.eu/legal-content/EN/TXT/PDF/?uri=CELEX:31996R2271; *Rules on Counteracting Unjustified Extra-territorial Application of Foreign Legislation and Other Measures,* Article 13. http://english.mofcom.gov.cn/article/policyrelease/announcement/202101/20210103029708.shtml.

53 Council Regulation (EU) 2020/1998, *Concerning restrictive measures against serious human rights violations and abuses,* [2020]OJ 1 410I/1, December 7, 2020. https://eur-lex.europa.eu/legal-content/EN/TXT/PDF/?uri=CELEX:32020R1998

human rights, and more legislation addressing negative human rights impact should be enacted with further efforts. Moreover, States should further provide specific instructions to business enterprises on whether to carry out the unilateral sanctions through legislative interpretation and/or judicial interpretation. States should also promote the formation of consistent rules on blocking the extraterritorial application of unilateral sanctions at the international level, with specific focus on the human rights protection stipulated in international law and basic norms of international relations.

According to para. 19.3 of the Guiding Principles,[54] a State can also address the illegality of unilateral sanctions and eliminate the negative human rights impact caused by the compliance through diplomatic channels. Some Western countries that impose unilateral sanctions tend to elevate their own illegal interpretations of the rules above that of international law. This provides home States with powerful tools to demonstrate the illegality of the sanctions and their negative impact on human rights.

Establishing Effective Supervisory Mechanisms To Prevent Human Rights Violations Caused by Compliance with Unilateral Sanctions

States, business enterprises and international organizations should work together to formulate effective monitoring and supervising mechanisms against the negative impact of human rights caused by compliance with unilateral sanctions. In implementing the monitoring of compliance policies as stipulated in para. 26.3 of the Guiding Principles, business enterprises should establish internal supervision mechanisms to collect data on the performance of internal departments on implementing unilateral sanction measures, the performance of human rights impact assessments, human rights consequences and remedial measures for business decisions causing negative human rights impact under unilateral sanctions. Analyzing the above data and information enables the business enterprises to continuously monitor the impact of business decisions on human rights and adjust the

---

54 Article 19.3 of the *Guiding Principles on Sanctions, Business and Human Rights* stated that: "States are obliged to take all measures necessary to protect businesses under their jurisdictions or control from any means of enforcement on the part of sanctioning States including through diplomatic protection and international adjudication, to prevent or minimize over-compliance."

methods and scope of human rights due diligence and human rights impact assessments to guide their decision-making process.[55]

Additionally, states shall refine the enforcement mechanism of anti-sanctions laws and establish monitoring mechanisms to evaluate the actual implementation of laws and further propose plans for improvement. As for the United Nations, it should establish corresponding monitoring mechanisms for the Guiding Principles to effectively identify and mitigate the negative impact of unilateral sanctions on human rights.

Guaranteeing Access to Remedy for Victims of Human Rights Violations

Due to the multiplicity of the sanctions regimes, the multiplicity of the perpetrators, the unavailability of legal remedies, the absence of available courts, and the impossibility of using UN treaty body complaint mechanisms,[56] people affected by unilateral sanctions do not have sufficient mechanisms to mitigate their damages or losses. To solve this problem, a relief mechanism should be established under the Guiding Principles. In further interpreting the Guiding Principles through soft laws, the laws should clarify the priority of the company when dealing with the conflicts of obligations under unilateral sanctions, which are internationally wrongful acts, and of human rights protection. Moreover, the mechanism should emphasize the state's obligation to mitigate the negative human rights impact caused by over-compliance. It is also possible to promote consensus among all parties on the issue of the obligation of companies to protect human rights under unilateral sanctions in drafting the Business and Human Rights Treaty.

The United Nations should provide informational and institutional supports to States in implementing the Guiding Principles. This can refer to the implementation mechanisms of UNGPs. Besides the guidance on National Action Plans developed by UN Working Group

---

55 Article 26.3 of the *Guiding Principles on Sanctions, Business and Human Rights* requires business enterprises to "monitor their compliance policies and strategies for abiding with human rights and to adjust them as soon as a negative humanitarian impact is identified."

56 See Douhan, Alena F., *supra* note 18.

on Business and Human Rights,[57] as well as the reports given during the annual sessions of the UN Forum on Business and Human Rights,[58] the UN treaty bodies also play an increasingly significant role. They may give advice of a more general nature in the form of General Comments or provide recommendations as part of the Universal Periodic Review or in concluding observations of the bodies. Upon request to a specific country, UN working groups can provide individual advice to countries on an ad hoc basis, and UN Global Compact and Global Compact Local Networks can also give directions and support. Besides, the OHCHR may cooperate with certain country missions to provide technical assistance. Furthermore, the International Court of Justice can fully leverage the role of existing human rights institutions and international and regional human rights bodies to receive and review communications submitted by representatives of victim countries affected by unilateral sanctions.

Business enterprises should also develop complaint mechanisms and make them available to people negatively affected by over-compliance to challenge the conducts of the company and seek compensation. In establishing the complaint mechanism of the companies, the requirements stipulated in UNGPs could be referred to.

Conclusion

The dilemma of deciding between complying with the unilateral sanctions and protecting human rights faced by the technology companies should be solved through cooperation among companies, States and international organizations. Companies should carry out human rights due diligence when performing the unilateral sanction requirements, namely assessing the human rights risks and weighing that against the risks of penalties for circumventing sanctions. The Guiding Principles play an important role in balancing the pressure

---

57 UN Working Group on Business and Human Rights, *Guidance on National Action Plans,* November 1, 2016. https://www.ohchr.org/en/documents/tools-and-resources/guidance-national-action-plans

58 UN Forum on Business and Human Right, Annual Forum on Business and Human Rights. https://www.ohchr.org/en/hrc-subsidiary-bodies/united-nations-forum-business-and-human-rights/reports

businesses experience in sanctions compliance policies and preventing and mitigating risks to people and to their rights.[59]

It obliges businesses to monitor, assess the impact and risks, mitigate and seek accountability for human rights harm in a sanctions environment.[60] Thus, companies should establish effective monitoring mechanisms in collecting information and data regarding the elimination and minimization of negative human rights impact to guide their decision-making process, as well as provide internal complaint mechanisms for victims to ensure effective remedy.

The Guiding Principles also obliged States with jurisdiction over the businesses "to take all necessary measures (administrative, legislative, operational etc.) to make sure that businesses under their jurisdiction and control do not violate human rights and to establish mechanisms of monitoring, access to justice and effective remedies for victims of violations."[61] Thus, states should provide more support to the companies by imposing hard laws against unilateral sanctions and issuing legislative or judicial interpretations. They can also seek non-legislative measures, such as diplomatic measures, in guaranteeing technology companies do not have to follow unilateral sanction requirements.

Regarding the access to remedy for victims whose rights are violated by companies when abiding by unilateral sanctions, States should ensure that victims get meaningful remedies, which include the adoption of appropriate and effective legislative and administrative procedures and other appropriate measures that provide fair, effective, and prompt access to justice; adequate, effective, prompt, and appropriate remedies, including reparation; and the provision of at least the same level of protection for victims as required by their international obligations.[62]

---

59 See the *Commentary of the Guiding Principles on Sanctions, Business and Human Rights,* 2025, p. 33: "It includes thus on the one hand an obligation of States to ensure a favorable environment enabling businesses to promote and protect human rights even in a sanctions environment, and on the other the obligation of businesses to exercise 'human rights due diligence' without any discrimination to the maximum possible extent." https://www.ohchr.org/sites/default/files/documents/issues/ucm/commentary-gpssbhr-2025.pdf

60 Ibid., p. 45.

61 Ibid., p. 59.

62 See *Access to justice in the face of unilateral sanctions and over-compliance: note,* by the Secretary-General, A/79/183, para. 30, cited in *Guiding Principles on*

Additionally, States should also cooperate with international institutions to mitigate adverse human rights impacts. United Nations and other international and regional human rights bodies should provide support to States in implementing the Guiding Principles through regular dialogue, engagement in monitoring and evaluating the negative human rights impact under the initiative of the mandate of the Special Rapporteur, capacity-building and awareness-raising to ensure that States fulfil their duty to protect against any human rights violations arising from compliance with unilateral sanctions and over-compliance.[63] All the above methods further guarantee a human rights-based approach by technology companies in preventing over-compliance and combating human rights violations caused by unilateral sanctions.

Sanctions, Business and Human Rights: Commentary, p. 110. https://www.ohchr.org/ sites/default/files/documents/issues/ucm/commentary-gpssbhr-2025.pdf

63 See *Guiding Principles on Sanctions, Business and Human Rights: Commentary, supra* note 62, at 113.

CHAPTER 9

Regional Integration and Trade Agreements in a Sanctions Environment

Tatsiana Mikhaliova[1]

Abstract

Regional integration plays a crucial role in shaping modern economic cooperation, yet it faces significant challenges in a world increasingly influenced by unilateral sanctions. With 373 regional trade agreements currently in force, according to the World Trade Organization, economic integration efforts often collide with restrictive measures that hinder trade, financial cooperation, and investment. This chapter explores how sanctions disrupt regional economic structures, weaken integration efforts, and challenge the fundamental objectives of regional organizations. The withdrawal of Burkina Faso, Mali, and Niger from ECOWAS following sanctions, the financial isolation of Iran within the SCO, and the challenges faced by EAEU member states due to economic restrictions highlight the detrimental effects of sanctions on regional economic stability.

Furthermore, the over-compliance of financial institutions exacerbates these issues, limiting the participation of sanctioned states in regional mechanisms. This chapter argues that regional organizations must adopt legal frameworks to counteract the negative impact of sanctions. The adoption of principles such as those outlined in the Guiding Principles on Sanctions, Business, and Human Rights can help regional organizations navigate the complexities of unilateral coercive measures while maintaining their commitment to economic cooperation and human rights protection.

---

1 Associate Professor of the Belarusian State University, Faculty of International Relations

Introduction

The modern political landscape of integration processes is influenced a lot by the sanctions environment for a range of general reasons. Firstly, regional integration is an instrument of a new strategy of economic cooperation and liberalized trade. According to the World Trade Organization (WTO), regional cooperation grows exponentially and today accounts for 373 regional trade agreements (RTAs), most of them forming a free trade legal framework for trade in goods.[2] Therefore, RTAs` functioning is inevitably interfered with by growing trade and financial sanctions because the objectives of RTAs and sanctions are colliding: to promote trade, and correspondingly to impede trade. Secondly, one of the main characteristics of regional integration is a tendency to form common markets—in goods, services, capital and investment, and labor.[3] An impact on one of the member States` economy will be definitely related to such common markets. Thirdly, countries that have already been involved in extensive trade are more likely to sign regional trade agreements; decreasing trade means decreasing chances of closer cooperation and integration in a region. Particular situations refer, as well, to special reasons for negative impacts, depending on the sphere and scope of sanctions in relation to spheres and scope of enhanced integration.

Internal sanctions within a region may cause a disruption of trade relations, and a termination of membership in a regional integration. In particular, in January 2024, Burkina Faso, Mali and Niger announced their withdrawal from the Economic Community of West African States (ECOWAS). A one-year notice is required according to art. 91 of the ECOWAS Treaty of 24.07.1993 (revised),[4] therefore they kept their membership until the end of January 2025.

While ECOWAS has been designed to promote regional economic integration, on several occasions it has adopted sanctions with reference to the changes of government in its member states. From

---

2 WTO notification data. In 1992, they counted 32. https://rtais.wto.org/UI/charts.aspx

3 C. Barnard, *The Substantive Law of the EU,* 3rd Edition (Oxford University Press, 2010), p. 674. T. N. Mikhaliova, *Legal Regulation of Regional Economic Integration: Challenges and Prospects* (in Russ.) (Minsk, 2016), p. 197.

4 Economic Community of West African States (ECOWAS): revised Treaty (accessed July 1, 2025). https://ecowas.int/wp-content/uploads/2022/08/Revised-treaty-1.pdf

2000 to 2023, several military coups took place in many African countries, including in six West African States, namely Mali (2020 and
2021); Guinea (2021); Burkina Faso (January and September 2022);
and Niger (2023).[5] A withdrawal request by three of these States, presented as a reaction to sanctions,[6] has been immediately referred to as
'Sahelexit.' These actions have had negative effects on most ECOWAS
member States, hindering economic cooperation and increasing trade
costs, thereby complicating regional integration efforts and increasing
humanitarian crises. Y.N. Adu and A.B. Mezyayev stress that "attempts
by ECOWAS to address political instability through normative means
can be encouraged," however, they "should be based on existing
community norms, humanity, and real facts in order to avoid dividing
the community."[7] As it can be assumed, this withdrawal presents a
complex set of challenges for the region for the long term. Regional
sanctions have not provided a solution to regional tension but rather
have multiplied it.

    In this context it is worth noting that the Guiding Principles on
Sanctions, Business and Human Rights[8] and the Commentary thereto[9]
refer to States and regional organizations, indicating regional obligations in compliance with universal human rights standards, including
economic rights, and the *jus cogens* character of fundamental principles of international law. "Fundamental principles of international law
are of peremptory character and as such enjoy priority over any other
norm of international and domestic law, including the law of regional
organizations, including the sanctions provisions of the Treaty of
the European Union, the Treaty on the Functioning of the EU, and

---

    5 Y. N. Adu, A. B. Mezyaev, "Political Turmoil in ECOWAS: "When Politics
Prevalis Over Law," *Journal of the Institute of African Studies* 67, no. 2 (2024): 102–
117.

    6 European Union, "'Sahelexit' in West Africa: Implications for ECOWAS and
the EU," *Think Tank*, April 26, 2024. https://www.europarl.europa.eu/thinktank/en/
document/EPRS_BRI(2024)762295

    7 Adu and Mezyaev, op cit.

    8 United Nations Human Rights Special Procedures, *Guiding Principles on
Sanctions, Business and Human Rights*, 2025. https://www.ohchr.org/sites/default/
files/documents/issues/ucm/events/international-conf-sanctions-business-hr/gps-
sanctions-business-hr.pdf

    9 United Nations Human Rights Special Procedures, *Guiding Principles on
Sanctions, Business and Human Rights: Commentary*, 2025, p. 17. https://www.ohchr.
org/sites/default/files/documents/issues/ucm/commentary-gpssbhr-2025.pdf

sanctions regulations and Directives." (Commentary to para.5) This approach proves an important axiom, which has been neglected in the recent sanctions marathon.

At the same time, regional integration helps to avoid coercion by making a region stronger. An example from FAO educational materials gives some interesting conclusions:

> Not only market power but also bargaining power can be increased by forming an RTA. To the extent that an RTA increases the joint bargaining power of its members, it may be more successful in obtaining tariff reductions from its trading partners (or avoiding the imposition of trade sanctions)... This assumes that the countries making up an RTA have a sufficient economic size relative to the third countries with which they must negotiate, and this requirement limits the relevance of this argument in the case of developing countries.[10]

In all cases proliferation of unilateral coercive measures and related over-compliance affects regional mechanisms of economic and financial cooperation and the implementation of integration agreements. In particular, the Organization of African, Caribbean and Pacific countries held a meeting on the situation around the COVID-19 pandemic in June 2020. Cuba is a member of the organization but was unable to participate in the forum via videoconference due to the denial of access to the U.S. Zoom platform, which was used to hold debates at the summit. It is quite reasonable that in its final statement, this organization demanded "an end to sanctions against its members, as they make it even more difficult to protect their countries and populations from the pandemic."[11]

Another example: despite Iran's full membership in the Shanghai Cooperation Organization (SCO), sanctions on banks and a number of restrictions prevent Iran's full participation in the work of the

---

10 Chapter 2. "Economic Aspects of Regional Integration." https://www.fao.org/4/y4793e/y4793e05.htm

11 "US blockade prevents Cuba from participating in a multilateral forum," *Granma*, June 5, 2020. https://www.granma.cu/hilo-directo/2020-06-05/hilo-05-06-2020-00-06-1

organization. Problems related to the SCO Interbank Consortium and trade restrictions exacerbate the situation.[12]

The tightening of the policy of economic coercion also affects the development of sub-regional ties, disrupting the structure of economic cooperation and hindering the conclusion of bilateral and multilateral agreements. Thus, some of the promising partners of the EAEU interrupted negotiations on cooperation and joined the sanctions regime (the Republic of Korea, New Zealand, Singapore).[13]

Taking into consideration the grave negative effects of sanctions on all the region and globally, SADC set October 25 as an Anti-Sanctions Day, with SADC calling for the immediate removal of all sanctions against Zimbabwe and pointing out the following regional impacts: mass emigration, dilapidation of critical rail and road networks traditionally utilized by neighboring countries, retardation of macroeconomic convergence within a community, reduction in capacities to take part in regional programs, and underperformance of agricultural sector posing threats to food and nutrition security.[14]

Assessing unilateral measures as coercion via a certain choice of mechanisms for the formation of foreign trade and foreign economic policy of States, it can be concluded that this is a violation of the principle of non-interference (art. 2(7) of the UN Charter).[15] As the International Court of Justice noted in the Nicaragua case (1986), interference becomes unlawful when it uses coercive methods against political, economic, social and cultural systems and in the formulation of a foreign policy that should be independent.[16]

---

12 M. Soltani, "The role of SOC in economic relations in the situation of sanctions with an accent to Russia and Iran" [in Russ., *Rol` ShOS v. elonomicheskih otnoshenijah v. uslovijah sanktsij s aktsentom na Rossiju I Iran*], in *International business [Mezhdunarodnyj biznes]* 6, no. 4 (2023): 59–72.

13 M. Krivoguz and D. Fesenko, "EAEU in world integration processes" [in Russ., *EAES v. mirovyh integratsionnayh protsessah*], 2024. https://www.imemo.ru/files/File/magazines/rossia_i_novay/2024_01/7-Krivogouz.pdf

14 *Statement by the Southern African Development Community Calling for the Immediate Removal of Sanctions Imposed on The Republic Of Zimbabwe*, June 2021. https://www.Sadc.Int/Sites/Default/Files/2021-06/Statement_By_Sadc_Calling_For_Immediate_Removal_Of_Sanctions_On_Of_Zimbabwe.pdf

15 *United Nations Charter* (full text). https://www.un.org/en/about-us/un-charter/full-text

16 International Court of Justice, *Military and Paramilitary Activities in and against Nicaragua* (*Nicaragua v. United States of America*), Judgment of 26 November 1984. https://www.icj-cij.org/case/70/judgments

In the context of an integration community, open domestic markets, a common customs and tariff policy, and a single non-tariff regulation, sanctions are aimed not only at worsening the situation in a particular state but also affecting the entire region. According to experts from the Higher School of Economics on the impact of sanctions on the EAEU, "the sanctions pressure on two out of five economies is aimed not only at their economic disarmament, but also at the erosion of socio-ideological integration platforms."[17]

Of course, there are a lot of factors influencing integration processes. While they are diverse, external unilateral restrictive measures disrupt regional trade, financial and even social ties, pose a threat to the development of close contacts, and are aimed at worsening the well-being of the population, thereby contradicting the main goal of an integration.

In addition, International Monetary Fund experts note that as a result of a new era of conflict in international relations, "a more discriminatory regional approach may be formed, designed to strengthen barriers to trade with non-member states of RTAs, rather than to reduce barriers to trade with member states of RTAs. This kind of regional approach will be less effective and ultimately weaker."[18]

Most regional integration organizations (RIOs), including the European Union and the Cooperation Council for the Arab States of the Gulf, do not have a single or uniform response mechanism.

The blocking statute of the EU was developed as a response to extraterritorial sanctions by the United States and other countries in order to avoid damage to European companies.[19] The main purpose

---

17 *Mechanisms of adoption of supranational decisions in the EAEU: contribution in strategic planning and anti-crisis management: Expert report to the XXIV Yasinskoj (April) international scientific conference on the problems of economy and society* [in Russ., *Mehanizmy promiatija nadnatsionalnyh reshenij v. EAES: vklad v. strategicheskoe planirovanie and antikrizisnoe upravlenie: ekspertnyj doklad k Yasinskoj (Aprelskoj) mezhdunarodnoj nauchnoj konferentsii po problemem razvitija ekonomiki i obschestva*], Moskva, 2023; D. V. Galushko, M. K. Glazatova, V. N. Zujev et al., ed. by T. A. Kolobashkina; National Research University, "High School of Economy," 2023, p. 234.

18 M. Ruta, *Discriminatory regional approach* [in Russ., *Rasprostranenije diskriminatsionnogo regionalnogo podhoda*]. https://www.imf.org/ru/Publications/fandd/issues/2023/06/the-rise-of-discriminatory-regionalism-michele-ruta

19 A. Abdullin and M. Keshner, "Application of coercive measures in the context of common foreign policy of the EU: conceptual approaches" [in Russ.,

of this act is to protect EU companies involved in international trade under EU law, to eliminate accusations of violating the sanctions regime imposed by third countries. The blocking statute of the EU allows European companies to compensate for losses from extraterritorial regulation.

It is often called a "paper tiger":[20] the main criticism of inefficiency comes down to issues of implementation, and the vague language. However, such an act has not only an economic protective purpose, but also a political and legal one, which consists in fixing the position of rejection (condemnation[21]) of the sanctions regime, which is extremely important both in the situational context and as the formation of a sustainable practice. Of course, it is important that the EU has the so-called "legal framework"—the norms of the Union's substantive and functional competence in terms of foreign policy, and not only foreign trade activities, which makes it possible to adopt such regulations relatively quickly and interpret the objectives of the statute quite broadly. Strict legal basis for an adoption of this Regulation refers exactly to provisions "engaging in international trade and/or the movement of capital and related commercial activities between the Community and third countries" (art. 1 para 1 of Regulation 2271/96).[22] Despite the serious threat of secondary sanctions and all the associated risks for commercial organizations, banks, etc., this act ensures the operation of the common market.

The example of cooperation between the Arab States of the Gulf is somewhat different, since sanctions on this organization were imposed from within the region (blockade of Qatar) and were due to the alleged violation of the so-called Riyadh agreements by Qatar.[23]

Primenenije ogranichitelnyh mer v. kontekste obshej vneshnej politiki ES], *ZhSE* no. 7 (2021): 72–83.

20 T. Ruys, "Secondary Sanctions: A Weapon Out of Control? The International Legality of, and European Responses to US Secondary Sanctions," T. Ruys, C. Ryngaert // *BYIL* (2020): 1–116.

21 O. Potemkina, *Blocking statute as an instrument of a sovereign trade policy* [in Russ., *Blokirujushij statut kak instrument suverennoj torgovoj politiki*]. http://www.instituteo-.feurope.ru/images/uploads/analitika/2018/an146.pdf

22 Consolidated text: Council Regulation (EC) No. 2271/96 of 22 November 1996 protecting against the effects of the extra-territorial application of legislation adopted by a third country, and actions based thereon or resulting therefrom. https://eur-lex.europa.eu/legal-content/EN/TXT/?uri=CELEX%3A01996R2271-20180807

23 A. Abusedra, "The Impact of Unilateral Sanctions on Regional Integration

Nevertheless, Qatar's experience in taking measures to remove sanctions pressure is valuable. Firstly, it is important that all decisions on the settlement were made within the region, maintaining its stability. Secondly, Qatar's active position in terms of protecting its interests in various universal jurisdictional bodies, among other things, led to a soft resolution of the conflict at the level of a regional declaration. Thirdly, it has "exposed" at the universal level, within the framework of specialized agencies and UN bodies, the connection between the complete rupture of economic and trade relations and the violation of the economic rights of private actors (pensions and insurance payments, property rights, etc.[24]).

In the Eurasian Economic Union, by the Disposition of the EEC Council dated March 17, 2022, No. 12, a list of measures to improve the stability of the economies of the Member States of the Eurasian Economic Union, including ensuring macroeconomic stability, was approved.[25] This list contains four groups of measures, although it is not exhaustive, and states can act in other directions. The first two groups relevant to customs regulation, domestic markets and cooperation are being implemented quite actively (16 and 29 measures, respectively). At the same time, measures related to international economic cooperation with third countries and financial markets contain several times fewer enforcement measures—that is, the first and fourth groups of measures, respectively, as evidenced by the EEC reporting materials as of April 1, 2024,[26] while the financial sector needs a more detailed and consistent response.

An economic union is based on a customs union and a common economic space. In the Treaty on the EAEU, these positions are laid down in Sections VI, IX and a number of annexes.[27] According to

Treaties with Special Reference to the Gulf Cooperation Council," in S.P. Subedi (Ed.), *Unilateral Sanctions in International Law* (Hart Publ., 2021), pp. 137–160.

24 Ibid.

25 *On the Implementation of Measures to Improve the Stability of the Economies of the Member States of the Eurasian Economic Union, Including Ensuring Macroeconomic Stability: Disposition of the EEC Council,* March 17, 2022, no. 12 (in Russ.). https://eec.eaeunion.org

26 *Key measures and decisions aimed at improving the stability of the economies of the EAEU Member States adopted by the EEC* (in Russ.). https://eec. eaeunion.org/upload/medialibrary/2ff/vlq1efd3vzogukhf6p0hjed08dprz0mj/Mery-EEK-01.04.2024.pdf

27 *Treaty on the Eurasian Economic Union.* https://docs.eaeunion.org/docs/en-us/0003610/itia_05062014

Russian scholars, the transformation of the global market manifested itself in changes in the formats of regional interaction and cooperation defined by the EAEU strategy.[28]

The key factor that made it possible to overcome the sanctions regime affecting trade within the Union was the promotion of import substitution, "zeroing of import customs duties in relation to more than 465 types of goods (more than 1300 codes of the Commodity Nomenclature of Foreign Economic Activity of the EAEU),"[29] and measures were also actively taken to organize duty-free import of goods by individuals for personal consumption.[30] Despite the difficulties, membership in the EAEU is one of the means to mitigate an external pressure.

Regional integration serves as a buffer that prevents isolation in the face of sanctions and the so-called "offshoring" of integration—business relocation, relocation of transport and logistics corridors from sanctioned countries to other member states.

The MGIMO expert points out that the difficulties associated with the movement of goods caused by sanctions, failures in the work of border control, cast doubt on the basic concept of a single customs space within the EAEU.[31] We cannot agree with the very approach that the movement of goods within the RIO is made dependent on the foreign policy of third countries. The objectives of the Treaty, found in Article 28 of the Treaty on the EAEU, lay out a number of special rules to provide for the functioning of the Union without exceptions and restrictions, and customs regulation refers to a single policy.

On the other hand, in the face of sanctions pressure, the issue of foreign trade is acute. In this area, we believe the EAEU possesses sufficient competence to develop joint measures to respond to threats to foreign trade. At the same time, not all possible measures have been

28 E. E. Bogdanova and V. A. Sapruka, *Impact of antiRussian sanctions on the state of integration processes in Eurasia* (in Russ.). https://elib.bsu.by/bitstream/123456789/322189/1/212-216.pdf

29 M. V. Myasnikovich and V. S. Kovalev, "New pages of integration in the Eurasian Economic Union" [in Russ., *Novyje stranitsy integratsii v. Evrazijskom ekonomicheskom sojuze*], in *Russia in a Global Politics* 21, no. 2 (2023): 207–218.

30 Bogdanova and Sapruka, op cit.

31 M. Soltani, "The role of SOC in economic relations in the situation of sanctions with an accent to Russia and Iran" [in Russ., *Rol` ShOS v. elonomicheskih otnoshenijah v. uslovijah sanktsij s aktsentom na Rossiju I Iran*], in *International Business* [*Mexhdunarodnyj biznes*] 6, no. 4 (2023): 59–72.

developed yet. In particular, it is necessary to develop a supranational mechanism to support the export of products jointly produced in the EAEU to third countries. This mechanism may include regulatory and institutional measures (with the exception of direct subsidy measures and similar measures regulated by WTO law). The former include the powers of the EAEU under art. 33 of the Treaty on the EAEU.

Thus, paragraph 1 of this article prescribes that the Union's foreign trade policy is aimed, among other things, at "promoting sustainable economic development of the Member States, diversification of economies, innovative development, increasing the volume and improving the structure of trade and investment." In accordance with para 2 art. 33 of the Treaty on the EAEU, the justification for the measures of foreign trade policy may also be the protection of the rights and legitimate interests of participants in foreign trade activities of the Member States, producers and consumers of services and a number of other so-called "legal frameworks," which can be the basis, if not of complex blocking statutes, then at least of trade countermeasures. Article 33 of the Treaty on the EAEU includes innovative development, increasing the volume of trade and investment. Thus, Article 33 of the Treaty on the EAEU provides a fairly wide range of powers without specifying measures (this, accordingly, is the choice of the organization) due to the specified goals and principles. Paragraph 3 of this article indicates the mechanisms for the implementation of such measures—joint and autonomous.[32] We believe that the potential of art. 33 of the Treaty has not yet been sufficiently realized in the framework of countering the impact of sanctions. The system of anti-sanctions legislation can represent interrelated norms of various branches of substantive and procedural law from the point of view of the mechanism of legal regulation and law enforcement, which are semantically combined in solving the problems of forming a legal mechanism for protection against economic sanctions, in combination with coordination with the legislation of the EAEU, for example, in terms of non-tariff regulation and customs policy.[33]

---

32 *Treaty on the Eurasian Economic Union.* https://docs.eaeunion.org/docs/en-us/0003610/itia_05062014

33 A. A. Kartskhiya, "Legal regime of public and private legal regulation," [in Russ., *Pravovoy rezhim publichnogo i chastnopravovogo regulirovaniya*], *Monitoring of Law Application* 43, no. 2 (2022): 2–9.

The tightening of sanctions has had a particularly strong impact on the financial sector. The formation of a common payment space has suffered significantly in 2024 not only due to the sanctions themselves, but also due to the over-compliance of banks. In these conditions, the general task is to reduce dependence on settlements through Western financial institutions. The mechanisms for this can be economic and legal—for example, the Eurasian Economic Commission proposed to create a universal payment system for the EAEU and BRICS member countries, which will unite the national payment systems of China (Union Pay), Brazil (Elo), India (RuPay), as well as the EAEU member states (Mir and Belkart systems).[34]

Also, the expert community discusses regulatory mechanisms for a long-term response: the EAEU acts indicate that the integration of financial markets should be carried out taking into account the principles of the Basel Committee on Banking Supervision, the International Organization for Insurance Supervision, the International Securities Organization, the Organization for Economic Cooperation and Development, and this "[t]he requires a prompt reassessment of the expediency of following all these standards."[35] Obviously, it is necessary to improve the mechanisms for the implementation of payments and mutual settlements, to give business entities a stable analogue of dollar settlement, and perhaps the most important thing is to ensure the freedom of individual settlements, so that citizens can feel the benefits of integration in relation to payment and financial transactions.

The EAEU has created a legal framework for these purposes. The Treaty on the EAEU of May 29, 2014, regulates a coordinated

---

34 "The EAEU and BRICS will work out the creation of a universal payment system and independent international institutions" (in Russ.). https://eec.eaeunion. org/news/eaes-i-briks-prorabotayut-sozdanie-universalnoy-platezhnoy-sistemy-i-nezavisimykh-mezhdunarodnykh-in/

35 *Mechanisms of adoption of supranational decisions in the EAEU: contribution in strategic planning and anti-crisis management: expert report to the XXIV Yasinskoj (April) international scientific conference on the problems of economy and society* [in Russ., *Mehanizmy promiatija nadnatsionalnyh reshenij v. EAES: vklad v. strategicheskoe planirovanie and antikrizisnoe upravlenije: ekspertnyj doklad k Yasinskoj (Aprelskoj) mezhdunarodnoj nauchnoj konferentsii po problemem razvitija ekonomiki i obschestva*], Moskva, 2023; D. V. Galushko, M. K. Glazatova, V. N. Zuje, et al., ed. by T. A. Kolobashkina (Higher School of Economics, 2023), pp. 27, 226–227.

policy in the field of financial markets, and defines seven goals of such a policy. Appendix 17 to the Treaty (Protocol on Financial Services) provides definitions, as well as the basis and restrictions for the application of national treatment and most-favored-nation treatment in mutual supplies of financial services. In 2014, the Agreement on the Exchange of Information, including Confidential Information, in the Financial Sector was signed in order to create conditions in the financial markets to ensure the free movement of capital.

In accordance with the Main Directions of Economic Development of the European Economic Union, approved by the Decision of the Supreme Eurasian Economic Council No. 28 of October 16, 2015, such areas include, among other things, cooperation of the Member States in the monetary and financial sphere, which is carried out through "coordinated regulation in the field of financial markets," "the implementation of a coordinated monetary policy," "the formation of an integrated exchange space, expanding mutual access of financial market participants (including ensuring direct access of investors and professional participants to the financial markets of the Member States)," "improving the regulation of the securities market infra-structure (including accounting for rights to securities)," "conducting settlements in the financial market of the Member States," etc.[36]

The Concept for the Formation of the Common Financial Market of the EAEU was approved by the Decision of the Supreme Council of the EAEU No. 20 dated October 1, 2019.[37] The main directions of this formation were the following: regulation of the common financial market; harmonization of the legislation of the Member States; ensuring mutual access of participants in the financial markets of the member states; supervision of the activities of participants in the common financial market; development of the infrastructure of the common financial market; formation of a common exchange space; protection of the rights and interests of investors and consumers; ensuring cyber-security; and development of a common payment space.[38]

---

36 The Main Directions of Economic Development of the European Economic Union, approved by the European Economic Union, by Decision of the Supreme Eurasian Economic Council of October 16, 2015, No. 28. https://eec.eaeunion.org/upload/medialibrary/923/broshyura_ONER-_final-05.05.2016_.pdf

37 *O Kontseptsii formirovanija obshego finansovogo rynka* (accessed 22.02.2025). https://docs.eaeunion.org/documents/348/4690/

38 The Concept of the Formation of the Common Financial Market of the

In accordance with clause 1.4 of the Strategic Directions for the Development of the Eurasian Economic Integration until 2025, approved by the Decision of the Supreme Council of the EAEU No. 12 dated December 11, 2020,[39] as well as with the Action Plan for the implementation of the Strategic Directions for the Development of the Eurasian Economic Integration until 2025, approved by the Disposition order of the EEC Council dated April 5, 2021, No. 4, the formation of a common financial market includes the following areas: development of an international agreement on a standardized license, harmonization of the legislation of the Member States, development of an international agreement on a special body for the regulation of the common financial market, monitoring of the use of national currencies for mutual settlements and the formation of proposals for expanding their use, development of a common payment space, conclusion of an international agreement on the exchange of information included in credit histories (concluded in 2021), conclusion of an international agreement on the admission of brokers and dealers of one member state to participate in organized trading of exchanges (trade organizers) of other member states, as well as an international agreement on mutual admission to the placement and circulation of securities in organized trading in the member states.[40]

A brief overview of the adopted and planned legal acts in this area demonstrates that the legal framework is still not fully adapted to the conditions of the sanctions environment. It is extremely important for financial actors and business entities participating in cross-border transactions to have an act of a legal nature that justifies their obligation to act on a non-discriminatory basis—revealing for States their obligation to loyal cooperation in the face of sanctions. The powers laid down by the Treaty on the EAEU make it possible to adopt recommendations at the Commission's level on the avoidance

---

EAEU, approved by the Ministry of Finance of the Russian Federation, by Decision of the Supreme Council of the EAEU dated October 1, 2019, No. 20. https://eec.eaeunion.org/upload/medialibrary/ddd/Kontseptsiya-OFR.pdf

39 Action Plan for the Implementation of the Strategic Directions for the Development of Eurasian Economic Integration until 2025, approved by the Ministry of Foreign Affairs of the Russian Federation, by the Disposition of the EEC Council dated April 5, 2021, No. 4 (in Russ.). https://eec.eaeunion.org/upload/medialibrary/820/Strategy_2025.pdf

40 Ibid.

of over-compliance in the organization of financial activities (as well as in the work of business entities in general).

In order to neutralize, minimize or prevent such an effect, it is important to determine the level, criteria, and forms of negative influence. We believe that it is necessary to develop a mechanism for assessing the impact of sanctions on regional trade and economic development, with a clear methodology for such an assessment.

From the point of view of ensuring interbank cooperation in countering sanctions pressure, we will cite the example of the Shanghai Cooperation Organization (SCO). The SCO, as a key player in the field of regional security, pays increasing attention to economic cooperation between the member states.[41] One of the important aspects of such economic cooperation is the SCO Interbank Consortium. The main goal of the Interbank Consortium, established as a nominal union of leading banks of the SCO countries, is to stimulate financial activities and attract investment for economic development. Despite its initial nominal importance, the Interbank Consortium has become an essential element of the SCO's economic landscape.[42]

While the Consortium has its advantages, such as establishing strong links between leading commercial banks and facilitating access to financial resources, its disadvantages, including its limited impact on economic development and the challenges posed by the current sanctions, call into question its effectiveness. The SCO Interbank Consortium has the potential to play a role in ensuring the resilience of the regional economy to external sanctions. However, according to experts, its success depends on solving internal problems and creating a more balanced and transparent structure of financial cooperation within the SCO.[43]

---

41 Zh. Yuelong, "Shanghai Cooperation Organization and Economic Security in Belarus and China," in Zh. Yuelong, *Belarus-China: Shaping innovation technological cooperation* (in Russ.) (Minsk: BNTU, 2023), pp. 37–40.

42 Olga G. Lebedinskaya, Svetlana G. Babich, Mikhail V. Karmanov, and Sergey S. Shituev. "The SCO Financial Mechanisms: Risk Analysis and Development Prospects," in *Proceedings of the External Challenges and Risks for Russia in the Context of the World Community's Transition to Polycentrism: Economics, Finance and Business (ICEFB 2019)* (Atlantis Press, 2019). https://www.atlantis-press.com/proceedings/icefb-19/125925157_

43 M. Soltani, "The role of SOC in economic relations in the situation of sanctions with an accent to Russia and Iran" [in Russ., *Rol` ShOS v. elonomicheskih otnoshenijah v. uslovijah sanktsij s aktsentom na Rossiju I Iran*], in *International*

As E. Arapova stresses, "international sanctions affect international trade significantly. They lead to a decrease in the trade flow between the sender and the target; when the political relationship is strained, it can negatively affect trade flows. Moreover, the threat of economic sanctions may be even more important than the actual imposition. The anticipation effect may bring controversial results for both the sender–target interactions and the target's relations with the third countries."[44] She points out an increase in credit risks, trade delay, etc.; however, "the threat of sanctions can act as an incentive for potential targets to stockpile against future negative effects of sanctions and result in short-term positive effects."[45]

Another important issue with regard to RIOs and sanctions concerns the limits and scope of their involvement in sanctions programs. As far as the RIO possesses an exclusive or a shared competence transferred by member-states in a range of trade and economic issues it becomes responsible for acts in this regard, and coercive measures are not excluded. As the Guiding Principles stressed and the Commentary explained, regional organizations, as subjects of international law, are under the obligation to act in full respect of their international obligations: "Whatever the scope of its competence, a regional organization is bound by universally recognized human rights, and when it takes measures which are binding for its members, it is under an obligation to act in conformity with international human rights standards" (Commentary to para. 4).

Conclusion

One can conclude there is a general negative distortion in relation to regional ties and stable economic, commercial, and social relations. In this context the decisions made within the framework of regional associations and interregional cooperation are becoming important. A jointly developed response and the consolidation of the legal position indicates the non-recognition of the practice of sanctions not

Business [*Mexhdunarodnyj biznes*] 6, no. 4 (2023): 59–72.

44 E. Arapova, "The Sanctions Dilemma: How Sanctions Against Russia Affect Regional Integration within the EAEU States," *Strategic Analysis* 47, no. 3 (2023): 267–280. https://www.tandfonline.com/doi/full/10.1080/09700161.2023.2196257

45 Ibid.

based on international law and leading to expanded approaches to extraterritoriality.

The understanding of the complex negative impact on all levels of the economy and stable social ties, the presence of already de jure designated legal positions within the framework of regional associations should find consolidated support from all international actors. Those regions where the practice of sanctions pressure is still applicable face serious disruptions in connections, which result in fundamental changes in the regional system of trade, economy and security. The regions that experienced the practice of sanctions and concluded on its ineffectiveness and threatening character were very effective in reaching consensus by regional peaceful means and restoring regional interstate and private connections.

An anti-sanctions agenda may be recommended for adoption within regional organizations of economic integration as far as sanctions are a serious deterrent to a stable economic development of regions and the welfare of their population. RIOs, in their effort to create and promote a strong economic community, shall act in conformity with those international universal standards, which provide for integrity of economic cooperation and universally recognized fundamental principles. The Guiding Principles can be guiding in this regard for RIOs in their attempts to form a correct and legitimate answer to sanctions.

PART III

....

HUMANITARIAN IMPACT OF UNILATERAL SANCTIONS AND BUSINESS OVER-COMPLIANCE

Unilateral Coercive Measures, the Private Sector and the Sustainable Development Goals

Gilles-Emmanuel Jacquet[1]

Abstract

Since the end of the Cold War, States have adopted numerous unilateral coercive measures in order to respond to violent crises (like in the case of Iraq, Syria and Libya) and as a way to avoid the use of force. This practice is debated with regard to its effects on the human rights of the civilian populations of targeted countries. While international or regional organizations and States adopt, implement and enforce unilateral coercive measures respectively, the private sector plays an important role in ensuring their effectiveness through compliance, as well as through what has been recently identified as "over-compliance," all having also negative effects on the human rights of targeted populations and contradicting at the same time the Sustainable Development Goals. Legal cases related to compliance or over-compliance with sanctions from companies and their negative effects on human rights of targeted populations were rare in the past but their number is currently growing. At the international level, the main legal corpus related to the role of the private sector with regard to human rights is mainly constituted by soft law (like OECD Guidelines) and it doesn't mention or address at all the issues related to unilateral coercive measures, compliance and over-compliance, as well as their effects on Human Rights.

---

1 Gilles-Emmanuel Jacquet holds a Licence in Political Science from the University of Geneva and a D.E.A. in European Studies from the European institute of the University of Geneva.

Introduction

Since the end of the Cold War, unilateral coercive measures are increasingly used by States in order to intervene in crises without any use of direct force (as it was the case for Iraq, Syria and Libya among many others). The use of UCMs is questioned by international lawyers and experts as it affects negatively the human rights of the civilian populations of targeted countries.

While international or regional organizations and states adopt, implement and enforce multilateral/autonomous sanctions and unilateral coercive measures respectively, the private sector plays an important role in their effectiveness through compliance and what has been recently identified as "over-compliance,"[2] with both also having negative effects on the human rights of targeted populations and contradicting at the same time the Sustainable Development Goals.[3] Even though the Sustainable Development Goals are of a non-binding nature, all the 193 UN member states have pledged to implement them but only 41 UN member states have actually registered their commitments.[4]

Traditionally legal cases against companies are related to criminal acts and serious violations of human rights, all prosecuted under national jurisdictions. The number of cases related to compliance or over-compliance with UCMs from companies and its negative effects on the human rights of targeted populations are growing. Cases are currently being opened in Switzerland and in EU countries by Russian citizens following the freeze or seizure of their properties or bank

---

2 Alena Douhan, Monitoring and assessment of the impact of unilateral sanctions and over-compliance on human rights – Report of the Special Rapporteur on the negative impact of unilateral coercive measures on the enjoyment of human rights, Alena F. Douhan, 57th session of the Human Rights Council, A/HRC/57/55, 09/08/2024.   https://www.ohchr.org/en/documents/thematic-reports/ahrc5755-monitoring-and-assessment-impact-unilateral-sanctions-and

3 United Nations, The 17 Goals, Sustainable Development, Department of Economic and Social Affairs. https://sdgs.un.org/goals

4 United Nations Climate Change, UN Member States Agree Sustainable Development Goals, UNFCCC, 03/08/2015. https://unfccc.int/news/un-member-states-agree-sustainable-development-goals;   United   Nations   Sustainable Development Group, Pact for the Future: World leaders pledge action for peace, sustainable development, 23/09/2024. https://unsdg.un.org/latest/stories/pact-future-world-leaders-pledge-action-peace-sustainable-development;   United   Nations, National Commitments to SDG Transformation, Department of Economic and Social Affairs. https://sdgs.un.org/SDGSummitActions/National

accounts. Similar legal actions were also launched in the USA by Iranian citizens against U.S. banks.[5] At the international level, the main legal *corpus* related to the role of the private sector with regard to human rights is primarily constituted by soft law, like the OECD Guidelines,[6] the UN Guiding Principles on Business and Human Rights,[7] and the more recent UN Guiding Principles on Sanctions, Business and Human Rights.[8] Hard law doesn't mention or address at all the issues related to unilateral coercive measures, compliance and over-compliance, as well as their effects on human rights.

The goal of this contribution is to address the relationship between the private sector / companies and unilateral coercive measures, and how—through compliance and over-compliance—they impact negatively the human rights of affected populations. This chapter analyzes the role of companies in the enforcement of unilateral coercive measures and demonstrates how compliance and over-compliance affect human rights and contradict the Sustainable Development Goals. This article will also explore the relevant legal frameworks related to the role of companies in the implementation of unilateral coercive measures and its effect on the human rights of the civilian populations of targeted countries.

Unilateral Coercive Measures: Definition and Legal Considerations on Their Impact

Since the end of the Cold War, international organizations and regional organizations have adopted numerous multilateral or autonomous sanctions in order to respond to crises (like in the case of Iraq,

---

5 NIAC Action, Bank of America is being sued for discriminating against Iranians, 05/03/2024. https://www.niacouncil.org/news_publications/bank-of-america-sued-for-discrimination-against-iranians/ ; Iran International, Bank Of America Dismisses Lawsuit Alleging Discrimination Against Iranians, 28/03/2024: https://www.iranintl.com/en/202403287604

6 OECD, OECD Guidelines for Multinational Enterprises on Responsible Business Conduct. https://mneguidelines.oecd.org/mneguidelines/

7 United Nations, Guiding Principles on Business and Human Rights, Office of the High Commissionner for Human Rights, 2011. https://www.ohchr.org/documents/publications/guidingprinciplesbusinesshr_en.pdf

8 United Nations, Guiding Principles on Sanctions, Business and Human Rights, *Office of the High Commissionner for Human Rights*, 25/02/2025. https://www.ohchr.org/sites/default/files/documents/issues/ucm/events/international-conf-sanctions-business-hr/gps-sanctions-business-hr.pdf

Syria and Libya) and as a way to avoid the use of force. This last point is debated with regard to the effects of multilateral or autonomous sanctions on the human rights of the civilian populations of targeted countries. In particular, in August 1999, UNICEF reported that UN sanctions had severely affected Iraqi children: malnutrition, related diseases and child mortality had increased significantly under the Oil-for-Food Programme, and available treatments were lacking.[9] Various experts, scholars, reporters, NGOs and former UN officials stated that UN sanctions had caused the additional death of 500,000 Iraqi children[10] but this figure was contested by a group of British researchers from the London School of Economics and the Royal Statistical Society, who argued the UNICEF survey was a fraud, based on rigged statistics instrumentalized by the Iraqi government, including Saddam Hussein himself.[11] In this case, it is useful to remember that Madeleine Albright had acknowledged, during an interview on *Sixty Minutes* in May 1996, that half a million Iraqi children had died as a result of the UN sanctions and she even replied that it was "A hard choice, but the price, we think the price is worth it."[12]

9 ReliefWeb, UNICEF Report: Sanctions Severely Affect Iraqi Children, 05/08/1999. https://reliefweb.int/report/iraq/unicef-report-sanctions-severely-affect-iraqi-children

10 Mohamed M. Ali and Iqbal H. 'Shah, "Sanctions and childhood mortality in Iraq," *The Lancet*, Volume 355, Issue 9218, 27/05/2000, pp. 1851–1857; World Health Organization, Technical discussion – Health under difficult circumstances: The impact of war, disasters and sanctions on the health of populations, Regional Committee for the Eastern Mediterranean, 49th session, EM/RC49/Tech.Disc.1, July 2002; Mohamed M. Ali, John Blacker and Gareth Jones, "Annual mortality rates and excess deaths of children under five in Iraq, 1991–98," *Population Studies*, 57(2), April 2003; Hans C. von Sponeck, *A Different Kind of War: The UN Sanctions Regime in Iraq*, Berghahn Books, 2006; Geneva International Centre for Justice, Razing the Truth About Sanctions Against Iraq. https://www.gicj.org/positions-opinons/gicj-positions-and-opinions/1188-razing-the-truth-about-sanctions-against-iraq; Ahmed Twaij, "Let's remember Madeleine Albright for who she really was," *Aljazeera*, 25/03/2022. https://www.aljazeera.com/opinions/2022/3/25/lets-remember-madeleine-albright-as-who-she-really-was

11 Michael Spagat, "Truth and death in Iraq under sanctions," *Significance*, Volume 7, Issue 3, September 2010, pp. 116–120; Tim Dyson and Valeria Cetorelli, *Changing views on child mortality and economic sanctions in Iraq: a history of lies, damned lies and statistics*, BMJ Global Health, 2(2), 24/07/2017. https://www.ncbi.nlm.nih.gov/pmc/articles/PMC5717930/

12 Jon Jackson, "Watch: Madeleine Albright Saying Iraqi Kids' Deaths 'Worth It' Resurfaces," *Newsweek*, 23/03/2022. https://www.newsweek.com/watch-madeleine-albright-saying-iraqi-kids-deaths-worth-it-resurfaces-1691193

Countries like the United States of America frequently use similar means known as unilateral coercive measures (UCMs), often called unilateral sanctions. Their legality can be debated but their negative effects on the human rights of the civilian populations are increasingly evidenced by the literature and reports from scholars, independent researchers or experts, reporters, UN experts,[13] the UN General Assembly, the UN Human Rights Council, the UN Special Rapporteur on Unilateral Coercive Measures,[14] and the Independent Expert on Human Rights and International Solidarity.[15] Their reports

---

13 Like Alfred de Zayas, Volker Türk, Mihir Kanade, Elena Gentili, Amir Saed Vakil, Jeffrey Sachs and Alena Douhan, the United Nations Special Rapporteur on the Impact of Unilateral Coercive Measures on the Enjoyment of Human Rights. Alena F. Douhan, " Unilateral Coercive Measures: Effects and Legality Issues," Symposium on Third World Approaches to International Law & Economic Sanctions, *Yale Journal of International Law*, 20/06/2023. https://www.yjil.yale.edu/unilateral-coercive-measures-effects-and-legality-issues/; Geneva International Centre for Justice, *HRC54: Unilateral Coercive Measures- A Risk to the SDGs and the Right to Development*, Biennial panel discussion on unilateral coercive measures and human rights (HRC res. 27/21 and 52/13), 14/09/2023. https://www.gicj.org/conferences-meetings/human-rights-council-sessions/discussion-reports/3619-hrc54-unilateral-coercive-measures-a-risk-to-the-sdgs-and-the-right-to-development; United Nations Information Service, High Commissioner for Human Rights to the Human Rights Council: Sanctions that Threaten People's Lives and Health Need to be Halted, 14/09/2023. https://www.ungeneva.org/en/news-media/meeting-summary/2023/09/le-conseil-des-droits-de-lhomme-se-penche-sur-limpact-quont-sur

14 Idriss Jazairy, Negative impact of unilateral coercive measures on the enjoyment of human rights: report of the Special Rapporteur on the Negative Impact of Unilateral Coercive Measures on the Enjoyment of Human Rights, Report of the Special Rapporteur on the negative impact of unilateral coercive measures on the enjoyment of human rights Idriss Jazairy, 42nd session of the Human Rights Council, A/HRC/42/46, 05/07/2019. https://digitallibrary.un.org/record/3823888/files/A_HRC_42_46-EN.pdf?ln=fr ; Alena Douhan, Monitoring and assessment of the impact of unilateral sanctions and over-compliance on human rights – Report of the Special Rapporteur on the negative impact of unilateral coercive measures on the enjoyment of human rights, Alena F. Douhan, 57th session of the Human Rights Council, A/HRC/57/55, 09/08/2024. https://www.ohchr.org/en/documents/thematic-reports/ahrc5755-monitoring-and-assessment-impact-unilateral-sanctions-and; see as well the other thematic reports available at : https://www.ohchr.org/en/special-procedures/sr-unilateral-coercive-measures/annual-thematic-reports

15 Virginia Dandan, Report of the Independent Expert on human rights and international solidarity, 72nd session of the United Nations General Assembly, A/72/171, 19/07/2017, p. 10. https://www.ohchr.org/en/documents/thematic-reports/a72171-report-independent-expert-human-rights-and-international; Obiora Chinedu Okafor, International solidarity in aid of the realization of human rights during and after the coronavirus disease (COVID-19) pandemic, Report of the Independent Expert on human rights and international solidarity, Obiora Chinedu Okafor, 47th

highlighted how unilateral coercive measures violate the UN Charter, customary international law, and fundamental principles and universal norms such as the sovereign equality of States, the right to self-determination, the prohibition of the use of force, the principle of non-intervention, as well as several treaties that codify the rights to life, food, water, shelter, education, development, privacy and property.[16]

More specifically, unilateral coercive measures contravene various resolutions of the UN General Assembly that affirm the principles of sovereignty, non-interference, friendly relations, free trade, and various political, social or economic rights, such as UN General Assembly resolution 2131 (XX) of 1965,[17] the International Covenant on Civil and Political Rights—UN General Assembly resolution 2200 A (XXI) of 1966,[18] the International Covenant on Economic, Social and Cultural Rights—UN General Assembly resolution 2200 A (XXI) of 1966,[19] UN General Assembly resolution 2625 (XXV) of 1970,[20] UN General Assembly resolution 3281 (XXIX) of 1974[21] and the World Summit Outcome of 2005.[22]

---

session of the Human Rights Council, A/HRC/47/31, 13/04/2021, pp. 15 and 18. https://docs.un.org/en/A/HRC/47/31

16 Alfred de Zayas, *Unilateral Coercive Measures in the Light of International Law, International Conference on Responsibility of States* hosted by the International Progress Organization, Vienna, 20–22/09/2023.

17 General Assembly of the United Nations, Declaration on the Inadmissibility of Intervention in the Domestic Affairs of States and the Protection of Their Independence and Sovereignty, UN General Assembly resolution 2131 (XX), 1965. https://www.refworld.org/legal/resolution/unga/1965/en/7120

18 General Assembly of the United Nations, International Covenant on Civil and Political Rights, UN General Assembly resolution 2200 A (XXI), 16/12/1966. https://www.ohchr.org/en/instruments-mechanisms/instruments/international-covenant-civil-and-political-rights

19 General Assembly of the United Nations, International Covenant on Economic, Social and Cultural Rights, UN General Assembly resolution 2200 A (XXI), 16/12/1966. https://www.ohchr.org/en/instruments-mechanisms/instruments/international-covenant-economic-social-and-cultural-rights

20 General Assembly of the United Nations, Declaration on Principles of International Law concerning Friendly Relations and Co-operation among States in accordance with the Charter of the United Nations, UN General Assembly resolution 2625 (XXV), 1970. http://un-documents.net/a25r2625.htm

21 General Assembly of the United Nations, Charter of Economic Rights and Duties of States, UN General Assembly resolution 3281 (XXIX), 1974. https://www.legal-tools.org/doc/3bf094/

22 General Assembly of the United Nations, Resolution adopted by the General Assembly on 16 September 2005, 60/1, 2005 World Summit Outcome, 24/10/2005.

The former United Nations Independent Expert on the Promotion of a Democratic and Equitable International Order, Alfred de Zayas, goes further in questioning the legality of unilateral coercive measures and considers that UCMs, due to the Human Rights violations they cause, are a form of collective punishment violating the Hague Conventions of 1899 and 1907, and the Geneva Conventions of 1949. He adds that "The deliberate economic and moral harm caused by UCMs raise many issues of State responsibility, both civil and penal. Indeed, they constitute prohibited 'use of force' within the meaning of article 2, paragraph 4, of the UN Charter, and because of their demonstrable 'intent,' they can be seen as 'crimes against humanity' for purposes of article 7 of the Rome Statute."[23]

It is believed here that these coercive measures adopted by States, as well as their negative effects on human rights are also in contradiction with most of the Sustainable Development Goals, that will be analysed in the last part of this chapter.

The Role of the Private Sector in the Implementation of UCMs and in Their Impact on the Human Rights of the Populations of Targeted Countries

Unilateral coercive measures are issued and implemented by a State but they require the compliance of other states in order to be effective with regard to their expected effects. The private sector plays an important role in the effectiveness of unilateral coercive measures through compliance (or enforcement) and its role in international trade (e.g. in global supply chains or for international financial transactions).

The effectiveness of unilateral coercive measures is ensured by compliance and in the light of the impact of multilateral sanctions on the Iraqi civilian population, it can be reasonably considered—by analogy—that compliance with UCMs can also lead to serious and massive violations of the human rights of the civilian populations of targeted countries. The effectiveness and the impact of UCMs do not depend for their implementation and their monitoring only on States

https://www.un.org/en/development/desa/population/migration/generalassembly/docs/globalcompact/A_RES_60_1.pdf

23 Alfred de Zayas, Unilateral Coercive Measures in the Light of International Law, International Conference on Responsibility of States hosted by the International Progress Organization, Vienna, 20–22/09/2023.

but also on the private sector and compliance by companies. Thus, States are not the only actors responsible for the violations of the human rights of the populations of targeted countries. As companies play a role in this phenomenon, they could be also held accountable for human rights violations caused by their compliance.

The negative effects on the human rights of civilian populations are also aggravated by another phenomenon known as "over-compliance," defined by UN Special Rapporteur Alena Douhan as "self-imposed restraints beyond the restrictions mandated by sanctions, applied as a part of the de-risking process (to minimize the potential for inadvertent violations or to avoid reputational or other business risks), and therefore, the widening of the scope of targets to include non-sanctioned individuals and entities, and sometimes entire populations."[24] Over-compliance by companies can be explained by various factors such as

> the multiple, complex, unclear, fast-evolving and overlapping sanctions regimes; the broad, unclear and confusing terminology and wording of sanctions regulations, which bring about uncertainty concerning their scope of application, the types of prohibited conduct and the negative spillover effects on critical sectors of the targeted State; the existence of secondary sanctions, and criminal and civil penalties provisions for circumvention of sanctions regimes; direct threats with sanctions; maximum pressure campaigns; uncertainty around the scope of humanitarian carve-outs; and the complex licensing procedures, even for the delivery of humanitarian goods, along with the burden

---

24 Alena Douhan, Report of the Special Rapporteur on the negative impact of unilateral coercive measures on the enjoyment of human rights, 78th session of the General Assembly of the United Nations, A/78/196, 04/09/2023, p. 4. https://digitallibrary.un.org/record/4023204/files/A_78_196-EN.pdf?ln=fr; Alena Douhan, Secondary sanctions, civil and criminal penalties for circumvention of sanctions regimes and over-compliance with sanctions, Report of the Special Rapporteur on the negative impact of unilateral coercive measures on the enjoyment of human rights A. Douhan, 51st session of the Human Rights Council, A/HRC/51/33, 15/07/2022, p. 5. https://www.ohchr.org/en/documents/thematic-reports/ahrc5133-secondary-sanctions-civil-and-criminal-penalties-circumvention

of proof of the humanitarian nature of the activities imposed on humanitarian actors.[25]

Waivers can be issued for humanitarian reasons or if companies can prove that the goods they deliver (imports or exports) are not dual-use items (their use is only for peaceful and civilian purposes).[26] However, the complex, bureaucratic and technical aspects of these procedures discourage many companies from doing business with sanctioned countries and it contradicts freedom of trade, as UCMs violate the principle of trade without discrimination. Moreover, countries issuing or complying with UCMs, while being members of the World Trade Organization, are in contradiction with the principles of this organization, with the General Agreement on Tariffs and Trade,[27] the Marrakesh Agreement,[28] the Agreement on Technical Barriers to Trade,[29] the Agreement on Trade-Related Investment Measures,[30] the General Agreement on Trade in Services[31] and the WTO agreements.[32]

Over-compliance is a growing practice and with regard to its impact on the Human Rights of affected populations, U.N. Special Rapporteur Alena Douhan argues that it must "be recognized as a significant new danger to international law and human rights."[33] She adds

---

25 Alena Douhan, Report of the Special Rapporteur on the negative impact of unilateral coercive measures on the enjoyment of human rights, 78th session of the General Assembly of the United Nations, A/78/196, 04/09/2023, p. 4. https:// digitallibrary.un.org/record/4023204/files/A_78_196-EN.pdf?ln=fr

26 It should be noted that sanctions are also imposed on various goods which cannot be considered as dual-use items.

27 World Trade Organization, General Agreement on Tariffs and Trade (GATT), 1994. https://www.wto.org/english/res_e/publications_e/ai17_e/gatt1994_e.htm

28 World Trade Organization, Marrakesh Agreement Establishing the World Trade Organization, 1995. https://www.wto.org/english/docs_e/legal_e/marag_e.htm

29 World Trade Organization, Agreement on Technical Barriers to Trade, 1995. https://www.wto.org/english/docs_e/legal_e/tbt_e.htm

30 World Trade Organization, Agreement on Trade-Related Investment Measures, 1995. https://www.wto.org/english/docs_e/legal_e/trims_e.htm

31 World Trade Organization, General Agreement on Trade in Services, 1995. https://www.wto.org/english/docs_e/legal_e/gats_e.htm

32 World Trade Organization, WTO legal texts. https://www.wto.org/english/ docs_e/legal_e/legal_e.htm

33 Alena Douhan, Secondary sanctions, civil and criminal penalties for circumvention of sanctions regimes and over-compliance with sanctions, Report of the Special Rapporteur on the negative impact of unilateral coercive measures on the enjoyment of human rights A. Douhan, 51st session of the Human Rights Council, A/

that "the provision of authorized humanitarian goods and services to sanctioned States often involves an extensive chain of participants in multiple countries, and that over-compliance by any of them, including manufacturers, exporters, financial service providers and transportation companies, can prevent essential goods from reaching persons in need."[34] Based on extensive information[35] received by affected countries, public institutions, companies, NGOs or persons, Alena Douhan reported that "over-compliance with unilateral sanctions has prevented, delayed or made more costly the purchase and shipment to sanctioned countries of food, medicine, medical equipment and parts for such equipment, even when the need is urgent."[36] Because of U.S. unilateral coercive measures, the Portuguese bank Novo Banco refused to process payments for medical supplies and medicines ordered by Venezuelan authorities.[37] Similarly, UCMs prevented *epidermolysis bullosa* patients in Iran to receive a proper treatment.[38] While compliance with UCMs generate negative effects on the human rights of the populations of targeted countries, over-compliance aggravates these negative impacts and this phenomenon can persist after UCMs are lifted.[39] Over-compliance from companies or private sector entities can result in the decision to stop or refuse to do business, even when it is not prohibited by sanctions. It can be motivated by reputational reasons, a perceived business benefit or by the refusal of intermediaries such as banks to conduct transactions.

Even when humanitarian exemptions or waivers can be granted, companies can refuse to carry out transactions (for the same reasons

---

HRC/51/33, 15/07/2022, p. 5. https://www.ohchr.org/en/documents/thematic-reports/ahrc5133-secondary-sanctions-civil-and-criminal-penalties-circumvention

34 Ibid.

35 Communications and reports by the Special Rapporteur on the negative impact of unilateral coercive measures on the enjoyment of human rights, "Communication report and search," Office of the High Commissioner for Human Rights. https://spcommreports.ohchr.org/TmSearch/Mandates?m=263

36 Alena Douhan, Secondary sanctions, civil and criminal penalties for circumvention of sanctions regimes and over-compliance with sanctions, Report of the Special Rapporteur on the negative impact of unilateral coercive measures on the enjoyment of human rights A. Douhan, 51st session of the Human Rights Council, A/HRC/51/33, 15/07/2022, p. 5. https://www.ohchr.org/en/documents/thematic-reports/ahrc5133-secondary-sanctions-civil-and-criminal-penalties-circumvention

37 Ibid.

38 Ibid.

39 Ibid., p. 6

as in the previous situation) and their decision has an impact on the human rights of the affected populations. After U.S. unilateral sanctions were reimposed on Iran in 2018, Swedish medical company Mölnlycke halted its exports to this country, including exempt products, and *epidermolysis bullosa* patients were not able to receive their treatment: "This led to greater suffering and even deaths among those children, compromising their rights to health and to life."[40] Mölnlycke stopped its exports to Iran as it was unable to find a bank willing to process the required financial transactions.[41] Other companies are also unable to deliver goods, like medicines and medical equipment, as insurance companies are reluctant to insure air cargos to Iran.[42]

Over-compliance from banks and financial institutions also plays an important role in this phenomenon, as these actors can refuse to process financial transactions and payments because of reputational or legal risks (e.g. if they operate branches in the USA or conduct transactions in U.S. dollars, they fall under U.S. extraterritorial jurisdiction). These decisions can have humanitarian consequences and can harm the Human Rights of affected populations: this "excessive de-risking by banks and other financial actors impedes the flow of humanitarian goods and services permitted under unilateral sanctions."[43] As reported by UN Special Rapporteur Alena Douhan, this

> over-compliance includes, inter alia, refusing to conduct authorized transactions; deterring authorized transactions by requiring onerous documentation or certification, charging higher rates or additional fees or imposing delays; freezing assets that are not targeted by sanctions; and denying individuals the possibility to open or maintain bank accounts or to conduct transactions on grounds that they are nationals of a sanctioned country, even if they are refugees from that country or because they were born there.[44]

---

40 Ibid., p. 7
41 Ibid.
42 Ibid.
43 Ibid., p. 8
44 Ibid.

These decisions violate the economic rights of affected persons, the freedom of trade, as well as the contractual obligations and the international obligations of states: the UN Special Rapporteur reported that the refusal by banks to process financial transactions prevented the Government of Venezuela from receiving $ 200 million from the Government of China.[45] She also noted that "that over-compliance by banks also impedes sanctioned States from carrying out sovereign functions; they face difficulties paying membership dues to international organizations and accessing debt markets to finance activities that can be critical to protecting the human rights of their nationals."[46]

Likewise, U.S. and EU sanctions against the Russian Federation and Belarus affected Russian and Belarussian citizens residing abroad. In Switzerland[47] and in various EU member states like France,[48] many banks closed bank accounts of Russian or Belarussian citizens who

---

45 Ibid.

46 Alena Douhan, Secondary sanctions, civil and criminal penalties for circumvention of sanctions regimes and over-compliance with sanctions, Report of the Special Rapporteur on the negative impact of unilateral coercive measures on the enjoyment of human rights A. Douhan, 51st session of the Human Rights Council, A/HRC/51/33, 15/07/2022, p. 9. https://www.ohchr.org/en/documents/thematic-reports/ahrc5133-secondary-sanctions-civil-and-criminal-penalties-circumvention

47 Yanick Corminbeuf, *Il règne un certain flou juridique en lien avec les sanctions russes*, Wilhelm Avocats. https://www.wg-avocats.ch/actualites/il-regne-un-certain-flou-juridique-en-lien-avec-les-sanctions-russes/; Arthur Rutishauser, «Les banques suisses mettent presque tous les Russes à la porte,» *La Tribune de Genève*, 16/06/2024. https://www.tdg.ch/suisse-les-banques-mettent-presque-tous-les-russes-a-la-porte-856879466757; Ombudsman des Banques Suisses, Suspension de transactions bancaires en raison des sanctions à l'encontre de la Russie, numéro de cas 2022/10, Banking Ombudsman, 22/05/2023. https://bankingombudsman.ch/fr/suspension-de-transactions-bancaires-en-raison-des-sanctions-a-lencontre-de-la-russie/

48 Camille Ducrocq, De simples ressortissants russes voient leurs virements bloqués par les banques en France, Capital, 01/04/2022. https://www.capital.fr/economie-politique/de-simples-ressortissants-russes-voient-leurs-virements-bloques-par-les-banques-en-france-1432744; Ouest France, Comptes bancaires bloqués: des Russes vivant en France déposent plainte pour discrimination, 25/08/2022. https://www.ouest-france.fr/monde/guerre-en-ukraine/comptes-bancaires-bloques-des-russes-vivant-en-france-deposent-plainte-pour-discrimination-f15dcc46-249e-11ed-b87a-5a37cb5b8d3c; Anthony Geran Hachon, «Guerre en Ukraine: Après leurs comptes bancaires bloqués, des «Russes» portent plainte pour discrimination,» *L'Indépendant*, 26/08/2022. https://www.lindependant.fr/2022/08/26/guerre-en-ukraine-apres-leurs-comptes-bancaires-bloques-des-russes-porte-plainte-pour-discrimination-10507040.php

had no ties to their respective governments, of French citizens with Russian origins, or of persons who had simply a Slavic family name.[49]

Numerous cases were reported in the media, such as the case of a Russian student at a French university whose request for credit housing funds was refused on the basis of "European sanctions" or of a Russian employee in Paris who was unable to access her salary, as her account had been blocked by her bank.[50] These decisions are a violation of the freedom of trade and can be considered as discrimination against the economic rights of these persons, as well as their rights to housing, food, education, and health. In 2022, 76 Russian citizens or French citizens of Russian origin whose bank accounts were blocked, filed complaints against French banks and online banks for this discrimination caused by over-compliance.[51] In Switzerland, some lawyers consider that the legal criteria used to close the bank accounts of Russian citizens are unclear.[52] Numerous cases are reported[53] and some Swiss lawyers consider these discriminatory decisions as an "unprecedented" violation of the rule of law.[54] Swiss lawyer Nicolas

---

49 Ouest France, Comptes bancaires bloqués: des Russes vivant en France déposent plainte pour discrimination, 25/08/2022. https://www.ouest-france.fr/monde/guerre-en-ukraine/comptes-bancaires-bloques-des-russes-vivant-en-france-deposent-plainte-pour-discrimination-f15dcc46-249e-11ed-b87a-5a37cb5b8d3c

50 Alena Douhan, Secondary sanctions, civil and criminal penalties for circumvention of sanctions regimes and over-compliance with sanctions, Report of the Special Rapporteur on the negative impact of unilateral coercive measures on the enjoyment of human rights A. Douhan, 51st session of the Human Rights Council, A/HRC/51/33, 15/07/2022, p. 5. https://www.ohchr.org/en/documents/thematic-reports/ahrc5133-secondary-sanctions-civil-and-criminal-penalties-circumvention

51 Ouest France, Comptes bancaires bloqués: des Russes vivant en France déposent plainte pour discrimination, 25/08/2022. https://www.ouest-france.fr/monde/guerre-en-ukraine/comptes-bancaires-bloques-des-russes-vivant-en-france-deposent-plainte-pour-discrimination-f15dcc46-249e-11ed-b87a-5a37cb5b8d3c;   Jocelyn Ziegler, «Des comptes russes bloqués par les banques françaises: quelle solutions?,» Village de la Justice, 27/09/2022. https://www.village-justice.com/articles/des-comptes-russes-bloques-par-les-banques-francaises-quelles-solutions,43783.html

52 Yanick Corminbeuf, Il règne un certain flou juridique en lien avec les sanctions russes, Wilhelm Avocats. https://www.wg-avocats.ch/actualites/il-regne-un-certain-flou-juridique-en-lien-avec-les-sanctions-russes/

53 Arthur Rutishauser, «Les banques suisses mettent presque tous les Russes à la porte,» La Tribune de Genève, 16/06/2024. https://www.tdg.ch/suisse-les-banques-mettent-presque-tous-les-russes-a-la-porte-856879466757

54 Marc Guéniat, «Sur les sanctions russes, les avocats genevois dénoncent une atteinte «sans précédent» à l'Etat de droit,» Le Temps, 23/05/2023. https://www.letemps.ch/suisse/sanctions-russes-avocats-genevois-denoncent-une-

Rouiller declared in that regard that the effects of over-compliance "can be particularly dramatic for the targeted persons."[55] This situation affecting Russian citizens or entities in Switzerland and EU countries pushed lawyers from Brussels, Paris and Geneva to launch in March 2023 a joint legal action at the Tribunal of the European Union against the EU prohibition to provide legal advisory services to public and private Russian companies.[56]

The author was also able to witness the effects of compliance and over-compliance on Russian citizens studying in various public and private universities in Geneva, who were unable to open bank accounts or whose bank accounts were blocked. These effects can be dramatic and absurd when they affect humanitarian projects and NGOs, as shown by the case of Swiss fashion designer and social entrepreneur Rania Kinge.[57] In 2013, she founded a social entrepreneurship project in Syria named "I Love Syria / Made by Women" and

atteinte-precedent-letat-droit?srsltid=AfmBOoqPcMu5ok2tjsSc3bfSgBCxLT_HHUpCr9gcSMK_9FMf_-RRo_qv

55 Alena Douhan, Targets of unilateral coercive measures: notion, categories and vulnerable groups, Report of the Special Rapporteur on the negative impact of unilateral coercive measures on the enjoyment of human rights, 76th session of the General Assembly of the United Nations, A/76/174/Rev.1, 13/09/2021, p. 20. https://www.ohchr.org/en/documents/thematic-reports/a76174rev1-report-targets-unilateral-coercive-measures-notion-categories

56 *Supra* note 54.

57 Jackie Abramian, "Rania Kinge's Social Enterprise 'I Love Syria' Transcends Nationalism," *The Huffington Post*, 25/08/2015. https://www.huffpost.com/entry/rania-kinges-social-enterprise-i-love-syria-transcends-nationalism_b_7994862; International Trade Centre, "Syrian designer taps online markets through pop-up souk in Geneva," *ITC News*, 12/02/2016. https://www.intracen.org/news-and-events/news/syrian-designer-taps-online-markets-through-pop-up-souk-in-geneva; Christian David, «Entre Damas & Genève: la guerre pacifique de Rania,» *Synergies Internationales*, 13/02/2016. http://www.synergies-internationales.ch/entre-damas-geneve-la-guerre-pacifique-de-rania/; Susanna Pak, "In line with going online: using e-commerce to tap new markets," *International Trade Forum*, n°2, 2016, pp. 30–31. https://www.proquest.com/openview/58029814f925ae66272b3eb0641e31ea/1?pq-origsite=gscholar&cbl=47429; Laure Gabus, Etablie à Damas, «Rania Kinge initie des femmes à l'artisanat traditionnel,» *Tribune de Genève*, 12/02/2016. https://www.tdg.ch/etablie-a-damas-rania-kinge-initie-des-femmes-a-lartisanat-traditionnel-162231581546; Jackie Abramian, "Empowering Syria's Internally Displaced Refugee Women," *Change Magazine*, 27/04/2018. https://www.seechangemagazine.com/empowering-syrias-internally-displaced-refugee-women/; Alexandra Nicolas, «Des bijoux pour changer le destin des Syriennes,» *Décodeurs 360*, 11/08/2021. https://decodeurs360.org/international/des-bijoux-pour-emanciper-les-femmes/

whose goal was to provide vocational training and paid job opportunities to Syrian displaced women. As sanctions were already enforced against Syria, her humanitarian activities faced various obstacles such as the refusal of an Italian company to sell and ship an enamelling kiln for jewellery and pottery, even though it could be used only for peaceful and civilian purposes.

She was also unable to import raw materials, to buy machines or simply to operate as the internet was not working and electricity shortages were almost permanent. In 2017, during the Geneva Peace Week, Rania Kinge was invited by the International Trade Center and the Permanent Mission of Japan[58] to participate to the "E-Caravan for Peace," and to present her concept and activities at the United Nations Office in Geneva.[59] Items were sold during the event but the revenues earned through online sales were seized by 2Checkout, the platform she used to process these transactions.[60] In 2018, the U.S. State Department invited her to participate to a TEDWomen event organized by the Artisan Alliance but she wasn't able to attend it, as the U.S. Embassy in Bern refused to grant her a visa and justified its decision by the location of her humanitarian project in Syria.[61]

The adoption of the Caesar Syria Civilian Protection Act by the United States of America in 2019 brought additional negative effects to Rania Kinge and her social entrepreneurship project. In February 2020, her NGO bank account was closed by PostFinance, Switzerland's main public postal and banking company and it severely hampered her

---

58 International Trade Centre, Partnering with Japan to connect displaced Syrian women to markets, ITC News, 08/08/2017. https://www.intracen.org/news-and-events/news/partnering-with-japan-to-connect-displaced-syrian-women-to-markets

59 Permanent Mission of Japan to the International Organizations in Geneva, "E-Caravan for Peace" at the United Nations Office at Geneva co-hosted by the ITC and the Permanent Mission of Japan, 09/11/2017. https://www.geneve-mission. emb-japan.go.jp/itpr_en/event_20171107.html; Digital Watch, E-caravan for peace: Promoting e-commerce in conflict and post-conflict situations, 13/11/2017. https://dig.watch/event/geneva-peace-week-2017/e-caravan-peace-promoting-e-commerce-conflict-and-post-conflict-situations; International Trade Centre, "Trade Compass: Creating quality jobs at home," 07/11/2017. https://www.facebook. com/InternationalTradeCentre/videos/trade-compass-creating-quality-jobs-at-home/841470059355482/; International Trade Center, "Geneva Peace Week 2017 – Rania Kinge," Flickr, 07/11/2017. https://www.flickr.com/photos/international-trade-centre/38184188916/in/photostream/

60 Interview with the author on *28/10/2024.*

61 Ibid.

humanitarian activities. Her personal bank account at PostFinance was also drastically constrained by restrictions prohibiting her to carry out financial transactions (even with companies located in the European Union) and until now she is only allowed to make basic payments, thus impacting negatively her living conditions and the enjoyment of her fundamental rights.[62] In 2020, Shopify closed her professional website and her professional Facebook page was suspended several times, while her Facebook business account was also blocked.[63] These obstacles forced Rania Kinge to recreate her project under the name "Made by Women"[64] and to not use the word "Syria" as it could again lead to the blockage of her pages on social media platforms and prevent her from using e-commerce services.[65]

As shown by the previous example, banks and financial institutions can practice over-compliance, "whether sanctions are comprehensive or limited."[66] In the case of Zimbabwe, "non-sanctioned individuals and entities have had long-established accounts closed by banks in Australia, the United Kingdom of Great Britain and Northern Ireland and the United States due to their nationality, and only 6 of 27 commercial banks in Zimbabwe still have foreign correspondent banks willing to handle transactions."[67] Thus, UCMs are discriminatory and violate the economic and human rights of citizens with other potential effects on their rights to food, health or education for example, as well as the economic rights of affected companies in targeted countries, while violating at the same time the economic rights, the economic sovereignty and the freedom of trade of targeted countries.

---

62 Ibid.

63 Ibid.

64 "Made by Women." https://www.raniakinge.com/collections/i-love-syria; "Rania Kinge – Made by Women." https://www.instagram.com/raniakingemadebywomen/?hl=fr; "Rania Kinge x Made by Women." https://www.facebook.com/RaniaKingeMadeByWomen/

65 Interview with the author on 28/10/2024.

66 Alena Douhan, Secondary sanctions, civil and criminal penalties for circumvention of sanctions regimes and over-compliance with sanctions, Report of the Special Rapporteur on the negative impact of unilateral coercive measures on the enjoyment of human rights A. Douhan, 51st session of the Human Rights Council, A/HRC/51/33, 15/07/2022, p. 8. https://www.ohchr.org/en/documents/thematic-reports/ahrc5133-secondary-sanctions-civil-and-criminal-penalties-circumvention.

67 Ibid., pp. 8–9.

Violations of Human Rights caused by Compliance or Over-compliance from Private Sector Entities with UCMs: What is the Relevant Legal Framework?

With regard to the negative effects and human rights violations caused by unilateral coercive measures, as well as their legality, UCMs violate most of the fundamental principles of international law (sovereignty and non-intervention, friendly relations among states, freedom of trade, prohibition of collective punishment) and related conventions (Charter of the United Nations, International Covenant on Civil and Political Rights, International Covenant on Economic, Social and Cultural Rights, several resolutions of the UN General Assembly).[68]

While states can be held accountable for their actions under international law and remain the main subjects of law under this legal framework, the role of companies and their accountability is not addressed, unless we take into consideration the relevant jurisprudence of the Nuremberg Tribunal related to German companies and their complicity in war crimes and crimes against humanity. The main legal framework concerning the accountability of private sector companies with regard to human rights violations relies mainly on domestic legislation. Legal cases against companies are usually related to criminal acts and serious violations of human rights, all prosecuted under national jurisdictions, which can include universal jurisdiction and / or extraterritorial jurisdiction, like in the U.S. for cases judged under the Alien Tort Statute (also known as the Alien Tort Claims Act).[69]

Legal cases related to compliance or over-compliance with sanctions from companies and its negative effects on the human rights of targeted populations were rare or virtually non-existent in the past

---

68 See the first part of this chapter.

69 *Dolly M. E. Filártiga and Joel Filártiga v. Americo Norberto Peña-Irala*, 630 F.2d 876 (2d Cir. 1980) and 577 F.Supp. 860 (D.N.Y. 1984); *Jose Francisco Sosa v. Humberto Alvarez-Machain, et al.*, 542 U.S. 692 (2004); *Doe v. Unocal Corp.*, 110 F.Supp.2d 1294 (C.D.Cal. 2000), 395 F.3d 932 (9th Cir. 2002), 395 F.3d 978 (9th Cir. 2003) and 403 F.3d 708 (9th Cir. 2005); *Wiwa et al v. Royal Dutch Shell Petroleum et al.*, 226 F.3d 88 (2d Cir. 2000); *Presbyterian Church of Sudan v. Talisman Energy*, 244 F. Supp. 2d 289 (S.D.N.Y. 2003); *Doe v. Nestle, S.A.*, No. CV 05-5133 SVW (JTLx) (C.D. Cal. Sep. 8, 2010); *Kiobel v. Royal Dutch Petroleum Co.*, 569 U.S. 108 (2013), *Jesner v. Arab Bank, PLC*, No. 16-499, 584 U.S. (2018); *Nestlé USA, Inc. v. John Doe I, et al. – Cargill, Inc. v. John Doe I, et al.*, 593 U. S. (2021).

but there is currently a growing number of cases being opened under domestic jurisdictions in Switzerland and in EU countries by Russian citizens following the freeze or the seizure of their properties or bank accounts.[70]

At the international level, the main legal *corpus* related to the role of the private sector with regard to Human Rights is mainly constituted by soft law, while some issues are indirectly addressed by some international conventions (whose main legal subjects remain states and not entities like private companies).

This international legal *corpus* is mainly based on the core conventions of the International Labour Organization[71] and its main soft law instrument, the Tripartite Declaration of Principles concerning Multinational Enterprises and Social Policy.[72] Concerning the Organization for Economic Co-operation and Development, the relevant legal framework is based on soft law instruments, with the Convention on Combating Bribery of Foreign Public Officials in International Business Transactions[73] (whose scope remains

---

70 Ouest France, Comptes bancaires bloqués: des Russes vivant en France déposent plainte pour discrimination, 25/08/2022. https://www.ouest-france.fr/monde/guerre-en-ukraine/comptes-bancaires-bloques-des-russes-vivant-en-france-deposent-plainte-pour-discrimination-f15dcc46-249e-11ed-b87a-5a37cb5b8d3c; Jocelyn Ziegler, Des comptes russes bloqués par les banques françaises: quelle solutions ?, Village de la Justice, 27/09/2022. https://www.village-justice.com/articles/des-comptes-russes-bloques-par-les-banques-francaises-quelles-solutions,43783.html; Yanick Corminbeuf, Il règne un certain flou juridique en lien avec les sanctions russes, Wilhelm Avocats. https://www.wg-avocats.ch/actualites/il-regne-un-certain-flou-juridique-en-lien-avec-les-sanctions-russes/; Arthur Rutishauser, Les banques suisses mettent presque tous les Russes à la porte, La Tribune de Genève, 16/06/2024. https://www.tdg.ch/suisse-les-banques-mettent-presque-tous-les-russes-a-la-porte-856879466757; Marc Guéniat, «Sur les sanctions russes, les avocats genevois dénoncent une atteinte 'sans précédent' à l'Etat de droit,» *Le Temps*, 23/05/2023. https://www.letemps.ch/suisse/sanctions-russes-avocats-genevois-denoncent-une-atteinte-precedent-letat-droit?srsltid=AfmBOoqPcMu5ok2tjsSc3bfSgBCxLT_HHUpCr9gcSMK_9FMf_-RRo_qv

71 International Labour Organization, ILO Conventions. https://www.ilo.org/resource/ilo-conventions

72 International Labour Organization, Tripartite Declaration of Principles concerning Multinational Enterprises and Social Policy (MNE Declaration). https://www.ilo.org/ilo-department-sustainable-enterprises-productivity-and-just-transition/areas-work/tripartite-declaration-principles-concerning-multinational-enterprises-and

73 OECD, Convention on Combating Bribery of Foreign Public Officials in International Business Transactions, 1999. https://legalinstruments.oecd.org/en/

limited to corruption-related offences) and the OECD Guidelines for Multinational Enterprises on Responsible Business Conduct[74] respectively.

The World Bank is also increasingly concerned by the activities of private companies in relation to human rights: it issued various guidelines[75] but like in the previous examples, the issue of human rights violations caused by compliance or over-compliance with UCMs by companies is not addressed or mentioned at all. In the United Nations framework, numerous soft law instruments, such as the resolutions of the General Assembly of the United Nations, address Human Rights issues or affirm principles that could be invoked but their legal effects or applicability remain extremely limited because of their nature.

The only resolutions from the UN General Assembly addressing the issue of UCMs and their impact on human rights are those asking since 1992 to lift U.S. unilateral sanctions against Cuba,[76] but until now they remain ineffective. In parallel, the only soft law instruments addressing the issue of human rights from the perspective of private sector actors like companies are the Norms of the Responsibilities of Transnational Corporations and Other Business Enterprises with Regard to Human Rights,[77] the Responsibilities of transnational cor-

---

instruments/OECD-LEGAL-0293; OECD recommendations issued in 2009, 2016, 2019 and 2021. https://www.oecd.org/en/topics/fighting-foreign-bribery.html

74 Organization for Economic Co-operation and Development, OECD Guidelines for Multinational Enterprises on Responsible Business Conduct, 2023. https://mneguidelines.oecd.org/mneguidelines/

75 World Bank, Guidelines on the Legal Framework for the Treatment of Foreign Investment, 1992. https://documents1.worldbank.org/curated/fr/955221468766167766/pdf/multi-page.pdf

76 General Assembly of the United Nations, Necessity of ending the economic, commercial and financial embargo imposed by the United States of America to Cuba, UN General Assembly revolution A/Res/47/19, 70th plenary meeting, 24/11/1992. https://daccess-ods.un.org/access.nsf/Get?OpenAgent&DS=A/Res/47/19&Lang=E; and more recently, General Assembly of the United Nations, Necessity of ending the economic, commercial and financial embargo imposed by the United States of America against Cuba, UN General Assembly revolution A/8/L.5, 11/10/2023. https://undocs.org/en/A/78/L.5

77 Commission on Human Rights, Norms of the Responsibilities of Transnational Corporations and Other Business Enterprises with Regard to Human Rights, Commission on Human Rights, Sub-Commission on the Promotion and Protection of Human Rights, Economic and Social Council, 55th session, E/CN.4/Sub.2/2003/12/Rev.2, 26/08/2003. https://digitallibrary.un.org/record/501576?v=pdf

porations and other business enterprises with regard to human rights[78] and the Guiding Principles and Business and Human Rights[79] but they don't address at all the issue of human rights violations caused by compliance or over-compliance by companies (the term "sanctions" is used only once in each document and with no connection to unilateral sanctions or unilateral coercive measures).

Many of the recent soft law instruments adopted by the United Nations tend to address human tights but they have only a declarative nature and depend on voluntary commitment, as is the case with the UN Global Compact[80] (involving companies but relying on the commitment of company CEOs). None of these instruments address or mention the issue of UCMs, their impact on human rights and the role of companies in this phenomenon. The connection between human rights, environmental protection, sustainability and all the various spheres of human life and activities is also acknowledged by the 2030 Sustainable Development Agenda[81] and its Sustainable Development Goals. The SDGs are presented like an unprecedented collective endeavour to build a better and more sustainable world in a critical context, through the commitment of states, companies, NGOs and citizens. Unfortunately, this noble endeavour remains declarative and even contradictory when it comes to the issue of human rights violations caused by UCMs and by companies' compliance or over-compliance (this issue will be analyzed in the last part of this chapter).

International soft law instruments do not mention or address at all the issues related to unilateral coercive measures, compliance

---

78 Office of the United Nations High Commissioner for Human Rights, Responsibilities of transnational corporations and other business enterprises with regard to human rights, Sub-Commission on the Promotion and Protection of Human Rights, Res. 2003/16, 13/08/2003. https://ap.ohchr.org/documents/E/SUBCOM/resolutions/E-CN_4-SUB_2-RES-2003-16.doc

79 Office of the United Nations High Commissioner for Human Rights, Guiding Principles and Business and Human Rights, 2011. https://www.ohchr.org/documents/publications/guidingprinciplesbusinesshr_en.pdf

80 United Nations Global Compact. https://unglobalcompact.org/

81 General Assembly of the United Nations, Transforming our world: the 2030 Agenda for Sustainable Development, UN General Assembly Resolution A/RES/70/1, 25/09/2015. https://undocs.org/en/A/RES/70/1; United Nations Department of Social and Economic Affairs, Transforming our world: the 2030 Agenda for Sustainable Development. https://sdgs.un.org/2030agenda; United Nations, The Sustainable Development Agenda. https://www.un.org/sustainabledevelopment/development-agenda/

and over-compliance, as well as their effects on the human rights of the civilian populations of targeted countries. Likewise, among the various voluntary codes of conduct and self-regulation measures adopted by industry associations, this issue is not addressed or mentioned at all. The same is true with most of the tools used to assess the impact of companies' activities on human rights, such as the Human Rights Compliance Assessment tool elaborated by the Danish Institute for Human Rights,[82] the Guide to Human Rights Impact Assessments issued by the International Finance Corporation, the International Business Leaders Forum and the UN Global Compact,[83] and the Human Rights Impact Assessments for Foreign Investment Projects published by the International Centre for Human Rights and Democratic Development.[84] This gap is partly covered by research databases on sanctions, such as the Global Sanctions Data Base developed by the Austrian Institute of Economic Research (WIFO), Drexel University's School of Economics, and the University of Applied Sciences of Konstanz (HTWG)[85] or the Targeted Sanctions Initiative led by the Geneva Graduate Institute and its "UN SanctionsApp."[86]

However, more comprehensive databases and tools provided by the United Nations Security Council,[87] by the Office of the United Nations High Commissioner for Human Rights[88] and the UN Special Rapporteur on unilateral coercive measures[89] enable the conduct of

---

82 Danish Institute for Human Rights, Human rights compliance assessment quick check, 2016. https://www.humanrights.dk/publications/human-rights-compliance-assessment-quick-check

83 United Nations Global Compact, Guide to Human Rights Impact Assessment and Management, 2010. https://unglobalcompact.org/library/25

84 International Centre for Human Rights and Democratic Development, Human Rights Impact Assessments for Foreign Investment Projects, Learning from Community Experiences in the Philippines, Tibet, the Democratic Republic of Congo, Argentina, and Peru, 2007. https://publications.gc.ca/collections/collection_2007/dd-rd/E84-21-2007E.pdf

85 "The Global Sanctions Data Base." https://www.globalsanctionsdatabase.com/

86 "Targeted Sanctions Initiative." https://www.graduateinstitute.ch/research-centres/global-governance-centre/targeted-sanctions-initiative; "UN Sanctions App." https://unsanctionsapp.com/

87 United Nations Security Council, "Sanctions." https://main.un.org/securitycouncil/en/sanctions/information

88 Office of the United Nations High Commissioner for Human Rights, "Sanctions Research Platform." https://sanctionsplatform.ohchr.org/

89 United Nations Special Rapporteur on unilateral coercive measures,

in-depth research, and provide considerable evidence on the impact of UCMs on human rights and more specifically on the role played by companies' compliance or over-compliance in this phenomenon. The existence of this significant gap was identified by UN Special Rapporteur on unilateral coercive measures Alena Douhan and it will lead to the adoption of the Guiding Principles—Sanctions, Business and Human Rights in 2025.[90]

Companies, Human Rights Violations and the Sustainable Development Goals

Twenty three years after Rio de Janeiro Conference of 1992 and 15 years after the Millenium Summit at the UN headquarters in New York in September 2000 that elaborated 8 Millenium Development Goals, the UN Sustainable Summit held in September 2015 in New York approved the 2030 Agenda for Sustainable Development and its 17 Sustainable Development Goals.[91] The achievement of the Sustainable Development Goals doesn't depend on the sole commitment of States as it involves citizens and the civil society at large, including the private sector:[92] "The private sector is critical to achieving the Sustainable Development Goals (SDGs)—by creating employment, building skills, spurring innovation, providing essential infrastructure, and supplying affordable goods and services. The private sector is also crucial to SDG achievement as an investor of

---

"Sanctions Monitoring & Impact Assessment Tool," Office of the United Nations High Commissioner for Human Rights. https://www.ohchr.org/en/special-procedures/sr-unilateral-coercive-measures/sanctions-monitoring-impact-assessment-tool

90 United Nations Special Rapporteur on unilateral coercive measures, "Guiding Principles—Sanctions, Business and Human Rights," Office of the United Nations High Commissioner for Human Rights. https://www.ohchr.org/en/special-procedures/sr-unilateral-coercive-measures/guiding-principles-sanctions-business-and-human-rights

91 United Nations Department of Economic and Social Affairs, The 17 Goals. https://sdgs.un.org/goals; United Nations, Take Action for the Sustainable Development Goals. https://www.un.org/sustainabledevelopment/sustainable-development-goals/; United Nations Development Programme, What are the Sustainable Development Goals? https://www.undp.org/sustainable-development-goals

92 Marcos Neto and Sahba Sobhani, Engaging the private sector to achieve the 2030 Agenda, Istanbul International Centre for Private Sector in Development, United Nations Development Programme, 03/10/2023. https://www.undp.org/policy-centre/istanbul/blog/engaging-private-sector-achieve-2030-agenda-0

much-needed capital."[93] The inclusion and involvement of the private sector is supported by the UNDP Private Sector Strategy 2023–2025,[94] while the effectiveness of their actions and those of the other partners towards the achievement of the SDGs is ensured by the Sustainable Development Goals Fund.[95]

The Sustainable Development Goals are not legally binding and "are not directly referred to in treaties, local laws, or case law."[96] The Sustainable Development Goals are soft law instruments but "with their wider scope and through the principle of integration (implying that, in the light of the interlinked aspect of the goals, any measures carried out towards the achievement of (a) goal(s) should integrate a view to achieve other goals in a coherent and balanced manner), the SDGs have the potential to create links between otherwise fragmented binding instruments at both international and national/local levels."[97] Moreover, as recognized in the legal doctrine "the SDGs, although not legally binding, have already had a rather substantial influence on local legislations and have indeed resulted in new laws and regulations at regional, national, and local levels."[98] The elaboration, implementation and assessment of the Sustainable Development Goals involved and still involve considerable resources and commitments from various actors (States, NGOs, companies, citizens), important publicity and media attention but their coherence can be seriously questioned with regard to the human rights violations caused by the enforcement of UCMs by States and by companies' compliance or over-compliance with UCMs.

As evidenced by the reports of the UN Special Rapporteur on unilateral coercive measures, the negative effects of UCMs impact more strongly "persons in vulnerable situations, including women, children,

---

93 United Nations Development Programme, UNDP and the Private Sector. https://www.undp.org/partners/private-sector

94 Marcos Neto and Sahba Sobhani, *supra* note 92; United Nations Development Programme, Ibid.

95 "Sustainable Development Goals Fund." https://www.sdgfund.org/private-sector and https://jointsdgfund.org/

96 Ariane Samson-Davisia, Revisiting the non-binding legal aspects of the SDGs, Oslo SDG Blog, Oslo SDG Initiative, University of Oslo, 06/01/2023. https://www.sum.uio.no/english/sdg/blog/guest/revisiting-the-non-binding-legal-aspects-of-the-sd.html

97 Ibid.

98 Ibid.

people with disabilities or with chronic or severe diseases, the elderly, refugees, internally displaced persons, migrants, people living in poverty and others who depend on social or humanitarian assistance."[99] Over-compliance and its negative impact on human rights also pose challenges or even obstacles to "the delivery of specialized life-saving medicine, medical equipment or in transferring money for medical operations to or from the countries under sanctions; risks for the delivery of humanitarian assistance to mitigate negative impacts of natural disasters (the Syrian Arab Republic and Türkiye); challenges in the implementation of humanitarian provisions of Security Council resolutions; (...); and challenges in academic research and cooperation."[100] In the light of these examples, the direct and indirect effects, as well as the immediate and long term effects caused by the enforcement of UCMs by States and companies' compliance or over-compliance with UCMs violate Sustainable Development Goals 1 (No poverty), 2 (Zero Hunger), 3 (Good health and well-being), 4 (Quality education), 6 (Clean water and sanitation), 8 (Decent work and economic growth), 9 (Industry, innovation and infrastructure), 10 (Reduced inequalities), 11 (Sustainable cities and communities) and 16 (Peace, justice and strong institutions).

Sanctions against Iran have disastrous effects on Iranians suffering from various diseases as they cannot obtain treatments: "The country faces a lack of vital medicine for thalassemia patients, as the supplier company Novartis stopped exporting them, due to the unclear U.S. sanctions regime."[101] Similarly, "in 2019, a Swedish medical products company told an Iranian NGO that provides free bandages to patients that, because of United States sanctions, it decided to suspend doing any business involving the Islamic Republic of Iran, including "business conducted under any form of exceptions" to

---

99 Alena Douhan, Secondary Sanctions, Over-compliance and Human Rights, Report of the Special Rapporteur on the negative impact of unilateral coercive measures on the enjoyment of human rights, 78th session of the General Assembly of the United Nations, UN General Assembly resolution A/78/196, 04/09/2023, p. 5. https://digitallibrary.un.org/record/4023204?ln=ru&v=pdf

100 Ibid.

101 Maira Sophie Müller, How (Over)Compliance by Private Actors Can Violate the Right to Health, Völkerrechtsblog, 30/06/2023. https://voelkerrechtsblog.org/how-over-compliance-by-private-actors-can-violate-the-right-to-health/

the United States economic sanctions."[102] This situation contradicts clearly commitment of States and companies under SDGs 3 and 10. U.S. sanctions against Cuba forced banks to suspend transactions with Cuba and companies to ship ordinary goods like food but also vital goods such as medicines, even during the COVID-19 crisis.[103] In this situation, states and activity of companies impedes the achievement of SDGs 1, 2, 3, 4, 6, 8, 9, 10, 11 and 16.

UN Special Rapporteur on unilateral coercive measures Alena Douhan reported that "Medical personnel, lawyers and others living in sanctioned countries, or who are citizens of sanctioned countries but no longer live there, are blocked from participating in online medical consultations and conferences that use the services of the communications technology company Zoom, under its terms of service."[104] This situation contradicts States' and companies' commitments, as well as people rights under SDGs 1, 2, 3, 4, 6, 8, 9, 10, 11 and 16.

The Sustainable Development Goals may be considered as a crucial and serious endeavour by the United Nations, its member states, civil society and the private sector but in the light of all these examples showing how States enforcing UCMs and companies complying or over complying with UCMs negatively affect the human rights of affected populations, their credibility can be seriously questioned, just like the credibility of the commitment and the good faith of concerned States and companies.

---

102 Alena Douhan, Targets of unilateral coercive measures: notion, categories and vulnerable groups, Report of the Special Rapporteur on the negative impact of unilateral coercive measures on the enjoyment of human rights, 76th session of the General Assembly of the United Nations, A/76/174/Rev.1, 13/09/2021, p. 21. https://www.ohchr.org/en/documents/thematic-reports/a76174rev1-report-targets-unilateral-coercive-measures-notion-categories

103 Alena Douhan, Secondary sanctions, civil and criminal penalties for circumvention of sanctions regimes and over-compliance with sanctions, Report of the Special Rapporteur on the negative impact of unilateral coercive measures on the enjoyment of human rights A. Douhan, 51st session of the Human Rights Council, A/HRC/51/33, 15/07/2022, p. 9. https://www.ohchr.org/en/documents/thematic-reports/ahrc5133-secondary-sanctions-civil-and-criminal-penalties-circumvention

104 Alena Douhan, Targets of unilateral coercive measures: notion, categories and vulnerable groups, Report of the Special Rapporteur on the negative impact of unilateral coercive measures on the enjoyment of human rights, 76th session of the General Assembly of the United Nations, A/76/174/Rev.1, 13/09/2021, p. 21. https://www.ohchr.org/en/documents/thematic-reports/a76174rev1-report-targets-unilateral-coercive-measures-notion-categories

Conclusion

Because of reputational risks, the fear of secondary sanctions and the complexity of exemption regimes when it comes to granting waivers, most companies prefer to not conduct business with countries under sanctions, even when it can negatively affect the human tights of the civilian populations of the targeted countries or even threaten their lives. In international law, this issue is not addressed by hard law but only by soft law, thus creating a gap and putting the accountability, as well as the legal responsibility of companies aside. These soft law instruments are unable to address effectively human rights violations caused by private sector actors complying or over complying with unilateral sanctions regimes and unilateral coercive measures. Recent global initiatives like the Sustainable Development Goals claim to connect better all the spheres of human life and activities in accordance with the principles of environmental protection and human rights but their coherence and consistency, as well as the role of States and companies, can be seriously questioned in the light of the available evidence of human rights violations caused by UCMs.

The UN Guiding Principles on Sanctions, Business and Human Rights address and supplement all these gaps in the field of the relevant soft law. These Guiding Principles may push the concerned private sector actors to reconsider and redesign their business policies towards sanctioned countries and affected populations. It could also push companies to be more consistent and coherent with regard to their corporate social responsibility strategies and their due diligence processes, by taking into consideration how business decisions towards sanctioned countries can negatively affect the human rights of civilian populations.

Lawsuits in Switzerland and in the European Union against banks or companies denying services to Russian citizens and violating their rights are increasing. These cases shed light on a wider phenomenon as the rights of civilian populations are also violated all around the world by UCMs. As long as a national jurisdiction considers itself as competent on these matters, domestic law can address these cases more effectively than the relevant soft law instruments in international law but both can't effectively address this phenomenon at the international level. It raises various questions, such as whether hard law could help, and which type of hard law instrument could be adopted.

While this gap remains in the field of hard law, it has been filled in the field of soft law with the publication of the *Guiding Principles on Sanctions, Business and Human Rights* in February 2025.[105] These Guiding Principles can play a crucial role in addressing the issue of human rights violations caused by compliance or over-compliance from companies, as they "remind States of their responsibility to abide by and uphold international human rights standards" and "reiterate States' responsibility to ensure through administrative and judicial measures that businesses under their jurisdiction and/or control, operating in sanctions contexts, do not violate human rights, including extraterritorially."[106] Moreover, as these Guiding Principles "explain how existing international legal standards shall be applied in the context of sanctions,"[107] they can effectively help States and companies to limit human rights violations caused by compliance or over-compliance with UCMs and thus, to be consistent with the Sustainable Development Goals.

---

105 United Nations, Guiding Principles on Sanctions, Business and Human Rights, Office of the High Commissionner for Human Rights, 25/02/2025. https://www.ohchr.org/en/press-releases/2025/02/un-expert-launches-guiding-principles-sanctions-business-and-human-rights

106 Ibid.

107 Ibid.

CHAPTER 11.

Economic Warfare and Civilian Casualties

Michael Swainston, KC[1]

Abstract

This chapter deals with the collision between unilateral sanctions and human rights. It explains the general incompatibility of such measures with the international obligations of States, including especially, human rights obligations, humanitarian norms, investment treaty obligations and trade obligations. It shows how rights and norms recognized in the aftermath of the Second World War apply directly or by analogy to protect civilians in the context of economic warfare, and how only obstructionism has prevented appropriate remedial action. Finally, it demonstrates how States and officials are nonetheless vulnerable where unilateral coercive measures (UCMs) cause economic harm and human suffering, with an outline of the scope for legal redress and personal accountability.

Introduction

It is difficult to catalogue the greatest evils in human history, but the Second World War and the events surrounding it must account for many of them. The rise of fascism in Germany brought new extremes of discrimination and genocide. The mass targeting of civilians using new weapons of mass destruction was another milestone of inhumanity. The veterans and survivors of World War II were acutely aware of the horrors of global conflict, and in the post war years, that awareness prompted a genuine effort by civilised people to prevent anything like it from happening again.

The most important step was the creation of the United Nations Organization in 1945, and constitution of a Security Council with

---

1 Barrister at Brick Court Chambers in London and a Bencher at Lincoln's Inn

responsibility for maintaining international peace and security.[2] To that end, the Security Council was given the exclusive power to authorize the use of force and to apply non-military enforcement measures including to impose economic sanctions on recalcitrant States. In accordance with art. 24–25, 41 of the UN Charter such measures must be implemented by the members of the United Nations. Regional organizations "dealing with such matters relating to the maintenance of international peace and security as are appropriate for regional action" can be used by the UN Security Council for "enforcement action under its authority," but "no enforcement action shall be taken under regional arrangements or by regional agencies without the authorization of the Security Council" (art. 52(1), 53(1) of the UN Charter). Without such authority, economic sanctions of both States and regional organizations constitute intervention in the domestic affairs of target States which is prohibited under art. 2(7) of the UN Charter as well as under later instruments.[3] The principle of non-intervention is regarded as one of the fundamental principles of international law and generally recognized to be of a peremptory nature.[4]

There were also measures to promote the conditions necessary for world peace. The General Agreement on Tariffs and Trade ("GATT") was concluded in October 1947[5] to encourage international development and to reduce the trade tensions that lead to conflict.

Human rights treaties and instruments guaranteed basic rights in the jurisdictions of signatory and other States: the right to life, freedom from torture, respect for home, family life and livelihood, the right to freedom of expression and freedom from discrimination on the basis of race or nationality.[6] The hope was that preventing internal

---

2 Charter of the United Nations, 1945

3 Delaration of principles of International law; Helsinki Final act 1975

4 Guerreiro A. "The Legal Status of the Principle of Non-Intervention, " *Moscow Journal of International Law*. 2022. No. 1, pp. 6–26.

5 World Trade Organization (WTO), General Agreement on Tariffs and Trade (GATT 1947), https://www.wto.org/english/docs_e/legal_e/gatt47_e.htm.

6 1948 Universal Declaration of Human Rights (UDHR)

1948 Genocide Convention

1950 European Convention on Human Rights

1951 Refugee Convention

1960 Discrimination in Employment Convention

1966 The International Convention on the Elimination of All Forms of Racial Discrimination (ICERD)

oppression would hinder the rise of another Hitler.

Progress faltered during the Cold War, but as the USSR fell behind economically, Russia, along with many developing States, concluded bilateral investment treaties (BITs) to promote investment and development. These guaranteed rights to property, which were controversial and not universally accepted at the time of the UN Charter and the International Covenant on Civil and Political Rights ("ICCPR" 1966).

International law provides some standards to promote and protect human rights of civilian population even in the period of military conflict. In particular, the Geneva Conventions of 1949 and Additional Protocols of 1977 sought, inter alia, to mitigate the impact on civilians, who must not be targeted in their own right and who must be left with means of sustenance.[7] Collective punishment—a favorite tool of the Nazis—was forbidden. Under Article 33 of the Fourth Geneva Convention: ". . .Collective penalties and likewise all measures of intimidation . . . are prohibited."[8] Article 33 derived from Article 50 of the Hague Convention (IV) on Laws and Customs of War on Land 1907: "No general penalty, pecuniary or otherwise, shall be inflicted upon the population on account of the acts of individuals for which they cannot be regarded as jointly and severally responsible."[9]

Time has passed since these principled legal developments. Especially in the West, awareness of the horrors of conflict has faded. War is something that happens abroad with no negative consequences at home and plenty of advantages abroad. Regional wars are fought by sponsored proxies. They weaken geopolitical opponents and give access to oil or to the rare-earth elements that sustain our

---

1966 The International Covenant on Economic, Social and Cultural Rights (ICESCR)

1966 The International Covenant on Civil and Political Rights (ICCPR)

1979 The Convention on the Elimination of All forms of Discrimination against Women (CEDAW)

1984 The Convention against Torture and Other Cruel, Inhuman or other Degrading Treatment of Punishment (CAT)

7 See eg Protocol 1 Arts. 51,54 and Protocol II Arts. 10–11, Arts. 13–14, Art. 16

8 Fourth Geneva Convention 1949

9 International Committee of the Red Cross (ICRC), Hague Convention (IV) Respecting the Laws and Customs of War on Land and Its Annex: Regulations concerning the Laws and Customs of War on Land, 1907, art. 50, https://ihl-databases. icrc.org/en/ihl-treaties/hague-conv-iv-1907/regulations-art-50?activeTab=.

media-saturated (and manipulated) age. For example, the Democratic Republic of Congo ("DRC") is presently in turmoil, the target of the M23 insurgency and a recent coup attempt in which American citizens were apparently involved. At the same time, the United States and the United Kingdom fund Rwanda, which in turn supports a brutal insurgency by M23 rebels, even sending its own soldiers to fight alongside them.[10] Meanwhile, Apple gets minerals from the East of DRC where M23 is dominant.[11]

The result of economic incentives for sponsoring conflict and the fading sensitivity to conflict are hugely unfortunate: The legal mechanisms and norms put in place to prevent and mitigate wars are failing. Indeed, it is increasingly clear that they were under threat from the very beginning.

Thus, in 2023, the Central Intelligence Agency (CIA) finally admitted its role in the displacement of the democratically elected President of Iran in 1953. Mohammad Mosaddegh was removed in a coup and replaced by the Shah: Mohammad Reza Pahlavi.[12] Indeed, the coup only succeeded because of the commitment of its agent, Norman Derbyshire, an MI6 officer based in Cyprus, whose agents got crowds onto the streets of Tehran.[13] Mosaddegh had nationalized the Iranian oil industry, which Britain had controlled since 1913. After the coup, he was imprisoned for three years and then held under house arrest until his death in 1967. The new Shah immediately granted concessions to Western oil companies.[14]

---

10 Vava Tampa, "Why Do the US and UK Still Fund Rwanda While Atrocities Mount Up in the DRC?," *The Guardian*, 14 February 2024, https://www.theguardian.com/global-development/2024/feb/14/why-us-and-uk-fund-rwanda-while-atrocities-mount-up-in-drc-vava-tampa.

11 "DRC Accuses Apple of Using Illegally Exploited Minerals from Conflict-Torn East *Le Monde*,," 25 April 2024, https://www.lemonde.fr/en/pixels/article/2024/04/25/drc-accuses-apple-of-using-illegally-exploited-minerals-from-conflict-torn-east_6669468_13.html#.

12 *CIA Finally Admits Role in 1953 Iran Coup Was "Undemocratic."* https://www.theguardian.com/us-news/2023/oct/13/cia-1953-iran-coup-undemocratic-argo

13 "Written Out of the History Books': The British Spy Who Planned the Iranian Coup," *The Guardian.*. https://www.theguardian.com/world/2023/aug/15/written-out-the-history-books-the-british-spy-who-planned-the-iranian-coup

14 Stephen Kinzer, *All the Shah's Men: An American Coup and the Roots of Middle East Terror* (Hoboken: John Wiley & Sons, 2003), 203–205.

Many coups and attempted coups have followed, mostly orchestrated by America and its allies. One of the most interesting attempted coups was exposed before the International Court of Justice in the Nicaragua Case in 1986.[15] This case was important because it revealed the West's algorithm for orchestrating regime change, which remains essentially unchanged even now, albeit that technology has allowed enhancements. Nicaragua brought proceedings against the United States alleging breach of a 1956 Treaty of Friendship, Commerce and Navigation. The USA declared a trade blockade against Nicaragua to destroy its economy, and mined Nicaragua's harbors to ensure its isolation. The USA also organized and sponsored a paramilitary opposition. As summarized by the Court:

> 20. The armed opposition to the new Government in Nicaragua, which originally comprised various movements, subsequently became organized into two main groups: the Fuerza Democratica Nicaragüense (FDN) and the Alianza Revolucionaria Democratica (ARDE). The first of these grew from 1981 onwards into a trained fighting force, operating along the borders with Honduras; the second, formed in 1982, operated along the borders with Costa Rica. The precise extent to which, and manner in which, the United States Government contributed to bringing about these developments will be studied more closely later in the present Judgment. However, after an initial period in which the "covert" operations of United States personnel and persons in their pay were kept from becoming public knowledge, it was made clear, not only in the United States press, but also in Congress and in official statements by the President and high United States officials, that the United States Government had been giving support to the contras, a term employed to describe those fighting against the present Nicaraguan Government. In 1983 budgetary legislation enacted by the United States Congress made specific provision for funds to be used by United States intelligence agencies for supporting "directly or indirectly military

15 Case Concerning Military and Paramilitary Activities in and against Nicaragua (*Nicaragua v. United States*) ICJ Reports 1986, p. 14

or paramilitary operations in Nicaragua." According to Nicaragua, the contras have caused it considerable material damage and widespread loss of life, and have also committed such acts as killing of prisoners, indiscriminate killing of civilians, torture, rape and kidnapping. It is contended by Nicaragua that the United States Government is effectively in control of the contras, that it devised their strategy and directed their tactics, and that the purpose of that Government was, from the beginning, to overthrow the Government of Nicaragua.

The ICJ was able to obtain and review a copy of a CIA "Psychological Operations" manual explaining, inter alia, how to foment civil unrest to bring down a target government.[16] The Court summarized part of the document as follows (with emphasis supplied):[17]

> The Court will . . . concentrate its attention on the other manual, that on "Psychological Operations." That this latter manual was prepared by the CIA appears to be clearly established: a report published in January 1985 by the Intelligence Committee contains a specific statement to that effect . . .
>
> In a later section on "Control of mass concentrations and meetings," the following guidance is given (inter alia): If possible, professional criminals will be hired to carry out specific selective 'jobs.' Specific tasks will be assigned to others, in order to create a 'martyr' for the cause, taking the demonstrators to a confrontation with the authorities, in order to bring about uprisings or shootings, which will cause the death of one or more persons, who would become the martyrs, a situation that should be made use of immediately against the régime, in order to create greater conflicts.

---

16 The manual appears to have been derived from similar techniques used in Vietnam. http://www.nytimes.com/1984/10/29/world/cia-manual-is-linked-to-vietnam-war-guide.html.

17 At para 118 of its Judgment

"Jobs" and "tasks" are clear euphemisms for killings, designed to create martyrs, whose deaths can be exploited to bring about violent protest. So much for non-interference in the internal affairs of other countries and the United States' special commitments in that regard.[18] So much for the Geneva Conventions. So much for human rights.

Since then, a series of suspected "colour [or color]" revolutions has followed a similar template. First the target government is branded a "regime," and accused of human rights abuses, often on the basis of false-flag operations or dubious digital evidence. Sanctions follow in the form of unilateral coercive measures (UCMs) imposed by individual States or groups of States, without Security Council endorsement. Their object is to undermine a target State's economy to cause social disruption and spur local discontent. Foreign "civil society" groups then encourage protest and harness it under an opposition brand, bringing crowds of protesters onto the streets. These protesters either displace the target government themselves or they provide cover for a professional coup. More false flags are conventional in the later stages—on the Nicaragua model—with the carnage relayed on social media to inflame local opposition and world opinion against the incumbent government.

The main entities accused of promoting regime change are American: Freedom House and the National Endowment for Democracy (NED). As an example, according to Victorian Nuland, America's former Assistant Secretary of State, the United States spent $5 billion on "promotion of democracy" and "related projects" in Ukraine between 1991 and 2013.[19] Substantial sums were funnelled through USAID,[20] Freedom House and the NED.[21]

Freedom House used to describe itself as an "independent non-governmental organization that supports the expansion of

---

18 The U.S. undertook not to interfere in the affairs of other States in the Charter of the Organisation of American States (1948), and it reiterated an intention to refrain in the Declaration on the Inadmissibility of Intervention in the Domestic Affairs of States (1965).

19 YouTube, Victoria Nuland Admits Washington has Spent $5 billion to "Subvert Ukraine" (9 February 2014), https://www.youtube.com/watch?v=U2fYcHLouXY

20 United States Agency for International Development (USAID), *Ukraine*, https://www.usaid.gov/ukraine.

21 National Endowment for Democracy, Ukraine, https://web.archive.org/web/20140831044648/http://www.ned.org/where-we-work/eurasia/ukraine

freedom in the world."[22] Now it has dropped "non-governmental,"[23] and its money still comes from the Federal budget. Before 1997, the money was delivered via government contracts. Thereafter it has been provided by way of grants from the U.S. State Department and USAID.[24] According to the *Financial Times*, Freedom House was one of the organizations selected by the U.S. State Department to receive funding for "clandestine activities" inside Iran.[25] Teams of specialists in regime change—including nominal diplomats—move from theatre to theatre—for example, from Georgia to Ukraine.[26]

Attempts of other countries to complain about the abovementioned behavior had no much effect. In May 2001, the Permanent Representative of Cuba to the UN lodged an objection with the NGO Committee,[27] resisting the consultative status that Freedom House was seeking with the Economic and Social Council. Freedom House was "a machinery of subversion, closer to an intelligence service than an NGO."[28] China seconded the charge of subversion.[29]

At the later stage the USA expanded the use of economic and other means (sanctions) to change the policy and behavior of the target state, despite their clear inconsistency with international legal standards. It shall be noted, in particular, that the UN General Assembly regularly passes resolutions rejecting the use of UCMs as a means of intervention in the domestic affairs of States and condemning their impact on human rights,[30] also without much effect.

---

22 Gmane (archived*).* Discussion from the mailing list "India ZestMedia.*"* *http://comments.gmane.org/gmane.culture.region.india.zestmedia/1387*

23 Freedom House. About Us. https://freedomhouse.org/about-us.

24 Freedom House. Official Website. https://freedomhouse.org/.

25 Financial Times. White House and EU Talk Peace and Defence. http://www.ft.com/cms/s/0/48d26298-c052-11da-939f-0000779e2340.html

26 Ian Traynor, "US Campaign Behind the Turmoil in Kiev," *The Guardian*, 26 November 2004, https://www.theguardian.com/world/2004/nov/26/ukraine.usa.

27 United Nations, "Iraq Sanctions Committee Lifts Restrictions on Oil Spare Parts, Approves Contracts Worth Over $1 Billion," *UN Press Release*, 14 August 2001, http://www3.scienceblog.com/community/older/archives/L/2001/B/un011050.html.

28 Ibid

29 Ibid

30 A/RES/79/167 Human rights and unilateral coercive measures
A/RES/78/202 Human rights and unilateral coercive measures
A/RES/77/214 Human rights and unilateral coercive measures
A/RES/76/161 Human rights and unilateral coercive measures

At the same time the consequences of UCMs for targeted populations and targeted individuals are appalling. UNICEF has drawn

A/RES/75/181 Human rights and unilateral coercive measures
A/RES/74/154 Human rights and unilateral coercive measures
A/RES/73/167 Human rights and unilateral coercive measures
A/RES/72/168 Human rights and unilateral coercive measures
A/RES/71/193 Human rights and unilateral coercive measures
A/RES/70/151 Human rights and unilateral coercive measures
A/RES/69/180 Human rights and unilateral coercive measures
A/RES/68/162 Human rights and unilateral coercive measures
A/RES/67/170 Human rights and unilateral coercive measures
A/RES/66/156 Human rights and unilateral coercive measures
A/RES/65/217 Human rights and unilateral coercive measures
A/RES/64/170 Human rights and unilateral coercive measures
A/RES/63/179 Human rights and unilateral coercive measures
A/RES/62/162 Human rights and unilateral coercive measures
A/RES/61/170 Human rights and unilateral coercive measures
A/RES/60/155 Human rights and unilateral coercive measures
A/RES/59/188 Human rights and unilateral coercive measures
A/RES/58/171 Human rights and unilateral coercive measures
A/RES/57/222 Human rights and unilateral coercive measures
A/RES/56/179 Unilateral economic measures as a means of political and economic coercion against developing countries
A/RES/56/148 Human rights and unilateral coercive measures
A/RES/55/110 Human rights and unilateral coercive measures
A/RES/54/172 Human rights and unilateral coercive measures
A/RES/53/141 Human rights and unilateral coercive measures
A/RES/52/120 Human rights and unilateral coercive measures
A/RES/51/103 Human rights and unilateral coercive measures
A/RES/50/96 Economic measures as means of political and economic coercion against developing countries
A/RES/48/168 Economic measures as means of political and economic coercion against developing countries
A/RES/46/210 Economic measures as means of political and economic coercion against developing countries
A/RES/44/215 Economic measures as means of political and economic coercion against developing countries
A/RES/42/173 Economic measures as means of political and economic coercion against developing countries
A/RES/41/165 Economic measures as means of political and economic coercion against developing countries
A/RES/40/185 Economic measures as means of political and economic coercion against developing countries
A/RES/39/210 Economic measures as means of political and economic coercion against developing countries
A/RES/38/197 Economic measures as means of political and economic coercion against developing countries

attention to the particular impact of sanctions on children, whose development is frequently damaged because of interference with the supply of essential goods, including medicines, food and the means to produce food. As one example: "A record 12.4 million Syrians—nearly 60 per cent of the population—are food insecure, according to the World Food Programme (WFP). Reports of severe bread and fuel crises indicate these shortages are in part caused by sanctions. Around 90 per cent of children need humanitarian aid to survive, with more than half a million stunted because of malnutrition."[31]

As another example, American sanctions against Iran have discouraged a Swedish company from supplying special dressings needed by thousands of patients in Iran with "butterfly skin" disease. Many of the victims are children. Ordinary dressings rip off their skin when removed once or twice per day, inflicting torture beyond imagining. Officials in the United States and European Union have been made aware of the problem.[32] They have done nothing to redress it.

Sanctions against individuals are also widely adopted and utterly pernicious in their impact. The United Kingdom's legislation and practice provides an illustration. In collaboration with the United States and the European Union, the United Kingdom has adopted sanctions against designated persons. Under its Sanctions and Anti-Money Laundering Act 2018 (SAMLA), a Minister may make sanctions regulations (inter alia) in the interests of national security, in the interests of international peace and security, or even just to "further a foreign policy objective of the government of the United Kingdom."[33] For now, that objective seems to be to pressure Russian civilians to influence their government in relation to the conflict with Ukraine.

---

31 Sanctions and their Impact on Children DISCUSSION PAPER Feb. 2022.

32 OHCHR, Mandate of the Special Rapporteur on the Negative Impact of Unilateral Coercive Measures on the Enjoyment of Human Rights, Ref. OL USA 14/2023, 6 December 2023, https://spcommreports.ohchr.org/TMResultsBase/DownLoadPublicCommunicationFile?gId=28386; OHCHR, Mandate of the Special Rapporteur, Ref. OL USA 13/2023, 30 November 2023, https://spcommreports.ohchr.org/TMResultsBase/DownLoadPublicCommunicationFile?gId=28385.; OHCHR, Mandate of the Special Rapporteur, Ref. OL USA 12/2023, 17 November 2023, https://spcommreports.ohchr.org/TMResultsBase/DownLoadPublicCommunicationFile?gId=28384.

33 UK Government, Sanctions and Anti-Money Laundering Act 2018, c.13, https://www.legislation.gov.uk/ukpga/2018/13/contents.

The consequences for those directly targeted are severe. "Designated Persons" lose access to their money. They lose their businesses and homes. Their children are thrown out of school. They face travel bans that break families. They can apply for subsistence (out of their own money) but, per HMG: "High-net-worth individuals should not expect ... continuation of their previous lifestyle."[34]

The targets, who are usually rich Russians, have done nothing wrong. Usually, they built a business in Russia when building businesses was encouraged by the West, especially with Western capital. Nonetheless, sanctions against entrepreneurs are extended to others. In particular, under the UK regime, relatives[35] or friends of primary designees become "involved persons" and open to sanctions in their own right, even though there was no original crime and nothing to be "involved" in. Rights formerly protected by the European Convention on Human Rights have vanished: specifically, rights to peaceful quiet enjoyment of property, the right to respect for one's family life and livelihood, the right to freedom of opinion and expression and the right not to be discriminated against.

Challenges to these measures have been difficult because for a long time, the restrictions included interference with legal representation.[36] The early cases have established an adverse and very disappointing precedent. Judges tell complainants that sanctions are "temporary," even though those same judges have accepted evidence that UCMs have destroyed businesses and driven children to suicidal thoughts.

---

34 OFSI guidance at https://www.gov.uk/government/publications/financial-sanctions-licensing/ofsi-licensing-designated-individuals-licensing-principles--2

"5. In most cases and unless there are mitigating factors or extenuating circumstances, licences will not enable a designated person to continue the lifestyle or business activities they had before they were designated. In particular high-net-worth individuals should not expect licences to allow continuation of their previous lifestyle."

35 See e.g. the listing for Elizaveta Peskova, the then 24-year-old daughter of the Russian President's spokesman: "Elizaveta Dmitriyevna PESKOVA is closely associated with Dmitry Sergeyevich PESKOV by virtue of being his daughter. Dmitry Sergeyevich PESKOV is an involved person under the Russia (Sanctions) (EU Exit) Regulation 2019."

36 An initial limit in the UK of £500,000 per case was impossible for legal representatives to apply—a barrister, for example, would not know how much of the cap had been used by other professionals. The limit has since been increased but some cases require bespoke attention from OFSI. When it looks at cases, it has reduced arbitrarily the usual professional fees of barristers.

There is nothing temporary about insolvency or suicide. "Significant" harm to individuals is said to be outweighed by a so-called "community interest" in maintaining sanctions, even though this community interest is never articulated and even though the British government has failed to demonstrate in any case that the personal sanctions at issue have any remote prospect of influencing the Kremlin.[37]

The West seems impervious to arguments and evidence that its UCMs breach international law and cause wholly unjustifiable harm. It is sensitive to its potential legal exposure, but instead of arguing the issues, it prefers to block argument or to circumvent legal process altogether. Thus, there has been obstruction of legal mechanisms that ought to provide redress, and when, rarely, personal sanctions are successfully challenged, they are frequently reimposed on different (equally specious) grounds.

As an example of obstruction, many UCMs against countries appear to breach the trade rules in GATT, administered by the World Trade Organization (WTO), as amplified below. However, no legal action is possible, at least at the WTO. In December 2019, the WTO Appeal Tribunal, which had enabled the losing side before a WTO first-instance tribunal to appeal a case to oblivion, lost its quorum. WTO dispute resolution no longer works. This has happened because the USA obstructed the appointment of replacement judges, with the clear objective of destroying the rules-based order in international trade.[38] The USA seems far keener on applying sanctions than on defending their legality.

---

37 See for example *Shvidler v. Secretary of State for Foreign, Commonwealth and Development Affairs* [2023] EWHC 2121 (Admin) Garnham J. The Judge accepted evidence of destroyed businesses but concluded "... the Secretary of State has had conscientious regard to the impact of designation on both the Claimant and his family. They have properly been taken into account but have been found insufficient to outweigh the community interest in the maintenance of sanctions in the Claimant's case." There was no definition of "community interest" or demonstration of potential influence if it meant affecting the decision making of the Russian government. See too: *Khan v. Secretary of State for Foreign, Commonwealth and Development Affairs* [2024] EWHC 361 (Admin), a decision of Cockerill J:

"...The youngest child, aside from having to change school, has suffered a considerable downturn in mental health, expressing suicidal ideas prompted by the loss of so much of the secure routine which is so important in childhood ..."

But this and other harm was outweighed by "the benefits of Ms Khan's sanctioning," which were not defined or proved.

38 Congressional Research Service. Legal Sidebar LSB10385. https://crsreports.

The absence of legal redress is unfortunate because the legal objections under GATT are compelling. Articles XI[39] and XIII[40] prohibit quantitative restrictions of trade (including "other measures") aimed at particular countries, and GATT also prohibits discrimination. There is an exception (in Art. XXI) for trade restrictions that must be implemented under the UN Charter: i.e. UN sanctions. There is no exception covering unilateral sanctions imposed by individual States or groups of States for obvious reasons. The WTO agreement would be futile if States could abrogate their obligations at will on the basis of national law or subjective public policy. The very clear implication is that only the UN Security Council can authorize sanctions.

Another exception (also in Art. XXI) allows measures that a State considers necessary for the protection of its essential security interests, but this exception is narrow. It is confined to measures concerning fissionable materials, trade in weapons and trade in time of war or other emergency in international relations. Moreover, the assessment of necessity is an objective one which WTO tribunals should be able to test, like in *Nicaragua v. United States* in the ICJ.[41] The friendship

---

congress.gov/product/pdf/LSB/LSB10385.

39 Article XI General Elimination of Quantitative Restrictions

1. No prohibitions or restrictions other than duties, taxes or other charges, whether made effective through quotas, import or export licences or other measures, shall be instituted or maintained by any contracting party on the importation of any product of the territory of any other contracting party or on the exportation or sale for export of any product destined for the territory of any other contracting party.

2. The provisions of paragraph 1 of this Article shall not extend to the following:

(a) Export prohibitions or restrictions temporarily applied to prevent or relieve critical shortages of foodstuffs or other products essential to the exporting contracting party ..."

40 Article XIII Non-discriminatory Administration of Quantitative Restrictions

"1. No prohibition or restriction shall be applied by any contracting party on the importation of any product of the territory of any other contracting party or on the exportation of any product destined for the territory of any other contracting party, unless the importation of the like product of all third countries or the exportation of the like product to all third countries is similarly prohibited or restricted.

2. In applying import restrictions to any product, contracting parties shall aim at a distribution of trade in such product approaching as closely as possible the shares which the various contracting parties might be expected to obtain in the absence of such restrictions ...":

41 International Court of Justice (ICJ), Military and Paramilitary Activities in and against Nicaragua (*Nicaragua v. United States of America*), Merits, Judgment, 27 June 1986, https://www.icj-cij.org/sites/default/files/case-related/70/070-19860627-JUD-01-00-EN.pdf

treaty in issue in that case contained scope for derogation in circumstances similar to Article XXI of GATT.

The Court said this:

> Secondly, the Court emphasizes the importance of the word "necessary" in Article XXI: the measures taken must not merely be such as tend to protect the essential security interests of the party taking them, but must be "necessary" for that purpose. Taking into account the whole situation of the United States in relation to Central America, so far as the Court is informed of it (and even assuming that the justification of self- defense, which the Court has rejected on the legal level, had some validity on the political level), the Court considers that the mining of Nicaraguan ports, and the direct attacks on ports and oil installations, cannot possibly be justified as "necessary" to protect the essential security interests of the United States. As to the trade embargo, the Court has to note the express justification for it given in the Presidential finding quoted in para- graph 125 above, and that the measure was one of an economic nature, thus one which fell within the sphere of relations contemplated by the Treaty. But by the terms of the Treaty itself, whether a measure is necessary to protect the essential security interests of a party is not, as the Court has emphasized (paragraph 222 above), purely a question for the subjective judgment of the party; the text does not refer to what the party "considers necessary" for that purpose. Since no evidence at all is available to show how Nicaraguan policies had in fact become a threat to "essential security interests" in May 1985, when those policies had been consistent, and consistently criticized by the United States, for four years previously, the Court is unable to find that the embargo was "necessary" to protect those interests ... (para. 282).

More generally, it highly unlikely that economic warfare on the other side of the world is justifiable under a test of whether measures are strictly necessary to protect national security interests.

In the same context it is striking that the United Kingdom and most States party to the European Convention on Human Rights[42] have not derogated from that Convention, under Article 15, to excuse their sanctions regimes. On the face of it, derogation would be necessary, because UCMs trample over fundamental human rights. However, the terms of Article 15 make legitimate derogation impossible. Article 15 provides as follows (with emphasis supplied):

ARTICLE 15
Derogation in time of emergency

1. **In time of war or other public emergency threatening the life of the nation** any High Contracting Party may take measures derogating from its obligations under this Convention **to the extent strictly required by the exigencies of the situation, provided that such measures are not inconsistent with its other obligations under international law**.

2. No derogation from Article 2, except in respect of deaths resulting from lawful acts of war, or from Articles 3 [torture], 4 (paragraph 1 [slavery or servitude]) and 7 [No punishment without law] shall be made under this provision.

3. Any High Contracting Party availing itself of this right of derogation shall keep the Secretary General of the Council of Europe fully informed of the measures which it has taken and the reasons therefor. It shall also inform the Secretary General of the Council of Europe when such measures have ceased to operate and the provisions of the Convention are again being fully executed.

It would be difficult for any of the countries applying personal sanctions to justify them on the basis of war (since they are not combatants) or face a national emergency threatening the life of the nation, since they are not on the receiving end of invasion.

---

42 Council of Europe, European Convention on Human Rights, https://www. echr.coe.int/documents/d/echr/convention_ENG.

On any view, it is difficult to see any necessity for what amount to grave penal measures against people innocent of any crime. That applies to the principals behind legitimate Russian businesses and *a fortiori* to their relatives and friends. There is no necessity to destroy the rights of individuals guaranteed under the European Convention on Human Rights: rights to peaceful enjoyment of property, rights to respect for family life and livelihood, the right not to be discriminated against, the right to freedom of opinion and expression. Indeed, the onslaught against designated persons amounts to psychological torture because of the destruction of all incidents of a normal family life.

Sometimes this entails physical torture where, for example, medical treatment is obstructed. This breaches a non-derogable Convention right under art. 3, 15 of the European Convention on Human Rights. Overall, this treatment of designated persons amounts to (very vindictive) punishment without a crime, in breach of another non-derogable right (art. 7, 15).

Of course, UCMs against populations and individual civilians also transgress some of the most sacred protections of ordinary people under international humanitarian law—in particular, the rules against using starvation as a weapon of war and the prohibition of collective punishment, cited above.

There is no doubt about this. The starting point when analysing purported countermeasures is the ILC work on Responsibility of States for Internationally Wrongful Acts. Article 49 of the ILC Draft Articles says this:

Object and limits of countermeasures
1. **An injured State may only take countermeasures against a State which is responsible for an internationally wrongful act** in order to induce that State to comply with its obligations under Part Two."
A targeted State is different from its people. Targeting civilians is therefore outside the scope of permissible countermeasures. Further, under Article 50:
"1. Countermeasures shall not affect:
. . .

    (b) obligations for the protection of fundamental human rights;

(c) Obligations of a humanitarian character prohibiting reprisals;

(d) other obligations under peremptory norms of general international law.

Unilateral coercive measures aimed at populations and designated individuals are totally incompatible with fundamental human rights. They come close to reprisals and they transgress peremptory norms of international law—including, especially, the rules of international humanitarian law against collective punishment.[43]

The ILC, in particular, dealt expressly with the case where sanctions interfere with the provision of food to a population. The commentary to Article 50 says this "In its general comment No. 8 (1997) the Committee on Economic, Social and Cultural Rights discussed the effect of economic sanctions on civilian populations and especially on children.... It stressed that "whatever the circumstances, **such sanctions should always take full account of the provisions of the International Covenant on Economic, Social and Cultural Rights**" ...

Analogies can be drawn from other elements of general international law. For example, paragraph 1 of article 54 of the Protocol Additional to the Geneva Conventions of August 12, 1949, and relating to the protection of victims of international armed conflicts (Protocol I) stipulates unconditionally that **"[s]tarvation of civilians as a method of warfare is prohibited."** Likewise, the final sentence

---

43 Note:

The 4th Geneva Convention, Article 33:

No protected person may be punished for an offence he or she has not personally committed. Collective penalties and likewise all measures of intimidation or of terrorism are prohibited.

Pillage is prohibited.

Reprisals against protected persons and their property are prohibited.

The Hague Convention (IV), Article 50:

No general penalty, pecuniary or otherwise, shall be inflicted upon the population on account of the acts of individuals for which they cannot be regarded as jointly and severally responsible.

Article 53 of the 1969 Vienna Convention on the Law of Treaties:

A peremptory norm of general international law is one which is "accepted and recognized by the international community of States as a whole as a norm from which no derogation is permitted and which can be modified only by a subsequent norm of general international law having the same character."

of paragraph 2 of article 1 of the International Covenant on Economic, Social and Cultural Rights and of the International Covenant on Civil and Political Rights states that **"In no case may a people be deprived of its own means of subsistence."**

Sadly, sanctions targeting populations often have precisely this effect, as attested by UN Agencies, including UNICEF. Similarly, measures that target individuals depriving them of their property, homes and livelihood and ruining their family life are totally impermissible under human rights law and international humanitarian law—particularly the prohibition of collective punishment.

Again, the West is impervious to criticism on these grounds, preferring to avoid debate and resisting the jurisdiction of relevant international tribunals. To the extent that America and its allies try to justify UCMs, they usually do so by reference to "retorsions" or "countermeasures." Retorsions are unfriendly acts that are not in breach of the international obligations of the State adopting them. Countermeasures are a proportionate response to an earlier international wrongdoing, but they must similarly comply with the international human rights and humanitarian obligations of the State adopting them.[44] States are not entitled to ignore their human rights obligations, which are typically owed to third States as well as the people protected. Nor can they ignore their obligations and responsibilities under peremptory norms of international law—like the rules against using starvation as a weapon, and against collective punishment.

Moreover, UCMs are used to victimize people with minimal to no legal and due process. Populations are targeted as an aspect of foreign policy. Individuals are designated with no opportunity to contest the purported grounds of their designation in advance, and even when a subsequent challenge succeeds, they are frequently relisted on different grounds, again without any prior opportunity to contest them. The result can be a cycle of sanctions and challenges in which the victim can never win. This breaches fundamental human rights principles requiring due process[45] and humanitarian principles forbidding punishment without personal responsibility for crime.

---

44 DARS, art. 50

45 Article 6 of the European Convention on Human Rights and Article 14 of the International Covenant on Civil and Political Rights (International Covenant ("ICCPR")

Conclusion

It follows that the States imposing unilateral coercive measures are only protected, as matters stand, by the absence of clear opportunities to establish their international responsibility before tribunals with compulsory jurisdiction. However, there is scope for that to change in four important respects.

First, the UN General Assembly is entitled to ask the International Court of Justice for an advisory opinion on UCMs, drawing attention to their impact on innocent people and their apparent inconsistency with international law. Such a request could usefully be added to the next resolution by which the General Assembly condemns unilateral coercive measures.

Second, various human rights tribunals have compulsory jurisdiction, including between States. Sanctions adopted and applied in Europe could be challenged before the European Court of Human Rights. Given the evidence of the appalling impact of unilateral coercive measures on populations, individuals and families, it would be open to that Court to declare them in breach of the Convention and to award compensation—after exhaustion of domestic remedies in one of the signatory States.

Third, given that the States adopting unilateral coercive measures have paid singularly little attention to their inconsistent international obligations generally, it is no surprise that in many cases, they have also ignored bilateral investment treaties that protect investors whose property has been seized. Typical provisions conferring protection include the following:

- Each Contracting Party shall ensure *fair and equitable treatment* to the investments of investors of the other Contracting Party and *shall not impair by unreasonable or discriminatory measures, the operation, management, maintenance, use, enjoyment or disposal thereof by those investors*. Each Contracting Party shall accord to such investments *full security and protection*.

- Neither Contracting Party shall take *any measures depriving investors of the other Contracting Party of their investments nor take any measures having similar effects unless* the following conditions are complied with:

(a) the measures are taken in the public interest and under due process of law;

(b) the measures are not discriminatory;

(c) the measures are accompanied by provisions for the *payment of just compensation*.

Bilateral investment treaties (BITs) allow investors to bring arbitration claims against States that breach them. Personal designations of individual investors in Europe under sanctions regimes quite clearly breach the protections in applicable BITs. They are unfair and inequitable, and they discriminate. They are specifically designed to interfere with the operation, management, maintenance, use, enjoyment or disposal of investments: they usually involve freezing targeted individuals out of management and stopping their access to dividends. Investments are frozen and liquidation and free transfer of proceeds are blocked. Sometimes there is forced divestment. In many cases, the seizure lasts for years and amounts to practical expropriation—and certainly deprivation. All of this is the opposite of the "full security and protection" generally promised under the relevant treaties, and there is no lawful excuse for ignoring them.

Of course, in some cases, there must be interference with property—where, for example, without discrimination, property rights are interfered with for the general good—like building a necessary road. However, when that occurs, it must be fair and equitable and in the public interest. Designation under unilateral coercive measures is usually discriminatory (on the basis of nationality from a State with an unpopular government) and always unfair (because of the obliteration of fundamental human rights and humanitarian standards). There is no public interest in abandoning basic human rights or peremptory norms of international humanitarian law. like the prohibition of collective punishment. It follows that there can be no public interest justification for UCMs in the sense required by bilateral investment treaties to justify a departure from strict protection of investments.

Even if a public interest exception could potentially apply, bilateral investment treaties invariably require payment of prompt and effective compensation. Western governments have so far provided none on a voluntary basis. Soon, under these treaties, they are likely to face arbitration awards for massive compensation.

Finally, the Prosecutor at the International Criminal Court (ICC) has recently shown signs of robust independence. The ICC has jurisdiction over crimes against humanity (under Article 7), including: "extermination" being "the intentional infliction of conditions of life, inter alia the deprivation of access to food and medicine, calculated to bring about the destruction of part of a population." Crimes against humanity also include: "Other inhumane acts of a similar character intentionally causing great suffering, or serious injury to body or to mental or physical health."

"Torture" is also included, but with the qualification that: ". . . torture shall not include pain or suffering arising only from, inherent in or incidental to, lawful sanctions. . . ."

For all of the reasons summarized above, UCMs are not "lawful sanctions" because there is minimal prospect of them qualifying as legitimate retorsions or countermeasures. They cannot do so when they breach the human rights and humanitarian obligations of the States adopting and applying them.

Given indisputable evidence that UCMs against countries do restrict access to food and medicine, do cause destruction of populations, especially children, and do cause great suffering and injury, the ICC Prosecutor could usefully direct his attention to the most egregious of them. He should also respond to any predictable tragedy as a result of personal sanctions on individuals. Public officials should understand that if they are complicit in humanitarian crimes, they can and will face prosecution, and personal retribution whatever their status or office.

It is a sad commentary on our times that for the time being, the only relevant retribution has been the adoption of sanctions by the USA against the ICC for doing its job.[46] Parallels with America's suppression of dispute resolution in the WTO are obvious.

The tools exist to fix this unfortunate situation and to enforce respect for human rights and humanitarian norms in the various ways set out above. Those with opportunities to do so have a responsibility to act. Basic human rights and minimum humanitarian standards were achieved at terrible cost. It is vital to protect them for us all.

---

46 White House, "Imposing Sanctions on the International Criminal Court," *The White House*, 14 February 2025, https://www.whitehouse.gov/presidential-actions/2025/02/imposing-sanctions-on-the-international-criminal-court/

CHAPTER 12

The Devastating Impact of Unilateral Coercive Measures
on Human Rights and *Jus Cogens*

Ali Rastbeen[1]

Abstract

Unilateral sanctions can be qualified as remnants of the system of a balance of power in which the powerful States imposed their laws on the weak, taking advantage of their political and economic ascendancy. These "acts of war" affect the legitimacy of public international law, the legal framework and responsibility of States and private actors, as well as human rights. The principles of State sovereignty, non-interference, free trade (including international shipping), the most-favored-nation status, and trade discrimination contrary to WTO rules are all targeted, with consequences for the sanctioned country and for third-party States, victims of extra-territorial impacts. Recent cases in Syria and Iran show that coercive measures affect the right to health, food and to development, an inalienable human right that encompasses all human rights and fundamental freedoms. Such collective punishment through unilateral coercive measures is prohibited by law, and is an attack on human rights, challenging the principles of the international legal order, sovereignty and the equality of States, and non-interference. It is an attack on the enjoyment of human rights in their most fundamental aspects.

Introduction

Two main characteristics of unilateral sanctions used within international society deserve to be studied and developed as part of a work of elucidation raising questions both as to the stability and as to

---

1 Dr., President of the Paris Academy of Geopolitics

the very existence of public international law, insofar as they are not developed via common law judicial decisions.

Unilateral sanctions reflect the establishment of a balance of power in which the most powerful imposes its law on the weakest with impunity, taking advantage of the political, economic and financial prerogatives and privileges at its disposal. These measures might have an effect similar to "acts of war," affecting both the legitimacy of public international law, and the legal framework and responsibility of private and state actors as it concerns human rights, guaranteed by *jus cogens*.

Thus, the principles of sovereign equality of states, of non-intervention into the domestic affairs of states, as well as freedom of trade, of international navigation, and prohibition of commercial discrimination contrary to WTO rules are called into question by these sanctions, which have consequences not only primarily on the country or countries sanctioned, but also on third-party States and actors, which are also victims in a "secondary" manner of the extraterritorial effects of these acts.

Furthermore, it should be emphasized that unilateral coercive measures make the entire population of the countries concerned pay the price of the dispute existing between their governments and the country that imposes sanctions.[2] Recent cases in Syria or Iran demonstrate this. Indeed, these measures aggravate the suffering of populations by directly affecting their right to health, food, and development, the latter being an inalienable right for every human being.

This situation is thus similar to collective punishment,[3] but in terms of measures or activities applied by States, groups of States or regional organizations without or beyond the authorization of the UN Security Council. It is is prohibited by international law. It constitutes an attack on the principle of legal certainty and that of minimizing the humanitarian impact in compliance policies.

Subsequent developments reveal an apparent paradox where the attack on public international law and human rights by unilateral

---

2 Cortright David, Lopez George A., *The Sanctions Decade. Assessing UN Strategies in the 1990s*, International Peace Academy, Boulder, Lynne Rienner, 2000, 274 p.; Mascala Corinne (dir.), À propos de la sanction (les travaux de l'IFR), Toulouse, Presses de l'Université Toulouse Capitole, Librairie générale de droit et de jurisprudence (LGDJ), 2007, 202 p.

3 Nossal Kim Richard, "International sanctions as international punishment," dans *International Organization*, Vol.43, Iss. 2, 1989, pp. 301–322.

coercive measures is asserted by the sender State to have a moral basis. Sanctions targeting Iran are among the many examples taken from recent international situations where we have noted such attacks on the principles of international law, in particular on those of respect for the sovereignty and equality of States, non-interference, and the enjoyment of human rights in their most fundamental aspects. This leads us to conclude that public international law is being called into question by the adoption of unilateral international sanctions, which are akin to countermeasures similar to acts of war.

Sanctions, Law and Force

While the emergence and existence of the concept of sanction is not in itself contestable since the beginnings of humanity up to the present; whether it is through the moral approach of anthropology and/ or in its inscription in law, nevertheless this concept naturally falls within the prudential virtue to which all authorities and governments of human society are bound. Thus, the concept of the surrounding context conditions its legitimacy.

Sanctions in principle are born and applied only in a very specific context of contestation by their repression and virtuous rectification of acts likely to disturb a natural or legal order. The notions of protection and proportionality must guide the decision to impose a sanction, because its aim is to put an end to the conditions that led to its implementation: not just the acts themselves, of course, but also the behavior that aims to repeat them over time.

Prudential virtue arises from the necessity to protect the community that is victim of these behaviors by the disciplinary anticipation of any recurrence; the safeguarding of the good of the community obliges the use of repression.

According to the principle of proportionality, the sanction must be graduated according to the seriousness of the breach of the rule in order to obtain a substantial change of the perpetrator responsible for these disorders. In all respects, the sanction integrates, is part of, the principle of justice: reparation of the prejudice, and prevention of social disorder due to its eventual repetition; hence, a penalty enacted by a legitimate authority whose decision is obviously taken in the interest of the community that is victim of the prejudice and for the common good.

The basis of the action of punishing and preventing by sanction lies in the common understanding by the members of the community of the reprehensible nature of the acts targeted, of the need for a decision of repression and of their agreement on the choice of an incontestable authority.

As we can see, the question of the environment and the context of general consensus on the principles of sociability and order is a prerequisite for legitimate action. In the opposite case of a privatization and a diversion of the meaning of the sanction, the sanction loses its status as an exercise of justice for and in the name of the community and enters the category of a unilateral act serving the interests of an individualized entity. It thus disconnects itself from the law, from which it draws its reason for being and which has defined the means of recognition of the offense as well as the conditions of the validity of its exercise of sanctioning it and preventing its possible repetition.

In short: for a sanction to be applied, there must first be agreement on a common, universal definition of guilt, then it must be recognized in a specific act having harmed the community sharing these *minimo-rum* legal principles. This, in public international law, has produced the "*Kelsenian*" definition of sanction: "sanction is a reaction to the illicit. It is the main consequence of illicit behavior."[4]

Indeed, in this context, public international law has developed an international legal order, based on the *jus cogens* norms and the Charter of the United Nations. *Jus cogens*, "imperative law" in French, applies universally to all peremptory legal norms of international law and without possibility for any derogation. *Jus cogens* is thus codified as a "peremptory legal norm of general international law [...] accepted and recognized by the international community of States in its entirety as a standard from which no derogation is permitted and which can only be modified by a new norm of general international law having the same character."[5]

---

4 Kelsen Hans, *The Law of the United Nations: A Critical Analysis of its Fundamental Problems – Volume 1*, New York, F. A. Praeger, 1950, p. 706 (903 p.); Kelsen Hans, *Allgemeine Theorie der Normen*, Vienne, Manz, 1979, p. 115 (362 p.).

5 Vienna Convention on the Law of Treaties, article 53, 1969.

States are therefore, in principle, required to apply and respect these rules by virtue of their imperative nature,[6] because they have a universal vocation, and are accepted and recognized as legal norms from which no derogation is possible by the international community of States as a whole.

This last characteristic signifies the strong difference between regular norms of international law and norms of *jus cogens*, the latter taking precedence over the former, and any international treaty contrary to a norm of *jus cogens* being deemed null, according to Article 53 of the Vienna Convention on the Law of Treaties (1969).[7] However, public international law is supposed to apply in the international community formed by its actors, namely the States, whose respect for sovereignty is a principle. Some States are seeking, in some cases disproportionately, to broaden their capacity to interpret norms of application at the heart of international relations, i.e. those involving the exercise of political, economic and military power.

The most powerful states in the international system, geopolitically influential but also very present in the formulation of legal systems, have long been accustomed to leaving the rule of law imprecise for the protection of their own interests, and to limiting the sanction to the political and moral levels. This capacity, external to common law, is reinforced by the absence of a vertical hierarchy in the international order capable of exercising the means of execution. The geopolitical characteristic based on the balance of power highlighted above and the difficulties specific to the structure of international law, raise the question of whether a few of the strongest States might be able to impose

---

6 Tomuschat Christian, Thouvenin Jean-Marc (éds.), *The Fundamental Rules of the International Legal Order:* Jus Cogens *and Obligations* Erga Omnes, Leiden, Martinus Nijhoff, 2006. Mandatory rules (or *jus cogens*) are those that order or prohibit a conduct without the subject being able to evade it, while supplementary laws, which are also mandatory, can be set aside by the subjects of law. In fact, they come to supplement the absence of expressed will and to apply themselves, by default, to legal situations.

7 "Draft conclusions on identification and legal consequences of peremptory norms of general international law (*jus cogens*) ," adopted by the International Law Commission at its seventy-third session, in 2022, and submitted to the General Assembly as a part of the Commission's report covering the work of that session (A/77/10, para. 43), *Yearbook of the International Law Commission, 2022*, vol. II, Part Two.

political and economic sanctions themselves,[8] exempting themselves from the rules of law concerning the taking of non-coercive measures, in application of the provisions of Article 41 of the Charter of the United Nations and of the international legal system intended for the framing of a sanction under the conditions of objectivity and justice necessary for its legitimacy.

This reminder of the relationship between what should be law and force on the international stage, up to the most recent crisis situations, allows us to shed more light on the attack on equity and human rights implied by extraterritorial sanctions enacted by leading international actors on the sole basis of their political and economic power, and according to their minority conception of the interpretation of the law.

The Nature of Extraterritorial Sanctions

When we talk about extraterritorial sanctions, what are we talking about? If States are indeed authorized by international law to enact sanctions against any act that undermines, on their territory, their internal public order, or even international public order,[9] or some of their nationals outside their territory, this is not the case when they target foreigners residing outside this territory. In the latter case, international public order is not respected by the prescriptive country, and international institutions are able to implement any legal process of condemnation or even sanction these illicit acts.[10]

---

8 Mulder Nicholas, *The Economic Weapon: The Rise of Sanctions As a Tool of Modern War*, New Haven, Yale University Press, 2022, 448 p.

9 Sanctions for violations of legal norms or principles of public international law. Such violations must constitute acts that are manifestly unlawful under international law; Frowein Jochen A., "Reactions By Not Directly Affected States to Breaches of Public International Law," in *Recueil des cours de l'Academie de droit international de La Haye*, Vol. 248, 1994, pp. 345–437 (93 p.); Hailbronner Kay, "Sanctions and Third Parties and the Concept of International Public Order," in *Archiv des Völkerrechts*, Vol. 30, N°1, 1992, pp. 2–15 (13 p.); Stein Thorsten, "International Measures Against Terrorism and the Sanctions By and Against Third States," in *Archiv des Völkerrechts*, Vol. 30, 1992, pp. 38–54; Akehurst Michael, "Reprisals by Third States," in *British Year Book of International Law*, Vol. 44, 1970, 36 p.

10 Sicilianos Linos-Alexandre, "The Classification of Obligations and the Multilateral Dimension of the Relations of International Responsibility," in *European Journal of International Law*, Vol. 13, 2002, pp. 1127–1145 (18 p.).

The Legal Materiality of Sanctions with Extraterritorial Effect

International society is made up of entities with international legal personality: States, international intergovernmental organizations (international organizations) as well as non-governmental actors. International organizations are established primarily by international treaties concluded by States, being primary subjects of public international law. In other words, the State is the main actor in international relations. It is the founder of public international law, which is said to be "the product of the will of States."

Furthermore, sovereignty, an attribute recognized by public international law to any legal person having the quality of a State[11] and the principle of independence that is applied to States, allows governmental institutions and their rulers to exercise effective power over the population, which the latter will have freely chosen or accepted, without at any time admitting any submission to a higher or foreign authority. This sovereign power is reflected in particular by the ability to freely enact its own legal standards for the administration of its state

---

11 Article 2 of the Charter provides that: "The United Nations and its Members, in pursuing the Purposes set forth in Article 1, shall act in accordance with the following principles:

The Organization is based on the principle of the sovereign equality of all its Members.

Members of the Organization, in order to ensure to all the enjoyment of the rights and benefits of membership, shall fulfill in good faith the obligations assumed by them under the present Charter.

Members of the Organization shall settle their international disputes by peaceful means in such a manner that international peace and security and justice are not endangered.

Members of the Organization shall refrain in their international relations from the threat or use of force against the territorial integrity or political independence of any State, or in any other manner inconsistent with the Purposes of the United Nations.

The Members of the Organization shall give the Organization full assistance in any action taken by it in accordance with the provisions of the present Charter and shall refrain from rendering assistance to any State against which the Organization is taking preventive or enforcement action.

The Organization shall ensure that States which are not Members of the United Nations act in conformity with these principles to the extent necessary for the maintenance of international peace and security.

Nothing in the present Charter shall authorize the United Nations to intervene in matters which are essentially within the domestic jurisdiction of any State or require Members to submit such matters to a procedure for settlement under the present Charter; however, this principle shall not prejudice the application of enforcement measures provided for in Chapter VII."

community and to impose sanctions on offenders on its territory or on nationals abroad, or even on foreigners responsible for reprehensible acts committed against nationals.

Furthermore, territorial jurisdiction allows certain States to impose sanctions on acts that have occurred abroad if they have an effect on their national territory, which is the case for certain criminal laws adopted in the United States of America or Canada,[12] but is not the same as applying sanctions exterritorialy. The extraterritorial characteristic of the legal norms is observed during the extraterritorial implementation of a territorial or extraterritorial norm and the direct extraterritorial application of a norm. Thus, the most attentive observer discerns a considerable number of distinct situations, within the framework of extraterritorial imputation and extraterritorial application of norms, *in which a State legitimately uses its own law with regard to situations or acts located outside its territory.*[13] On the other hand, and in a completely separate setting, the prescription of legal norms by States with extraterritorial effect is detrimental to the principle of State sovereignty and thus destabilizes the international system so profoundly that it creates fragilities in the balance of economic exchanges as well as large-scale belligerent risks. This may be the case for legal norms that sanction a foreign State in pursuit of political influence or economic interests, and which will be executed by being extended to persons who have no direct link with the prescriptive State.

Perhaps the most emblematic examples of this practice are American, such as the Helms-Burton laws package of 1996, consisting

---

12 Similarly, given the internationalization of phenomena and the accumulation of regulations in economic relations, private international law allows certain national standards to have extraterritorial application, without affecting the sovereignty of the State that "imports" them, depending on the distribution of powers between States. In this case, this is an extraterritorial implementation of a territorial standard by the courts: a judge of a court of State (A) may be required to apply the law of State (B) to a situation or an act that occurred on the territory of the latter (State B). Or, there may be an extraterritorial implementation of an extraterritorial standard when a foreign court of State (A) applies a standard of State (B) to facts or a situation that occurred on the territory of State (C), based on the nationality of the parties (nationals of State B). Similarly, a State may proceed to an extraterritorial application of its law (in matters of private international law) by applying its standards to facts located outside its territory. This situation is identical to that applicable in criminal law.

13 Stern Brigitte, "L'extraterritorialité 'revisitée': où il est question des affaires Alvarez-Machain, Pâte de Bois et de quelques autres," *Annuaire français de droit international*, Vol. 38, 1992, pp. 239–313 (76 p.).

of extraterritorial U.S. sanctions that were applied to commercial transactions with Cuba, Libya and Iran; or the laws against Iran after Washington's withdrawal from the Iranian nuclear treaty.[14]

The abusive and excessive nature of these standards lies not only in their application to nationals, but also to anybody using the dollar or having business ties with the United States. This has obviously resulted in colossal financial sanctions being applied to foreign companies. This extension of legitimate sanctions towards national residents or companies to physical or legal foreign entities not residing in the United States is an abuse of the law. The sovereignty of third States and, as a result, their diplomatic and economic independence, is literally called into question since their nationals outside the United States territory are subject to retaliatory measures (penalties, fines, threats and seizures of assets on the U.S. territory, expenses for compliance with the requirements of the authorities,[15] etc.) in the event of non-application of the unilateral measures taken by Washington against a State with which these nationals have nevertheless legitimately established lawful relations.

The U.S. objective is coupled with a capacity to appropriate exorbitant sums in the form of fines, coupled with asset recovery or even obstacles to competition, especially since the determination of the connecting factor of foreign companies with the United States is very broad: a simple transaction in dollars or the use of American technology would authorize, according to Washington, the application of its extraterritorial powers.[16] A very large number of companies

---

14 Department of the Treasury, Office of Foreign Assets Control, 31 CFR Part 560, *Iranian Transactions and Sanctions Regulations*, Office of Foreign Assets Control, Treasury. "The Department of the Treasury's Office of Foreign Assets Control (OFAC) is amending the Iranian Transactions and Sanctions Regulations (ITSR) to implement the President's May 8, 2018 decision to end the United States' participation in the Joint Comprehensive Plan of Action (JCPOA) on Iran's nuclear program, as outlined in National Security Presidential Memorandum-11 of May 8, 2018 (NSPM–11) ."

15 Which by coincidence, with no doubt, made the budget for these expanses to be often equivalent to the amount of the fine which could be inflicted on the companies that have not considered this legislation with extraterritorial effect.

16 There are many examples of companies that had to submit to American jurisdictions, including French ones: Technip (a French oil services group) was ordered to pay $338 million by the US Department of Justice (DoJ) and stock exchange authorities following proceedings brought against Technip in Nigeria (for example Archives, US department of Justice, Technip S.A. Resolves Foreign

around the world have been forced to pay billions of dollars to the American Treasury by the unilateral application of its extraterritorial power. In view of the numerous financial and commercial exchanges of the targeted countries, the latter submit themselves in order to avoid a conviction: the attack on the sovereignty of third States, and therefore on their independence, through the attack on their freedom of trade, of competition or of establishment of diplomatic relations, or other relations, is obvious. The legal rhetoric used poorly masks the economic and geopolitical instrumentalization, as well as the imposition of a policy of influence resulting from the balance of power of superpowers that does not fit well with legal arguments, which are sometimes even neglected by American political leaders themselves.[17]

Corrupt Practices Act Investigation and Agrees to Pay $240 Million Criminal Penalty, June 28, 2010, Criminal Division, Number: 10-751); Total fined was $300 million in 2013 and 1997 when it signed two gas contracts in Iran (for example Archives, US Department of Justice, French Oil and Gas Company, Total, S.A., Charged in the United States and France in Connection with an International Bribery Scheme, May 29, 2013, Criminal Division, Number: 13-613; https://www.justice. gov/iso/opa/resources/9392013529103746998524.pdf and https://totalenergies.com/ fr/medias/actualite/communiques/total-sa-confirme-la-fin-amiable-de-lenquete-americaine); ALSTOM was fined $772 million in 2014 for contracts in Africa (for example Archives, US Department of Justice, Alstom Pleads Guilty and Agrees to Pay $772 Million Criminal Penalty to Resolve Foreign Bribery Charges, December 22, 2014, Criminal division, number14-1448); BNP Paribas was fined $8.9 billion in 2014 during unilateral US embargoes targeting Sudan, Cuba and Iran and, in 2018, another fine of $90 million for a monetary agreement (for example, Archives, US Department of Justice, BNP Paribas Agrees to Plead Guilty and to Pay $8.9 Billion for Illegally Processing Financial Transactions for Countries Subject to U.S. Economic Sanctions, June 30, 2014, Criminal Division, number 14-686); Crédit Agricole was fined $787.3 million for dollar transactions between 2003 and 2008 on behalf of Sudanese, Iranian, Cuban and Burmese entities and then hit by unilateral US sanctions (US Department of Justice, Crédit Agricole Corporate and Investment Bank Admits to Sanctions Violations, Agrees to Forfeit $312 Million, October 20, 2015, USAO – District of Columbia); Société Générale two fines of $1.34 billion in 2018 for contracts in Libya, as well as for transactions on the Libor rate, (US Department of Justice, Société Générale S.A. Agrees to Pay $860 Million in Criminal Penalties for Bribing Gaddafi-Era Libyan Officials and Manipulating LIBOR Rate, June 4, 2018, Criminal Division), etc.

17 The observers did not miss the fact that U.S. President Donald Trump justified his withdrawal from the Iranian nuclear treaty by a desire to "exert financial pressure on the Iranian regime with a view to a global and lasting solution to all the threats posed by this country: ballistic development and proliferation, regional aggression, support for terrorist groups, pernicious activities of members of the Revolutionary Guards and its auxiliaries"; subjective motives and political analysis without proof, outside the protocols of international law.

International unilateral sanctions push for the individualization of the interpretation of the law because the member States of the international community can at any time claim their subjectivity to prescribe it according to their exclusive and irreducible vision; the international legal order is thus lastingly affected in its foundations and principles.

The Return of the Balance of Power

The Iranian case is likely to be retained as it combines elements illustrating the return of the balance of power used as a strategic means, essentially by the United States.[18] A former ambassador (1989–1992) of the United States to Saudi Arabia, Charles Friedman, declared in a debate on the accession of Saudi Arabia to the WTO: "One of the great ironies of the moment is that the United States, which was for so long opposed to secondary boycotts, has become the first user. As for Iran for example, on which the United States has imposed unilateral sanctions, where we penalize anyone who wants to trade with this country, without any international legal basis for doing so. Thus, this principle that we once defended with so much vigor, we systematically violate it."[19]

Indeed, Iran has been sanctioned by the West since 1979, and the comparison of the political calendar of the Islamic Republic since its establishment in 1979 with the calendar of discussions and sanctions of the "international community" demonstrates explicitly that sanctions have become a real obsession for America and the West, to the point of appearing to be their only "diplomatic" instrument; it then appears that it was to "trap" Iran that the Europeans, acting as "proxies" of America, itself under very strong pressure from Israel, proposed to Iran in 2003 to begin exchanges, then discussions concerning its nuclear program. The ulterior motive was to try to draw Tehran into an escalation of concessions under penalty of massive sanctions, the overall goal being the reduction to a minimum of its civil nuclear ambitions and to force it to give up its military prospects.

---

18 Garapon Antoine, Servan-Schreiber Pierre (dir.), *Deals de justice. Le marché américain de l'obéissance mondialisée* (Paris, Puf, 2013); Fayazmanesh Sasan, *The United States and Iran: sanctions, wars and the policy of dual containment* (Londres: Routledge, 2008).

19 Charles Friedman, Middle East Policy Council, January 23, 2006.

The external application of this *geopoliticization* of the law of sanctions by the West, essentially the United States, has borne fruit vis-à-vis third countries, its European allies. Indeed, Europe's losses in the face of American secondary sanctions against Iran are counted in multiple areas.

In particular, Iran has signed contracts with three French car brands: Peugeot, Renault and Citroen. After the nuclear deal, Peugeot and Renault were among the most important European companies that entered the Iranian market but were forced to leave Iran following the U.S. withdrawal from the deal. The Peugeot group had announced in its statement that its global sales volume decreased by 15.7% in the first quarter of 2019, the main reason for it being the suspension of the group's activities in Iran. Likewise, the Italian brand Fiat, which had sought to acquire a 15% stake in the Iranian national automobile industry, was also forced to leave Iran.

However, there is a great desire in Iran to use foreign cars due to the lack of quality in the domestic automobile industry, as well as to the challenges to the delivery of spare parts due to the U.S. sanctions. National companies need partnerships with foreign automobile companies for spare parts, technology transfer and to restore their images.

Another example refers to gas supplies. Iran has the capacity to produce more than 1 billion cubic meters of gas daily. Total had launched a $5 billion project for the development of South Pars field.[20] If the U.S. sanctions were lifted, Iran could have become Europe's most important gas partner.[21] However, given the U.S. sanctions,[22] the risk of transporting oil and gas to international destinations is great. The 90% dependence of the maritime insurance industry on Western companies (such as Astral and Parismet France), has caused a decrease in the sale of Iranian oil and an increase in demand and price. Other examples include the solar industry with Saga's $3 billion deal to build a solar power plant, and the Airbus aviation sector which had a $25

---

20 Reilly Tristan S., "Extinguishing gas flaring at the "Supergiant" South Pars gas field; Can Iran replicate Qatar's LNG success story?," in *Petroleum Exploration Society*, Mai 2018, pp. 58–61.

21 Szabo John, "EU-Iran natural gas cooperation potential?," *Challenges,* N° 214, Center for Economic and Regional Studies, Institute of World Economics, 2015, pp. 1–15.

22 Carter Stephen G., "Iran, natural gas and Asia's energy needs: A spoiler for sanctions," *Middle East Policy* 21, N°1, Mars 2014.

billion contract to supply jets to Iran Air. According to statistics from the International Monetary Fund (IMF) and the European Commission in 2017, China, the European Union, India, the United Arab Emirates (UAE) and South Korea were Iran's top five partners, respectively. Thus, the value of total trade between Iran and the European Union was equal to $20.9 billion, of which $10.8 billion represented the value of EU exports to Iran and $10.1 billion the value of EU imports from Iran.

Yet the attitude of the United States of America illustrates the pattern of power according to which the strongest imposes its law on the weakest, resorting to illegal maneuvers, exercising blackmail on all the actors of international society and resorting to a series of sanctions with extraterritorial effects in violation of the principles of public international law, the opposite of what would be true countermeasures in recent years.

Current unilateral coercive measures constitute true acts of economic war. For example, Washington has chosen the path of the blockade against Iran, which is similar to a real state of siege using the "weapon of secondary sanctions."[23] Dominating the global economic system since the establishment of the Bretton Woods system, the United States has used this unchallenged ascendancy to establish, through unilateral extraterritorial measures, monetary hegemony through the use of the U.S. dollar in international transactions, control over *Swift*, etc. and its political authority over international bodies and authorities such as the UN Security Council, NATO, etc.

With the new world order resulting from the fall of communism, and its status as the only hyperpower since the early 1990s, the United States has led the entire international society to become accustomed to its domination and practice, as much towards those States that it considers its enemies as towards its competitors and even its allies, engaging in true acts of political and economic war, affecting both the sanctioned States or entities in a direct manner, as well as

---

23 United Nations General Assembly Resolution 3314 of 14 December 1974; Resolution 2625 of 24 October 1970 on friendly relations and cooperation among States, which states that the States have the duty to "refrain in international relations from the use of military, political, economic or any other coercion against the political independence or territorial integrity of any State"; United Nations General Assembly Resolution 69/5 of 28 October 2014 on the embargo against Cuba.

other States and international actors in an indirect (secondary) manner.[24] The unilateral measures taken by this country cannot borrow the
terminology of "sanctions" in view of the objective and purpose of
these sanctions. The U.S. is supplementing legality with an attempt
to claim legitimacy, but their measures are not legal. In addition to
legality, they must have a legitimate objective, in accordance with that
of the United Nations and the principles of public international law,
which the United States constantly violates.

The example of the progressive sanctions pressure applied
against Iran illustrates this denial of law and return of political violence. Against Iran (to which we can now add Russia), this strategy
of accumulating "sets of sanctions" will not cease. In March 1995,
Washington decreed an oil embargo against the Islamic Republic,
followed by an economic one, and in 1996 by the vote approving the
Amato–Kennedy law, which prohibits any contract exceeding 20 million dollars. In 2003, Washington took on aeronautical and scientific
issues and raised suspicions concerning the existence of a nuclear and
military program developed by Tehran. It was its European allies who
proposed a dialogue in the form of exchanges of views or information
on non-proliferation, but, in reality, the Iranian nuclear issue was thus
"created" in 2003 with the real objective of a rapid escalation, the
conditions imposed on the negotiators becoming increasingly harsh to
the point of no longer being acceptable.

In 2005, the Iranian president would cancel the concessions
made by his predecessor concerning restrictions on the civil nuclear
program, inspections, etc. The United States entered the process by
demanding the tightening of pre-existing sanctions and new embargoes in 2006, then 2007, on weapons, equipment for communication,
law enforcement and nuclear power, in particular reactors, but also

---

24 Douhan Alena F., Sanctions secondaires, peines civiles ou pénales en cas de
contournement des régimes de sanctions et application excessive des sanctions, Report
of the Special Rapporteur on the negative effects of coercive unilateral measures on
the exercise of Human Rights, A/HRC/51/33, Human Rights Council of the United
Nations, 2022; Secondary sanctions are used to secure the extraterritorial application
of unilateral sanctions and, together with domestic enforcement measures and other
factors, have led to widespread over-compliance with unilateral sanctions and thereby
significantly expanded the reach of such sanctions and their negative impact on the
human rights of individuals, and even entire populations not directly targeted by the
initial sanctions. The nature of these practices, their questionable legality and the
various rights at risk lead to human rights violations arising from their application.

financial services, etc.: it is therefore a question of forcing Iran to sign an agreement in line with the demands of the West since Russia and China offer a series of more balanced proposals, taking up those of the Iranian theses, factors of appeasement. The punitive methodology of sanctions has been put in place and likely will never fall back since the escalation continues. With the imposition of a new wave of measures in 2012 designed to asphyxiate Iran if it does not give in, the true design of the West is revealed. The European Union decreed an embargo on hydrocarbons, mining equipment, naval equipment, precious metals, as well as a block on the assets of the Iranian state and its banks. Access for air freight transport from Iran is prohibited, as is the supply of aircraft spare parts, etc. Then came the restriction on Iran's use of foreign financial services for oil exports, then the transfer of technology in terms of armament related to "nuclear weapons." In 2013, the U.S. Congress voted for a new strengthening of sanctions: the cumulative effect of the sanctions revealed the desire not just to establish a balance of power but a destructive intention. But on July 14, 2015, Iran, the five permanent members of the Security Council plus Germany and the European Union signed the Joint Comprehensive Plan of Action (JCPoA) in Vienna: the UN and EU embargoes were to be eased, and by the way replaced by measures that strengthened the control of the Security Council.

The freeze on financial assets and those concerning the trade in hydrocarbons were lifted by the European Union, but they were maintained by the United States. Two and a half years later, in March 2018, the American president decided to unilaterally withdraw from the nuclear agreement: all sanctions were reinstated (embargo on oil, aeronautics and the mining sector, as well as the ban on the use of the dollar in transactions with Iran). In July 2018, the Iranian Minister of Foreign Affairs filed and addressed a complaint to International Court of Justice (ICJ), but the United States challenged its jurisdiction. Nevertheless, on October 3, 2018, fifteen judges of the ICJ ruled that the withdrawal from the JCPOA constituted a violation of the treaty of friendship signed in 1955 between the United States and Iran. In 2019, new sanctions were imposed: the revenues of the Central Bank of Iran and the sovereign wealth funds of the National Development Fund were frozen, decisions that the American president claims are the most severe sanctions ever imposed on a country.

On February 21, 2020, in Paris, the FATF (Financial Action Task Force, responsible for legal standards and measures to combat money laundering and terrorism financing) called on its members to take countermeasures against Iran based on Palermo convention.[25] Washington announced the unilateral reestablishment of all sanctions. However, the agreement concluded in 2015 after twelve years of negotiations on a global scale with six major powers had seen all the signatory States of the agreement commit to preserve and maintain financial circuits with Iran, as well as to ensure the continuation of Iranian oil and gas exports, and in 2016 the International Atomic Energy Agency (IAEA) indicated that Iran had cooperated satisfactorily and that sanctions could be lifted.[26] The United Nations Security Council even adopted Resolution 2231 lifting the six resolutions voted between 2006 and 2010 against Iran. Without any consideration of this action based on public international law, the change of American presidents has not brought any substantive change to the radical American position against Iran, destabilizing even a bit more the international legal order.

It seems that the American superpower knows how to create sanctions and how to wage war, but it appears that it has lost the methodology of public international law which requests that States elaborate a diplomatic approach for the resolution of conflicts in a pacific manner. The White House has given the impression of exploiting sanctions to maintain and preserve its global leadership, seeking precisely to eliminate Iran's strategic depth.[27]

In summary, sanctions and economic pressures can in the short term influence the actions of politicians in targeted countries; they can also disrupt international cooperation, call into question the common interests of States and harm international peace and stability. This issue poses a significant challenge to international law and contradicts the goals sought by the creation of the United Nations. From the

---

25 https://www.fatf-gafi.org/en/publications/Fatfgeneral/Outcomes-fatf-plenary-february-2020.html

26 AIEA, *Nuclear Law: The Global Debate*, La Haye (Pays-Bas), T.M.C. Asser Press, 2022, 333 p.; Labbé Marie-Hélène, *La quête nucléaire de l'Iran*, Paris, Sorbonne Université Presses, 2020, 160 p.

27 Kirkham Ksenia, *The political economy of sanctions: Resilience and Transformation in Russia and Iran*, International Political Economy Series, Cham ed., Springer International Publishing, 2022, 1 p.

perspective of international law based on neoclassical economic principles, it seems that economic sanctions are in clear contradiction with freedom of trade and State sovereignty. The unilateral action of the United States constitutes an obstacle to the establishment of fair and equitable international relations, based on the International Covenant on Economic, Social and Cultural Rights. Europe's priority in the democratization process that it is trying to develop, with a revaluation of the economic transition and economic and political cooperation, obviously reflects the European culture of crisis management. Faced with the multiplication of strategic actors in the Middle East region, it asserts itself as a major sponsor of stability. But then Europe aligns its position with that of the United States and consequently fails to respect the very foundation of its own policy, which should be focused on the development of democracy, the defense of universal values, individual freedoms and the maintenance of the dialogue necessary for solidarity between peoples.

Economic sanctions serve first of all as a punishment by putting the targeted State out of the international game (by limiting its access to certain resources or services, or even by seeking to disconnect it completely from international trade) with the aim not only of punishing the State deemed deviant[28] by the prescribing State, but also of perpetuating a hegemonic relation towards the third States. The purpose of sanctions is therefore to exclude targeted states from the international community. Economic sanctions[29] are used to indicate to the population that their government must be overthrown, since its bad behavior deprives it of economic prosperity and well-being. The idea is that the exasperated population will revolt and bring about a change of regime. On the other hand, if the population does not revolt, then it is just as guilty as its government and deserves the deprivations. This is all the more true as there is a tendency to merge decision-makers with their populations.[30] It will then also be necessary to defeat the

---

28 Sidani Soraya, *Intégration et déviance au sein du système international*, Paris, Presses de Sciences Po, 2014, 240 p.

29 Leblanc-Wohrer Marion, " Le droit, arme économique et géopolitique des États-Unis," in *Politique Étrangère*, Nº 4, Hiver 2019, pp. 37–48 (13 p.); *Op. Cit.* Mulder Nicholas *The Economic Weapon: The Rise of Sanctions As a Tool of Modern War* …

30 Post Jerrold M. (ed.), *The Psychological Assessment of Political Leaders: With Profiles of Saddam Hussein and Bill Clinton*, Ann Arbor, University of Michigan

population, to punish it, in order to be able to bring it to surrender to the conditions of the prescribing state.

The Effects of Extraterritorial Sanctions

Extraterritorial sanctions undermine the international legal order, in particular *jus cogens*, like for example the Human Rights enshrined in the United Nations Universal Declaration of Human Rights.

The Violation of Human Rights

The fundamental rights of the Iranian people, such as the right to health, the right to food and the right to development have been affected[31] by the enactment of these measures which in reality constitute massive violations of fundamental rights, which we have been witnessing for decades.

The reality of sanctions is not limited to the freezing of bank assets or the blocking of fund transfers; it raises the question of the survival of an entire population, in particular its weakest and most deprived fringe, in light of both the intensity and the duration of the application of the sanctions affecting the country. The right to development is an inalienable human right by which every human person and all peoples have the right to participate and contribute to an economic, social, cultural and political development in which all human rights and fundamental freedoms are respected. These fundamental rights have been directly affected by the hostile and unilateral actions of the United States, which have worrying effects on human rights.

Regarding Iran.[32] Mike Pompeo declared in November 2018 that the government in Tehran will have to make the right choice regarding U.S. sanctions "if it wants its people to eat." Sanctions can be deadly. Those taken against Iraq under the leadership of the United States and Israel cost the lives of more than a million people between 1991

Press, 2005, 480 p.; Horowitz Michael C., Stam Allan C., Ellis Cali M., *Why Leaders Fight*, Cambridge, Cambridge University Press, 2016, 228 p.

31 *Op. Cit.*, Douhan Alena F., Sanctions secondaires, peines civiles ou pénales en cas de contournement des régimes de sanctions et application excessive des sanctions ...

32 Cuynet Joris, *L'Iran sous sanction. Une société sous pression*, Paris, L'Harmattan, 2022, 212 p. ; Coville Thierry, *L'Iran, une puissance en mouvement*, Paris, Eyrolles, 2022, 192 p.; Therme Clément (dir.), *L'Iran et ses rivaux. Entre nation et révolution*, Paris, Passés/composés, 2020, 208 p.

and 2003, including nearly 500,000 children (according to UNICEF figures). For Madeleine Albright, "the price was worth it."[33] This means in both cases that, for the United States, the idea of making a civilian population suffer as a collective punishment for the actions of its governments is compatible with the legal principles governing the decision of unilateral extraterritorial sanctions. This process of coercive diplomacy gives a clear conscience without risk, which Michael Mandelbaum summarized as "Punishing the innocent to express one's indignation to the guilty."[34] Today, sanctions come directly from hell ("sanctions from hell," or "apocalyptic" as the Americans say), because the goal is to create an untenable situation, real suffering for civilian populations so that they rebel against their government, or even overthrow it—means and objectives totally opposed to the objectivity and prudential virtue of justice inherent in decisions emanating from public international law.[35]

The return of power relationships in place of law via the framework of unilateral coercive measures—now deteriorated in all its facets (intrinsic violence, escalation, successive and cumulative effects, permanence of the embargo situation, indirect destruction of infrastructures, etc.)—leads to consequences in practical order.

The populations concerned see that the impact on economic issues such as small industry, the import of basic necessities and agriculture, but also social and cultural areas such as the health care system, the environment and education are subject to an impact external to common law. The punishment by rejection, the brutal and disproportionate downgrading of an entire society, the humanitarian impact and the social repercussions at the personal and collective level of the sanctions against Iran in the service of dominant American geopolitical

---

33 "Sixty Minutes" (TV show), *CBS*, 12 mai 1996.

34 David Charles-Philippe, *La guerre et la paix: approches contemporaines de la sécurité et de la stratégie* (2ème éd.), Paris, Presses de Sciences Po, 2006, p. 222 (463 p.).

35 The use of economic sanctions for the purpose of illicit balance of power use has already been stated by US President Woodrow Wilson in a speech in Indianapolis, in 1919: "A nation that is boycotted is a nation that is in sight of surrender. Apply this economic, peaceful, silent, deadly remedy and there will be no need for force. It is a terrible remedy. It does not cost a life outside the nation boycotted, but it brings pressure upon a nation which, in my judgement, no modern nation can resist," quoted in: Padover (dir.), *Wilson's Ideals*, Washington, American Council on Public Affairs, 1942, p. 108.

interests is a negation of international human and economic rights. The coercion resulting from the sanctions has indeed multiple aspects and violates international economic and social law on a daily basis in that it blindly generalizes the effects on all industrial, commercial and craft sectors while the aspects of transport (taxes and insurance costs), distribution, export (customs duties) and spare parts are particularly targeted, and are suffocating and disappearing without the appearance of subsistence replacements. Coercion and hindrance to trade and transactions by direct effect (currency) or indirect effect (impoverishment of the State's social services), do not respect international economic and social law—they push heads of families to despair at not being able to ensure the minimum subsistence of their loved ones. The real impact on populations[36] when their government is the target of these sanctions multiplies and is embodied in all aspects of their daily lives, whether it is the health system, as neonatal and early childhood services are the most affected, or the lack of places, resources, care materials, particularly in surgery, and medicines. But the shortage due to lack of cash—the side effect again—obviously also affects the ability to ensure the financing of emergency social housing as well as the reception of refugees, estimated to be 5 million on Iranian territory.[37]

Due to sanctions—particularly on spare parts—food security and human rights, which should include the right to maintenance, are difficult to ensure in Iran. They seriously threaten the food supply of populations as it concerns storage and detection of natural disasters—drought and floods.

---

36 Iran: Unilateral sanctions and over-compliance constitute serious threat to human rights and dignity, Haut-Commissariat des Nations Unies pour les Droits de l'Homme (site internet), May 19, 2022. https://www.ohchr.org/en/press-releases/2022/05/iran-unilateral-sanctions-and-over-compliance-constitute- serious-threat-human.

37 UNHCR, *Afghanistan Situation Regional Refugee Response Plan, January–December 2022*; Organisation internationale pour les migrations (OIM), " Mobility Dynamics: Afghanistan One Year After August 15," *IOM Displacement Tracking Matrix*, 22 août 2022, available at: https://dtm.iom.int; *Global trends – forced displacement in 2021*, UNHCR, 2022 ; UNHCR, *Afghanistan Situation: Emergency Preparedness and Response in Iran, 16 May–15 June 2022*, juillet 2022; J. Mackenzie, "Aid Group Says 4,000–5,000 Afghans Crossing into Iran Daily," *Reuters*, November 10, 2021. https//www.reuters.com; Organisation internationale pour les migrations (OIM), *Movements in and out of Afghanistan*, 2022. https://displacement.iom. int; Samuel Hall, *Education and Livelihoods of Afghan Youth to Inform Voluntary Repatriation*, November 2015. https://static1.squarespace.com;

The Attack on the International Legal Order

The international legal order was formed to respond to the eternal violence existing between the different human communities. At the end of the Thirty Years' War (1618–1648), the Peace Treaties of Osnabrück and Münster, the Treaties of Westphalia, introduced the guiding concepts of classic public international law: just war (*justa causa*),[38] and balance of power laid grounds for the possibility of collective response to aggression. Articles 1–2 of the United Nations Charter introduced the prohibition to the use of force with the exception of self-defense exercised on a provisional basis, until the Security Council takes the necessary measures;[39] the principle of non-intervention in the domestic affairs of other states; and the principle of sovereign equality of states, as peremptory norms of international law.

The free adhesion of States to this international legal order gave them an obligation to respect its rules. This is the famous *pacta sunt servanda*, resulting from bilateral and multilateral treaties in which States participate or adhere,[40] and their ratification by States integrates them into their internal legal order and makes them binding on their communities. At the same time, the "international community" is subject to other imperative rules from which even treaties cannot derogate. These are the *jus cogens* legal norms (inalienable sovereignty of States, sovereign equality between them, non-interference in the internal affairs of countries).

This legal equality of States established by the Charter of the United Nations obliges States that have free enjoyment of it to respect the legal personality, independence and therefore the sovereignty of the other States by not interfering in their right to freely choose and develop their own political, legal, economic, social and cultural systems. Each State is thus free and sovereign to legislate on any issue

---

38 The prohibition to use force/ to start war has been set forth in the UN Charter only

39 This principle has been confirmed, repeatedly and explicitly, by a great number of resolutions, the goal of which is to avoid open conflicts by the use of preventive rules. The Security Council has thus become the only body in the international order able to authorize or even order the use of force under the provisions of Chapter VII of the Charter of the United Nations, but also to order sanctions against States, entities or even persons who commit internationally illicit acts.

40 Art. 26 of the Vienna Convention of 1969: "Every treaty in force is binding on the parties and must be performed by them in good faith."

that falls within its political, economic and territorial space, to decide on the nature of its regime, its political institutions, its foreign policy, etc. Any measure taken with the aim of exerting pressure on the exercise of these prerogatives constitutes a violation of the principle of sovereign equality of states as well as that of self-determination and the freedom of peoples to self-determination.[41] The consequence is clear: non-intervention in the domestic affairs of States constitutes a fundamental principle as stated by the Declaration of principles of 1970 or Helsinki final act 1975,[42] each State having the right to exclusively exercise its powers within its national domain, without external constraint. According to this principle, each State must respect the internal sovereignty of other States.

As we can see, these constitutive principles of the international legal order are flouted by the extraterritorial sanctions of States against other States,[43] whose sovereign capacity and independence they call into question, as well as the status of equality from which they must benefit. Only the United Nations would be able to guarantee the objectivity of possible decisions on measures[44] to be taken against certain international disorders. The only legal sanctions from the point of view

---

41 Paragraph. 2 of the Preamble to the Charter of the United Nations on the purposes of the global organization: "To develop friendly relations among nations based on respect for the principle of equal rights and self- determination of peoples, and to take other measures to consolidate world peace." Similarly, Article 55 of the Charter, inserted in Chapter IX on international economic and social cooperation, adds: "With a view to creating the conditions of stability and well-being necessary for peaceful and friendly relations among nations based on respect for the principle of equal rights and self-determination of peoples, the United Nations shall promote:

Raising standards of living, full employment and conditions of economic and social progress and development;

Solving international economic, social, public health and related problems, and international cooperation in the fields of intellectual culture and education;

- Universal respect for and observance of human rights and fundamental freedoms for all, without distinction as to race, sex, language or religion."

42 Art. 2 paragraph 7, *ibidem*.: "Nothing in the present Charter shall authorize the United Nations to intervene in matters which are essentially within the domestic jurisdiction of any State or shall require Members to submit such matters to a procedure for settlement under the present Charter; but this principle shall not prejudice the application of coercive measures under Chapter VII."

43 "Le rapport de la Commission de Droit International sur les travaux de sa trente et unième session," *Annuaire CDI 1979*, Vol. II, deuxième partie, 1980.

44 These are in fact "sanctions" even if this expression is not used in the Charter of the United Nations which speaks of "non-coercive measures" on this subject.

of public international law are those of the United Nations Security Council. This is not the case for the sanctions currently decided by the United States in particular and the Western powers in general, which are unilateral and reflect a balance of power of a geopolitical nature.[45]

The use of the term "sanctions" in political speeches requires, in order to understand what is left unsaid in these speeches, that we distinguish between sanctions adopted within a multilateral institutional framework (United Nations, etc.) and countermeasures decided unilaterally by States. In both cases, these are coercive measures aimed at influencing the behavior of a State deemed to be contrary to international rules.

However, the term "sanctions" must be reserved for coercive measures adopted by an organ of an international organization in accordance with its constituent treaty.[46] This conclusion is necessary because the measures are taken by an organ having the competence to adopt them in order to ensure that member States respect the legal order of the organization. Therefore, the taking of sanctions by States derives from the decision of the organization.[47]

Article 41 of the Charter thus authorizes the Security Council, on the one hand, to take all measures not involving the use of force that are likely to "give effect to its decisions" and, on the other hand, to "invite Member States to implement these measures." The latter are grouped under the generic term of sanctions, which are, as indicated in the report *A More Secure World: Our Shared Responsibility*, an indispensable, if imperfect, tool for preventing threats to international peace and security. They represent an essential middle ground between

---

45 Coates Benjamin Allen, *Legalist Empire: International Law and American Foreign Relations in Early Twentieth Century*, New York, Oxford University Press, 2016, 298 p.

46 Abi-Saab Georges, "De la sanction en droit international. Essai de clarification," p. 63, dans Jerzy Makarczyk (éd.), *Theory of International Law at the Threshold of the 21st Century. Essays in Honour of K. Skubiszewski*, La Haye, Londres, Boston, Kluwer Law International, 1996, pp. 61–77 (868 p.); Leben Charles, "Les contre-mesures interétatiques et les réactions à l'illicite dans la société internationale," *Annuaire Français de Droit International* (AFDI), Vol. 28, Éds. du CNRS, 1982, pp. 9–77.

47 Sicilianos Linos-Alexandre, "Sanctions institutionnelles et contre-mesures: tendances récentes," p. 17, in Forlati Laura Picchio, Sicilianos Linos-Alexandre (éds.), *Les sanctions* économiques *en droit international*, (série Les livres de droit de l'Académie), Leiden, Martinus Nijhoff, 2004, pp. 3–98.

armed intervention and discourse in cases where countries, individuals and rebel groups violate international legal standards and where the absence of intervention would have the effect of undermining these standards, encouraging other offenders, or would be interpreted as complicit silence.[48]

In its resolution 67/170 of March 20, 2013, the UN General Assembly condemned these unilateral sanctions measures, considering in its preamble that such "unilateral coercive measures and laws are contrary to international law, international humanitarian law, the Charter of the United Nations and the legal norms and principles governing peaceful relations among States."

In its paragraph 4, this resolution states that the Assembly "strongly opposes the extraterritorial nature of unilateral coercive measures which, moreover, threaten the sovereignty of States and, to this end, calls upon all Member States not to recognize them, not to apply them and to take administrative or legislative measures, as appropriate, to counteract their application and their extraterritorial implications."

After recalling and reaffirming the principles under which such measures are unlawful,[49] this resolution condemns, in its paragraph 5,

the maintenance in force and execution of unilateral coercive measures by certain Powers and denounces these measures, as well as all their extraterritorial implications, as means of exerting political or economic pressure on countries, in particular developing countries, with the aim of preventing them from exercising their right to choose, in full freedom, their own political or economic and social systems, and because of their harmful impact on the realization of all human rights of large groups of their population, in particular children, women, older persons and persons with disabilities.

---

48 Report of the High-Level Panel on Threats, Challenges and Change: Un monde plus sûr: notre affaire à tous, A/59/565, Assemblée générale des Nations Unies, 2 décembre 2004, p. 55, par. 178 (109 p.).

49 Preamble to this resolution and §8 in which this resolution reaffirms "the right of all peoples to self- determination, by virtue of which they freely determine their political status and freely organize their economic, social and cultural development."

Finally, this resolution, which underlines the illegal nature of these measures that call into question the principles of public international law, calls on Member States "that have taken such measures to respect the principles of international law, the Charter, the declarations of United Nations conferences and world conferences as well as the relevant resolutions, and to fulfil the obligations and responsibilities imposed on them by the international human rights instruments to which they are parties by repealing these measures as soon as possible."[50]

Conclusion

Regarding the *Jus cogens*, we can highlight Georges Scelle's observation: "There is an international public order within the society of States just as there is an internal public order within one same State community. The treaties that States make between them cannot derogate from these principal rules."[51] Similarly, States have the duty to "refrain in international relations from using military, political, economic or other constraints directed against the political independence or the territorial integrity of any State." Similarly, the Declaration on Principles of International Law concerning Friendly Relations and Cooperation among States in accordance with the Charter of the United Nations of 1970 stipulates:

> no State or group of States has the right to intervene, directly or indirectly for any reason whatsoever, in the internal or external affairs of another State. Consequently, not only armed intervention, but also any other form of interference or threat directed against the personality of a State or against its political, economic and cultural elements, is contrary to international law. No State may apply or encourage the use of economic, political or any other kind of measures to compel another State to subordinate the exercise of its

---

50 Paragraph 7 of the said Resolution A/RES/67/170 of March 20, 2013 (United Nations general Assembly).

51 Scelle Georges, Cours de Droit International Public, Paris, Domat-Montchrestien, 1948, p. 640 (1008 p.). This statement coincides with the provisions of Article 103 of the United Nations Charter.

sovereign rights or to obtain from its advantages of any kind whatsoever.[52]

This legal framework allows us to conclude that sanctions taken unilaterally by States against other international actors, without going through the UN mechanism, and which also affect third parties in a secondary manner, violate the principles recalled by the United Nations General Assembly in its aforementioned resolution. These measures doubly harm the sanctioned State and the international community and, consequently, the international legal order.[53] This attitude should lead other actors, who consider themselves victims of this situation, to react unilaterally, individually or collectively, to help restore the international legal order affected by these measures.

---

52 Provisions of Resolution 2625 of the United Nations General Assembly of 24 October 1970 on friendly relations and cooperation among States.

53 Sicilianos Linos-Alexandre, *Les réactions décentralisées à l'illicite: des contre-mesures à la légitime défense*, Paris, LGDJ, 1990, 532 p.; Brownlie Ian, "International Law at the Fiftieth Anniversary of the United Nations," in *Recueil des cours de l'Académie de droit international de La Haye*, Vol. 255, La Hague, La Hague Academy of International Law, 1995, p. 220; Weil Prosper, «Le droit international en quête de son identité: cours général de droit international public,» in *Recueil des cours de l'Académie de droit international de La Haye*, Vol. 237, La Haye, Nijhoff, 1996, 370 p.; Makarczyk Jerzy (dir.), *Theory of International Law at the Threshold of the 21st Century: Essays in Honour of Krzysztof Skubiszewski*, La Haye, Kluwer, 1996, 868 p.; Dupuy Pierre-Marie, «Responsabilité et légalité,» in Société Française pour le Droit International (SFDI) (dir.), *La responsabilité dans le système international* (colloque du Mans), Paris, A. Pedone, 1991, 338 p.

CHAPTER 13.

Égalité de tous les droits de l'homme

Amal Yazji-Yakoub[1]

Abstract

Ce chapitre va être consacré à la relation si fragile mais si fondamentale entre sanctions et droit fondamentaux de l'être humaine.

Le texte va analyser la relation entre les fondements de la notion des droits le l'homme et la nature des sanctions qui peuvent entraver le seuil minimum des libertés et droits consacrés par les règles du droit international coutumier et conventionnel, en mettant l'accent sur la catégorie des droits considéré comme étant le noyau dur des droits de l'homme, et en soulignant la nécessité de conserver le noyau dur de ces droits et libertés de toute entrave.

Donnez des exemples sur les procédures que les Etats utilisent via les sanctions imposées aux sociétés multinationales, si elles collaborent avec le pays sanctionné, et expliquer le rôle de ces sociétés multinationales dans l'encouragement de certaines sanctions, profitant de l'absence de tout texte international infligeant leurs responsabilités internationales sur leurs actes illicite.

Introduction: Égalité de tous les droits de l'homme

La question de l'égalité de tous les droits de l'homme est une question fondamentale en soi, et l'idée même de distinguer des catégories de droits moins implorantes que les autres, touche le cœur du concept originaire des droits de l'homme conçu et développé au cour de ces dernières décennies.

---

1 Doctorat en Droit International, Université Paris X, Nanterre, La Sorbonne, France, 1996. Professeur à la Faculté de Droit, Département de Droit International, Université de Damas, 2018. Chef du Département de Droit International, Faculté de Droit, Université de Damas: 2009–2013, 2016–2020, 2021–2024

A partir de ce constat, on va tenter de démontrer les liens effectifs entre ces droits et pourquoi ils doivent être garantis sur un pied d'égalité entre tous, à travers trois axes: l'idée de l'égalité de droits d'homme et comment peut garantir cette égalité, de l'égale jouissance des droits inaliénables de l'homme, et enfin les devoirs des acteurs appliquant les mesures coercitives ou des sanctions émises par les Nations Unies.

Si la Charte des Nations Unies de 1945, est le point de départ implicite de la notion contemporaine des droits de l'homme,[2] la consécration de ces droits était entamée par la déclaration universelle des droits de l'homme[3] et les deux pactes,[4] et par l'intégration dans les législations nationales, accordant ainsi un vrai sens à la notion des droits l'homme.

La littérature des droits de l'homme avancés et développés dans deux générations, la première concernant les droits politiques et civiles, et la deuxième génération concernant les droits économiques, sociaux et culturels, reflètent son caractère d'armure, qui protègent l'être humain indépendamment de son origine, sa race, ses convictions religieuses et culturelles, et son niveau de vie et ses besoins essentielle; Tous ces piliers sont couronnés par le principe de non distinction entre les êtres humains par tout dans le monde.

Ce constat concernant cet ensemble de règles de droit, reconnus sans hésitation par tous, reste, malheureusement, théorique et loin de la réalité vécue par les êtres humains dans les quatre coins du monde, pour la simple raison que les notions de droit et de devoir ne sont pas standardisées en pratique, même si en théorie on définit le droit comme étant une revendication justifiée, et le devoir comme une réponse à une revendication justifiée; Cette divergence entre théorie et réalité

---

2 La notion des droits de l'homme est citée dans les articles:1, 13, 54, 62, 68, 76. Voir le texte sur site de de l'organisation, disponible à: https://treaties.un.org/doc/Publication/CTC/uncharter-all-lang.pdf

3 Déclaration universelle des droits de l'homme, Assemblée Générale des Nations Unies, A/RES/217 (III), disponible à: https://www.un.org/fr/universal-declaration-human-rights/

4 Le Pacte International relatif aux droits Civils et Politiques de 1966, disponible à: https://treaties.un.org/doc/Treaties/1976/03/19760323%2006-17%20 AM/Ch_IV_04.pdf; Le Pacte International relatif aux droits 2conomiques, Sociaux et Culturels, de 1966, https://treaties.un.org/doc/Treaties/1976/01/19760103%20 09-57%20PM/Ch_IV_03.pdf

se cristallisent au tour de la notion des droits de l'homme, surtout les droits définis par la Charte internationale des droits de l'homme.

De nos jours, il faut repenser les droits cités dans la Charte en rajoutant la dimension interétatique à la dimension nationale, et étudier les impacts, de certains actes extraterritoriaux, sur les droits définis par cette Charte, et rendre les effets destructrices des actes commis par des acteurs non nationaux plus visibles pour tout le monde, comme dans le cas des actes de tout Etat sur ses nationaux; Ces actes se traduisent, de nos jours, via les sanctions et les mesures coercitives, prises par certains Etats et Organisations Internationales, que ce soit avec les meilleure intention ou prétendue meilleure intention, de façon que tout acte, prit sans respecter un minimum de précaution avant qu'il soit appliqué, illégal.

Toutefois, avant d'entrer dans le vif du sujet et examiner la question de «l'égalité de tous les droits de l'homme» sous tous ses aspects, il faut souligner que les mesures coercitives unilatérales sont dépourvues, par principe, de tout consentement de la part des Etats sanctionnés, tandis que les sanctions prises par n'importe quelle organisation internationale a le mérite que ses membres ont eu connaissance au paravent de leurs engagements et des pouvoirs que cette organisation a sur eux. Une situation étrange que certains Etats lésés décrivent comme une nouvelle sorte de colonialisme, bravant ainsi le droit d'auto-détermination qui est un des principes fondamentaux de droit international de du droit international des droits de l'homme.

Égalité de droits de l'homme

Le concept contemporain des droits de l'homme est né lorsque les Etats ont adoptés la déclaration des droits de l'homme en 1948, sans faire aucune distinction entre les droits et les libertés assurés; Les deux pactes de 1966, de droits civils et politiques et des droit sociaux, économiques et culturels, ont essayer de leur côté de traduire cette volonté si claire et sincère des Etats apparu en 1948, et construire ainsi un ensemble de droits appelé communément la Charte internationale des droits de l'homme.

L'idée sur laquelle est bâti la Charte internationale des droits de l'homme, est celle de consacrer: des droits, des libertés et une certaine valeur de la dignité humaine si bafouée et peu définie. Ce mélange de valeurs ne facilite pas le principe de contrôle efficace sur les sanctions prises par le Conseil de Sécurité ou sur les mesures coercitives, prises à titre de sanction par une Organisation Régionale ou par Etat envers un autre Etat souverain.

Quels sont les droits consacrés dans la Charte internationale des droits de l'homme?

Le principe que tous les droits de l'homme sont indivisibles et interdépendants[5] est un postulat nécessaire à la comprenions de la notion des droits de l'homme. Une énumération rapide des droits essentiels cités dans la déclaration de 1948 et les deux pactes de 1966 est nécessaire, où plusieurs questions en découlent faisant l'objet actuel du droit international des droits de l'homme: le droit à la vie, le droit à la dignité humaine qui implique que nul ne sera soumis à la torture, le droit au travail, à l'éducation, à la santé, le droit à la liberté qui ils implique que chacun a le droit à la liberté d'opinion et d'expression, jusqu'à le principe que nul ne sera tenu en esclavage, ... ces droits sont des exemples parmi d'autres que l' Charte a consacré.

Il n'est point rare d'entendre la question: pourquoi est-ce mal d'enfreindre le droit à la vie des autres? surtout quand une Organisation Internationale pose cette question avec une gravitée certaine, comme si d'enfreindre le droit à la vie, en tant qu'un droit essentiel des droit de l'homme, a un sens bien claire pour tout le monde, et des moyens bien déterminés pour l'enfreindre, et que le droit à la vie a été bien expliquer pour aller de la peine de mort, à la torture, en passant au droit à l'avortement ou plus dernièrement l'Euthanasie ... Mais ce droit à la vie au sens stricte du terme peut être provoqué par des sanctions ou des mesures coercitives imposant un embargo sur des produits comme le «chlore» considéré comme composant d'certaine arme, en négligeant que le «chlore gazeux» est l'agent oxydant et bactéricide

---

5 Droits Indivisibles et interdépendants, c'est-à-dire: droit «indissociable ou inséparable» et «tous les droits sont liés les uns aux autres de sorte la satisfaction de l'un contribue à la satisfaction des autres, de même que la violation d'un droit aura des conséquences sur les autres.»

Voir : Indivisibilité et interdépendance des Droits de l'Homme: Que peut-on comprendre? par Olivier Dismas Ndayambaje, Enseignant à l'Ecole Nationale d'Administration du Burundi. https://zeraction.over-blog.com/article-indivisibilite-et-interdependance-des-droits-de-l-homme-113535035.html

le plus universel pour rendre l'eau potable, causant ainsi la mort de centaine voir des millier des personnes.

Cet exemple parait choquant, mais il est réal et il n'est pas le seul, ajoutez à cet exemple d'autres formes de sanctions, comme l'embargo sur les matériels médicaux, ou plus simplement le gel des avoirs financiers de certains pays, leurs interdisant l'achat des générateurs électriques ou d'autres pièces de rechanges de peur de les utiliser de manière choque ceux qui imposent les sanctions, tout en sachant que ces derniers jouaillent de toutes la capacité de produire et vendre toutes les armes dont les mines anti personnes que l'on puisse les interdire mondialement sans causer du tort à qui ce soi ... Une politique appelée «deux poids deux mesures.»

Après plus de quarante-huit ans de la naissance de cette Charte, dans ce climat d'incertitude et de conflits armés de toute sorte, et le constat de violation des règles impératives considérées comme étant des principes du droit international dont les principes avancés dans la Charte des Nations Unies, surtout le principe de non-ingérence dans les affaires intérieures des autres Etats,[6] et les principes du droit international relatifs aux relations amicales et à la coopération entre les États[7] principes considérés par la Charte des Nations Unies comme étant un de ses buts essentiels,[8] plusieurs constats s'imposent:

- La nature des droits consacrés ne pose aucun problème de légitimité et de mondialité.

- Le niveau de compréhension et du teneur de ces droits par les Etats ne fait aucun doute.

- Les moyens de contrôle effectifs de «respecter et faire respecter» ces droits sont variés et variable, et la question des droits de l'homme perd de jour en jour sa valeur essentielle au profit des enjeux politiques, dans le contexte de l'absence d'un véritable équilibre des forces politiques mondiales et de la transformation des droits de l'homme en un outil d'ingérence

---

6 Article 2, alinéa 7, de la Chartre des Nations Unies.

7 Déclaration relative aux principes du droit international touchant les relations amicales et la coopération entre les Etats conformément à la Charte des Nations Unies (A/8082), 2625(XXV). Du 24 octobre 1970, disponible à: https://documents.un.org/doc/resolution/gen/nr0/350/22/pdf/nr035022.pdf

8 Article premier de la Charte, alinéa 2.

dans les affaires intérieurs d'autres pays, sans prêter égard au fait que les dommages collatéraux[9] ont commencé à dépasser les limites du concept de dommage collatéral, et se transformant en violations des droits essentiels des êtres humains qui s'élèvent au niveau de violations graves.

- Faire respecter les droits de l'homme est le devoir de chaque Etat, et si le contrôle de ce devoir est exécuté, plus au moins bien, par les mécanismes et organes des Nations Unies, la liberté que certains Etats directement ou via une Organisation Régionale s'octroient d'imposer des mesures coercitives dépassent toute attente de la notion des droits de l'homme.

Les sanctions de nature économiques imposées en application du chapitre VII, article 41, de la Charte des Nations Unies suscitent de nombreux défi, et les Comités de sanctions rattachés au Conseil de Sécurité,[10] créés en vertu de l'article 29 de la Charte et l'article 28 du Règlement intérieur provisoire du Conseil de sécurité,[11] ont pour finalités de surveiller l'application des décisions contenant des sanctions et de s'assurer que des procédures équitables et claires sont en place, et œuvrer pour la levée des sanctions; Sans qu'ils puissent plier le Conseil de Sécurités et ses résolutions si les intérêts des grandes puissances ne se convergent pas. Tandis que les mesures coercitives unilatérales, imposées par un Etat ou une Organisation Régionale, échappent à tout contrôle, ce qui rend les impacts de ces mesures et la possibilité de les lever, sous réserve de l'évolution politique et de conditions qui ne répondent pas souvent aux intérêts des pays contre lesquels ces mesures ont été imposées, ce qui encouragent certains Etats et Organisations internationales à aller trop loin dans leurs exigences a connotations purement politique, et de faire les sourd d'oriels et négliger non seulement les violations de droits de l'homme en général, mais et surtout les noyaux durs de ces droits.

---

9 Les dommages collatéraux : «Dégâts ou dommages causés involontairement ou inconsciemment.» La langue française – 2025, https://www.lalanguefrancaise. com/dictionnaire/definition/dommage-collateral#0

10 Nations Unies, Conseil de Sécurité, Sanctions et autres comités, disponible à: https://main.un.org/securitycouncil/fr/content/repertoire/sanctions-and-other-committees

11 Nations Unies, Conseil de Sécurité, Organes subsidiaires, disponible à: https://main.un.org/securitycouncil/fr/content/subsidiary-bodies

Déclarer le respect des droits fondamentaux des personnes et des peuples et adhérer aux traités internationaux en la matière sous la forme actuelle ne suffit plus. Un nouveau et dangereux type de violation des droits fondamentaux de l'être humain dans l'espace des relations interétatiques est devenu une réalité, et la création d'un nouveau système juridique pour y faire face est une question urgente au niveau international. Il faut agir d'une sorte où on distingue entre les droits de l'homme et leurs applications au niveau national, et des droits de l'homme dans l'espace interétatique.

La solution de l'impasse actuel ne peut être proposée par une convention internationale, ou un traité, qui aura comme objet principal le plein respect des droits de l'homme, toutes les libertés, et toute la dignité consacrée par la Charte internationale des droits de l'homme, car c'est déjà fait; La solution peut prendre la forme d'un ensemble de règles de droit imposé par une résolution du Conseil de Sécurité semblable, par sa force et son étendue, à la résolution 1373 (2001)[12] qui a été appelée le «Code anti-terrorisme» mondial, et créer un «code des droits essentiels de l'homme dans l'espace interétatique»; Il est vrai que très peu de résolutions du Conseil de Sécurité ou de l'Assemblée Générale dictent de nouvelles règles de droit international, mais cette catégorie de règles de droit existe bel et bien, et elle est considérée comme faisant partie des sources du droit international actuel.

Quelle forme et quel est le contenu d'une telle résolution?

Le principe sur lequel repose cette éventuelle résolution est de protéger, autant que possible, l'homme et ses droits, contre les abus des États autres que celui de sa nationalité ou de sa résidence éventuelle, une protection de toute violation commise directement par un Etat étranger ou via le Conseil de Sécurité ou une Organisation intergouvernemental. Le monde d'aujourd'hui ne distingue plus entre les mesures coercitives et les sanctions prises en vertu du chapitre VII de la Charte des Nations Unies, vu le poids inhumain que les peuples subissent à cause de ces sanctions et mesures à leurs égard.

L'idée principale de cette résolution serait de «respecter et faire respecter» les droits de l'homme essentiels lord de n'importe quelle

---

12 Nations Unies Conseil de Sécurité, résolution 1373 (2001), du 28 septembre 2001, S/RES/1373 (2001), disponible à: https://www.unodc.org/pdf/crime/terrorism/res_1373_french.pdf

sanction prise à l'encontre de n'importe quel Etat, à travers un ensemble de normes qui exclut toute sanction ou mesure prise dans le cadre des Nations Unies, ou par un État, ou une Organisation internationale à l'encontre d'un autre État, et qui pourrait porter atteinte aux droits humains fondamentaux définis dans le cadre des relations interétatique; Ces règles ou normes différent des droits accordés normalement à l'être humain dans le cadre national, et à ce fin il faut que ces droits soient explicitement définis, surtout: le droit à la vie, à l'égalité devant la loi, le droit au travail, la non-discrimination, le droit à la dignité humaine, et de considérer que les règles avancées par cette résolution comme des règle impératives du droit international, si c'est possible. De cette manière, il est possible de garantir les droits des peuples en tant que groupes et des individus en tant que personnes physiques, et cela fait des droits de l'homme une question qui dépasse les slogans brandis par certains pays le cas échéant, bien évidement sans décharger les États de leurs devoirs fondamentaux envers leurs peuples, et sans porter préjudice aux mécanismes internationaux qui traquent les violations de la Charte internationale des droits de l'homme que ces États pourraient commettre.

Quelles sont les précotions à prendre avant l'émissions de sanctions ou des mesures coercitives unilatérales?

Si l'idée sur laquelle nous travaillions, concernant les sanctions et les mesures coercitives, est d'avoir un instrument non conventionnel mais ayant un caractère obligatoire, est acceptée, dans ce cas les précautions et certains d'autres critères doivent être inclus dans cet instrument.

Il est incontestable que presque tous les États ont ratifié au moins un, voire plusieurs, des principaux traités relatifs aux droits de l'homme et certains de leurs protocoles additionnels facultatifs. Cela signifie que les États ont l'obligation et le devoir de respecter et faire respecter leurs engagements, conventionnels ou coutumiers, en protégeant et mettant en œuvre les droits de l'homme en vertu du droit international public. Mais la question qui se pose ici est de savoir quel est la nature et l'étendue des obligations des Etats? est-ce c'est comme les définit le Haut-Commissariat des Droits de l'Homme? pour le Haut-Commissariat ces obligations sont:[13]

1. L'obligation de respecter des droits pour le Haut-Commissariat «signifie que les États doivent s'abstenir de s'ingérer dans l'exercice des droits de l'homme ou de restreindre ces derniers.»

2. L'obligation de protéger exige des États «qu'ils protègent les personnes ou groupes de personnes contre les violations des droits de l'homme.»

3. L'obligation de mettre en œuvre «signifie que les États doivent prendre des mesures positives pour faciliter l'exercice des droits de l'homme.»

Ne doit-t-on pas élargir le champ de responsabilité pour intégrer les Etats avec leurs actes extraterritoriaux? L'idée que les droits de l'homme dégagent des obligations *erga omnes*, visent défendre les droits de l'homme d'autrui, ou en d'autres termes, l'existence d'un intérêt commun impliquant que les obligations conventionnelles et coutumières s'imposent à tout Etat à l'égard des autres Etats; L'ensemble des Etats concernés par la Charte internationale des droits de l'homme ont donc «un intérêt juridique» à ce que les droits en cause soient protégés, ce principe ne doit-il pas exclure les Etats ou les organisations internationales qui émettent des sanctions ou des mesures coercitives, pour qu'ils fassent attention avant l'adoptions de telles sanctions ou mesures, et non pas après pour rattraper quelques effets négatifs?

La doctrine internationale et certaines jurisprudences,[14] avancent non seulement que la nature philosophique de obligations découlant

---

13 Que sont les droits de l'homme? disponible à: https://www.ohchr.org/fr/what-are-human-rights

14 La responsabilité pour violation alléguée d'obligations envers toutes les parties (erga omnes partes) peut être invoquée en intentant une action en justice devant le tribunal, indépendamment de la possibilité de prouver un intérêt privé ... «Pour ces raisons, la distinction que [l'accusé] a tenté d'établir entre le droit d'invoquer la responsabilité en vertu de la Convention sur le génocide et la capacité juridique d'engager des poursuites à cette fin devant le tribunal n'a aucun fondement en droit.» Questions concernant l'obligation de poursuivre ou d'extrader (Belgique c. Sénégal), arrêt, C.I.J. Recueil 2012, p. 449, para. 69; Cour internationale de Justice. *Affaire n° 178 – Arrêt du 22 juillet 2022 (français).* https://www.icj-cij.org/sites/default/files/case-related/178/178-20220722-jud-01-00-fr.pdf

des violations des droits de l'homme, doivent être à la charge des Etats sur plan national, mais ils poussent loin leur reflétions, en parlant non seulement d'obligations de nature d'*erga omnes*, mais «erga omnes partes,» c'est-à-dire que tous les Etats ont des intérêts vitaux à défendre les droits de l'homme, or si ce principe trouve des admirateurs, pour quoi on ne l'applique pas sur des Etats et des organisations internationale qui adoptent des sanctions et des mesures qui violent gravement les droits essentiels de l'homme, pour qu'ils assument la responsabilité de leurs actes?

En réalité, les sanctions et les mesures coercitives visent, en tous les cas, d'opérer des changements politiques dans certaines régions dans le monde, ce fait est claire et limpide, et l'états de violation des règles de droit international en temps de paix et de guerre n'est caché à personne, ce qui crée un sentiment de désespoir, de plus en plus croissant, auprès des personnes lésées par les sanctions et les mesures coercitives unilatérales, et qui ne comprenant pourquoi eux qui sont punies de la sorte. . . . Cette situation rende l'idée si admirable des droits de l'homme, vue et détaillée par la Charte internationale des droits de l'homme, moins mondiale et impartiale comme les prêcheurs des droits de l'homme le prétend. Cette approche juridique de la nécessité d'opérer des changements au niveau de responsabilité de chaque entité internationale et non pas la responsabilité de certains, va donner confiance aux peuples de croient aux droits de l'homme à nouveau.

Il est vrai que les droits de l'homme sont liés les uns aux autres, mais cela ne doit pas empêcher que le noyau dur soit soustrait à toutes sortes de sanctions ou de mesures coercitives, en effet aujourd'hui,

---

Application de la convention pour la prévention et la répression du crime de génocide (Gambie c. Myanmar), exceptions préliminaires, arrêt, C.I.J. Recueil 2022, p. 516, para. 108.

«Cet intérêt commun implique que les obligations en question s'imposent à tout Etat partie à la convention à l'égard de tous les autres Etats parties. L'ensemble des Etats parties ont «un intérêt juridique» à ce que les droits en cause soient protégés, Les obligations correspondantes peuvent donc être qualifiées d'(obligations erga omnes partes), en ce sens que, quelle que soit l'affaire, chaque Etat partie a un intérêt à ce qu'elles soient respectées.»

Application de la convention pour la prévention et la répression du crime de -génocide (Gambie c. Myanmar), exceptions préliminaires, arrêt, C.I.J. Recueil 2022, p. 516, para. 108, disponible à: https://www.icj-cij.org/sites/default/files/case-related/144/144-20120720-JUD-01-00-FR.pdf

les États sont libres de faire ce qu'ils veulent, sans se soucier du droit international ou de la communauté internationale.

Égalité de jouissant des droits

Toutes les personnes doivent jouir de tous les droits de l'homme consacrés par la Charte internationale des droits de l'homme; Ce constat parait évident, mais il est en réalité plus compliqué à réaliser qu'apparaitre. La notion des droits inaliénables de l'homme a fait un long chemin avant d'être cristallisé,[15] mais si on examine l'état le monde d'aujourd'hui, on remarque que le noyau dur de ces droits n'est pas le même par tout, et cela sur tous les niveaux: au niveau politique et la question de la démocratie et le partage du pouvoir, au niveau social, l'égalité et la justice sociale, et enfin et surtout au niveau économique où certaines personnes dans beaucoup de régions dans le monde, se contentent de n'importe quel travail précaire, si ce travail leur donne de quoi manger. Aujourd'hui, un regard impartial et non superficiel sur l'existence d'un ensemble de droits inaliénables, nous pousse à constater que l'idée de droits inaliénables ne sont qu'un leurre ou une simple illusion. Les disparités économiques, sociales et culturelles, se creusent d'une décennie à l'autre, et rendent la simple affirmation que la notion de droits inaliénables est bel et bien une réalité mondiale difficile à réaliser.

Sans porter préjudice à la distinction faite plus haut entre les droits qui doivent être accordés aux personnes et aux peuples au niveau interétatique et les droits inaliénables de l'homme, il faut dire que les garanties accordées à l'être humain sur le plan international, de nos jours, concerne seulement les obligations l'Etat de sa nationalité ou de son pays de résidence. Toutefois ces idées pessimistes doivent nous pousser à l'optimisme de la volonté, et de recommencer à réfléchir à nouveau au sens des termes utilisées concernant les droits essentiels de l'homme, et de redéfinir le sens que l'on va leurs donner, en gardant en esprit que la notion des droits de l'homme est un ensemble de principes relatifs à l'égalité et à l'équité, comportant des droits et des devoirs.

---

15 Nations Unies, Droits humains, Questions thématiques, disponible à: https://www.un.org/fr/global-issues/human-rights

Le principe de l'égalité de jouissance en droits est une notion assez complexe, certains voient en elle une idée contre nature, tandis que d'autres la considèrent trop utopique pour être vrai, mais l'état actuel du droit international des droits de l'homme considère que ce principe repose sur trois piliers essentiels.

Le premier pilier se cristallise autour des valeurs essentielles à partie desquelles on a bâti l'ensemble de droits de l'homme, où chaque être humain a en soi de la dignité et de la valeur humaine. A partir de cette valeur on peut reconnaître et de respecter des droits aux personnes et aux peuples.

Le deuxième pilier repose sur ceux qui doivent assurer ces droits, la capacité d'une personne à jouir de ses droits de l'homme dépend du respect de ces droits par les autres. Certains juristes considèrent que ces sont des droits et de responsabilités partagés et réciproques; Cela signifie que la jouissance des droits de l'homme implique une responsabilité et des devoirs envers les autres et la communauté. Or le rôle principal est joué par les gouvernements qui ont une responsabilité particulière de veiller les droits sont protéger par des lois, et mis en œuvre par des institutions qui veillent à la bonne marche des droits octroyées aux personnes, pour permettre une jouissance d'une vie dans laquelle les droits de l'homme soient respectés et protégés.

Le troisième pilier concerne le champ que couvrent le droit des droits de l'homme, au premier lieu on trouve les règles de droit couverts par la déclaration des droits de l'homme, qui constitue un tronc commun, transformée en règles coutumières obligatoires, ensuite le premier pacte de 1966 concernant les droits civils et politiques qui assurent aux personnes la reconnaissance due, et la capacité à participer à la vie publique en respectant en même temps la vie privé. Le deuxième pacte couver des droits économiques, sociaux et culturels, allant d'avoir un travail, à la santé, au logement adapté, à l'accès à l'eau potable, et passant aux droits à sécurité sociale et une vie culturelle et la protection des biens culturels. Un très large éventail de droits bien repartis en catégories, mal repartis sur les êtres humains.

Toutefois, si le principe de l'égalité de jouissance des droits de l'homme peut être, plus ou moins, bien défini, le principe de l'équité dans la jouissance des droits de l'homme, est plus difficile à cerné; l'idée de l'équité en soi est, en réalité, plus subjective qu'elle est objective. L'équité peut être définie comme un principe modérateur du droit selon lequel chacun peut prétendre à un «traitement juste, égalitaire et raisonnable»[16] tout en prenant en considération la possibilité de traiter certaines personnes différemment si la situation l'exige. D'ici vient la difficulté en matière de jouissant des d,roits de l'homme, nul ne peut prétendre avoir les critères de la droiture, de l'honnêteté de l'impartialité ou de le la justice.

Les droits humains sont un ensemble de principes liés aux concepts d'égalité et équité. Sur le plan des individus il est concevable de reconnaitre la liberté de faire des choix concernant la vie et de développer un potentiel en tant qu'êtres humains qui visent à vivre une vie, sans harcèlement ni discrimination. Mais dès que l'on sort du cercle individuel au cercle des devoirs des Etats, cela devient plus problématique, et si on passe aux conséquences des sanctions ou des mesures coercitives, l'égalités de traitement et l'équité dans les actes, les notions d'égalité et d'équité entrent dans l'improbabilité d'être réalisées.

Cela nous mène à constater que les droits inaliénables de l'hommes, prescrits dans la Charte des droits de l'homme, ne trouvent pas encor un espace commun avec les sanctions ou avec les mesures coercitives prises en application de la même Charte, si l'on ne le crée pas. Toutes personnes physiques et morales doivent jouir de tous les droits de l'homme consacrés par la Charte, indépendamment des objectifs de toute politique de sanctions. Ceci est un vrai dilemme, les pires textes de droits c'est celles qui essaient de servir une certaine politique, au lieu que la politique se conforme avec les textes du droit et à leurs esprits, surtout le droit des droits de l'homme.

En examinant de près toutes les résolutions du Conseil de Sécurité à propos des sanctions, on trouve quelles sont conformes à la Chartes des Nations Unies et elles sont tout à fait légales, mais sont-elles juste? cela va de même aux mesures coercitives, est-ce ces procédures sont illégales? ou le problème réside dans l'application de ces sanctions et mesures est dépourvue de mécanismes adéquates. La réponse à ces questions est relative et non pas catégorique.

Si on décide de laisser tomber tout discours démagogique, et de voir le monde comme il est, un monde dur et partisan où les rapports

---

16 Définition de Équité, par Serge Braudo, Conseiller honoraire à la Cour d'appel de Versailles, Dictionnaire Du Droit Privé, disponible à: https://www.dictionnaire-juridique.com/definition/equite.php

de force jouent un rôle déterminant, on est forcé à constater que la politique et les politiciens aurons toujours la main, et un certain degré de réalisme est nécessaire pour arriver à des buts réalisables. Les questions des droits de l'homme, même si elles sont intransigeantes, utopiques pour certaines personnes, elles méritent que l'on soit un peu réaliste en les traitant, et que nos solutions soient plus modestes et réalisables.

La théorie de «l'abus de droit» peut offrir une porte de sortie de ce dilemme, une porte sous l'égide du réalisme politique qui est une méthode incitante «à garder la tête froide, et à observer le monde tel qu'il est, et non à l'imaginer tel que nous voudrions qu'il fût.»[17] On peut définir «l'abus de droit» comme étant le fait, pour une personne physique ou morale dont les Etats, «de commettre une faute par le dépassement des limites d'exercice d'un droit qui lui est conféré, soit en le détournant de sa finalité, soit dans le but de nuire à autrui.»[18] Le champ de cette théorie est restreint aux cas où le droit est exercé légitiment et non pas avec intention de nuire ou punir ou de faire plier un adversaire à des fins politiques, où il faut prouver que l'intérêt défendu est légitime.[19] où il faut prouver que l'intérêt défendu est légitime. Et comme nul ne peut soutenir la possibilité que les sanctions ou les mesures coercitives sont prises avec l'attention de nuire à un Etat ou à plusieurs Etats et apporter des preuves tangibles à sa thèse, ou au moins, les exemples concrets sur ces cas ne sont pas disponibles, en notant que tous ce que la communauté internationale a réussi à développer c'est la légalité des actes sans prétendre pouvoir arriver à la légitimité des actes pris légalement. On prétend que les actes constituant l'objet des sanctions ou des mesures coercitives, tout au plus, peuvent être exécutés avec maladresse ou malhabileté ou négligemment.

Pour cette raison la théorie de «l'abus de droit» est un bon moyen de démasquer les méfaits des sanctions et des mesures coercitives, à condition qu'on ne laisse pas les mesures coercitives hors toute possibilité de contrôle comme c'est le cas d'aujourd'hui, si non on ne

---

17 Théories des relations internationales, Par Jean-Baptiste Jeangène Vilmer, que sais-je, 128 pages, p. 23.

18 Abus de droit – Juillet 2024, Fiches d'orientation, Dalloz.fr., disponible à: https://www.dalloz.fr/documentation/Document?id=DZ%2FOASIS%2F001515

19 Pour plus d'information sur cette théorie voir: L'abus de droit en droit international public, Marie Lemey, 2021, LGDJ, Lextenso, ISBN: 978-2-275-08837-2 ISSN: 0520-0261, P. 447.

pourra pas appliquer cette théorie qu'en ce qui concerne les sanctions que Conseil de Sécurité prendra, et le résultat va être aussi catastrophique sur l'état des droits de l'homme qu'il est aujourd'hui, car les même Etats partis au Conseil vont prendre des mesures coercitives au lieu de faire jouer les mécanismes de sanctions comme c'est le cas actuellement dans certains cas.

L'application de cette théorie, propose les moyens de faire face à l'exercice des sanctions et des mesures qui portent préjudice à l'Etat contre lequel ces actes ont été pris, où il faut interdire l'exercice abusif d'un droit qui nuit malicieusement à l'Etat concerné ou lui porte préjudice, sans qu'existe par ailleurs un intérêt sérieux et légitime à l'exercice de ce un droit. Cette théorie propose ainsi des solutions aux préjudices hors proportion causés par des sanctions ou mesures coercitives, en précisant que toute atteinte aux droits essentiels de l'homme doit être sanctionnées sans tolérance. Ce principe peut être considéré comme un moyen de prévention efficace contre tout abus de droits que souvent les sanctions et les mesures coercitives en comportent, en se basant sur la violation des principes de paix et de sécurité internationale, principes indéfinis clairement par une règle impérative, et restent au grès des Etats et Organisations Internationales.

Le dernier volet de la pleine égalité de jouissance des droits de l'homme, ou comment peut-on associer les droits de l'homme et la politique des sanctions ou des mesures coercitives? La meilleure solution sera par la mise en œuvre des sanctions pertinentes, ou par un regard permanant sur les sanctions ou mesures, pour éviter le respect excessif qui négligent le principe d'équité que doit comporter toute sanction ou mesure coercitive. La mise en œuvre des sanctions ou des mesures pertinentes, peut avérer juste si le terme «pertinent» est défini en ayant en optique les droits essentiels de l'homme. Plusieurs catégories de peuvent être avancées à titre d'exemple:

- L'identification rigoureuse des personnes physiques ou des entités en relation directe avec le fait qui justifie les sanctions ou les mesures coercitives; Ce lien direct souvent n'existe pas ou très peu démontré.

- L'éloignement de généraliser les sanctions ou les mesures coercitives, surtout quand ces actes frappent des entités publiques qui offrent des services indispensables à vie courante et la vie économique, comme le fait de généraliser des sanctions contre les ministères des sources d'eaux ou le ministère de l'électricité, voire l'imposition d'un embargo sur les pièces détachées pour équipements médicaux ou l'imposition d'un blocus sur l'importation de ces équipement ...

- L'examen périodique des sanctions ou des mesures coercitives en présence de la personne physique ou morale ou qui la représente.

- Dresser des listes directrices de produits ou des services que les sanctions ou les mesures coercitives doivent éviter, au risque si non, de violer des droits essentiels de l'être humain.

- Avoir des éléments de preuve tangible que cette entité ou cette personne commettent des actes illicites engageant une responsabilité internationale. Tout en sachant qu'une preuve tangible C'est la preuve qui «n'a pas pour seule fin de libérer une proposition du doute; elle permet en outre de pénétrer la dépendance relative des vérités.»[20]

- Avoir des justificatifs comme quoi l'interruption des services offerts par cette personne, physique ou morale, ou cette entité ne conduira pas à une aggravation des droits de l'homme.

- Développer et encourager le recours aux moyens pacifiques définis dans le sixième Chapitre de la Charte des Nations Unies, pour faire face aux infractions prétendues aux obligations dictées par les règles du droit internationale, c'est-à-dire trouver d'autres moyens que ceux la Charte a défini dans son septième Chapitre, article 41, pour faire face aux cas de menace contre la paix, de rupture de la paix et d'acte d'agression, sans prendre le soin de définir le sens ou la portée d'aucun de ces termes, en laissant aux neuf des quinze Etats membres de décider si un de ces trois cas existe réellement.

---

20 Chateauraynaud, Francis. «L'épreuve du tangible.» *La croyance et l'enquête*, edited by Bruno Karsenti and Louis Quéré, Éditions de l'École des hautes études en sciences sociales, 2004, disponible à: https://doi.org/10.4000/books.editionsehess.11215.

Rares sont les situations qui atteignent le niveau d'une violation ou d'une menace contre la paix et la sécurité internationales, ou encore un état d'agression. Généraliser les solutions émises pour des cas si graves, et cela sur toutes les divergences entre nations, surtout dans les cas d'ingérence dans les affaires intérieures des Etats, et utiliser les moyens cités dans l'article 41 de la Charte pour régler des divergences d'ordre politique, sans prêter égard aux conséquences sur les droits essentiels de de l'homme, peut être considéré comme un crime de gravité certaine.

Les solutions avancées plus haut ne sortent pas du déjà vue et connu, pour cela s'il n'existe pas un corps indépendant responsable de l'examen des sanctions ou des mesures coercitives périodiquement, un corps doté de moyen de pression réelle sur les institutions des Etats ou sur les Organisations Intergouvernementales qui éditent ces sanctions ou mesures, la situation des victimes des violations de droits de l'homme va s'aggraver, en engendrant plus et misères et de violence. Violer le principe d'égalité de jouissance des droits de l'homme, surtout ceux qui touchent à la dignité humaine, sera une des causes principales du terrorisme, du repli sur soi, du fanatisme, d'émigration incontrôlée pour échapper à la misère sociale et économique... Il faut vivre cette situation pour la comprendre.

Devoirs des acteurs appliquant les mesures coercitives

En partant du postulat comme quoi tous les acteurs publics et privés doivent respecter et donner la priorité à tous les droits de l'homme, sans discrimination lors de la formulation et de la mise en œuvre de sanctions et les politiques de conformité, peut nous pousser à constater que tout va pour le mieux dans le monde, mais ce n'est pas un postulat, c'est un chalenge que l'on doit gagner par ceux qui ont une bonne volonté.

Très peu de moyens sont possédés par ceux qui imposent des sanctions ou des mesures coercitives pour contrôler et limiter les méfaits de ces actes et procédures. Même les Nations Unies avec leurs moyens divers surtout le mécanisme de vote au Conseil de Sécurité qui peut jouer un rôle modérateur de temps en temps d'un côté, et les Comités des sanctions, créés par le Conseil de Sécurité, et qui possèdent une armada de résolutions et de procédures et des experts en droit de l'homme de l'autre, les effets négatifs sur les droits essentiels de l'homme ne sont pas assez contrôlés dans beaucoup de cas, et les violations, de plus en plus, sont constatées par d'autres organes des Nations Unies et par des organisations internationales non gouvernementales, et les Etats victimes.

Le rôle des agents de tout Etat, soit aux seins des Nations Unies ou toute autre Organisation Internationale, ou auprès de leurs gouvernements, est de faire entendre aux politiciens les limites et les dangers à violer les droits essentiels de l'homme, voir même demander expressément la suppression de certaines demandes de sanctions ou des mesures coercitives à prendre. Cela bien évidement exigent que les Etats disposent d'un groupe d'experts et de conseillers dans le domaine des droits de l'homme, en plus des spécialistes des affaires intérieures des pays susceptibles d'imposer des sanctions contre ils, ou de prendre des mesures coercitives à leur encontre.

Bien évidemment le rôle des conseillers est appréciable, néanmoins ce rôle dans la prise de décision reste limité, le Conseil de l'Union Européenne, par exemple, précise sur son site officiel que «Les mesures restrictives sont définies dans les décisions du Conseil en matière de politique étrangère et de sécurité commune,»[21] donc la politique prime sur tout autre question, et le droit n'est qu'un outil en service de la politique de l'Union,[22] il n'a y qu'à voir les efforts déployés à élaborer ces sanctions et les résultats au final pour s'en convaincre du rôle de la politique et du droit en la matière.

Toutefois, est-ce l'imposition des sanctions ou des mesures coercitives engendre-elle une responsabilité internationale des Etats et des Organisations Internationales qui s'impliquent dans ces processus? cette question doit être poser, pour qu'au moins on laisse la juste place de l'honnêteté morale et académique. La prise des sanctions par une Organisation Internationale visant un de ses membre, est un acte licite en soit, car il est légal et souvent ces Organisations se basent sur leur Charte ou leur traité constituant pour justifier de tels actes, mais

---

21 Comment l'UE adopte-t-elle et réexamine-t-elle les sanctions? Disponible à: https://www.consilium.europa.eu/fr/policies/sanctions-adoption-review-procedure/

22 Lignes directrices relatives aux sanctions – mise à jour, Bruxelles, le 4 mai 2018, (OR. en), 5664/18, LIMITE, CORLX 39, CFSP/PESC 68, FIN 69, RELEX 376, CONUN 139, COARM 156, disponible à: https://www.tresor.economie.gouv.fr/Institutionnel/Niveau2/Pages/f3234489-26a1-48f7-8a05-f31d34551f13/files/a39128a7-0c1f-4ff6-88cb-09c43715023

s'il résulte de ces actes des violations graves des droits essentiels de l'homme, que doit-on faire ou penser? Peut-on tout le temps penser et agir aux termes de légalité ou doit-on laisser place à la légitimité des actes émanant de grandes institutions ? A titre d'exemple, il existe trois types de régimes de sanctions que l'Union Européenne peut mettre en œuvre: les sanctions des Nations unies, les sanctions mixtes et les sanctions autonomes de l'Union.[23] Cette expression politique, en soi, ne pose point un problème d'ordre légal, mais encor une fois ce n'est pas une question de légalité de la procédure, mais une question de légitimé des actes et de leurs conséquences, la réponse ne peut être la même dans les deux cas de figure; il est courant que des droits essentiels soient bafoués par des mesures et sanctions de l'Union Européenne et par les Nations Unies; Enfin «dans l'espace de l'Organisation de Sécurité et de Coopération en Europe, des embargos peuvent être imposés sur l'achat et la vente de produits liés à la défense et de biens à double usage,»[24] ces embargos peuvent conduire à des violations graves, car la liste des produits à double usage est très longue; Tout cela sème un désordre juridique mondial, entre ce qui est légal et ce qui est légitime, dont nous sommes tous des témoins, mais en attendant, les victimes potentielles parmi les peuples perdent de plus en plus de leurs droits essentiels l'homme, sans que la situation de ces peuples puisse opérer un changement radical et immédiat du comportement des décideurs de la scène internationale, pour qu'il se calque sur leurs discours humanitaires.

De la même façon, pour les mesures prisent par un Etat contre un autre Etat, comme c'est le cas, et à titre d'exemple, de l'embargo économique, commercial et financier imposées par les Etats Unies contre Cuba, depuis 1960,[25] qui est officiellement toujours en place; Ces mesures sont des actes souverains et légale voir légitime en certaines cas, où chaque Etat a le pouvoir d'organiser ses relations internationales librement, à conditions que ses actes souverains ne

23 Types de sanctions adoptées par l'UE, Conseil de l'Union Européenne ? disponible à: https://www.consilium.europa.eu/fr/policies/sanctions-different-types/

24 Ministère des Affaires étrangères, de l'Union européenne et de la Coopération espagnole, disponible à: https://www.exteriores.gob.es/fr/PoliticaExterior/Paginas/SancionesInternacionales.aspx

25 Salim Lamrani «Rupture dans la stratégie anticastriste de Washington, A Cuba, vers la fin de l'embargo,» Le Monde diplomatique, disponible à: https://www.monde-diplomatique.fr/2015/01/LAMRANI/51971

soient pas de nature illicite, ce qui loin du cas l'embargo américain sur Cuba, vue l'impact sur les droits essentiels du peuple cubain.

Le projet d'articles de la sixième Commission de de l'Assemblée Générale des Nations Unies, concernant la responsabilité des Etats sur leurs actes illicites de 2001,[26] précise dans son premier article que: «Tout fait internationalement illicite de l'Etat engage sa responsabilité internationale,» tout en sachant que ce principe est un principe coutumier faisant partie de droit international,[27] l'acte est considéré illicite selon l'article deux de ce projet si deux conditions se réunissent: «une action ou une omission est attribuable à l'Etat en vertu du droit international» et cette action ou omission «constitue une violation d'une obligation internationale de l'Etat.»[28] Ce projet peut nous aider à bien déterminer la responsabilités des Etats sur actes dont les mesures coercitives.

En 2011, la même Commission a préparé un projet sur la responsabilité des Organisations Internationales[29] pour des faits internationalement illicites; La Commission n'a opéré des changements par rapport aux principes juridiques avancés dans le projet de la responsabilité des Etats sur leurs actes illicites, toutefois elle a ajouté un point essentiel

---

26 Le projet d'article de la sixième Commission de l'Assemblée Générale des Nations Unies sur la responsabilité de l'Etats pour fait internationalement illicite, de 2001, disponible à: https://legal.un.org/ilc/texts/instruments/french/draft_articles/9_6_2001.pdf

27 "Les articles 16 à 18 sur la responsabilité de l'État pour fait internationalement illicite couvrent les cas dans lesquels un État aide ou assiste, dirige et contrôle ou contraint un autre État dans la commission d'un fait internationalement illicite. L'article 16 a été considéré comme exprimant une «règle coutumière» par la Cour internationale de Justice dans l'arrêt sur le fond qu'elle a rendu en l'affaire relative à l'Application de la Convention pour la prévention et la répression du crime de génocide,» Commentaire (1) sur l'article 16 du projet des responsabilités des organisations internationale, p. 28, disponible à: https://legal.un.org/ilc/reports/2011/french/chp5.pdf

28 "Comme dans le cas de la responsabilité des États, l'expression «obligation internationale» s'entend d'une obligation imposée par le droit international, «quelle [que] soit l'origine» de l'obligation concernée. Comme indiqué dans le commentaire de l'article 12 des articles sur la responsabilité de l'État pour fait internationalement illicite, cette formule signifie que les obligations internationales «peuvent être établies par une règle coutumière de droit international, par un traité, ou par un principe général de droit applicable dans l'ordre juridique international.» Commentaire (1) sur l'article 10 du projet des responsabilités des organisations internationale, p. 26.

29 Le projet d'article de la sixième Commission de l'Assemblée Générale des Nations Unies sur la responsabilité des Organisations Internationales de 2011, disponible à: https://legal.un.org/ilc/texts/instruments/french/draft_articles/9_11_2011.pdf

sur la responsabilité internationale de l'État pour un fait internationalement illicite à raison du fait d'une organisation international. A partir de ce projet on peut poser les mêmes questions que l'on avait posé sur la responsabilité des Etats concernant des sanctions qui entraînent des violations des droits fondamentaux humains, peuvent être posées à l'encontre des organisations internationales, toute en sachant, que ce dernier projet a expliqué la signification du terme comportement d'une organisation internationale, dans son sixième article, comme étant le «comportement d'un organe ou d'un agent d'une organisation internationale dans l'exercice des fonctions,» ce qui signifie que dans le cas où l' exercice des fonctions mène à l'adoption des sanctions, ou au moment de l'application des sanctions, par cet organe ou cet agent, cette exercice est considérée «comme étant un fait de cette organisation d'après le droit international.»

La Commission ne s'est pas arrêtée à l'invocation de la responsabilité des Etats sur leurs actes illicites ou celui de la responsabilité des Organisations, mais elle a rajouté dans l'article 50, du premier projet, et l'article 52 du deuxième projet, que les contre-mesures[30] prises par un Etat ou une organisation internationale face à un acte illicite émanant d'un autre Etat ou d'une autre organisation internationale «ne peuvent porter aucune atteinte: . . . Aux obligations concernant la protection des droits fondamentaux de l'homme.» D'autre part, la doctrine se prononce dans sa nette majorité, concernant le droit qu'ont les Organisations Internationales d'invoquer la responsabilité d'un Etat dans le cas d'une violation d'une obligation due à la communauté internationale dans son ensemble, en faveur de la notion d'*erga omnes*, et il semble bien que l'obligation *erga omnes* s'appliquera aussi au cas d'une violation commise par une Organisation Internationale, surtout dans les cas de violations graves des droite essentiels de l'homme.[31] D'ici vient l'importance du travail de ceux qui sont concernés par la mise en application des sanctions ou des mesures coercitives.

---

30 Une contre-mesure est une «mesure s'opposant à une mesure précédente jugée mauvaise,» Encyclopædia Universalis, https://www.universalis.fr/dictionnaire/contre-mesure/

31 Rapport de la Commission du droit international sur les travaux de sa soixante-troisième session, Chapitre V Responsabilité Des Organisations Internationales, disponible à: https://legal.un.org/ilc/reports/2011/french/chp5.pdf

Il est très intéressant de mettre en œuvre ces deux projets, et de les utiliser comme un outil juridique pour contrôler les sanctions et les mesures coercitives, en recourant à des cas réels pour mesurer les méfaits voir les catastrophes que les peuples subissent à cause de ces sanctions. La théorie de l'abus de droit peut expliquer dans ce cas pourquoi il est inconcevable d'établir le principe de bonne foi aux Etats quand ils agissent de la sorte, soit directement quand ils prennent eux-mêmes des mesures coercitives, ou indirectement via les sanctions émises par des Organisations Internationales.

Outre le fait que la notion d'abus de droit n'est que rarement consacrée par la jurisprudence internationale ce qui l'affaiblit cette théorie, il est vrai aussi que dans les relations internationales, les États se prévalent de l'abus de droit, en exerçant leur droit d'une façon arbitraire, ou d'une manière à infliger aux autres États un préjudice qui ne peut être justifié, et cela par une considération légitime de leurs propres intérêts; Tout cela est fort possible, mais pas au point de violer des droits essentiels à la vie des êtres humains, la doctrine et la jurisprudence doivent œuvrer dans ce sens. En tous les cas pour qu'une allégation d'abus de droit soit retenue, il faut au moins établir l'existence d'un droit qui aurait fait l'objet d'un abus, et dans la pratique de sanctions il est facile de constater le droit bafoué, mais il reste d'établir si un État ou l'Organisation Internationale, ont agi de bonne ou de mauvaise foi, ce qui reste une question relative et sujette à diverses interprétations politiques.

Cet état de laxisme concernant les violations des droits de l'homme résultat des sanctions, doit être changer, malgré les exemples frappants de ces dernières décennies, l'état de droit en la matière demeure inchangé, et c'est un des devoirs des agents de l'Etat ou les fonctionnaires au près des Organisations internationales et surtout les Comités de sanctions de changer la donne. Les mauvais exemples ne manquent pas: si on examine les sanctions des Nations unies prises contre l'Irak en 1990 par la résolution 661[32] et les résolutions ultérieures pertinentes, du Conseil de Sécurité, qui a installé un embargo économique le plus radical que les Nations Unies ou n'importe quelle autre organisation internationale ont imposés à ce jour;

---

32 La résolution 661(1990), adoptée le 6 août 1990 , à la 2933 séance par 13 voix contre zéro, avec 2 abstentions (Cuba et Yémen), disponible à: https://documents.un.org/doc/resolution/gen/nr0/575/48/pdf/nr057548.pdf

Où ce pays a vécu une descente en enfer, même avec le programme «Pétrole contre nourriture» et avec le travail de deux Comités des sanctions, le premier a été créé par la résolution 661 (1990), ce Comité était chargé de superviser le programme «pétrole contre nourriture» et d'identifier les besoins humanitaires, et le deuxième Comité a été créé par la résolution 1518 (2003),[33] et était chargé de continuer à identifier, conformément à la résolution 1483 (2003) du 22 mai 2003,[34] des personnes et des entités dont les fonds et autres avoirs financiers et les ressources économiques devraient être gelés et transférés au Fonds de développement pour l'Iraq, tout ce travail n'a abouti à rien aux regards du peuple irakien, qui a vu sa situation en matières de droit de l'homme s'empirait. Mais on mettant de cotes toutes les affaires de corruption d'agents publics étrangers et d'abus de biens sociaux,[35] et les mensonges conduisant à l'occupation militaires de ce pays, on peut après tous cela constater que ces sanctions n'ont arrivé qu'à empirer la situation de peuple irakien, qui a perdu non seulement de sa richesse, mais aussi de sa dignité humaine. C'est un bon exemple qui peut constituer un cas d'école pour mettre en œuvre les règles du projet de la Commission du droit international concernant la responsabilité des organisations internationales sur les actes illicites.

Or si la démonstration faite plus haut n'est pas assez convaincante, le cas des mesures coercitives prises contre la Syrie par plusieurs Etats et organisations internationales, dont l'Union Européenne en 2011,[36] et en 2020, tout en déclarant que le régime de mesures restrictives «prévoit un grand nombre de d'exemptions ou de dérogations au

---

33 La résolution 1518 (2003), S/RES/1518 (2003), du 24 novembre 2003, disponible à: https://documents.un.org/doc/undoc/gen/n03/631/02/pdf/n0363102.pdf

34 La résolution 1483 (2003), S/RES/1483 (2003), du 23 mai 2003, disponible à: https://documents.un.org/doc/undoc/gen/n03/368/54/pdf/n0336854.pdf

35 Corruption d'agents publics étrangers dans le cadre du programme «Pétrole contre nourriture»: une incrimination prévisible, Par Ambroise Vienet-Legué, Avocat, disponible à: https://www.village-justice.com/articles/corruption-active-agents-publics-e%CC%81trangers-principe-legalite,47984.html

36 Règlement (UE) n ° 442/2011 du Conseil du 9 mai 2011 concernant des mesures restrictives en raison de la situation en Syrie, Conseil de l'Europe, disponible à: https://eur-lex.europa.eu/legal-content/FR/TXT/?uri=celex%3A32011R0442

Mesures restrictives de l'UE en raison de la situation en Syrie, Union Européenne, disponible à: https://eur-lex.europa.eu/FR/legal-content/summary/eu-restrictive-measures-in-view-of-the-situation-in-syria.html

bénéfice des activités humanitaires,»[37] et le dernier paquet de mesures européen en 2024;[38] ou la succession des mesures prises par les Etats Unis D'Amérique qui ont commencé en 1979, suivies d'une deuxième vague en 2004,[39] de retour avec une fréquence plus élevée depuis 2011,[40] et le dernier paquet a eu lieu en 2019,[41] constituant un blocus total et continu sur le pays; Sans se soucier, sauf en parole seulement, de l'état des droits de l'homme du peuple syrien, qui perd, d'année en année, de niveau de vie et de sa sureté.[42] Ce qui est en commun entre la situation en Irak et en Syrie, c'est que ceux qui éditent des sanctions ont accompagné leurs actes par une agression armée contre ces deux pays, appelée mesures coercitives militaires, ce qui rend la situation des droits essentiels de l'homme dans un pire état. Ce point

37 Les sanctions européennes: un instrument de lutte contre la répression en Syrie, ministère de l'Europe et des Affaires Étrangères. Conseil de l'Europe, disponible à: https://www.diplomatie.gouv.fr/fr/dossiers-pays/syrie/les-sanctions-europeennes-un-instrument-de-lutte-contre-la-repression-en-syrie/

38 Voir les détails sur le site du Conseil de l'Union Européenne, disponible à: https://www.consilium.europa.eu/fr/press/press-releases/2024/01/22/syria-council-adds-six-persons-and-five-entities-to-eu-sanctions-list/

39 Décret présidentiel 13338, signé le 11 mai 2004: «Gel des biens de certaines personnes et interdiction de l'exportation de certaines marchandises vers la Syrie (date d'entrée en vigueur: 12 mai 2004),» Renseignements sur le document: Federal Register, volume 69, numéro 93, jeudi 13 mai 2004, disponible à: https://ofac.treasury.gov/media/6456/download?inline

40 Décret présidentiel 13572 du 29 avril 2011: «Gel des avoirs de certaines personnes en lien avec des violations des droits de l'homme en Syrie.» Renseignements: Federal Register, volume 76, numéro 85, mardi 3 mai 2011, disponible à: https://ofac.treasury.gov/media/6481/download?inline

Décret présidentiel 13573 du 18 mai 2011: «Gel des avoirs des hauts responsables du gouvernement syrien,» Renseignements: Federal Register, volume 76, numéro 98, vendredi 20 mai 2011, disponible à: https://ofac.treasury.gov/media/6486/download?inline

Décret présidentiel 13582 du 17 août 2011: «Geler les biens du gouvernement syrien et empêcher certaines transactions liées à la Syrie.» Renseignements sur le document: Federal Register, volume 76, numéro, 162 lundi 22 août 2011, disponible à: https://ofac.treasury.gov/media/5941/download?inline

41 Loi César de 2019 sur la protection des civils en Syrie (entrée en vigueur le 17 juin 2020).

Site officiel du Senat disponible à: https://www.congress.gov/bill/116th-congress/house-bill/31/text; site officiel du secrétariat au Trésor, disponible à: https://ofac.treasury.gov/media/57351/download?inline

42 Voir le Rapport de la Rapporteuse spéciale sur les effets négatifs des mesures coercitives unilatérales sur l'exercice des droits de l'homme, Symbol: A/HRC/54/23/Add.1, adopté par l'Assemblée Générales le: 03 juillet 2023. A/HRC/54/23/Add.1, disponible à: https://documents.un.org/doc/undoc/gen/g23/127/58/pdf/g2312758.pdf

de ressemblance ne s'arrête pas à ces deux Etats, mais il gagne, tôt au tard, tous les pays qui vivent une situation de blocus.

Il est difficile de comprendre dans les démarches décrites plus haut où se trouvent la notion des droits de d'homme? ou où il est le rôle des conseilleurs ou agents de l'Etat ou les grands fonctionnaires des Organisations Internationales en question? Ce n'est point un reproche, mais le peu de poids constaté de leurs influences rend très difficile de décrire le type d'actes ou de conseils qu'ils prodiguent et qui peuvent constituer une méthode à suivre; Tout cela n'empêche pas d'essayer d'agir d'une manière plus efficace. Toutefois, si on faisait cette démonstration en droit, et on a réussi à prouver les atteintes graves aux droits de l'homme, on peut faire avancer la cause de rationaliser les sanctions ou mesures coercitives.

Encor une fois, les possibilités actuelles de changer les comportements de puissances actives dans le monde sont quasi nul, pour cette raison et en attendant mieux, il faut encourager les points forts dans le travail des Comités de sanctions, et essayer de mettre en lumière les points de faiblesse, en faisant le maximum pour opérer des changements d'attitudes. Il convient donc de proposer, une fois encore, une nouvelle résolution du Conseil du Sécurité, en vertu de l'article 29 selon laquelle le Conseil a créé précédemment des tribunaux internationaux indépendants, et sans qu'il puisse intervenir dans leurs affaires, une résolution définissant un code de conduite obligatoire aux membres des Nations Unies concernant les sanctions prises par le Conseil et les mesures coercitives prises par les Etats membre aux Nations Unies en dehors du Conseil, et exécuté par un Comité directeur, un code de conduite bâti, entre autre, sur les principes suivants:

Objet du Code

1. Mettre une liste des actes exclus expressément des sanctions et mesures coercitives.
2. Définir les valeurs et principes fondamentaux de l'éthique professionnelle pour les membres du Comité.
3. Définir les limites minimales des droits garantis aux dont les violations sont considérées comme des actes prohibés, et identifier les formes qui pourraient constituer une violation de ces droits.

4. Définir les moyens de dédommagement aux Etats lésés par ces sanctions ou mesures coercitives.
5. La possibilité de créer de sous-comités spécialisés en sanctions et en régions géographiques.

Les obligations fondamentales de ce code et du Comité directeur

1. Total indépendance au Conseil de Sécurité et tout autre organe principal de l'organisation.
2. La considération dominante dans le recrutement des membres de ce comité doit être la nécessité d'assurer la présence des personnes possédant les plus hautes qualités de compétence et d'intégrité et de haute connaissance en matières du droit de l'homme.
3. Prendre en compte la répartition géographique et culturelle dans la sélection des membres de ce dit Comité.
4. Les membres sont élus par les Etats au sein de l'Assemblée Générale, et pour une durée déterminée.
5. La Répartition géographique des membres.
6. Totale indépendance de ce corps financièrement.

Conclusion

Il est indispensable pour garantir à l'humanité et la paix et la sécurité internationales que le seuil minimum de droits de l'homme soit assuré, pas verbalement seulement, mais pratiquement aussi. Les méfaits des sanctions prisent conformément aux règles du droits international et les mesures coercitives unilatérales dépassent en réalité leurs buts initiaux, et les pays sanctionnés cités plus haut montrent à quels degrés les ce concept est en réalité ne respecte pas le seuil minimum des droits de l'homme. Pour cette raison l'organisation des Nations Unies essaie de souligner les dangers de certains types de ces sanctions ou mesures prises par les organisations internationales ou par des Etats.

Dans cette étude, certaines solutions ont été avancées, comme le développement du rôle des conseillés aux prés des politiciens, tout en sachant que ce rôle n'influence pas beaucoup la prise de décision ; ou

de souligner la responsabilité des organisations internationales ou des
Etats sur leurs actes concernant des sanctions ou des mesures coercitives qui entraînent des violations des droits fondamentaux humains.

Le rôle à jouer par les Nations Unies dans le domaine des
sanctions et les mesures coercitives reste déterminant, et les idées en
la matière ne manquent pas, comme l'adoption d'une résolution du
Conseil de sécurité définissant un code de conduite obligatoire aux
membres des Nations Unies concernant les limites des sanctions ou
les mesures unilatérales.

La légalité doit être accompagnée par l'équité en droit des droits
de l'homme; Il y a assez de textes en la matière, il faut seulement
changer d'optique, de regarder ceux qui souffrent quotidiennement au
lieu de continuer à voir le monde avec un regard condescendant. Les
divergences politiques entre Etats motivent les sentions et les mesures
et les victimes collatéraux ne sont pas prises en comptes.

CHAPTER 14

Assessing the Impact of Sanctions

An FBO perspective

Floriana Polito,[1] *Peter Prove,*[2] *Emmanuel Tronc*[3]

Abstract

Faith-based organizations (FBOs) have a distinctively multi-sectoral experience and perspective on the impact of sanctions and related economic measures, covering the spectrum of professional international and national level humanitarian operations, to local community-based essential service provision, to the basic functions of community life and organization.

This experience has not, however, been systematically mapped or researched. An initiative to begin addressing this gap was taken by a group of church-related membership-based organizations, focusing on their experience of negative impacts of sanctions on their constituents' engagement in humanitarian response and social service provision. Syria provided one of the key case studies for this research.

In addition to specific technical strategies and recommendations arising from this research, broader policy questions arise regarding the gap between legitimate purpose and practical consequence. A thorough 'cost-benefit' analysis of the current utilization of sanctions and related measures is warranted.

---

1 Humanitarian and Human Rights Advocacy Officer, Caritas Internationalis
2 Director, International Affairs, World Council of Churches
3 Syria Country Office Director, HEKS/EPER

Introduction

The past three decades have witnessed a significant increase in the use of both unilateral and multilateral sanctions.[4] While policymakers have attempted to mitigate the negative impacts of these measures by designing targeted sanctions aimed at specific actors and entities and/ or by providing carve-outs and exemptions, many sanctions regimes continue to negatively affect ordinary people. This is largely due to their restrictive impact on humanitarian response and essential social services, as well as their consequences for the lives and work of communities and people in general.

Sanctions often negatively affect—directly and indirectly— humanitarian organizations' ability to provide life-saving assistance to people of concern in affected countries. This is contrary to the spirit of international cooperation and international solidarity embodied in the UN Charter, and to the principle of *"Do no harm."*

In addition to the impacts on humanitarian assistance, sanctions regimes frequently affect the capacity of communities and people to pursue their normal lives and work unrelated to the stated purposes of the sanctions, especially due to the indirect effects of such measures and/or to over-compliance. Faith-based organizations and communities have experienced both aspects of this problem.

While humanitarian organizations—faith-based and otherwise—play a crucial role in providing humanitarian aid and social services worldwide, their work is often hindered by sanctions, which can prevent funds from being transferred due to the direct impact of sanctions or banks' over-compliance and risk-aversion. Moreover, local communities and related organizations frequently struggle to obtain relevant exemptions due to inaccessible, costly application procedures or a lack of publicly available information. This situation further exacerbates the vulnerability of affected populations in already complex humanitarian settings, is detrimental to human rights, and often undermines the stated purposes of sanctions.

---

4 Ian Kenneth Bolton, *Deterrence and the use of Sanctions*, c/o King's College London Centre for Science and Security Studies, War Studies Department (Strand, London), p. 1. https://www.sto.nato.int/publications/STO%20Meeting%20 Proceedings/STO-MP-SAS-141/MP-SAS-141-10.pdf

The COVID-19 pandemic provided a painful reality-check on economic and financial sanctions and their negative impact on people's human rights, as well as on the provision of humanitarian aid. The pandemic presented unprecedented challenges to entire humanitarian and health systems. Among other things, during this period we observed how seriously sanctions undermined sanctioned countries' capacity to respond effectively to the pandemic, hindering the delivery of life-saving humanitarian aid and health assistance, exacerbating the suffering of vulnerable populations, and highlighting the urgent need to re-evaluate the use of sanctions.[5]

As is sadly too often the case, it is the most vulnerable, including women and children, elderly, people with disabilities, refugees, migrants and internally displaced people (IDPs) who paid the highest price and suffered the most devastating consequences of the COVID-19 pandemic, and this suffering was amplified by the effects of sanctions regimes.[6]

Researching Faith-Based Organizations' Experience

The experience of faith-based organizations with regard to the impact of sanctions is distinctively multi-dimensional, insofar as it encompasses professional international and national level humanitarian operations, local level social service provision, and the basic functions of community life and organization.

As a contribution to gathering a more robust and systematic overview of the impact of sanctions from this multi-dimensional perspective, a coalition of international church-related organizations—Caritas Internationalis (CI), the World Council of Churches (WCC), the World Evangelical Alliance (WEA) and ACT Alliance (ACT)—partnered with the Geneva Graduate Institute on a research project on the issue.

---

5 A/75/209 Report of the Special Rapporteur on the negative impact of unilateral coercive measures on the enjoyment of human rights, Alena Douhan, Negative Impact of unilateral coercive measures on the enjoyment of human rights in the coronavirus disease pandemic, 21 July 2020. (https://www.ohchr.org/en/documents/thematic-reports/a75209-report-impact-unilateral-sanctions-human-rights-during-state)

6 Caritas Internationalis internal webinar held on 18 June 2020.

Semi-structured interviews[7] conducted by the research team of the Geneva Graduate Institute with twenty practitioners working for the affected constituencies and five sanctions experts indicated that sanctions have indeed posed serious operational and administrative challenges that have limited their ability to provide humanitarian assistance and social services in an effective and timely manner. The report further explored pathways for addressing the negative impact of sanctions and attempted to compile a set of recommendations and practical tools to facilitate humanitarian and social service work in sanctioned environments.

Key Findings

A report entitled *"Assessing the Impact of Sanctions on Humanitarian Work"*[8] was released by the Geneva Graduate Institute in December 2022 in collaboration with CI, WCC, WEA and ACT, as part of the Applied Research Projects Interdisciplinary Masters programme of the Graduate Institute. The report draws on the direct experience of CI, WCC, WEA and ACT constituencies in navigating the complexity of sanctions and provides a systematic overview of sanctions-related challenges.

The report clearly indicates that sanctions have posed serious obstacles limiting the ability to deliver effective and timely humanitarian assistance and essential social services. The overall set of sanctions is generally aimed at specific targets, designed to minimize negative impacts on other individuals, communities and entities. The reality the report describes is, however, clearly different in practice. We witness that such coercive measures have substantial and far-reaching

---

7 Built on anecdotal evidence, the research project team conducted semi-structured interviews aimed at creating a firm foundation for future action by answering the following research questions: 1. What are the challenges that the national constituencies of our partner organizations experience in their humanitarian work resulting from sanctions? 2. How can our partner organizations address these sanctions-related challenges?

8 Geneva Graduate Institute, *Assessing the Impact of Sanctions on Humanitarian Work*, Applied Research Project in partnership with Caritas Internationalis, World Council of Churches, World Evangelical Alliance and Act Alliance, December 2022. https://www.caritas.org/wordpress/wp-content/uploads/2023/03/Final_Report_ARP_Sanctions-2.pdf and https://www.oikoumene.org/resources/documents/report-assessing-the-impact-of-sanctions-on-humanitarian-work

unintended consequences and that, once again, it is the most vulnerable who suffer the amplified impacts.

The research builds on practical experience and seeks to create a firmer foundation for future action by identifying the main challenges experienced by members of the co-sponsoring organizations' constituencies in their humanitarian and social service work resulting from sanctions and suggesting possible ways of addressing these sanctions-related challenges.

The report identifies four main **administrative challenges** that humanitarian organizations face while working under the constraints of sanctions:

(i)   *Understanding the scope of sanctions.* Sanctions legislation often contains vague language and complex legal terminology, making it difficult for organizations and local communities to fully understand their obligations. This lack of clarity as regards the terminology and multiple references to other legal documents poses significant challenges in understanding how to comply with sanctions correctly in the respective operational environments to implement humanitarian and social service projects effectively.

(ii)   *Legal repercussions and derisking.* The report indicates that while humanitarian organizations have rarely been targeted for legal investigations due to violations of sanctions requirements, there remains a real risk of legal consequences for non-compliance with sanctions regimes. Additionally, such violations could potentially lead to reputational harm.

(iii)   *Obstacles faced in applying for humanitarian licences.* In order to operate effectively, organizations delivering humanitarian aid may need to apply for licences that exempt them from certain sanctions requirements. For instance, within the U.S. sanctions system, humanitarian organizations typically require two licences: one from the Commerce Department (Bureau of Industry and Security/ BIS licences) and another from the Treasury Department (OFAC licences). The application for humanitarian licenses causes heavy administrative burdens, generates extra costs and is time consuming.

(iv) *Enhanced due diligence requirements and processes.* Banks, suppliers and donors often demand rigorous due diligence processes to ensure that humanitarian organizations do not engage with sanctioned individuals or entities. These processes can be time-consuming and may involve specific requirements concerning the use of funds, ranging from monitoring project implementation to mandating the use of specific IT equipment. All these measures generate additional costs and bottlenecks for humanitarian organizations due to the need to hire new staff with relevant expertise, seek external legal counsel and divert existing staff to fulfil due diligence requirements and license applications, instead of focusing on project implementation and providing critical life-saving assistance.

These added burdens also impede efforts to pursue a localization agenda,[9] which aims to support and promote effective local leadership and response. Instead, sanctions impose additional burdens and risks on local organizations.

To mitigate these challenges, several strategies could be considered, including:

1. *Capacity building*: Providing training and resources to help local organizations understand and navigate the complexities of sanctions regulations. This could include workshops, webinars, or online resources.
2. *Legal assistance*: Establishing a pool of pro bono legal experts who can provide advice and guidance to local organizations. This would help them comply with sanctions without incurring significant costs.
3. *Advocacy*: Engaging in dialogue with policymakers to ensure that sanctions regulations do not unduly burden humanitarian organizations. This could involve advocating for exemptions or special provisions for these organizations.

---

9 International Federation of Red Cross and Red Crescent Societies, *The Grand Bargain. Workstream 2: Localisation.* https://gblocalisation.ifrc.org/

4. *Partnerships*: Encouraging partnerships between local
    and international organizations. The latter could pro-
    vide resources and expertise to help the former navigate
    sanctions regulations.

The report also highlights three major **operational challenges**:

1. *Importing and exporting humanitarian goods.* There
    are considerable difficulties in importing and exporting
    humanitarian goods, especially dual use goods, to or
    from sanctioned countries. Over-compliance with sanc-
    tions by service providers and key suppliers often leads
    to delays or denials in the shipment of essential items.
    This can result in shortages of critical humanitarian aid
    for vulnerable populations.
2. *Travel restrictions.* Travel to sanctioned countries is
    often restricted, requiring time-consuming visa appli-
    cations that are frequently rejected. This operational
    challenge often hinders the rapid deployment of person-
    nel and resources, further exacerbating the challenges
    faced by affected communities.
3. *Bank derisking and over-compliance.* A significant chal-
    lenge, finally, is the reluctance of banks and financial
    institutions to transfer funds to local and international
    humanitarian NGOs operating in sanctioned countries.
    Despite humanitarian exemptions being in place, banks
    often fail to apply these exceptions, leading to delays in
    fund transfers.

For instance, since 1985 CI has been managing a collective
humanitarian pooled-funding mechanism known as the Caritas
Emergency Appeal. The Emergency Appeal is designed to support
national Caritas member organizations to respond to major humanitarian crises. As it has received more and more requests for this service,
CI has gained more direct experience of the challenges faced when
dealing with the international banking system's over-compliance
and its unwillingness to immediately recognize the exemption of
funds for humanitarian assistance from sanctions regimes. While this

phenomenon has received some public attention regarding transfers in the Middle East, it affects a range of countries in other regions as well.

Several Caritas member organizations spend an increasing amount of time in providing administrative proof to banks about the use of their funds. This results in a significant waste of staff time, and months of delay in receiving funds dedicated to critical life-saving activities on the ground.

Strategies/Recommendations

When responding to rapidly worsening humanitarian crises, detecting and addressing obstacles that might hinder timely, effective and principled humanitarian action is of critical importance. This includes the unintended negative impact of sanctions. To address these challenges, the report makes a set of recommendations to help humanitarian organizations navigate the complexities of sanctions and their impact on humanitarian work.

1. *Advocacy for general humanitarian exemptions and more accessible, clear, timely and standardized licensing processes.* By leveraging networks of humanitarian organizations located in sanctioning countries and engaging directly with relevant governments, FBOs can promote a unified ethically-grounded message and coordinate advocacy efforts.

2. *Strengthen collaboration with UN bodies and other NGOs.* Collaborating with key UN bodies and other NGOs facing sanctions-related challenges can help organizations exchange experiences and coordinate advocacy measures.

3. *Multi-stakeholder consultations.* Engaging in multi-stakeholder consultations with sanctioning governments, financial institutions and affected humanitarian organizations can help identify practical solutions to over-compliance and bank derisking. Wherever tri-sector working groups do not yet exist, national networks can help advocate for their creation.

4. *Documenting the impact of sanctions.* Continuing to document the impact of sanctions on humanitarian work and essential social services can strengthen and inform general advocacy and engagement with sanctioning governments by providing robust evidence.

5. *Coordinated information-sharing.* Coordinating information-sharing within and among organizations on sanctions-related challenges can help all stay informed and prepared. Organizing regular webinars and forums with relevant external sanctions experts may facilitate discussions and address sanctions-related issues.

6. *Creation of a sanctions focal point within the organizations.* Consider creating the position of a focal point on sanctions from which to seek advice and guidance on sanctions-related challenges. Staff working in this position could produce relevant fact sheets on sanctions requirements to guide the work of national constituencies. If the required resources are not available, consider requesting staff working on related issues, such as risk and compliance, to allocate time to address sanctions-related challenges.

To further support the work of partner organizations in sanctions-affected environments, the report suggests several practical tools, including:

- a comprehensive list of resources to help understanding sanctions and their impact on humanitarian work, and

- a sanctions impact assessment survey

The proposed assessment survey aims to systematically document the effects of sanctions on the humanitarian and social service efforts of members and constituents. Data gathered through this survey can significantly strengthen advocacy and engagement with sanctioning authorities.

Syria: A Case Study

One of the case studies included in the research project, but which has gained even greater significance in light of subsequent political developments in the country, is that of the co-sponsoring organizations' experience with regard to the impact of sanctions on their members and constituents in Syria, and on their humanitarian and social service work in that country.

In addition to its humanitarian complexity and specificities, Syria has been described as a country facing "some of the most complicated and far-reaching sanctions regimes ever imposed."[10] Even if the challenges have mostly affected actors operating from Damascus, other responders across the country and in the region have faced similar issues since, for example, over-compliance does not respect borders or areas of control.

The direct operational impact is characterized by four basic challenges:

- First, restrictions in interacting with some suppliers and service providers, for example major telecom companies or airlines.

- Second, lack of clarity regarding the level of permitted interactions with the public sector, including for example capacity building for public servants.

- Third, restrictions in project scope, in particular related to heavy infrastructure works and activities related to the energy sector.

- Fourth, recurrent challenges in bank transfers, including lengthy and time-consuming due diligence processes and frequent transactions rejections.

These challenges are also linked to the over-compliance of the private sector, especially bank derisking strategies leading to a constantly shrinking number of banking channels, putting at risk the

---

10 Justine Walker et al., *Humanitarian Impact of Syria-related unilateral Restrictive Measures, National Agenda for the Future of Syria*, Office of the United Nations Resident Coordinator in the Syrian Arab Republic, ESCWA, 2016, p. 6. https://theintercept.com/document/humanitarian-impact-of-syria-related-unilateral-restrictive-measures/

continuity of the delivery of aid. In parallel, limitations in international procurement have been experienced due to the reluctance of the private suppliers to engage in transactions with Syria for fear of the sanctions.

Over-compliance is not limited to the private sector. Many governmental and institutional donors have also imposed "red lines" going beyond the restrictions actually prescribed by the sanctions. Humanitarian organizations have themselves become more cautious and conservative for fear of the consequences of actual or alleged non-compliance with sanctions regimes, developing an internal "chilling effect."

Theoretically, different **licensing processes** seek to address such challenges.

The first category of processes is managed at organization level to engage with specific activities or designated service providers. However, those mechanisms are complex and unclear, consuming a lot of time and resources. Moreover, while they are difficult to handle for regular programming, they are absolutely inapplicable during an emergency response. Above all, they do not provide enough assurances to the private sector to avoid over-compliance on their side.

The second category of licensing processes is related to the actions of international suppliers, taken in order to be compliant with export control restrictions especially regarding to dual use goods procurement. Similarly to the ones managed by humanitarian organizations, those processes are complex, lengthy and disincentivizing for suppliers.

In parallel to derogations and specific licencing mechanisms, several humanitarian exemptions are in place. However, their scope is too restricted, they are not harmonized between jurisdictions, and do not protect against potential exposure to U.S. secondary sanctions and thus do not resolve the over-compliance challenges.

In addition to their direct impacts, the indirect impact of sanctions on the delivery of humanitarian aid on the population of Syria and on the Syrian public sector have been grave. Even if sanctions cannot be considered responsible for all the issues affecting the population, they have undeniable direct and indirect impacts on different sectors, in particular through a 'waterfall effect'—whereby the impact on a targeted sector has consequences for a non-targeted one.

By their accumulation and combination with other factors, in particular conflict and its consequences and natural disasters, sanctions have been a major aggravating factor for the suffering of the population and have increased the need for humanitarian aid, while at the same time obstructing it.

Sanctions have increased the cost and complexity of humanitarian response in Syria by:

- increasing the volume of work

- creating goods scarcity, and increasing the cost of imported goods and insurance

- increasing reliance on unregulated ('black') market

- adding extra layers of compliance control

- forcing adjustment of activities to compensate, for example, for the lack of energy supply.

Moreover, as a necessary consequence of their political dimension and being imposed by governmental entities, sanctions undermine fundamental humanitarian principles by tacitly or explicitly including references to parties to the conflict and thereby introducing double standards that are political in nature.

Even less well recognized than the impact on professional humanitarian access and response is the impact that sanctions have had on local community-based, often informal humanitarian and social service provision by, among others, Syrian religious actors, as well as on the ordinary regular internal functions of such communities upon which Syrian social architecture is substantially based.

In general, the Syrian case study illustrates, the attempt to distinguish the impact of sanctions on humanitarian aid delivery from the impact on the population is not relevant, as both are closely interlinked, and humanitarian aid and essential social service provision is at the service of the population. Further, available exemptions and derogations have had a limited impact on the daily practical challenges, and do not tackle any of the deeper issues related to sanctions in terms of the creation or aggravation of humanitarian need. In addition to the legitimate questions regarding sanctions' legality, there is an urgent need to alleviate the suffering of the Syrian population by lifting the sectoral measures negatively impacting access to water, food, health, education and employment, in particular by lifting measures targeting the energy sector.

Since the fall of the Assad regime at the end of 2024 and the establishment of a transitional government, some sanctioning authorities have begun to respond to this urgent necessity. For example, the European Union has recently suspended a range of sanctions against Syria, including restrictions related to energy, banking, transport and reconstruction.[11] While this news is welcome, sanctions by other authorities, especially the USA, continue to pose significant challenges to humanitarian assistance and support for democratic institutional development in Syria despite efforts to ease some restrictions.[12]

Conclusion

Though sanctions are generally and understandably seen as preferable to measures for the restoration of international peace and security that entail the use of armed force, in the collective experience of CI, WCC, WEA and ACT this presumption warrants much closer examination and reconsideration. In practice, sanctions—whether unilateral or mandated by the UN Security Council—often produce human suffering and other consequences at least as severe, and generally more widespread, than the use of armed force. In terms of their humanitarian impacts, such measures can often be considered as tantamount to warfare by economic means. This is particularly true in the case of comprehensive 'maximum pressure' sanctions regimes.

An aspect not explored in this paper, but which may reward further study is the possibility that the imposition of such measures risks poisoning the political environment for negotiations and other initiatives for peace (including civil society initiatives), thereby creating obstacles to the resolution of conflict.

The concern regarding the negative impacts of sanctions is exacerbated when, as is often the case, they fail to achieve their stated aims

---

11 Reuters, *EU suspends sanctions against Syria including on energy, banking,* 24 February 2025. (https://www.reuters.com/world/middle-east/eu-suspends-sanctions-against-syria-including-those-energy-banking-2025-02-24/)

12 Reuters, Exclusive: US sanctions hold up Qatari support for Syria, sources say, 27 February 2025. (https://www.reuters.com/world/middle-east/us-sanctions-hold-up-qatari-support-syria-sources-say-2025-02-26/)

but continue to be imposed. A thorough 'cost-benefit' analysis of the current utilization of sanctions and related measures, weighing their success (or lack thereof) in achieving their legitimate political/security aims against their negative humanitarian, human rights and political impacts, is therefore warranted.

Unilateral sanctions can have far-reaching consequences on various aspects of the life of affected communities. By anchoring programs and activities in international humanitarian and human rights law and adhering to the recently published Guiding Principles, it is possible to minimize these negative impacts. The Guiding Principles on Sanctions, Business and Human Rights[13] and its Commentary[14] provide a comprehensive legal framework for addressing the human rights implications of unilateral sanctions and emphasize the need for transparency, accountability, and due process in international relations to ensure unimpeded access to humanitarian assistance.

---

13 Mandate of the Special Rapporteur on the negative impact of unilateral coercive measures on the enjoyment of human rights, *"Guiding Principles on Business, Sanctions and Human Rights,"* United Nations Human Rights Special Procedures, 2025. https://www.ohchr.org/sites/default/files/documents/issues/ucm/events/international-conf-sanctions-business-hr/gps-sanctions-business-hr.pdf

14 Mandate of the Special Rapporteur on the negative impact of unilateral coercive measures on the enjoyment of human rights, *"Guiding Principles on Business, Sanctions and Human Rights – Commentary,"* United Nations Human Rights Special Procedures, 2025. https://www.ohchr.org/sites/default/files/documents/issues/ucm/commentary-gpssbhr-2025.pdf

PART IV

....

INTERNATIONAL ADJUDICATION IN THE FACE OF UNILATERAL SANCTIONS

CHAPTER 15

Access to Justice in the Face of Unilateral Sanctions and Over-compliance

Alena F. Douhan[1]

Abstract

Access to justice plays a double role in international human rights law. Viewed from one side access to justice is viewed as an independent right to be ensured for every human being; from the other it plays the role of safeguards for protection of all other human rights affected.

Today the world is facing the expanding use of unilateral sanctions applied by States and regional organizations without the authorization of the UN Security Council, as well as the means of their enforcement and implementation by States and businesses, and the consequent over-compliance by all international actors. The above factors are affecting the broad scope of human rights of the directly targeted individuals, population in general, as well as interests of states and businesses.

The article addresses contemporary challenges to access the right to meaningful remedy, justice, accountability and redress for those affected by unilateral sanctions, the means of their enforcement and over-compliance at the international, regional and domestic levels.

---

1 Professor, Dr., Dr. habilitat, Professor of International Law Department of Belarusian State University, UN Special Rapporteur on the negative impact of unilateral coercive measures on the enjoyment of human rights

Introduction

The multifold nature of the access to justice is generally recognized in modern international and human rights law. On the one hand, access to justice alongside the right to remedy is viewed as an integral part of the right to fair trial and the rule of law standards. On the other, as repeatedly announced by the UN treaty bodies, access to justice is a known safeguard for all other human rights. Every individual has a right to access justice to protect any of his/her rights, violated by the activity of states.

Traditionally, access to justice is analyzed either within the scope of criminal process or when the rights of an individual are infringed by the State of its residence. Unilateral sanctions and over-compliance, however, affect human rights extraterritorially, providing no or very vague and partial mechanisms for protection in remedy. Due to the multiplicity of subjects' rights of which are affected by unilateral sanctions and over-compliance, those who are not directly designated are often affected the most. Moreover, in the absence of specific acts affecting their rights, judicial mechanisms usually deny the existence of jurisdiction in such cases.

This chapter provides the legal grounds, nature and content of the access to justice in international human rights law, addresses specifics of that access in the face of unilateral sanctions and over-compliance and identifies challenges faced by different categories of targets (affected actors) to get access to adjudication in various unilateral sanctions regimes.

Notion and elements of the access to justice

Content of access to justice in the face of unilateral sanctions

The right of every individual to be protected by the law is inherent in many international human rights documents as a means to ensure that other human rights are protected properly.[2] Art. 26 of the International Covenant on Civil and Political Rights (hereafter, ICCPR) explicitly refers to equality of all persons before the law and sets forth their entitlement "without any discrimination to the equal protection of the law." Additionally, art. 14 lists the safeguards in the event of criminal charges against the person with special

---

2 ICCPR, art. 6 (1), 17 (2), 18 (3); CEDAW, art. 2 (c).

emphasis on ensuring the presumption of innocence. The primary challenges and impacts as well as main conclusions and recommendations have been reflected in the report on the impact of UCMs and over-compliance to the access to justice presented to the UN General Assembly in October 2024.[3]

I note with concern, thus, the traditional approach of sanctioning States to qualify unilateral sanctions as a foreign policy tool, administrative rather than criminal mechanism,[4] to prevent the use of due process, presumption of innocence and fair trial guarantees. This approach does not correspond with the content, nature and measures imposed, as will be presented here, but unfortunately, leaves many human rights affected by unilateral sanctions unprotected. As a result, the actuality of the current research cannot be doubted or underestimated.

Content of the access to justice has been repeatedly addressed in a number of UN documents. According to General Recommendation No. 33 of the CEDAW, access to justice encompasses "justiciability, availability, accessibility, good quality and accountability of justice systems, and provision of remedies for victims."[5] General Comment No. 32 includes as its integral part access to legal assistance, access to the documents, evidences and other relevant materials; access to the "duly reasoned written judgement of the trial court"; and access to the tribunal at the appeal level.[6] Guidance on the Access to justice for women additionally refers to: non-discrimination; widespread legal awareness and literacy among the population; affordable and quality legal advice and representation; accessible, affordable, timely, effective, efficient, impartial, corruption-free and trustworthy dispute settlement mechanisms; respect to the human rights standards; availability of efficient and impartial mechanisms for the enforcement of judicial decisions.[7]

---

3 UNGA   Report.   A/79/183.   https://documents.un.org/doc/undoc/gen/n24/213/84/pdf/n2421384.pdf

4 A/HRC/48/59, paras. 50–51; 2022; *2022 Economic Sanctions Year in Review and Outlook for 2023*. https://www.akingump.com/en/insights/alerts/2022-economic-sanctions-year-in-review-and-outlook-for-2023.

5 CEDAW, General recommendation No. 33.

6 HRC, General Comment No. 32, Article 14: Right to equality before courts and tribunals and to a fair trial (CCPR/C/GC/32); A/60/147, para. 12 (c, d); 67/187. United Nations Principles and Guidelines on Access to Legal Aid in Criminal Justice Systems (2013), para. 3.

7 Framework for measuring access to justice including specific challenges

Access to justice constitutes also an integral part of the adherence to the rule of Law. The UN Secretary General in his report "The rule of law and transitional justice in conflict and post-conflict societies" (2004), reflects that "the rule of law shall rely on measures to ensure adherence to the principles of supremacy of law, equality before the law, accountability to the law, fairness in the application of the law ... legal certainty, avoidance of arbitrariness and procedural and legal transparency [. . .], capacity, performance, integrity and accountability."[8]

The right of individuals to judicial protection of their rights is guaranteed both in international practice and legal doctrine. All procedural guarantees, including the right to due process[9] and the right not to be held guilty for any offense that was not an offense at the moment of its commission[10]—are considered inalienable by human rights institutions,[11] legal scholars[12] and international treaties.[13] Violating these rights is qualified even in time of war as a serious breach of international humanitarian law.[14]

---

facing women, Guidance note, 2016, p. 7.

8 Security Council Report. PCS S/2004/616. https://www.securitycouncilreport. org/atf/cf/%7B65BFCF9B-6D27-4E9C-8CD3-CF6E4FF96FF9%7D/PCS%20S%20 2004%20616.pdf; The United Nations Rule of Law indicators: Implementation Guide and Project tools (2011), p. v, United Nations Peacekeeping. UN Rule of Law Indicators. https://peacekeeping.un.org/sites/default/files/un_rule_of_law_indicators. pdf; the need for the existence of the right to appeal and legal certainty is supported even by those institutions which support sanctions: submission by the Association of reunification of Ukraine.

9 ICCPR, art. 14 (2–7).

10 ICCPR, art. 15 (1).

11 HRC, CCPR General Comment No. 29: Article 4: Derogations during a State of Emergency (CCPR/C/21/Rev.1/Add.11), para. 16.

12 Roberta Arnold, "Human Rights in Times of Terrorism," *66 Zeitschrift für ausländis-chesöffentlichesRecht und Völkerrecht*, 2006, p. 305; Yvon Dandurand, *Handbook on Criminal Justice and Responses to Terrorism*, Criminal Justice Handbook Series (New York: United Nations, 2009), pp. 40–41.

13 Geneva Convention Relative to the Protection of Civilian Persons in Time of War, 1949, 75 *UNTS* 287, art. 72–73, 146 (4); Geneva Convention Relative to the Treatment of Prisoners of War, 1949, 75 *UNTS* 135, art. 105–108, 129 (4); Protocol Additional to the Geneva Conventions of 12 August 1949, and relating to the Protection of Victims of International Armed Conflicts, 1977, *UNTS* 3, art.75; Protocol Additional to the Geneva Conventions of 12 August 1949, and relating to the Protection of Victims of Non-International Armed Conflicts, 1977, *UNTS* 609, art. 76.

14 Fourth Geneva Convention, art. 147; Protocol I, art. 85 (4e).

It is generally agreed in international legal practice and doctrine that every right must be accompanied by the availability of an effective remedy in case of its violation.[15] As a result this is relevant not only to the obligation of States to provide effective remedies for the victims of crimes or abuse of power in accordance with the UN Declaration of Basic Principles of Justice for Victims of Crime and Abuse of Power 1985,[16] but also to the possibility to get judicial protection for all human rights as an exercise of the due diligence obligation of States.[17] This obligation also refers to the obligation to protect economic, social and cultural rights as reflected in a number of General Comments of the Committee on economic, social and cultural rights (hereafter, CESCR).[18]

Additionally, the Human Rights Committee (hereafter, HRC) admits in its General Comment No. 32 that the right to access courts as an integral part of the right to fair trial shall be guaranteed in criminal cases for any individuals "who may find themselves in the territory or subject to the jurisdiction of the State party."[19] The same protection shall be provided even if rights are violated extraterritorially.[20] Despite the qualification of unilateral sanctions by sanctioning States

---

15 Adjudicating Economic, Social and Cultural Rights at National Level, Practitioners Guide No. 8, para. 24.

16 Declaration of Basic Principles of Justice for Victims of Crime and Abuse of Power. https://www.ohchr.org/en/instruments-mechanisms/instruments/declaration-basic-principles-justice-victims-crime-and-abuse.

17 Access to Justice for Economic, Social and Cultural Rights, Module 3. https://www.icj.org/wp-content/uploads/2021/09/Module-3-Access-to-justice-for-economic-social-and-cultural-rights.pdf; Adjudicating Economic, Social and Cultural Rights at National Level, Practitioners Guide No. 8, p. 14; International Principles and Guidelines on Access to Justice for Persons with Disabilities (2020), p. 6.

18 CESCR, General Comment No. 9 (E/C.12/1998/2), paras. 2, 3, 10; CESCR, General Comment No. 12; Adjudicating Economic, Social and Cultural Rights at National Level, Practitioners Guide No. 8, para. 24; ICESCR, art. 2; CESCR, General Comment No. 20 (E/C.12/GC/20.

19 HRC, General Comment No. 32, Article 14.

20 Adjudicating Economic, Social and Cultural Rights at National Level, Practitioners Guide No. 8, pp. 64–67; Maastricht Principles on Extraterritorial Obligations of States in the area of Economic, Social and Cultural Rights, principles 8–9; O. de Schutter, et al., Commentary to the Maastricht Principles on Extraterritorial Obligations of States in the area of Economic, Social and Cultural Rights (2012), p. 1089; Jessica Almqvist, "Human rights critique of European judicial review: Counter-terrorism sanctions," *International and Comparative Law Quarterly* 57, no. 2 (2008): 308.

as foreign policy tools, means to protect security, and references to their administrative rather than criminal nature, it is believed here that reasons cited by sanctioning States as a ground for unilateral sanctions do not change their status from the perspective of legal perception.

The consequences of designations—criminal and civil charges for circumvention of sanctions regimes—are much higher than those for minor administrative delicts, therefore sanctioning States are obliged to ensure access to justice for protection of rights affected by sanctions' civil, administrative, criminal or other penalties. Already in 2007 PACE criticized the humanitarian impact of targeted sanctions, even of those imposed by the UN Security Council, and referred to the obligation to guarantee procedural standards, including the rights to be fully informed of the charges and of the decision taken; to be heard and to be able to defend oneself; to appeal; and to redress and compensation in the case of targeted sanctions.[21]

Additional problems arise from the over-lapping unilateral sanctions of various types, confusing wording of sanctions regulations, and the risk of severe penalties for their violation. All the above constitute serious challenges for access to justice, access to meaningful remedies and redress. Designated individuals or companies are often prevented from submitting a case to the foreign court, as well as facing challenges to get proper legal assistance, to travel to present a case, and to transfer money to cover legal expenses, court or commercial arbitration fees. Courts or arbitration tribunals refuse to accept payments for fear of coming under sanctions enforcement or sanctions circumvention penalties.[22]

Extraterritorial application of secondary sanctions leading to civil and criminal cases for circumvention of sanctions regimes results in prosecution for acts often not criminalized in the country of nationality/residence. The above approach raises a range of legal problems, including low standards of proof, non-justiciability of cases and even

---

21 United Nations Security Council and European Union blacklists: rep. of the Comm. on Legal Affairs a. Human Rights, 16 Nov. 2007, Doc 11454 // PACE [Electronic resource]: Parliamentary Assembly. – Mode of access : http://assembly.coe.int/main.asp?Link=/documents/workingdocs/doc07/edoc11454.htm. – Date of access: 15.08.2011

22 Expert consultations of the SR with lawyers; Belarusian legal forum. Impact of sanctions on business processes, 28.11.2024; International Conference Sanctions, Business and Human Rights, 21-22.2024.

extradition without any legal grounds.[23] Legal practitioners report that the evidences can be either not presented at all, be substantially blocked or be represented by the collection of publications in media and social media.[24]

Practitioners also refer to the high risk of arbitrary interpretations of alleged circumventions of unilateral sanctions which, on a proper analysis, do not constitute any offence,[25] even under sanctions regulations. In such cases, penalties for alleged circumvention and designation of individuals as a result of such alleged conduct violate standards of fair trial, presumption of innocence, and the right to not be punished for activities which do not constitute a crime.

The politization of sanctions decision-making and sanctions assessment becomes so extensive that sanctioning States ignore all argumentation on the illegality of the use of unilateral coercive measures, challenges to access justice, as well as evidences provided for by different actors, including humanitarian organizations, individuals and the general population about the negative humanitarian impact of unilateral sanctions and over-compliance.[26] It is all the more concerning that despite the obvious illegality of unilateral coercive measures, and the official position of sanctioning States that unilateral sanctions do not constitute criminal penalties, such sanctions are nevertheless implemented and enforced by third states, businesses and even the UN organs. All actors prefer to comply or to find the way around limitations, rather than to oppose the imposed measures due to the challenges of bringing a case for international or national adjudication.

Another challenge reported to prevent proper access to justice is the high costs of sanctions-related cases that make use of judicial institutions affordable for huge corporations only, leaving small and

---

23 The Record. US Fails in Bid to Extradite Brit for Helping North Korea Evade Sanctions with Cryptocurrency. https://therecord.media/us-fails-in-bid-to-extradite-brit-for-helping-north-korea-evade-sanctions-with-cryptocurrency; Enforcement of Financial Sanctions and Extradition Risk. https://corkerbinning.com/enforcement-of-financial-sanctions-and-extradition-risk/.

24 Expert consultations with lawyers.

25 Enforcement of Financial Sanctions and Extradition Risk. https://corkerbinning.com/enforcement-of-financial-sanctions-and-extradition-risk/.

26 Arria Formular meeting. Impact of unilateral coercive mesures and over-compliance on the delivery of humanitarian assistance, 25.11.2024. https://webtv.un.org/en/asset/k1v/k1vg1356ui

medium businesses and individuals unprotected.[27] From the legal perspective the right to judicial protection and to remedies in full conformity with fair trial and procedural standards belongs to every individual without any discrimination. Therefore, sanctioning States are obliged to ensure that every individual affected by unilateral sanctions can protect their rights in court within a reasonable time and at reasonable affordable costs, including affordable legal assistance.[28] otherwise their activity can already be qualified as a violation of the access to justice due to the procedural impediments.

It is also extremely concerning that geopolitical concerns rather than legal ones are increasingly more taken into account by sanctioning States, when the rhetoric/ presumption of legality of unilateral sanctions, alongside the refusal of their punitive nature is broadly introduced in the media, official statements and court decisions. That results in the violation of the presumption of innocence of designated individuals[29] and seeks to transfer the burden of proof to the targets of sanctions. It is necessary to take into account that the presumption of innocence constitutes a peremptory norm of the law of human rights and cannot be derogated even in a time of emergency in accordance with art. 4(2) of the ICCPR.

In accordance with international law neither national law nor interests of domestic policy can be used to justify non-fulfillment of international obligations.[30] Any unilateral measures can only be taken without authorization of the UN Security Council if they do not violate any international obligations, or the illegality is excluded as countermeasures. The burden of proof of legality of any unilateral activity lays thus on the imposing or enforcing actors rather than on designated State, company or individual. No reference to "high goals" or "common concerns," provides for any legality, legitimacy or justification to otherwise illegal activity and can be used to hinder access to justice. As the cited grounds for designations often do not have anything to do with possible violations and are extremely broad and vague, e.g.

---

27 Report, China country visit, paras. 57, 86.

28 Framework for measuring access to justice including specific challenges facing women, Guidance note, 2016, p. 7; CEDAW, General Recommendation No. 3.

29 Submissions by Venezuela, Guatemala.

30 VCLT, art. 26–27.

the "need to ensure protection of national security,"[31] and secondary sanctions are imposed for "circumvention/ alleged circumventions/ assistance in circumvention of sanctions regimes," the burden of proof is shifted de facto to the targets of unilateral sanctions, even if they are not explicitly designated, and have just nationality, place of residence or registration or any other nexus with the country, territory or entity under sanctions that constitutes inter alia discrimination on the ground of nationality, place of residence or birth.

The introduction of the concept of "rebuttable presumption" of wrongfulness in the U.S. sanctions regulations used to supplement the presumption of innocence, and shifting the burden of proof of legality of activity taken to the individual or an entity[32] shall also be qualified as extremely concerning and not compatible with international law. In particular, the ULFPA is based on the rebuttable presumption that "any goods, wares, articles, and merchandise mined, produced, or manufactured wholly or in part in the Xinjiang Uyghur Autonomous Region of the People's Republic of China or produced by" designated entities are produced with the use of forced labor, shifting the burden of proof of non-use of the forced labor to the entities (sec. 3),[33] similar to the Countering America's Adversaries through sanctions act, sec. 321 towards North Korea,[34] without any clear instructions as to what can be used as evidences of the latter, clearly contradicts the very idea of the presumption of innocence.

Additionally, numerous reports are received about non-transparency of the grounds for listing with no evidences given for any type of designation or penalties, including via seizure of cargoes, administrative and civil charges. Sanctions regulations are traditionally uncertain as concerns their scope, means of implementation, interpretation via non-binding acts and contradicting statements. As reflected in the country visit report to China, Chinese business reported on its efforts to

---

31 United States, Executive Order 13959, November 2020; Countering American's Adversaries Through Sanctions Act 2017.

32 Uyghur Forced Labor Prevention Act: Are You Ready? CBP Issues Hints. https://www.afslaw.com/perspectives/alerts/uyghur-forced-labor-prevention-act-coming-are-you-ready-cbp-issues-hints-the; Countering America's Adversaries Through Sanctions Act, sec. 321.

33 An Act (Public Law 117–78 – DEC. 23, 2021), Public Law No: 117-78. https://www.congress.gov/117/plaws/publ78/PLAW-117publ78.pdf

34 Countering America's Adversaries Through Sanctions Act, sec. 32.

engage with the U.S. authorities through the Administrative Procedure Act[35] by filing a Modification Petition for its removal from the list and produced more than 10,000 pages demonstrating the absence of any nexus with Xinjiang in its supply, but the Petition was denied without any indication that the submitted evidence was reviewed and assessed, or any explanation of the denial decision[36] that constitutes a clear violation of the right to get full access to materials used as a ground for accusations.

The presumption of wrongfulness of any nexus to a specific country, region, sphere of economy, company or individual contradicts the very idea of presumption in criminal or administrative law. In particular, the burden of proof of illegality of action lies on the prosecution and constitutes an integral part of the presumption of innocence in accordance with General Comment 13 (para. 7) and General Comment 32 (para. 30), therefore the State shall establish the fact of violation without reasonable doubts.[37] In administrative law the State is to provide clear and sufficient evidences to support the accusation.[38] The burden of proof in customs law lies on customs authorities.[39] As for the access to information and limitations on the mass media, the burden of proof of the wrongfulness of information also lays on the State.[40]

Due Diligence Obligation in the Face of Shifting Responsibility

Another problem which is traditionally not addressed from the legal perspective is shifting the burden of proof from sanctioning

---

35 Act PL 79-404. https://www.justice.gov/sites/default/files/jmd/legacy/2014/05/01/act-pl79-404.pdf

36 Report, China country visit, paras. 55, 59.

37 HRC, General Comment 13, Article 14, (HRI/GEN/1/Rev.1), para. 7; HRC, General Comment No. 32, Article 14, para. 30.

38 5 CFR §2423.32 – Burden of proof before the Administrative Law Judge. https://www.law.cornell.edu/cfr/text/5/2423.32

39 Commissioner of Customs (Preventive) Vs Rajendra Kumar Damani @ Raju Damani (Calcutta High Court), read more at: https://taxguru.in/custom-duty/case-analysis-burden-proof-customs-law-commissioner-customs-vs-rajendra-kumar-damani.html; Guidelines on the consequences of the Judgment of the Court of 9 March 2006 in Case C-293/04 "Beemsterboer," Taxation and Customs Union. Beemsterboer Case Study. https://taxation-customs.ec.europa.eu/system/files/2016-09/beemsterboer_en.pdf

40 A/HRC/29/32, paras. 32–35 and A/67/357, paras. 41, 45; A/66/290, para. 24; A/67/357, para. 45; A/77/296, paras. 70, 83.

States to third States, regional organizations and businesses if human rights are violated as a result of enforcement of e.g. of U.S. sanctions by European companies.[41] Sanctioning States refer to the existence of humanitarian exemptions; enforcing / tolerating State of registration / functioning of the company appeal to the existence of Guidances requesting businesses not to comply with sanctions of the third States, without providing them, however, with any protection. All States reject their responsibility, appealing to the freedom of business activity and as a result businesses refer to the high risk of bankruptcy and punishment without any protection from the side of the sanctioning States.[42]

As a result, humanitarian actors are obliged to bear the burden of proof of purely humanitarian nature of humanitarian deliveries to the businesses of the countries under sanctions[43] to prove that they fully complied with unilateral sanctions regimes, especially when it comes to the deliveries of life-saving goods from monopolist producers.[44] All the above hinders the possibility of identifying the accountable actor (as everyone pretends not to bear any responsibility for the losses) or competent court, resulting in impunity for human rights violations, and thereby preventing the victims to get access to effective remedies and redress.

The recently adopted Directive of the European Union on corporate sustainability due diligence[45] is just increasing the risks, requesting businesses to make an assessment of the human rights situations in the countries where they operate, insofar as sanctions risks are requested to be taken into account[46] that may result in the additional withdrawal

---

41 AL USA 25/2023; AL SWE 3/2023; AL OTH 108/2023; responses of states; AL SWE 3/2023.

42 A/78/196, paras. 22–27. https://documents.un.org/doc/undoc/gen/n23/260/44/pdf/n2326044.pdf

43 A/78/196, paras. 9, 71, 77.

44 A/54/23. https://documents.un.org/doc/undoc/gen/g23/148/52/pdf/g2314852.pdf, paras. 31–34

45 Directive (EU) 2024/1760 of the European Parliament and of the Council of 13 June 2024 on corporate sustainability due diligence and amending Directive (EU) 2019/1937 and Regulation (EU) 2023/2859 (Text with EEA relevance). https://eur-lex.europa.eu/legal-content/EN/TXT/PDF/?uri=OJ:L_202401760

46 Directive (EU) 2024/1619 of the European Parliament and of the Council of 31 May 2024 amending Directive 2013/36/EU as regards supervisory powers, sanctions, third-country branches, and environmental, social and governance

from the relevant markets as a part of their business corporate due diligence due to uncertainty and fear.

At the same time the above situation does not conform to international standards of due diligence. In particular, in accordance with art. 2(1) of the ICCPR and technically pursuant art.2(1) of the ICESCR, States are responsible for ensuring the efficacy of human rights within their territory or jurisdiction.[47] This obligation extends to each branch of State authority (whether legislative, administrative or judicial),[48] all of which are bound to protect human rights when giving effect to implementation of any UN sanctions (which shall thus be interpreted strictly in accordance with authorization given) or when acting unilaterally. As the HRC underlines in its GC 31 "the obligations of the Covenant in general and article 2 in particular are binding on every State Party as a whole" (para. 8),[49] "despite the fact states are not per se responsible for human rights abuse by private actors, their obligation to protect against such abuses in fact extend to acts of private persons and entities." "When a State Party fails to prevent, punish, investigate or redress the harm caused by such acts by private persons or entities by permitting or failing to take appropriate measures or to exercise due diligence that gives rise to violations by this respective State Party its obligations under article 2 of the ICCPR."[50]

The obligation to protect human rights must be addressed by States through all relevant State authorities, including legislative, judicial, administrative, educative and others as appropriate.[51] States also have a duty to protect and promote the rule of law, including by taking steps to ensure equality before the law, fairness in its application, and

---

risks (Text with EEA relevance). https://eur-lex.europa.eu/legal-content/EN/TXT/PDF/?uri=OJ:L_202401619

47 International Covenant on Economic, Social and Cultural Rights (ICESCR), Article 2. https://humanrights.asn.au/ICESCR#article-2; F. Coomans, "The Extraterritorial Scope of the International Covenant on Economic, Social and Cultural Rights in the Work of the United Nations Committee on Economic, Social and Cultural Rights." https://www.corteidh.or.cr/tablas/r26506.pdf

48 Conclusion 5. https://legal.un.org/ilc/texts/instruments/english/commentaries/1_13_2018.pdf

49 CCPR/C/21/Rev.1/Add. 13, 26 May 2004. https://documents.un.org/doc/undoc/gen/g04/419/56/pdf/g0441956.pdf para. 4.

50 General comment No. 31 (2004), para. 8. https://www.refworld.org/legal/general/hrc/2004/en/52451

51 Ibid., para. 7.

by ensuring legal certainty, procedural fairness, transparency of law and legal process, accountability for wrongs and effective redress via appeals to the judicial institutions.[52]

Failure to deliver essential and especially life-saving goods, especially when the business is a monopolist supplier of the goods, services, equipment, and spare parts, cannot be justified by references to the freedom of contract or commercial activity, or fear of, or reluctance due to, unilateral sanctions or the means of their enforcement. It constitutes a violation of the generally recognized "duty of care," coming from the common law—"as a legal obligation requiring adherence to a standard of reasonable care, while performing any act which can foreseeably harm others," or "a legal obligation to act towards others with prudence and vigilance in order to prevent any risk of foreseeable damage,"[53] which in its nature is a part of the due diligence obligation in a broader human rights context.[54]

Access to Justice for Different Targets of Unilateral Sanctions

From the perspective of international law access to justice in the face of unilateral sanctions shall be guaranteed for all groups of actors: people and companies, including those directly designated by primary or secondary sanctions; those facing civil and criminal charges for circumvention of sanctions regimes; those affected by sanctions against specific States or sector of the economy or region; the general population of countries under sanction; people affected by reputational pressure campaigns as the means of sanctions enforcement; humanitarian actors; and lawyers.

The impact of primary and secondary unilateral sanctions on the directly designated individuals and companies is rather straightforward and includes the "right to property, to freedom of movement, to liberty and security, to privacy and family life, to freedom of expression, to

---

52 GPBHR, commentary to the first principle. https://www.ohchr.org/sites/default/files/Documents/Publications/GuidingPrinciplesBusinessHR_EN.pdf

53 ICRC Duty of care: elements of definition. https://unsceb.org/sites/default/files/imported_files/ICRC%20-%20Duty%20of%20Care%20ICRC%20definition.pdf

54 What is the duty of human rights vigilance in the supply chain? https://www.yvea.io/en/services/quality-compliance/product-quality-standard/human-rights-duty-of-care-in-the-supply-chain

work, the rights to health, to life," and to reputation.[55] The sanctions deprive targeted individuals of the entire range of due process rights, including the right to a fair trial, to be presumed innocent until proven guilty, to be informed promptly about the nature of any accusations, the right to defend oneself, to defend one's reputation, to an effective remedy, and to accessibility of legal assistance.[56]

Numerous reports refer to the challenges individuals and companies face to get access to adjudication at the national level, including identification of a competent country of adjudication; uncertainty of the means of judicial protection: administrative, civil, criminal, customs, constitutional law mechanisms, high costs and lengthy process to get access to legal advice;[57] non-transparency of the grounds for designation; reluctance of lawyers in both sanctioning and targeted countries to represent sanctions cases;[58] getting visas and travelling to the sanctioning country for the adjudication; reluctance of banks to engage in transactions for paying the fees to lawyers representing targeted clients[59] or unfreezing money to pay judicial fees, etc.

Regretfully targeted unilateral sanctions are used as a substitute for criminal penalties in the absence of criminal jurisdiction of the sanctioning State and with lower standards of proof. From the perspective of criminal law, if a crime has been committed, a criminal case shall be started if a State owes necessary jurisdiction over the case with full respect to the standards of due process to avoid impunity from one side and prevent any violation of human rights and reputational risks of the alleged suspects.[60] Today, however, there are multiple reports on the expanding lists of those subjected to secondary sanctions, facing administrative and criminal charges, civil suits and seizure of goods by customs as a part of sanctions enforcement[61] upon information received. Such designations and charges are open

---

55 A/76/174, para. 19.

56 Submissions by Venezuela.

57 Submissions by Syria.

58 Eastern Caribbean Supreme Court, "*JSC VTB Bank v. (1) Sergey Taruta (2) Arrowcrest Ltd.,*" BVIHC (COM) 2014/0062, para. 16.

59 SRA Guidance, November 2022. https://sra.org.uk/solicitors/guidance/financial-sanctions-regime/

60 A/77/296, paras. 56–59.

61 A/78/196, paras. 20–24.

for extensive and broad interpretation,[62] and do not provide any legal certainty. Information about civil, criminal or other charges is very fragmentary and non-transparent. Therefore, States do not have any ground to impose sanctions as a supplement of the criminal proceedings due to the absence of jurisdiction, non-transparency, non-transparency of evidences and violation of other standards of due process.

It is believed here that challenges caused to the reputation of the directly affected individuals, lawyers[63] and other people subjected to reputational pressure to enforce sanctions[64] shall also be taken into account. At the moment there is legal procedure or even a judicial case aimed at the protection of reputation, but as reputational campaigns in sanctions cases are held by cyber means mostly, starting a case of defamation might be very problematic. Any attempt to protect the right to reputation via judicial means will be limited to civil suits on the protection of dignity and reputation, with all the abovementioned challenges to achieving access to the court.[65]

Targeted sanctions regimes against high state officials are interpreted increasingly often based on geopolitical concerns and affect the whole country or the whole sphere of targeted individuals responsible for it. In particular, the UK court of the first instance qualified everything happening in Russia to be under effect of targeted sanctions against Russian president due to the "command economy" in the country.[66] The Official Governmental response to the situation requests to review this situation of control case-by-case,[67] does not provide much clarity, requests courts to take additional usually lengthy assessments,

---

62 AL DE 1/2024.

63 Bob Seely: Vladimir Putin, Libel Law, and Parliamentary Privilege. https://www.standard.co.uk/news/uk/bob-seely-vladimir-putin-libel-law-russia-parliamentary-privilege-b985500.html.

64 Over 1,000 Companies Have Curtailed Operations in Russia – Some Remain. https://som.yale.edu/story/2022/over-1000-companies-have-curtailed-operations-russia-some-remain;

65 Довгань Е.Ф. Репутационные риски, как механизм обеспечения применения односторонних санкций государствами и региональными организациями // Право.by. – 2024. – № 4. – С. 97-106

66 *PJSC National Bank Trust and Bank Otkritie Financial Corporation v. Mint* [2023] EWHC 118; *Litasco SA v. Der Mond Oil & Gas Africa SA & another* [2023] EWHC 2866.

67 E-alert of the UK Foreign, Commonwealth and Development Office. https://content.govdelivery.com/accounts/UKFCDO/bulletins/375e351.

and prevents access to judicial review as affected companies and individuals might be not directly designated.

Apparently the impact on the population of other types of unilateral sanctions, including economic, trade, financial, transportation, sectoral, as well as sanctions against state property and assets of central banks might be even more serious; however, access to judicial protection in such cases is very limited. In particular, a dispute on Venezuelan gold in the Bank of England has been requalified from the international public law dispute on immunity of state property to the private law dispute about the authority.[68] The immunities of central bank reserves were lifted in the U.S. with reference to the domestic qualification of the State as a sponsor of terrorism, in violation of the principle of the sovereign equality of States.[69] Immunities of diplomats are refused in violation of the Vienna Convention on Diplomatic Relations (1961) by the decisions of district level judges; this resulted in particular in the arrest, extradition and lengthy detention in a U.S. prison of Venezuelan special envoy Alex Saab, despite the decision of the African Court on Human and Peoples' Rights.[70]

The devastating comprehensive effect of sanctions regimes on the whole population of the countries affected,[71] violating a broad range of civil, economic, social and cultural rights, multiplying mortality rates and reducing life expectancy, have been reflected in multiple reports and communications.[72] In some cases, due to the severity of the consequences, this author believes that the people affected might be qualified as victims of gross human rights violations.[73] As a result sanctioning States are obliged to respect their obligation to ensure meaningful remedies for the victims of such violations, including: adoption of the appropriate and effective legislative and administrative procedures and other appropriate measures that provide fair, effective and prompt access to justice; adequate, effective, prompt and

---

68 Submission by Venezuela; AL GBR 12/2021 and AL OTH 259/2021 of 16 December 2021.

69 AL USA 6/2022 of 6 April 2022; AL USA 31/2023 of 6 February 2024.

70 AL USA 23/2023 of 19 September 2023.

71 A/78/196; A/HRC/51/33; A/HRC/54/23. Add. 1; A/HRC/51/33 Add.1; A/HRC/51/33 Add.2; A/HRC/4859 Add. 2

72 A/HRC/54/23.

73 General Assembly resolution 60/147, 15.12.2005, paras. 2(b-d), 3(c-d), 11, 13.

appropriate remedies, including reparation; and provision of at least the same level of protection for victims as that required by their international obligations.

At the same time members of the general population are traditionally deprived of any possibility to protect their rights as they are not directly affected by any specific sanctioning act. Existing judicial mechanisms do not provide for any possibility to address extraterritorial impact of unilateral sanctions.[74] The attempts of Iranian thalassemia and EB patients severely affected by unavailability of necessary medicines to bring a suit to the U.S. court to protect their right to life were dismissed with reference to the "lack of subject matter jurisdiction."[75]

Effect of Unilateral Sanctions on Judges and Lawyers

Unilateral sanctions also have a twofold effect on judges and lawyers, affecting representatives of legal professions directly and hindering the right to legal aid of the individuals affected by unilateral sanctions. The independence of judges and lawyers constitutes an important inalienable mechanism to ensure the right to fair trial and access to justice. The privileges and immunities of lawyers and judges are provided to ensure the independence of the judiciary and ensure proper access to justice for all those whose rights are affected. The Principles and Guidelines on Access to Legal Aid in Criminal Justice Systems explicitly requests not to treat them "with prosecution or administrative, economic or other sanctions for any action taken in accordance with recognized professional duties, standards and ethic" (principle 12).[76]

In particular, U.S. sanctions against judges and officials of the International Criminal Court (ICC)[77] constitute a clear violation of their privileges and immunities, undermine the ICC's efforts to

---

74 Submission by Broken Chalk; Özdamar, Ö. Shahin, E, "Consequences of economic sanctions: The state of the art and paths forward," *International Studies Review* 23, no. 4 (2021): 1646–1671; Submission by Venezuela.

75 Iran Thalassemia Society; *EB Home [et al.] v. OFAC* decision of 1.05.2023. https://cases.justia.com/federal/district-courts/oregon/ordce/3:2022cv01195/168501/32/0.pdf?ts=1683194528.

76 UNODC, 67/187. UN Principles and Guidelines on Access to Legal Aid in Criminal Justice Systems (2013), principle 12.

77 E.O. 13928. https://home.treasury.gov/system/files/126/13928.pdf .

investigate, prosecute and sanction international crimes and thwart victims' access to justice, giving rise to the impunity of the wrongdoers.[78] The Bill S.4484 passed by the House of Representatives on June 5, 2024, imposing sanctions with respect to foreign persons of the ICC engaged in any effort to investigate, arrest, detain or prosecute any protected person of the U.S. and its allies,[79] contravenes the standards of the judicial profession.

Upon several rounds of expert consultations with lawyers, a number of challenges faced by lawyers, when dealing with sanctions cases have been reported, including but not limited to:

- the need to get a license for every sanctions-related case, insofar as the general license issued for lawyers e.g. in the UK is qualified to be non-sufficient and not-efficient, while the U.S. general licenses are only provided under specific sanctions regimes;[80]

- lengthy and uncertain process of getting licenses to represent clients under sanctions and to be entitled to be paid for the services (UK,[81] U.S.,[82] EU[83]) even when it refers to international adjudication, including the International Court of Justice;[84]

---

78 JAL USA 15/2020 of 22 June 2020.

79 U.S. Congress. *S.4484 – Bill Text, 118th Congress.* https://www.congress.gov/bill/118th-congress/senate-bill/4484/text

80 Dogra S., Wilhelm K., Darling S., Bowen J., Denton J., Key Sanctions Issues in Civil Litigation and Arbitration. https://globalinvestigationsreview.com/guide/the-guide-sanctions/fourth-edition/article/key-sanctions-issues-in-civil-litigation-and-arbitration

81 Designated persons face delays of many months in receiving licences even for subsistence. https://www.lawgazette.co.uk/practice-points/time-for-a-general-licence-to-cover-basic-needs/5117856.article. There is massive obstruction of businesses. https://www.bloomberg.com/news/articles/2022-09-13/investors-fume-at-uk-treasury-s-license-delays-for-russian-firms. Lawyers face lengthy delays in obtaining licences to represent clients. https://corkerbinning.com/russian-sanctions-and-the-law-of-unintended-consequences/

82 U.S. Code of Federal Regulations, Title 31, §542.201, 542.507, 542.508, 594.517. https://www.treasury.gov/resource-center/sanctions/Documents/legal_fee_guide.pdf

83 Claire DeLelle, Nicole Erb, "Key Sanctions Issues in Civil Litigation and Arbitration," *Global Investigation Review,* 2020 (submission by Partners for transparency). https://globalinvestigationsreview.com/guide/the-guide-sanctions/first-edition/article/key-sanctions-issues-in-civil-litigation-and-arbitration

84 Submission by M. Swainston.

- geopolitical motivation in licensing decision-making, "even where the grounds of a licensing purpose have been satisfied";[85]

- challenges to get payment for the work done as banks are blocking the accounts of clients, relevant bank transfers or already transferred money;

- fear of being subjected to criminal prosecution due to adoption of legislation on the criminalization of circumvention of sanctions regimes, providing for higher responsibility of legal professionals;[86]

- requests to report on the content of their discussion with clients and monitor all details of the clients' structure, including piercing of the corporate veil;

- obligation to report on the violation of EU unilateral sanctions, "when providing services in the context of professional activities," as there "is a clear risk of the services of those legal professionals being misused for the purpose of violating Union restrictive measures";[87]

- reputational risks, including accusations in amorality or qualification of efforts to challenge the legality of unilateral sanctions as defamation or disinformation;[88]

- prohibition to provide legal advisory services to certain types of clients, including "the Russian Government, or legal persons, entities or bodies established in Russia even those which do not fall under acting sanctions regimes" without certainty about what can be qualified as "legal advice";[89]

---

85 Guidance on the principles its licensing caseworkers follow to assess license applications. https://www.gov.uk/government/publications/financial-sanctions-licensing/ofsi-licensing-designated-individuals-licensing-principles--2

86 Directive (EU) 2024/1226 of the European Parliament and of the Council of 24 April 2024 on the definition of criminal offences and penalties for the violation of Union restrictive measures and amending Directive (EU) 2018/1673, art. 8 (c).

87 Directive (EU) 2024/1226, preamble (18).

88 *Bob Seely: Vladimir Putin, Libel Law, and Parliamentary Privilege.* https://www.standard.co.uk/news/uk/bob-seely-vladimir-putin-libel-law-russia-parliamentary-privilege-b985500.html

89 Regulation (EU) No. 269/2014 concerning restrictive measures in respect of the actions undermining or threatening the territorial integrity, sovereignty and

- Limited exemptions from the prohibition to provide legal services under art. 5n of Council Regulation (EU) No. 833/2014, referring mostly to the "services that are strictly necessary for the exercise of the right of defense in judicial proceedings and the right to an effective legal remedy."[90]

It is believed here that the above challenges constitute a clear violation of the presumption of innocence, right to reputation[91] and standards aimed to guarantee impartiality and the independence of legal professionals.[92]

Access to Justice in Sanctions Cases in Judicial Institutions
International Courts

At the moment the use of international courts as the means of settlement of international disputes in sanctions cases is rather limited due to objective and subjective criteria. In the absence of a special international court authorized to review sanctions-related cases, any adjudication is only possible as regards violation of other international legal norms in force between parties to the dispute. Due to the inter-state character of proceedings, the countries involved mostly refer to violations of non-human rights treaties, in particular the Bern Treaty concerning the formation of a General Postal Union of October 9, 1874 before the Universal Postal Union,[93] the TRIPS agreement concerning intellectual property rights, 2020,[94] the International Air Services Transit Agreement of 1944,[95] the Treaty of Amity, Economic

---

independence of Ukraine, art. 2.

90 A/79/183, para. 34.

91 A/77/296, paras. 10, 20.

92 OL OTH 75/2023 of 9.06.2023.

93 Qatar's Resolution on Postal Services Gets UPU Backing. https://www.gulf-times.com/story/657181/Qatar-s-resolution-on-postal-services-gets-UPU-bac.

94 "Saudi Arabia –Measures Concerning the Protection Of Intellectual Property Rights," Report Of The Panel, WT/DS567/R, 2020, https://docs.wto.org/dol2fe/Pages/SS/directdoc.aspx?filename=q:/WT/DS/567R.pdf&Open=True.

95 ICJ, Appeal Relating to the Jurisdiction of the ICAO Council under Article II, SECTION 2, of the 1944 International Air Services Transit Agreement, 14.07.2020. https://www.icj-cij.org/public/files/case-related/174/174-20200714-JUD-01-00-EN.pdf

Relations, and Consular Rights of 1955,[96] and customary international law on the immunity of state property.[97]

Unfortunately, in the case of the Treaty of Amity, neither the order on interim measures nor the decision itself[98] have been implemented and enforced by the U.S. In Certain Iranian Assets the Court ruled on the obligation of the U.S. to compensate damages caused by freezing assets in violation of the Treaty of Amity after the unilateral qualification of Iran as a State sponsoring terrorism.[99] It is also regretful that the NY court took a decision to use frozen money being the matter of the dispute, instead of releasing it at the time when the decision was to be taken by the ICJ,[100] as well as the U.S. denunciation of the Treaty in the process of adjudication to avoid fulfillment of the request to restart fulfillment of its obligations in breach.

In some other cases, one could observe a discrepancy between the interpretation of the UN Human rights treaty bodies and decisions of the International Court of Justice due to the novelty of the problem. In particular, in the Application of the Convention on Elimination of All Forms of Racial Discrimination case (*Qatar v. UAE*), the Court noted the persistent position of the Committee on the Elimination of Racial Discrimination, which prohibits discrimination based on current nationality as a part of the prohibition of discrimination based on national origin, but concludes, however,[101] that "national or ethnic

---

96 ICJ, Alleged Violations of the 1955 Treaty of Amity, Economic Relations, and Consular Rights (*Iran v. USA*), Preliminary Objections, Judgment, I.C.J. Reports 2021, p. 9; ICJ, Certain Iranian Assets (*Iran v. USA*), Judgement, 30.03.2023.

97 ICJ, Alleged violations of State immunities (*Islamic Republic of Iran v. Canada*), Application instituting proceedings, 23 June 2023; World Trade Organization. Dispute Settlement Report WT/DS567R. https://docs.wto.org/dol2fe/Pages/SS/directdoc.aspx?filename=q:/WT/DS/567R.pdf&Open=True.

98 ICJ, Alleged Violations of the 1955 Treaty of Amity, Economic Relations, and Consular Rights (*Iran v. USA*), Preliminary Objections, Judgment, I.C.J. Reports 2021, p. 9.

99 Certain Iranian Assets (*Iran v. USA*), Judgement, 30.03.2023.

100 U.S. Judge Orders $1.68 Billion Payout to Families Over 1983 Beirut Bombing. https://www.reuters.com/world/us-judge-orders-168-bln-payout-families-over-1983-beirut-bombing-2023-03-22/

101 Application of the International Convention on the Elimination of All Forms of Racial Discrimination (*Qatar v. United Arab Emirates*), Preliminary Objections, Judgment, I.C.J. Reports 2021, p. 71; International Court of Justice. Case No. 172 – Judgment of 4 February 2021 (paras. 99–100). https://www.icj-cij.org/sites/default/files/case-related/172/172-20210204-JUD-01-00-EN.pdf

origin denote, respectively, a person's bond to a national or ethnic group **at birth**, whereas nationality is a legal attribute which is within the discretionary power of the State and can change during a person's life-time" (para. 81).

We would disagree, however, with the reasonableness of the Court's reference to art. 1(2, 3) of the Convention as regards differentiation between its own nationals and non-nationals (para. 82). In the case of unilateral sanctions, as noted in reports on over-compliance, discrimination may result from any nexus with the country under sanctions, including the current nationality. Reference to the Nottebohm case shall not be applicable here, as the case assessed the issue of nationality in wartime,[102] that was not/not in the case between Qatar and UAE.

In February 2020 the ICC had a submission from Venezuela contending that the use of unilateral sanctions against the country constitutes a crime against humanity.[103] At the same time, the Court has not taken decision on the admissibility of the case yet,[104] as such a decision might become a good precedent for the possibility to use the ICC as a means to prevent the negative effect of unilateral sanctions and ensure proper remedy. In the country visit report to Syria, I addressed the devastating effect of unilateral sanctions and recommended their similar assessment with regard to the qualification of "other inhuman acts of the similar character intentionally causing great suffering or serious injury to body or to mental and physical health" under art. 7(k) of the Rome Statute.[105]

It is believed here that data on the catastrophic impact of unilateral sanctions and over-compliance, reflected in the country visit reports to Venezuela and Syria; the absence of reaction to the findings to minimize such impact; announcement of a maximum pressure campaign against Venezuela and enactment of the so-called Syria

---

102 Nottebohm (*Liechtenstein v. Guatemala*), Second Phase, Judgment, ICJ Reports 1955.

103 International Criminal Court. Venezuela Referral Document, 12 February 2020. https://www.icc-cpi.int/sites/default/files/itemsDocuments/200212-venezuela-referral.pdf

104 Preliminary Examination. Venezuela II, ICC 01/20, International Criminal Court. Situation in Venezuela II. https://www.icc-cpi.int/venezuela-ii.

105 A/HRC/54/23/Add.1.

Anti-normalization act[106] to prevent any reconstruction and re-building of the country; adoption of legislation on criminalization of circumvention of sanctions regimes, which reportedly make work of humanitarian organizations delivering humanitarian assistance to the countries very complicated;[107] narrow interpretation of humanitarian needs and humanitarian goods despite repeated calls to lift all sanctions against critical infrastructure and critical services;[108] all testify to the intentional character of the humanitarian damage caused and therefore this activity might fall under the criteria of article 7.

Taking into account that no decision has been taken since nearly five years, despite the openness of Venezuela for discussion, including to the visit of the president of the ICC to the country in June 2023 and signing of the Memorandum of understanding with the country,[109] it is very surprising that no decision on the preliminary examination has been taken yet, although the hearing was scheduled for December 3, 2024.[110]

Several attempts to use the WTO dispute settlement mechanism for adjudication of unilateral sanctions related cases shall also be noted. Although the discussion on the possibility to use security exemptions of art. XXI(b(iii)) as a justification of non-application of the WTO rules due to unilateral sanctions was only reflecting the long difference in approaches of member States,[111] recent practice demonstrates another tendency.[112] The WTO ruled on the duty of States to respect their obligations under the WTO law and interpret security concerns

---

106 Assad Regime Syria anti-normalization bill, 18.06.2023, *S.2342 – Bill Text, 118th Congress.* https://www.congress.gov/bill/118th-congress/senate-bill/2342/text/is?overview=closed&format=xml.

107 A/78/196, paras. 10–13, 67–71.

108 Syrian country visit reports, para. 88(b); A/78/196, para. 78(e) etc.

109 International Criminal Court. ICC Prosecutor Karim A.A. Khan KC Concludes Official Visit to Venezuela with the Signing of an MoU on the Establishment of a Country Office. https://www.icc-cpi.int/news/icc-prosecutor-karim-aa-khan-kc-concludes-official-visit-venezuela-signing-mou-establishment.

110 Venezuela II, 2024. International Criminal Court. Official Document. https://www.icc-cpi.int/node/220037.

111 Article XXI Security exemptions. Interpretation, World Trade Organization. GATT Analytical Index – Article XXI. https://www.wto.org/english/res_e/booksp_e/gatt_ai_e/art21_e.pdf

112 Voon T., "Testing the limits of security exemptions," East Asia Forum Quarterly, 2023, pp. 13–15.

under international law[113] rather than via domestic "self-judging."[114] The Special Rapporteur notes with regret that since November 2020 the WTO dispute settlement body is not able to function[115] as vacancies are not filled due to blockage by the United States[116] that undoubtedly limits access to justice at the WTO.

UN Human Rights Institutions

UN Human rights treaty bodies as quasi-judicial institutions not authorized to review the substance of the case, however, provide some possibilities for remedies and redress, especially when it cannot be achieved via domestic courts. In view of the challenges to access justice in the face of unilateral sanctions, it is believed here that individuals whose rights are affected by unilateral sanctions shall have the possibility to submit a complaint to the relevant treaty body against a sanctioning State to protect affected rights.

While recognizing existing challenges, including the multiplicity of sanctioning and enforcing States, the violation of human rights by over-compliance of private actors, and shifting responsibility between public and private actors, I would insist that the UN treaty bodies should admit complaints when the causal link between the unilateral sanctions and over-compliance from one side and human rights violations can clearly be established. It is also possible to refer to the steady practice of lenient approach to domestic remedies in treaty bodies[117] and insist that the requirement to exhaust national remedies shall not be applicable for the sanctions situations due to the reasons identified

---

113 World Trade Organization. Dispute Settlement Case DS544 – United States – Certain Measures on Steel and Aluminium Products. https://www.wto.org/english/tratop_e/dispu_e/cases_e/ds544_e.htm; World Trade Organization. Dispute Settlement Case DS597 – United States – Origin Marking Requirement. https://www.wto.org/english/tratop_e/dispu_e/cases_e/ds597_e.htm.

114 D. Boklan and A. Bahri, "The First WTO's Ruling on National Security Exception: Balancing Interests or Opening Pandora's Box?," *World Trade Review* 19 (2020): 129, 135.

115 World Trade Organization. Appellate Body. https://www.wto.org/english/tratop_e/dispu_e/appellate_body_e.htm.

116 Office of the United States Trade Representative. Appellate Body Report – February 2020. https://ustr.gov/sites/default/files/enforcement/DS/USTR.Appellate.Body.Rpt.Feb2020.pdf

117 Shikhelman V., "Access to Justice in the United Nations Human Rights Committee," *Mich J. Int's L* 39 (2018): 461.

in Part 2. Complaints on the violation of access to justice directly shall be reviewed by the HRC under articles 14, 15 of the ICCPR.

It also seems reasonable to request the UN treaty bodies to assess the impact of unilateral sanctions while reviewing reports submitted by targeted States, as sanctions hinder their ability to implement their international obligations under relevant human rights treaties, sanctioning states are in breach of the prohibition to violate human rights set forth in relevant treaties extraterritorially and an obligation to cooperate.

Regional Courts

Regional courts rarely address the issue of the impact of unilateral sanctions on the relevant conventions, as sanctioning countries are not their parties.[118] The sole decision of the ECOWAS court of human rights requesting the release of Venezuela special envoy Alex Saab[119] has been ignored.[120] As a result, only the European court of justice (ECJ) and European Court of Human Rights (ECHR) have an intensive sanctions-related practice.

Access to justice encompasses the right to a fair trial, the right to an effective remedy under articles 6, 13 of the ECHR and article 47 of the Charter. At the same time, jurisdiction over sanctions-related cases for both the ECJ and ECHR is still restricted. Both courts are focusing on the application of the law of relevant international organizations only, and do not properly take into account provisions of international public law.

In accordance with art. 275 of the Treaty on the Functioning of the European Union (TFEU), natural and legal entities subjected to restrictive measures of the EU may apply to the General Court of the

---

118 Unilateral Coercive Measures, Sanctions, and the African Continental Free Trade Area (AfCFTA). https://afribar.org/wp-content/uploads/2023/08/PP-05-Unilateral-Coercive-Measures-Sanctions-and-the-African-Continental-Free-Trade-Area-ACFTA.pdf; L. E. M. Lisboa, Direitos Humanos em um mundo de sanções, para além da distinção entre o legal e o ilegal: O DireitoaoDesenvolvimento e as MedidasCoercitivasUnilaterais, p. 150.

119 Judgment ECW/CCJ/JUD/07/21 – *Alex Nain Saab Moran v. Republic of Cape Verde* (15 March 2021). http://www.courtecowas.org/wp-content/uploads/2021/08/JUD-ECW-CCJ-JUD-07-21-Alex-Nain-Saab-Moran-vs-.-Rep-of-CAPE-VERDE-15_03_21.pdf

120 JAL USA 23/2023 of 19.09.2023.

EU (GCEU) to annul their inclusion into the sanctions lists, with an appeal to the ECJ. National courts of the EU member states are not authorized to declare EU sanctions' acts invalid.[121] It is necessary to note, however, that the ECJ took a rather restrictive approach towards access to justice and review of designations. Its practice can be summarized as the following:

- designated individuals have the right to defense and to access judicial institutions;[122]

- sanctions shall not violate international legal norms obligatory to the EU,[123] but the ECJ is not reviewing the legality of the EU sanctions from the international law perspective;

- restrictive measures are presumed to be legal under European law;

- the European Council has a broad discretion to decide on the grounds for restrictive measures as a part of EU foreign policy[124] including when acting beyond the authorization of the UN Security Council;[125]

- assessment of the appropriateness or the reasonableness of the grounds for designations is not consistent: the European council shall approve the existence of good reasons to designate a person in targeted cases,[126] but in many others it is the obligation of the applicant to demonstrate sanctions "manifest inappropriateness" in a view of their general objective;[127]

---

121 Pantaleo L., "Sanctions cases in the European Courts," *Economic Sanction and International Law* (Hart Punlishing, 2019); Barnes R., "United States Sanctions: Delisting Applications, Judicial Review and Secret Evidence," *Economic Sanctions and International Law* (Hart, 2016), pp. 171–196.

122 CJEU, Joined Cases C-402/05 P and C-415/05 P (*Yassin Abdullah Kadi and Al Barakaat International Foundation v. Council and Commission*).

123 *Parliament v. Council (Smart Sanctions)*, C-130/10, ECLI:EU:C:2012:472; Lonardo L., "Challenging EU Sanctions against Russia: The Role of the Court, Judicial Protection, and Common Foreign and Security Policy," *Cambridge Yearbook of European Legal Studies* (2023), pp. 1–24.

124 *RT France*, T-125/22, para. 52; Case T-55/12, *North Drilling v. Council*, judgment of 12 November 2013, para. 25; Case T565/12, *National Iranian Tanker Company v. Council*, para. 58; Case T-715/14, *Rosneft*, para. 159.

125 Case T-65/18 RENV, *Venezuela v. Council*, Judgement of 13.09.2023, paras. 95–96.

126 Ibid.

127 Case C-732/18 P, *Rosneft and others v. Council*, ECLI:EU:C:2020:727.

- provisions of the HRC and UN General Assembly resolutions on the illegality of unilateral coercive measures are not recognized as customary norms of international law by the court;[128]

- groups of individuals can be listed but listing shall be limited, however, to the leaders of the groups and those associated with them;[129] the existence of association with leaders of the group shall be based on the criteria of the "commonality of interests,"[130] which is rather uncertain and provides for broad discretion;

- a person shall be informed about the reasons for designation at the moment of designation rather than in the court room;[131]

- standards on the documentation collected and used as ground for designation varies and may include unverifiable materials, including media statements;[132]

- individuals and companies not directly designated by the EU cannot appeal to the ECJ even if they are affected by the EU sanctions enforcement measures and over-compliance;[133]

- states affected by EU sanctions do not have *locus standi* to seek judicial remedy;[134]

- existence of family links on its own is recognized as insufficient ground for listing, therefore the majority of delisting decisions refer to the family ties designations;[135]

- delisting judgements usually do not provide for penalties or lifting conditions; that can lead to issues of effective judicial

---

128 Ibid., para. 97.
129 *Tay Za II*, C-376/10 P, ECLI:EU: C:2012:138, paras. 62–65; *Rosneft*, para. 152.
130 Prigozhina, para. 93.
131 Case T-496-10, *Bank Mellat v. Council*, paras. 47, 49; Case T-390/08, *Bank Melli Iran v. Council* [2009] ECR II-3967, para. 80.
132 Zelyova, N., "Restrictive measures – sanctions compliance, implementation and judicial review challenges in the common foreign and security policy of the European Union," *ERA Forum* 22 (2021): 159–181.
133 *Ville de Paris, Ville de Bruxelles and Ayuntamiento de Madrid v. Commission*, T-339/16, T-352/16 and T-391/16, judgment of 13.12.2018, para. 50.
134 Case T-65/18, *Bolivarian Republic of Venezuela v. Council of the European Union*, ECLI:EU:T:2019.
135 Tomana, T-190/12, para. 235.

protection.[136] In rare instances when the Court granted compensation for an error in imposing restrictive measures, the awarded compensation was relatively low.[137]

As a result, although the ECJ provides for some elements of access to justice, it is not able to ensure the efficient access to justice, right to fair trial, right to adequate remedy and redress for protection of rights violated by the EU restrictive measures.

National Courts of Sanctioning Countries

Although states bear primary responsibility to ensure access to justice within their jurisdiction under international law, domestic practice of judicial review of sanctions cases in sanctioning States is fragmentary, limited and inconsistent. Challenges start from the possibility of getting access to jurisdiction, as traditionally only directly designated individuals and companies can apply to the court. Non-directly designated individuals are usually prevented or hindered from bringing a suit to protect their rights affected by unilateral sanctions or over-compliance. Applicants often report physical impediments to get to the country of adjudication, unwillingness of courts to accept payments from the designated individuals or companies, discrimination, unequal treatment and the geopolitical motivation of courts.[138]

It is also concerning that in many instances directly designated individuals and companies are prevented from submitting an appeal to the court due to the executive or administrative mechanism used for their designation.[139] In the U.S. the use of judicial constitutional

---

136 H. Over De Linden, "The Court of Justice's Difficulty with Reviewing Smart Sanctions as Illustrated by Rosneft," *European Foreign Affairs Review*, no. 3 (2019), p. 28.

137 CJUE, Safa Nicu Sepahan c. Conseil de l'Unioneuropéenne, T-384/11, Arrêt du Tribunal de l'UE (première chambre), 25.11.2014, paras. 68, 69; *CJUE, Safa Nicu Sepahan v. Conseil de l'Unioneuropéenne*, Arrêt de la Cour de Justice (Grande Chambre), 30.05.2017, paras. 55, 111.

138 Dogra S., Wilhelm K., Darling S., Bowen J., Denton J., "Key Sanctions Issues in Litigation and Arbitration."

139 White D, "Autonomous and Collective Sanctions in the International Legal Order," p. 21; *Research Output*. https://nottingham-repository.worktribe.com/OutputFile/926485; Barnes R., "United States Sanctions: Delisting Applications, Judicial Review and Secret Evidence," *Economic Sanctions and International Law* (Hart, 2016), p. 206.

protection is only possible when the applicant proves the existence of close ties with the U.S.[140] It has been reported that even when access to adjudication is possible, it is limited to the review of procedural aspects of designation rather than its substance and is based on the non-transparent classified materials provided by the executives,[141] shifting the burden of proof to the applicant and accepting ex post facto oral justifications as corresponding to due process standards.[142] Additional challenges cited include difficulties to get access to legal advice and its high cost, fear of lawyers, non-disclosure of documents and grounds for designation, uncertainty of legal regulation and interpretation, use of non-binding explanations, challenges to unfreeze and transfer money, to enforce rare delisting or de-freezing decisions,[143] and many other elements addressed above.

Another tendency affecting international trade relations and cooperation arises from the attempts of targeted States to move trade and private law cases to their jurisdiction to protect rights of individuals and companies affected by unilateral sanctions, including due to so-called sanctions clauses.[144] However, the efficacy of such measures is rather low due to the refusal of sanctioning States to apply agreements on mutual recognition of judicial decisions, to recognize and enforce judicial and arbitration decisions[145] providing for anti-suit injunctions[146] "to prevent circumvention of sanctions regimes by judicial means."[147]

---

140 Leagle. *Court Decision: 251 F.3d 192 (2001)*. https://www.leagle.com/decision/2001443251f3d19216.; *Al-Haramain v. U.S. Department of the Treasury*. https://www.bernabeipllc.com/wp-content/uploads/sites/1500928/2020/03/Al-Haramain-v-U-S-Dept-of-the-Treasury.pdf

141 Barnes R., "United States Sanctions: Delisting Applications," pp. 210–211.

142 Ibid., pp. 208–209.

143 E. Chachko, "Symposium On Unilateral Targeted Sanctions Due Process Is in the Details: U.S. Targeted Economic Sanctions And International Human Rights Law," *AJIL* 113 (2019): 159.

144 Submission by Venezuela; *Law Countering Foreign Sanctions 2021, China.*

145 Report, China country visit; Submission by Dominicana; Submission ин Broken Chalk.

146 *Renaissance Securities (Cyprus) Ltd v. Chlodwig Enterprises Ltd & Others* [2023] EWHC 2816; US Court Grants JPMorgan Anti-Suit Injunction Against VTB in Sanctions Case. https://globalsanctions.co.uk/2024/05/us-court-grants-jpmorgan-anti-suit-injunction-against-vtb-in-sanctions-case/

147 EU Sanctions: Response to Article 24(8). https://www.linklaters.com/en/insights/blogs/arbitrationlinks/2024/june/eusanctionsreponsetoarticle248;   EU

It is necessary to mention that this approach results in the development of relevant legislation by countries under sanctions, moving jurisdiction from so-called "unfriendly jurisdictions," but also issuing anti-suit injunctions in response to same injunctions in the sanctioning States and introducing a presumption of impediments to access justice and meaningful remedies in the unfriendly jurisdictions due to the very fact of being listed or being relevant to sanctions countries, as different from the approach that existed, in particular in the Russian Federation before 2021.[148]

The above approach reflects the challenges to access justice and the meaningful remedies identified in this article.

International Commercial and Investment Arbitration

The negative impact of unilateral sanctions on arbitration institutions and procedures is also reported by many lawyers, although arbitration institutions reportedly mostly follow the position on arbitrability of sanctions-related cases.[149] Besides the general challenges to get access to adjudication as regards, travel and visa restrictions, licenses to participate in the proceedings in any capacity, clearance from banks,[150] legal representation,[151] IT-sanctions[152] addressed above,

---

Council regulation 2024/1745 of 24 June 2024, art. 5ab

148 Order of the Supreme Court of Russian Federation No. 309-ЭС21-6955 (1–3)of 9.12.2021 (*Uraltransmash v. PECA Bydgoszcz*). https://kad.arbitr.ru/Document/Pdf/99ce7aa2-7f06-4615-baa5-94473b980771/1f0d228b-cefb-435f-a5f1-8950060144da/A60-36897-2020_20211209_Opredelenie.pdf?isAddStamp=True.

149 Szabados T., "EU Economic Sanctions in Arbitration," *Journal of International Arbitration* 35, no. 4 (2018).

150 Managing Sanctions in International Arbitration; Vienna International Arbitral Centre. Arbitration Rules – Section II.e. https://viac.eu/en/arbitration/content#II.e; How Can U.S. Secondary Sanctions as Foreign Overriding Mandatory Rules Intervene in Arbitration Disputes Arising from the Ukraine-Russia Conflict? https://arbitrationblog.kluwerarbitration.com/2022/10/08/how-can-u-s-secondary-sanctions-as-foreign-overriding-mandatory-rules-intervene-in-arbitration-disputes-arising-from-the-ukraine-russia-conflict/

151 Obiter in *Barclays Bank PLC v. VEB.RF*, High Courts of Justice London Circuit Commercial Court, of 10 May 2024, with regard to LCIA arbitration in London, para. 46.

152 Managing Sanctions in International Arbitration. https://www.acerislaw.com/managing-sanctions-in-international-arbitration/#_ftn15; *Linde GMBH v. Ruschemchemalliance* (2023), pp. 24–25; Case No. A40-155367/2020, judgement of the Moscow City Arbitration Court, 20.04.2021. https://www.garant.ru/files/5/6/1539065/reshenie_arbitragnogo_suda_g_moskvi_ot_20_aprelya_2021_g_

difficulties are also reported in the choice of legal regimes or arbitral institutions, appointment of the arbitrators,[153] political and geopolitical motives of the latter, a growing presumption of non-impartiality of arbitrators from sanctioning States or States under sanctions, an increasing number of breaches of contracts with reference to unilateral sanctions/ fear of unilateral sanctions as force-majeure,[154] disputes concerning jurisdiction of arbitral tribunals with reference to sanctions regulations[155] and submission of disputes to several arbitration centers[156] that results in parallel proceedings.[157]

Additional challenges are reported concerning the enforcement of arbitral awards. In the EU, while the arbitration proceedings themselves are made possible through the derogation granted in Article 4.1(c) of Regulation 269/2014, the impact of such derogation is negated by Article 5(1)(a) of the same regulation when an arbitral award is rendered against a party after that party's inclusion in the list.[158] As a result, unilateral sanctions hinder performance of contractual obligations, and also *prohibit the satisfaction of claims* "in connection with any contract or transaction the performance of which has been affected, directly or indirectly, in whole or in part, by the measures imposed under Regulation 833."[159]

---

po_delu_n_a40_155367_2020.rtf.

153 *La Compagnie Nationale Air France v. Libyan Arab Airlines,* Court of Appeal, judgement of 31 March 2003, para. 15.

154 International Chamber of Commerce. *Force Majeure and Hardship Clauses – March 2020.* https://iccwbo.org/wp-content/uploads/sites/3/2020/03/icc-forcemajeure-hardship-clauses-march2020.pdf; Council Regulation No. 833/2014, Art. 11.1.

155 *Stati v. Kazakhstan* case, Award of 19 December 2013, pp. 154–161. https://www.italaw.com/sites/default/files/case-documents/italaw3083.pdf

156 E. A. Katrovskaya, "Sanctions challenges in the field of international commercial arbitration in 2022 and the ways to overcome them," *International Law* 1 (2023): 3.

157 International arbitration in 2024, Freshfields, p. 9.

158 Vienna International Arbitral Centre. Enforcement of Arbitral Awards. *https://viac.eu/en/arbitration/content#c_Enforcement_of_arbitral_awards*; Ordonez M., Aubry L., "Impact of Russian Sanctions on International Arbitration," *Legal Industry Review* 3 (2023): 28.

159 *Linde v. RusChemAlliance,* HKIAC Case No. A23039, decision of the Hong Kong Court. https://www.italaw.com/cases/documents/10857.

National Capacity to Ensure the Right to Fair Trial

Besides challenges existing to achieving access to justice for individuals and companies affected directly or indirectly by unilateral sanctions, the means of their enforcement and over-compliance, it is also necessary to assess challenges caused by unilateral sanctions to the judicial systems of States, which become more vulnerable in the face of political and economic pressure and scarcity of resources.[160]

Country visits and submissions demonstrate the high level of vacancies in the police, investigation, secretaries, experts, judges, prosecutors and other legal professionals (up to 50 per cent); the absence and insufficiency of spare parts, machinery and reagents for forensic expertise; of logistical and transportation resources and supplies; of resources and software for proper online judiciary; the stockpiling of court materials; the absence of resources for establishment of new courts;[161] hindered access to courses, experiences, techniques and technologies, and exchange of information preventing the staff from getting skills and qualifications;[162] decreasing State capacities to provide legal aid free of charge;[163] and the need to use alternative, often telecommunications means for court proceedings[164] that is also problematic due to connectivity, soft-ware and operational challenges.[165]

The above reasons together with the need to look for alternative ways to process transactions and money transfers increase the risk of influencing judicial decisions and corruption.[166] Multiple reports

---

160 Zimbabwe country visit, paras. 58–59; A/79/183, paras. 51–56.

161 Submissions by Syria, Venezuela.

162 Venezuela country visit. Submissions by Syria; Gerritsen, A. E., "The Value And Limitations Of The European Union's Restrictive Measures/Sanction Regimes As A Foreign Policy Tool To Achieve Objectives (2022). https://diposit.ub.edu/dspace/bitstream/2445/187005/1/TFM_CEI_Alexander_Gerritsen_%202021-2022.pdf

163 Submission by Syria, Dominicana.

164 Submission by Venezuela.

165 *Довгань Е.Ф. Борьба с трансграничной преступностью в условиях применения односторонних санкций и овер-комплаенса //* Право.by. 2023. – №6. – С. 124–134; Довгань Е.Ф. Основные угрозы применения односторонних санкций с точки зрения достижения целей устойчивого развития и обеспечения международного мира и безопасности // *Противодействие современным вызовам и угрозам в контексте права международной безопасности и устойчивого развития* / под ред Е.Ф. Довгань – Минск: Колорград, 2023. – 11–38

166 Submission by Dominicana; Zimbabwe country visit, paras. 58–59; Venezuela country visit, para. 58.

reflect on the unwillingness of individuals and companies to use judicial mechanisms of protection of their rights in sanctions cases, due to the absence of trust in the courts in sanctioning countries or due to the impossibility to enforce decisions taken by national courts in the country of residence.[167]

There is also the impact of unilateral sanctions on international cooperation, especially on criminal matters. Reports testify that sanctions affect exchange of information, collection of evidences abroad, extradition, collective operations to suppress terrorism and other types of transboundary crimes undermine implementation of the UN global counter-terrorism strategy and suppression of transboundary crimes conventions, treaties on cooperation and mutual assistance in criminal matters, resulting in impunity and affecting access to justice for the victims of crimes.[168]

Designation of high judicial officials and other legal professionals is reported to affect proper cooperation in criminal and judicial matters, prevent active engagement at the international fora, limit establishment and implementation of inter-institutional cooperation agreements and other relevant conventions.[169] Such designations as political decisions usually do not provide for any possibility of appeal, reportedly violating the presumption of innocence, property rights, right to reputation, freedom of movement, and right to fair trial.[170]

Conclusion

The right to meaningful remedy, to access to justice alongside the right to fair trial and presumption of innocence constitute a primary system for protection of all categories of human rights, including economic, social and cultural rights in all situations, including in the face of all types of unilateral sanctions. The right to judicial protection, including the right to access justice for protection of violated rights, is not limited to situations of criminal charges against the individuals concerned.

---

167 China country visit.
168 Submissions by Dominicana, "Due process and unilateral targeted sanctions," *Research Handbook on Unilateral and Extraterritorial Sanctions* (Edward Elgar Publishing, 2021), pp. 405–423.
169 Submission by Guatemala.
170 Ibid.

Access to justice as a primary safeguard of all categories of human rights shall be understood broadly and include:

- Equal protection of the law without any discrimination;
- Presumption of innocence;
- Due process in the face of penalties and other elements of fair trial guarantees;
- Justiciability of all categories of human rights;
- Access to the means of protection of human rights via adjudication;
- Access to affordable legal assistance;
- Access to documents and evidences, transparency;
- Access to duly reasoned written judgements;
- Access to appeal;
- Awareness of the means to access justice;
- Respect to the rule of law rather than a rules-based order;
- Legal certainty;
- Access to remedies and redress.

Primary sanctions, means of their enforcement and consequent over-compliance have a detrimental effect on all categories of human rights not only of directly designated people but also of those who have any nexus to the country under sanctions, including the general population. The main concerns are due to the fact that none of these rights are safeguarded by effective access to justice as an integral part of the universally recognized right to remedy in the case of human rights violations.

The general population as well as non-designated companies with nexus to the countries, individuals or companies under sanctions are fully deprived of any access to justice, including access to courts and therefore to meaningful remedies, compensations and redress.

Access to justice as well as the consequent right to remedy for human rights violations in the face of unilateral sanctions constitute an integral part of human rights protection, which is currently under-developed at the universal, regional and national levels. It also forms an important means for establishment of mechanisms of restitution, compensations and redress for human rights violations by unilateral sanctions, the means of their enforcement and over-compliance.

As unilateral sanctions are qualified as a means of foreign policy, the use of civil and criminal penalties for their circumvention contradicts the universal standards of criminal law. Non-criminal measures cannot be enforced by criminal means, especially insofar as the primary unilateral sanctions themselves are against international law. States cannot impose punishment if they are not able to exercise jurisdiction over specific cases in accordance with international treaties or standards of jurisdiction. Unilateral expansion of jurisdiction with reference to any "high goals," "joint concern," payment in the USD etc., has no ground in international law.

Imposing primary sanctions with reference to crimes committed by designated individuals undermine the whole system of international justice, providing for impunity from one side for not starting a criminal case if a crime has really been committed under State jurisdiction. It violates the standards of fair trial, presumption of innocence, the right not to be punished for activity which does not constitute a crime, the right to reputation and other rights in all other cases.

Unilateral coercive measures, the means of their enforcement and over-compliance result in the gross violation of the human rights of the general population of the country under sanctions; therefore UN norms on the remedies in gross human rights violations shall be fully applicable by all UN organs.

Uncertain and extensive compliance requirements; non-transparency of decision-making, non-transparency and non-disclosure of information used as a ground for designation on designations and seizure of property by customs; lengthy, expensive and inefficient process of appeals for delisting or administrative processes; challenges to get access to any form of protection in sanctioning and other countries; and the unwillingness of legal professionals in the sanctioning countries to represent cases of companies and individuals affected by unilateral sanctions constitutes violation of the access to justice and right to effective remedies.

Presumption of the legality of unilateral sanctions, as well as rebuttable presumption of the guilt of entities and individuals under sanctions are contrary to international law, including principles of responsibility for wrongful acts at the international and national levels, including the presumption of innocence being a peremptory norm of international law. States shall not shift the burden of proof of the legality of their activity to the individuals/ entities under sanctions. The burden of proof of illegality of acts or omissions of the entities and individuals subjected to any types of penalties lies on the States and only if the existence of State jurisdiction is properly grounded.

The current development of legislation on provision of legal assistance, suppression of defamation and disinformation, criminalization of circumvention of sanctions regimes and relevant policies undermine principles and standards of the exercise of the legal profession and turn lawyers into victims of sanctions rather than guarantors of the promotion and protection of human rights. They are therefore prevented from the possibility of properly exercising their functions, that in turn affects the human rights of those they seek to protect.

International Courts, including the International Court of Justice, International Criminal Court, and the WTO dispute settlement bodies have a very limited practice in sanctions cases, although potentially they can play an important role in assessing sanctions-related activity from the perspective of international law, international criminal law and international trade law.

Despite the existence of intensive unilateral sanctions-related case law, neither the Court of Justice of the European Union nor national courts of sanctioning States provide for the adequate access to justice, right to remedy and redress in accordance with international legal standards. It also ignores the fact that the European Union as an autonomous legal regime is functioning within the realm of international law and can neither affect the rights of the third States nor expand the EU and EU member-states jurisdiction, similarly to the national jurisdiction of States.

The introduction of rebuttable presumption of the wrongfulness of behavior of any individual and/or company with any nexus to the country affected by unilateral sanctions, and impediments in getting access to evidences, legal assistance, challenges to pay, fear to be paid in sanctions-related cases even by international arbitral tribunals in challenges to get access to justice and meaningful remedies results in the adoption of national legislation providing for the possibility of moving jurisdiction in the cases to the countries under sanctions for issuance of anti-suit injunctions by the courts of both parties (under sanctioning and sanctioned jurisdiction), as well as development of the presumption of the impediments for the access to justice. All the above affect the access to justice, provide for the possibility of manipulation, and impede normal international trade relations.

Impediments caused to the cooperation in criminal and civil matters between sanctioning States, States under sanctions and third States, and the refusal to enforce judicial decisions, collect evidences abroad, or develop and enhance national judicial systems, affects not only access to justice in the countries under sanctions, but instead creates additional impediments for the suppression of transboundary crimes, gives rise to corruption and impunity, and undermines the right to meaningful remedy and redress for victims of crimes.

CHAPTER 16

Unilateral Coercive Measures and Crisis of Cross-border Dispute Resolution

Vladislav Starzhenetskiy[1]

Abstract

Massive and ever-increasing use of unilateral coercive measures (UCMs) considerably affects the sphere of international trade and investment. It also inevitably produces disruptive side-effects for cross border dispute resolution. In Russia–West relations it triggered the erosion of rules and procedures aimed at creating neutral and reliable dispute resolution mechanisms, resulted in unequal treatment of parties to commercial and other disputes, ignorance of res judicata and lis pendens rules designed to prevent conflicts of jurisdiction, and risks of contradictory and incompatible judgements.

Jurisdictional battles, anti-suit and anti-anti-suit injunctions leave little or no space for international comity, reciprocity or mutual recognition and enforcement of court judgements in civil and commercial matters. UCMs have also become an existential threat to international arbitration as parties to a dispute regularly face severe difficulties in implementing arbitration agreements, using arbitration infrastructure and in the subsequent enforcement of arbitration awards. This chapter illustrates emerging disruptive trends and provides analysis of the main problems related to the impact of UCMS on access to justice.

---

1 PhD in Law, Associate Professor of the International Law Department, HSE University, Moscow, Russia; vstarzhenetskiy@hse.ru

Introduction

It is well known that the fair and effective resolution of disputes has fundamental importance for international trade, investment and other types of cross-border relations involving private parties. The lack of fair and equitable dispute resolution generates critical legal and commercial risks for business actors as the results of potential disputes become uncertain and unpredictable.

Over centuries, the international community has developed rules and procedures aimed at creating neutral and reliable dispute resolution mechanisms, at overcoming prejudice to foreigners and granting them access to justice without any discrimination.

International hard and soft law documents[2] contain important provisions that serve as essentials of cross border dispute resolution in civil and commercial matters. For the purposes of this study the most relevant ones are the following.

Firstly, parties to a dispute must be treated equally, without any discrimination, and should have reasonable opportunity to defend their rights in a court or arbitration.

Secondly, courts involved in cross-border litigation should respect and apply *res judicata* and *lis pendens* rules in order to avoid conflicts of jurisdiction, mitigate risks of repetitive litigation or contradictory and incompatible judgements.[3]

Thirdly, it is widely accepted that international commercial arbitration plays a vital role in the speedy and effective resolution of cross-border commercial disputes.[4] Therefore, States should take

---

2 Article 14 of the International Covenant on Civil and Political Rights, Articles 6 and 14 of the European Convention for the Protection of Human Rights and Fundamental Freedoms, numerous conventions administered by the Hague Conference of Private International Law (Convention of 1 March 1954 on civil procedure, 1965 Service Convention, 1970 Evidence Convention, 1980 Access to Justice Convention, 2005 Choice of Court Convention, 2019 Judgments Convention. https://www.hcch.net/en/instruments/conventions), United Nations Convention on the Recognition and Enforcement of Foreign Arbitral Awards, UNCITRAL Model Law on International Commercial Arbitration, Ell/UNIDROIT Model European Rules of Civil Procedure, etc.

3 ALI/UNIDROIT 2005 Principles of Transnational Civil Procedure, Principle 28; Ell/UNIDROIT Model European Rules of Civil Procedure, Section 3.

4 International commercial arbitration "provid[es] a neutral, speedy and expert dispute resolution process." Born, G. B. (2020). *International commercial arbitration.* Kluwer Law International, p. 172; *See also* Born, G. B. (2018). "The New York Convention: A Self-Executing Treaty," *Michigan Journal of Intl. Law* 40, 115, p. 127.

measures to support the use of international commercial arbitration within their jurisdictions, *inter alia*, by respecting parties' choice related to selection of forum, recognizing legal consequences of arbitration agreements concluded between private parties, and establishing rules for the recognition and enforcement of arbitral awards.[5]

Fourthly, based on international comity and reciprocity principles, national courts should provide international judicial assistance re service of documents, obtaining evidence abroad for courts of other states.[6] Likewise, the mutual recognition and enforcement of court decisions is also strongly encouraged in civil and commercial matters.[7]

All of these key provisions have been recently seriously weakened or distorted by the application of unilateral coercive measures (UCMs) by states and regional organizations without authorization of the UN Security Council.[8]

---

5 "Most States in Europe, North America and parts of Asia have adopted legislation that [...] provides effective and stable support for the arbitral process [...]. Over the past 50 years, virtually every major developed country has substantially revised or entirely replaced its international arbitration legislation, in every case, to facilitate the arbitral process and promote the use of international arbitration [...] This includes legislation in France, Switzerland, Germany, Italy, Spain, Portugal and all other Continental European states. It also includes England, Scotland, Ireland, Canada (and its provinces), Australia and New Zealand, as well as Singapore, Hong Kong, India, Malaysia and Saudi Arabia." Born, G. B. (2020). *International commercial arbitration*. Kluwer Law International, pp. 198–199.

6 ALI/UNIDROIT 2005 Principles of Transnational Civil Procedure, Principle 31; Discovery in International Civil Litigation: A Guide for Judges, Federal Judicial Center, 2015, pp. 22, 30–31; Markus, T. (2024). Mutual Legal Assistance Treaties and Letters Rogatory: Obtaining Evidence and Assistance from Foreign Jurisdictions, Federal Judicial Center. Mutual Legal Assistance Treaties and Letters Rogatory, US Federal Judicial Center, 2nd, p. 17.

7 "The corollary concept of mutual recognition of judgments is also universally accepted." ALI/UNIDROIT 2005 Principles of Transnational Civil Procedure, Introduction, p. 3; UN Human Rights Special Procedures, Guiding Principles on Sanctions, Business and Human Rights: Commentary, 2025, pp. 111–112; "Unilateral sanctions, means of their enforcement and over-compliance violate the broad scope of international treaties in various areas of international law, including [...] the mutual enforcement of court decisions ..." Report of the Special Rapporteur on the negative impact of unilateral coercive measures on the enjoyment of human rights, Alena Douhan on Access to justice in the face of unilateral sanctions and over-compliance, A/79/183, 18 July 2024, p. 22.

8 In this chapter we will use the term "UCMs" as covering unilateral sanctions, economics sanctions, restrictive measures taken without authorization of the UN Security Council. These terms are used interchangeably.

The massive and ever-increasing imposition of UCMs has considerably affected the sphere of international trade[9] and investment by making many transnational business activities illegal and creating serious impediments to the performance of international commercial contracts.[10] It also inevitably produced disruptive side-effects for cross border dispute resolution as we will explain further.

This fact is usually overlooked and underestimated by policymakers and legal practitioners from sanctioning States. Restrictions triggered by UCMs and directed against businesses from sanctioned States are generally perceived in sanctioning States as necessary and legitimate.

For example, in the joint statement of the leading arbitration centers, the ICC, the LCIA and SCC titled "The potential impact of the EU sanctions against Russia on international arbitration administered by EU-based institutions" (June 2015), it is stressed that "sanctions—while they may result in some additional administrative steps—do not preclude parties from referring their disputes to arbitration at an EU-based institution. As such, it is very much business as usual for both the institutions and the parties."[11]

This indicates the presumption that existing carve-outs and exemptions related to transactions necessary to ensure access to judicial, administrative, or arbitral proceedings[12] usually lead to access to

---

9 A/HRC/55/42, Summary of the biennial Human Rights Council panel discussion on unilateral coercive measures and human rights, 21 December 2023, paragraph 42

10 "Actually, the major legal challenge, which is not clearly decided for now, consists in controlling contractual practices such as unilateral termination of contracts on the grounds of the risks generated by extraterritorial sanctions . . ." Beaucillon, C. (2021). "An introduction to unilateral and extraterritorial sanctions: definitions, state of practice and contemporary challenges," in *Research handbook on unilateral and extraterritorial sanctions* (pp. 1–17). Edward Elgar Publishing, p. 10; "The prohibitive amount of penalties for unilateral sanctions breaches, particularly in the United States, often has an impact on international contracts." Eeckhoudt, M. (2021). "Resisting from the bench: an overview of French and UK courts jurisprudence on unilateral and extraterritorial sanctions," in *Research Handbook on Unilateral and Extraterritorial Sanctions*, 306–322, p. 313.

11 London Court of International Arbitration, *The potential impact of the EU sanctions against Russia on international arbitration administered by EU-based institutions,* June 17, 2015. https://www.lcia.org/News/the-potential-impact-of-the-eu-sanctions-against-russia-on-inter.aspx

12 Art. 5aa(3)(g) of Council Regulation (EU) No. 833/2014 concerning restrictive measures in view of Russia's actions destabilizing the situation in Ukraine

justice and due process for sanctioned parties and can be reconciled with the restrictions of the relevant sanction regimes.[13]

However, from the perspective of targeted states and affected entities, the situation looks the opposite. Sanctions place affected individuals and entities beyond the bounds of law and justice. For example, according to the Russian Supreme Court, there is a strong presumption that UCMs defeat the essence of the right to access to justice and therefore extraordinary means of protection are needed to safeguard economic and procedural rights of persons negatively affected by UCMs.[14]

Due to these profoundly different views on UCMs and their compatibility with access to justice we can now observe relentless jurisdictional battles among states, courts, arbitration tribunals, and parties to the disputes. This may call into question the credibility of existing dispute resolution mechanisms and undermine attempts to create uniform rules of transnational civil procedure.

In this chapter, we will illustrate emerging disruptive trends and analyze the main problems related to impact of UCMS on access to justice, the enjoyment of human rights (i.e. effective remedy and fair trial) with a focus on the resolution of civil and commercial disputes affected by UCMs imposed against Russia.

---

allows EU persons to provide services to sanctioned Russian persons in the form of representation, consultation, preparation or verification of documents in judicial, arbitration and administrative proceedings and mediation.

The U.S. sanctions regime also authorizes provision of legal services to or on behalf of persons whose property and interests in property are blocked via specific license. 31 C.F.R. §587.506 (the Russian Sanctions Regulations). https://www.ecfr.gov/current/title-31/subtitle-B/chapter-V/part-587/subpart-E/section-587.506.

13 For example, Mark Dr. J., Oliinyk O., "Sanctions against Russia: How to ensure due process of sanctioned parties in court or arbitral proceedings while at the same time enforce the sanctions regime," *Global Arbitration News,* December 14, 2022. https://www.globalarbitrationnews.com/2022/12/14/sanctions-against-russia-how-to-ensure-due-process-of-sanctioned-parties-in-court-or-arbitral-proceedings-while-at-the-same-time-enforce-the-sanctions-regime/

14 Ruling of the Supreme Court of the Russian Federation dated 09.12.2021 N 309-ЭC21-6955(1–3) in case N A60-36897/2020.

UCMs, the Weaponization of the International Economy, and Risks for Access to Justice

UCMs have recently become an overwhelmingly popular foreign policy tool used primarily by Western States. They represent a set of various restrictions on economic activity, ranging from trade and financial bans, including asset freezes, to the establishment of price caps, sectoral sanctions that target vital and sensitive sectors of the economy of sanctioned States.[15]

UCMs have a complex negative impact on economic relations, both from the view of substantive and procedural law. In essence, they exemplify deliberate and comprehensive discrimination on the basis of nationality, when legal entities and individuals from sanctioned States become subject to repressive and punitive measures such as the freezing of assets, restrictions on the disposal of civil rights, bans on trade, financial and other transactions. The effect of UCMs can vary from all sorts of barriers to access the market of the sanctioning States, to doing business there, and the expropriation of property (direct or indirect) to various procedural hurdles in the context of access to justice.

From the legal perspective UCMs are defined as overriding mandatory provisions[16] that are placed at the top of the hierarchy of legal norms due to their link to national security and the public order of a State. They have direct application to relations between private parties[17] regardless of the law applicable to a contract.

The implementation of UCMs is complex and accompanied by various anti-circumvention provisions,[18] secondary sanctions,[19] "no

---

15 Timofeev, I. (2022). "Sanctions on Russia: a new chapter,." *Russia in Global Affairs, 20*(4), 103–119, p. 104.

16 Szabados T. *Economic sanctions in EU private international law.* Hart Publishing, 2019.

17 Beaucillon, C. (2021). "An introduction to unilateral and extraterritorial sanctions: definitions, state of practice and contemporary challenges," in *Research handbook on unilateral and extraterritorial sanctions* (pp. 1–17). Edward Elgar Publishing, pp. 13–14.

18 For example, Article 9 of Council Regulation (EU) No. 269/2014 of 17 March 2014 prohibits to participate knowingly and intentionally in activities that attempt to circumvent the measures referred to in Article 2 of said regulation (asset freeze). Council Regulation (EU) 2023/1215 of 23 June 2023 added to the listing criteria natural persons facilitating infringements of the prohibition against circumvention.

19 For example, under the U.S. sanctions regime, secondary sanctions may be

claims,"[20] "no liability clauses,"[21] and criminal liability[22] for violation of the corresponding restrictions. The cumulative effect of these provisions results in the maximization of compliance and the extraterritorial expansion of UCMs to any trade and investments relations with entities from targeted States.

Heavy reliance on the applicable Western law in commercial contracts (e.g., English, Swiss, Swedish, German), on Western arbitration centers and institutions often used for dispute resolution (ICC, LCIA, SCC and others), on the services of law firms and arbitrators having nationality, domicile or other close affiliation with sanctioning jurisdictions make sanction compliance easy to achieve and place entities from targeted States in a particularly vulnerable position.

In the context of access to justice, UCMs have triggered serious problems in two dimensions—procedural and substantive.

Firstly, persons from targeted countries (not only those who were directly affected by UCMs and blacklisted but actually all having the nationality of a targeted State) face numerous difficulties of an organizational and procedural character if they resort to dispute settlement in sanctioning States, such as the retention of a legal counsel or expert

---

imposed on any person (including a non-U.S. person) that provides material assistance or financial, material, or technological support to, or supplies goods or services to, a person subject to U.S. personal sanctions. Sec. 1(a)(vi) of Executive Order 14024 of 15 April 2021; OFAC Determination Pursuant to Section 1(a)(i) of Executive Order 14024. https://ofac.treasury.gov/media/931771/download?inline.

20　"No claims in connection with any contract or transaction the performance of which has been affected, directly or indirectly, in whole or in part, by the measures imposed under this Decision, including claims for indemnity or any other claim of this type, such as a claim for compensation or a claim under a guarantee, notably a claim for extension or payment of a bond, guarantee or indemnity, particularly a financial guarantee or financial indemnity, of whatever form, shall be satisfied, if they are made by: [designated persons, entities, etc]"; Guidelines on implementation and evaluation of restrictive measures (sanctions) in the framework of the EU common foreign and security policy. https://data.consilium.europa.eu/doc/document/ST-5664-2018-INIT/en/pdf

21　Ibid. "The freezing of funds and economic resources or the refusal to make funds or economic resources available, carried out in good faith on the basis that such action is in accordance with this Regulation, shall not give rise to liability of any kind on the part of the natural or legal person, entity or body implementing it, or its directors or employees, unless it is proved that the funds and economic resources were frozen or withheld as a result of negligence."

22　For example, Directive (EU) 2024/1226 of the European Parliament and of the Council of 24 April 2024 on the definition of criminal offences and penalties for the violation of Union restrictive measures and amending Directive (EU) 2018/1673.

especially in light of the deliberate stigmatization of the sanctioned entities, subjecting them to different forms of corporate boycotts and refusals of representation,[23] payment of arbitration/court fees, going through a compliance procedure within an arbitration institution, the formation of an arbitration tribunal free from the impact of sanctions, getting a visa and other forms of access to the country of the seat of arbitration, and the enforcement of the award.[24]

In most cases these difficulties can be solved via special licenses from competent organs allowing the transfer of funds for the payment of arbitration fees or the remuneration to lawyers, via mandatory appointment of a party's representative by a bar/association of lawyers, etc.[25] However, it may take months or even years to get such licenses,[26] turning arbitration or litigation to an unreasonably time and cost consuming procedure. Moreover, it may frustrate the whole arbitration if its initiation is necessary to preclude expiration of the statute of limitations to corresponding contract claims. However, what is even more important is that such discriminatory treatment places parties to a dispute in a considerably unequal position where persons from targeted States are disadvantaged and may lack equivalent access to

---

23 "Dutch law firm Houthoff drops Russian clients, including Kremlin," Reuters March 3, 2022. https://www.reuters.com/legal/legalindustry/dutch-law-firm-houthoff-drops-russian-clients-including-kremlin-2022-03-03/; Kinstellar, Public statement on Kinstellar's policy to work for "Russian clients," 29 March 2022. https://www.kinstellar.com/news-and-insights/detail/1650/public-statement-on-kinstellars-policy-to-work-for-russian-clients; JSC *VTB Bank v. Alexander Katunin et al.* (15 March 2022), where Ogier, the legal representatives of the claimant ("VTB") applied to come off the record because continuing to act for them would damage its reputation. The Court held that "the fact that a legal practitioner does not want to act for an existing client because of matters as to the client's character or reputation have come to light may not in itself be a good ground for allowing the legal practitioner to come off the record" and "legal practitioners owe a client a duty to act in the client's best interests."

24 V. Khvalei, "Impact of sanctions on International Arbitration," in G. Affaki, V. Khvalei (eds.), *Overriding Mandatory Rules and Compliance in International Arbitration. International Chamber of Commerce* (2022). E. Rubinina, "Impact of sanctions on arbitration," *Practical Law. UK Practice Note* w-030-4886, p. 8–9, 11–12.

25 Recommendations of the International Association of Lawyers, "Economic Sanctions and Arbitration: A Practical Guide for Parties, Counsel and Arbitrators," (2023). https://www.uianet.org/sites/default/files/uia_-_economic_sanctions_and_arbitration_guide_en.pdf

26 Report of the Special Rapporteur on the negative impact of unilateral coercive measures on the enjoyment of human rights, Alena Douhan on Access to justice in the face of unilateral sanctions and over-compliance, A/79/183, 18 July 2024, par.34.

critical legal services of comparable quality. The principle of equality of arms is thus seriously diminished.

Secondly, from the substantive point of view, the overriding mandatory nature of the UCMs and the mode of their extraterritorial enforcement leave little chance for effective remedy to persons negatively affected by UCMs, especially if the dispute is subject to resolution in one of the sanctioning States and/or the law applicable to a contract is the law of a State that imposed UCMs. Any result of dispute resolution contrary to what UCMs prescribe is effectively blocked or excluded on various grounds such as the non-arbitrability of a dispute,[27] the strong presumption of UCMs legality[28] that often results in non-justiciability of claims challenging lawfulness of sanctions, ban on satisfaction of claims in favor of sanctioned persons,[29] non-liability rules protecting those who implement UCMs in violation of their contract obligations, the freezing of funds that can be used for enforcement of judgement or award, etc.

Despite the fact that there are examples where persons from targeted States were able to obtain awards or judgements on the merits in their favor in UCM-related disputes,[30] and were even able to initiate

27 De Brabandere, E.C.P.D.C.; Holloway, D. "Overriding mandatory provisions and arbitrability in international arbitration: the case of multilateral and unilateral sanctions," in Affaki G., Khvalei V. (eds.). *Overriding Mandatory Rules and Compliance in International Arbitration. International Chamber of Commerce,* 2022. De Brabandere E., Holloway D. *Sanctions and International Arbitration,* p. 8.

28 As it was stressed by the European Court of Justice "the legality of a measure [...] can be affected only if the measure is manifestly inappropriate having regard to the objective which the competent institution is seeking to pursue," *PJSC Rosneft Oil Company v. Her Majesty's Treasury and Others,* C-75/12, ECLI:EU:C:2017:236, para 147.

29 *Stankoimport v. Reibel,* Judgment, Svea Court of Appeal, November 18, 2024, referred a dispute between Russian and Belgian companies for a preliminary ruling to the European Court of Justice for clarification regarding law. In the initial dispute, Stankoimport requested that Reibel be ordered to repay the advance payment and interest to the company due to Reibel's failure to deliver the goods to Stankoimport in accordance with the agreement.

30 For example, in *PJSC National Bank Trust v. Mints,* a claim brought by Russian banks Trust and FC Otkritie to recover US$850 million from O1 Group founder Boris Mints and his sons, the English court directly recognized the possibility of a judgment in favor of a sanctioned person. In 2022, the UK imposed blocking sanctions on FC Otkritie, including a freeze on its assets; Trust was not sanctioned. The defendants sought a stay of the proceedings in view of the UK sanctions, which they considered applicable to Trust due to its control by two sanctioned persons. The judge found that UK sanctions against Russia did not prevent judgments in favor of

relevant enforcement proceedings,[31] the main criterion here is still not the possibility of appealing to a court or arbitration as such, but the achievement of the final result in the form of effective enforcement of the award/judgement made. And even in the most optimistic scenario, one should not forget that the disputed assets, or sums awarded by the court/arbitration tribunal, would remain blocked in the sanctioning State for a potentially indefinite period of time and would not be made available to a sanctioned party if this is prescribed by the UCMs' substantive provisions.[32]

Consequently, attempts to get access to justice in a sanctioning State may prove to be ineffective and/or unreasonable in light of the efforts and resources needed in the vast majority of cases. The enforcement of UCMs is thus hardly compatible with guarantees related to

---

sanctioned Russian persons. The judge considered that the debt awarded under the judgment would be a "fund" within the meaning of the UK sanctions regulations, but that the entry of the judgment would not be "dealing with a fund/economic resource" within the meaning of the sanctions regulations. The judge noted that although sanctions are intended to restrict certain rights (such as property rights), they do not override the fundamental right of access to justice unless there is a clear statement of that purpose of the sanctions; *PJSC National Bank Trust v. Mints* [2023] EWHC 118 (Comm).

31 For example, in *Angophora Holdings Limited v. Ovsyankin*, Angophora Holdings Limited, an indirectly owned company of the Russian JSC Gazprombank, initiated enforcement proceedings in Canada on an arbitration award against Andrey Ovsyankin. In 2022, Canada imposed sanctions on Gazprombank, and Ovsyankin sought a stay of enforcement of the arbitration award, since it would entail an indirect provision of assets in favor of a company controlled by the sanctioned Gazprombank. The Canadian court acknowledged that Angophora is controlled by Gazprombank but noted that since both the arbitration award in Angophora's favor and the order for its recognition and enforcement were issued prior to the inclusion of the controlling person on Canada's sanctions list, enforcement of the award through the sale of seized assets does not violate sanction regulations. The court also stressed that the sanctions are not intended to be relied upon by debtors to avoid fulfilling their obligations. The debtor's motion to stay the enforcement of the arbitration award was rejected. *Angophora Holdings Limited v. Ovsyankin* [2022] ABKB 711.

32 For example, in *MODSAF v. IMS*, the Iranian Ministry of Defense (MODSAF) sought to enforce arbitration awards in its favor in the UK. The English courts of first instance and appeal held that interest accrued on the awards while MODSAF was under EU sanctions could not be recovered due to a no-claim clause. The judge ruled that in some cases the interest could still be paid to the sanctioned person, provided that the person had a relevant account in the EU (i.e. effectively frozen in a special account). As a result, MODSAF was unable to enforce the awards. *Ministry of Defense and Support for the Armed Forces of the Islamic Republic of Iran v. International Military Services Ltd.* [2019] EWHC 1994 (Comm).

access to justice for private entities and individuals. In fact, this is exactly the outcome that sanctioning regimes aim to achieve when they exercise economic coercion and outlaw sanctioned persons.

Reaction of the Targeted States: The Case of Russia

Given the abovementioned consequences in the form of discrimination on the basis of nationality, the violation of property and other fundamental rights,[33] the punitive character of UCMs, the lack of effective access to justice, UCMs are increasingly perceived as the equivalent of collective punishment.[34] UCMs may also intend to degrade the economy of targeted states[35] and are perceived per se as illegal[36] and representing a vital and systemic challenge to national sovereignty, economic security, macroeconomic stability, and sustainability of targeted States, to their populations, economy, and future in general.

It is not surprising that targeted States respond by creating their own anti-sanction legal mechanisms designed to eliminate or mitigate negative consequences for victims, other vulnerable social groups and

---

33 UN HRC Reports of the Special Rapporteur Alena Douhan on the negative impact of unilateral coercive measures on the enjoyment of human rights: A/HRC/48/59, 8 July 2021; A/HRC/51/33; 15 July 2022; A/78/196, 4 September 2023; AL USA 15/2020 // UN OHCHR, 23 June 2020

34 Weisbrot M., Sachs J. Economic Sanctions as Collective Punishment: The Case of Venezuela, Center for Economic and Policy Research. 2019.

35 The statements of the EU and the U.S. in context of sanctions against Russia. European Commission, "EU Sanctions Against Russia Following the invasion of Ukraine." https://eu-solidarity-ukraine.ec.europa.eu/eu-sanctions-against-russia-following-invasion-ukraine_en; US Department of Treasury Press Release, "US Treasury Announces Unprecedented & Expansive Sanctions Against Russia, Imposing Swift and Severe Economic Costs" (24 February 2022), Press Release JY0608. https://home.treasury.gov/news/press-releases/jy0608; Executive Order (EO) 14024.

36 XVI BRICS Summit Kazan Declaration, XV BRICS Summit Johannesburg II Declaration, BRICS and Africa: Partnership for Mutually Accelerated Growth, Sustainable Development and Inclusive Multilateralism Sandton, Gauteng, South Africa // BRICS Information Centre, 23 August 2023; New Delhi Declaration of the Council of Heads of State of Shanghai Cooperation Organization // Government of India: Ministry of External Affairs, 4 July 2023; "The Declaration of the Russian Federation and the People's Republic of China on the Promotion of International Law," Lawfare, 25 June 2016; "SA, Brazil and others want COP28 to tackle 'unilateral, coercive' trade measures," News 24, 28 November 2023. https://www.news24.com/fin24/climate_future/news/sa-brazil-and-others-want-cop28-to-tackle-unilateral-coercive-trade-measures-20231128.

businesses as well as to contribute to increasing the resilience of their national economies.[37]

Turning to the Russian experience in the area of countering UCMs in the context of access to justice, we can observe two main legal instruments that mitigate the negative impact of UCMs within the Russian legal system.

Blocking the Legal Effect of the UCMs

The Russian domestic legal order contains the presumption of the illegality of the UCMs against Russia and the impossibility of their exerting extraterritorial effect on its territory. UCMs, in the opinion of the Russian parliament, pose a threat to its territorial integrity and are aimed at the economic and political destabilization of Russia.[38] As it was stated by the Russian Constitutional Court, "UCMs are imposed without proper international legal procedure and in contradiction with multilateral international treaty obligations."[39] Given this fundamental point, Russian law enforcement agencies refuse to apply foreign law or give legal force to the provisions of contracts[40] or enforce foreign judgements or awards, if this entails the explicit or implicit implementation of UCMs in Russia. The legal basis for such qualification is the broad interpretation of the public order clause contained in Russian substantive and procedural law.[41]

---

37 There is special anti-sanctions regulation emerging in countries affected by UCMs. For example, in Russia it is, inter alia, the Federal Law of 04.06.2018 No. 127-FZ "On measures of influence (counteraction) against unfriendly actions of the United States of America and other foreign states." China has also recently introduced analogous legislative provisions in Anti-Foreign Sanctions Law in 2021.

38 Article 1 (1) of the Federal Law of 04.06.2018 No. 127-FZ "On measures of influence (counteraction) against unfriendly actions of the United States of America and other foreign states"

39 Judgement of the Constitutional Court of the Russian Federation dated 13.02.2018 No. 8-P.

40 For example, in cases involving Siemens Group companies (No. A40-126531/17-68-571 and No. A40-171207/17-111-1562) courts declined to enforce contract provisions that prohibited use of Siemens gas turbines equipment in locations other than those specified in the contract (i.e. in Crimean Peninsula) in violation of relevant sanction clauses. Moreover, in case No. A40-171207/17-111-1562, courts came to the conclusion that "de jure application of economic sanctions imposed by the European Union on the territory of the Russian Federation" "would clearly contradict the public order of the Russian Federation, damaging the sovereignty of the state."

41 Article 1193 of the Civil Code of the Russian Federation, paragraph 5 of Part 1 of Article 412 and paragraph 2 of Part 1 of Article 417 of the Civil Procedure Code

Right to Transfer Disputes to Domestic Courts

Another legal instrument is of a procedural nature and provides for special remedy for persons affected by UCMs. Federal Law No. 171-FZ of 08.06.2020 introduced amendments to the Commercial Procedure Code of the Russian Federation (hereinafter, CPC), expanding the exclusive jurisdiction of Russian commercial courts.

CPC Article 248.1 provides for the exclusive jurisdiction of Russian commercial courts over disputes: 1) involving sanctioned persons; 2) disputes relating to UCMs imposed by foreign states, state associations and/or unions, and institutions of foreign states on Russian citizens or legal entities.

It follows from the explanatory note to the draft Federal Law No. 171-FZ that the purpose of adopting these amendments was to establish guarantees for ensuring the rights and legitimate interests of persons negatively affected by foreign UCMs, since such measures effectively deprive them of the opportunity to defend their rights in the courts of foreign states or arbitration tribunals located outside the territory of the Russia.

Main features of these amendments can be summarized as follows.

Firstly, the main purpose of CPC Article 248.1 is not to delimit the jurisdiction of different courts in civil and commercial matters, as is usually the case with classic exclusive jurisdiction of courts, but to grant access to justice for the victims of anti-Russian sanctions. It is this public interest that is decisive here. CPC Article 248.1 allows Russian courts, subject to a number of conditions, to exercise jurisdiction despite concurrent jurisdiction of foreign courts and international arbitration tribunals.

Secondly, the application of CPC Article 248.1 and the activation of the relevant jurisdiction of Russian courts are directly dependent on the "victim" status of the person seeking protection. Not just anyone can apply to a Russian court on this legal basis, but only those whose rights have been negatively affected by UCMs.[42] This feature correlates

---

of the Russian Federation, paragraph 7 of Part 1 of Article 244 of the Commercial Procedure Code of the Russian Federation, subparagraph 2 of paragraph 2 of Article 36 of the Law of the Russian Federation of 07.07.1993 No. 5338-1 "On International Commercial Arbitration."

42 In the ruling of the Tenth Appeals Commercial Court dated 16.06.2022 in

with the goals and purpose of CPC Article 248.1 and explains why the subject matter of disputes under this article is not expressly defined or limited. Potentially, a very wide range of disputes fall under the scope of CPC Article 248.1, including contractual, corporate, IP, tort and other kinds of disputes that are predominantly of a private law nature.

Thirdly, the exclusive jurisdiction under CPC Article 248.1 is of relative, not absolute, nature. Persons in respect of whom UCMs have been introduced retain broad discretion regarding the appropriate forum and procedure of dispute resolution; they are not prevented from using forum selection clauses that have been previously agreed upon in international contracts if they so wish. In addition, the provisions of this article do not automatically exclude the recognition and enforcement of a foreign court judgement or arbitration awards made with the consent of the person against whom UCMs have been imposed.

Fourthly, CPC Article 248.1 presumes, as it was interpreted by the Russian Supreme Court in 2021,[43] that forum selection clauses (arbitration and choice of court agreements) in favor of "unfriendly" jurisdictions[44] are unenforceable because "the application of UCMs in itself creates obstacles to the Russian party's access to justice" and prevent it from enjoying the same level of protection as their opponents in foreign proceedings. To transfer the dispute to the jurisdiction of Russian courts, the unilateral application of a party under sanctions to the Russian court is sufficient. In a recent ruling,[45] the Russian Supreme Court clarified that a party can activate provisions of CPC Article 248.1 if there are any obstacles to access to justice in a foreign jurisdiction in the form of (a) "reasonable doubts as to impartiality of the arbitrators or judges who are obliged to enforce UCMs against Russian party"; (b) "burdensome requirements related to access to

---

case No. A41-70235/2021, it was noted: "CPC Article 248.1 was introduced to protect persons against whom sanctions were imposed, and not to protect persons who make claims against persons under sanctions."

43 Ruling of the Supreme Court of the Russian Federation dated 09.12.2021 N 309-ЭC21-6955(1–3) in case N A60-36897/2020

44 Under Russian law jurisdictions that introduced anti-Russian UCMs are considered "unfriendly." Order of the Government of the Russian Federation of 05.03.2022 N 430-r "On approval of the list of foreign states and territories committing unfriendly actions against the Russian Federation, Russian legal entities and individual."

45 Ruling of the Supreme Court of the Russian Federation dated 28.11.2024 N 305-ES24-13398 in case N A40-214726/2023

justice, including unreasonable financial, time, reputational expenditures that a person must fulfill to initiate, continue, or complete proceedings" and that put such person in a deliberately unfavorable position. There could be difficulties with paying the arbitration fee or State duty for initiating a case, a lack of financial or other actual opportunity to engage a foreign representative, restrictions on physical presence at the place of consideration of the dispute (visa issues), etc.

Fifthly, another feature of exclusive jurisdiction under CPC Article 248.1 is that it can be reinforced by anti-suit injunctions under CPC Article 248.2. Russian commercial courts can issue an injunction prohibiting the initiation or continuation of foreign proceedings (litigation or arbitration) against persons on whom UCMs have been imposed and can also award the amount sought by the other party in the foreign proceedings as a penalty for failure to comply with the injunction.

The Crisis of Cross-border Dispute Resolution

Since 2022, economic and political pressure on Russia via UCMs escalated to an unprecedented scale. The familiar landscape of cross-border dispute resolution has been shaken and the situation with access to justice has quickly deteriorated for all parties involved.

Being unable to protect and restore their rights negatively affected by UCMs in Western jurisdictions, a significant number of the Russian businesses switched to the domestic remedy under CPC Article 248.1 and anti-suit injunctions under CPC Article 248.2. These measures have quickly become popular among Russian parties affected by UCMs.[46] A substantial number of disputes were transferred to the Russian commercial courts despite relevant provisions of forum selection clauses providing for the resolution of disputes outside Russia. Russian parties massively filed lawsuits in Russian courts for the recovery of damages, to refund advance payments paid to foreign parties, to resolve contractual and non-contractual matters, etc. Due to the presence of substantial commercial assets of Western businesses in

---

46 Research conducted by the Russian law firm KIAP provides for more than 480 cases where CPC articles 248.1 and 248.2 were applied by Russian commercial courts by September 2024. The text of the research is https://kiaplaw.ru/upload/iblock/f0a/ uobf64mr2u6d7qoha72azgo12dxmca8t/KIAP-Alert-po-Zakonu-Lugovogo-RU_s-prilozheniem_16.09.2024.pdf

Russia, the enforcement of the Russian court judgements in such cases has a high chance of success.

Defendants on their part engaged in different procedural tactics to counter the negative consequences of Russian court proceedings that included anti-anti-suit injunctions,[47] anti-enforcement injunctions,[48] blocking the recognition and enforcement of Russian court judgements, initiating parallel proceedings in local courts and arbitration tribunals,[49] and ignoring forum selection clauses in favor of Russian jurisdiction.[50]

Within the fourteenth sanctions package, Article 5ab was added to Regulation (EU) No. 833/2014.[51] The new provision introduced another kind of economic sanctions in the form of a transaction ban on Russian parties "meddling with arbitration and court competence rules." It prohibited EU persons "to directly or indirectly engage in any transaction with a legal person, entity or body that lodged a claim

---

47 Orders of the UK and Hong Kong courts: *SQD v. QYP* [2023] EWHC 2145 (Comm.), *Deutsche Bank AG v. RusChemAlliance LLC* [2023] EWCA Civ. 1144, *Commerzbank AG v. Ruschemalliance LLC* [2023] EWHC 2510 (Comm.), *G v. R* [2023] EWHC 2365 (Comm.), *Linde v. RusChemAlliance* [2023] HKCFI 2409 and others.

48 *Google LLC v. Nao Tsargrad Media* [2024] EWHC 2212 (Comm). In this case the UK judge granted the anti-enforcement injunctions sought by Google, preventing the enforcement of the Russian court's orders in foreign jurisdictions; *Ziyavudin Magomedov & Ors v. PJSC Transneft & Ors* [2024] EWHC 1176 (Comm). In this case the Court in London granted the AEI sought by the Claimants against Russian ASIs.

49 Decision of 1 June 2023 (Case No. 12 SchH 5/22) of the Higher Regional Court of Berlin (Kammergericht). Judgement of the Court of Appeal of England and Wales in *Deutsche Bank AG v. RusChemAlliance LLC,* where the court found that England is the proper place in which to bring the claim and granted ASI and AEI because "there is no good reason not to." This case was simultaneously considered by Russian Court; *UniCredit Bank GmbH (Respondent) v. RusChemAlliance LLC* (Appellant) [2024] EWCA Civ 64, where the English Court of Appeal found its jurisdiction, and etc.

50 The Commercial Court has handed down judgment in *Zephyrus Aviation Partners v. Fidelis Underwriting Limited* [2024] EWHC 734 (Comm), dismissing jurisdiction challenges brought by aviation reinsurers relying on Russian exclusive jurisdiction clauses. Henshaw J held that (among other things) the claimants were unlikely to obtain a fair trial in Russia.

51 The Council of the European Union, Council regulation (EU) 2024/1745 of 24 June 2024 amending Regulation (EU) No. 833/2014 concerning restrictive measures in view of Russia's actions destabilizing the situation in Ukraine, OJ L, 24 June 2024.

before a Russian court against a natural or a legal person, entity or body [. . .] to obtain an injunction, order, relief, judgment or other Court decision pursuant to CPC Article 248 or equivalent Russian legislation, in connection with any contract or transaction the performance of which has been affected, directly or indirectly, in whole or in part, by the measures imposed under this Regulation or under Regulation (EU) No. 269/2014, as listed in Annex XLIII." Another new provision, namely article 11a, introduced the right of those entities that were sued in Russian courts in connection with EU sanctions to "recover, in judicial proceedings before the competent courts of the Member State, any damages, including legal costs" from the Russian counterparty.

The fifteenth sanctions package in December 2024 introduced Article 11c that prohibited the recognition and enforcement in the EU of Russian court injunctions, orders, reliefs, judgments pursuant to or derived from CPC Article 248. 1.[52]

The sixteenth sanctions package in February 2025 amended articles 11a, 11b and 11c[53] and extended the right to recover both direct and indirect damages caused not only to that EU operator, but also to any EU entity it owns or controls. Furthermore, it has been clarified that the damages may be recovered from the persons and entities that benefitted from or are responsible for the damage caused.

A similar legislative amendment was later initiated in the U.S. The Protecting Americans from Russian Litigation Act of 2024[54] was aimed at protecting U.S. companies and their interests so that they are not subject to litigation for compliance with U.S. sanctions and export

---

52 The Council of the European Union, Council regulation (EU) 2024/3192 of 16 December 2024 amending Regulation (EU) No. 833/2014 concerning restrictive measures in view of Russia's actions destabilizing the situation in Ukraine Council regulation (EU) 2024/3192 of 16 December 2024, OJ L, 16 December 2024.

53 The Council of the European Union, Council Regulation (EU) 2025/395 of 24 February 2025 amending Regulation (EU) No. 833/2014 concerning restrictive measures in view of Russia's actions destabilizing the situation in Ukraine, Council regulation (EU) 2025/395 of 24 February 2025, OJ L, 24 February 2025.

54 Matthew Topolski, For Immediate Release: Rep. Wesley Hunt Introduces The Protecting Americans from Russian Litigation Act, 12 September 2024. https:// hunt.house.gov/media/press-releases/immediate-release-rep-wesley-hunt-introduces-protecting-americans-russian. A BILL To amend title 28, United States Code, to limit the availability of civil actions affected by United States sanctions, and for other purposes.

controls by limiting the availability of civil actions affected by U.S. sanctions (still a draft law at the time of writing).

Another consequence of UCMs against Russia was the denunciation of legal assistance agreements between Russia and the Baltic States (Latvia, Estonia, Lithuania) in 2024–2025. It was clearly a political decision allegedly justified by "lack of trust."[55] These international agreements came into effect in the 1990s and regulated important issues such as the national treatment principle in legal matters, mutual assistance in civil, family, and criminal law cases, the jurisdiction of courts, the recognition and enforcement of judgements, the status of official documents, etc. With the denunciation of these agreements, courts and other governmental organs of Baltic States and Russia would no longer have any firm legal basis for cooperation and assistance to interested private parties in civil and commercial matters.

Summing up the devastating effect of UCMs on cross-border dispute resolution in Russia-West relations we may witness a serious erosion of the rules and procedures aimed at creating neutral and reliable dispute resolution mechanisms. Discrimination triggered by UCMs has not bypassed the sphere of dispute resolution. The unequal treatment of parties to a dispute and the stigmatization of those affected by UCMs is becoming a new reality. Principles of *res judicata* and *lis pendens* designed to prevent conflicts of jurisdiction and risks of contradictory and incompatible judgements are now largely ignored by courts and parties that want to secure a decision in their favor in sanctioning/sanctioned jurisdictions. Moreover, jurisdictional battles, anti-suit and anti-anti-suit injunctions leave little or no space for international comity, reciprocity or the mutual recognition and enforcement of court judgements in civil and commercial matters.

UCMs have also become a "serious threat to the very existence"[56] of international arbitration as parties to a dispute regularly face severe

---

55 "Latvia, Estonia to end legal pacts with Russia," *Insider Paper,* January 18, 2024. https://insiderpaper.com/latvia-estonia-to-end-legal-pacts-with-russia/

56 As it was observed by Vladimir Khvalei, "The existing system of obtaining permissions from the regulatory authority before taking virtually any step in the course of international arbitration in no way facilitates the implementation of arbitration agreements. It appears that a possible solution could be found in obtaining from regulatory authorities, such as OFAC and/ or competent authorities of EU Member States, a general license for submitting sanctions related disputes to international arbitration. Such license should cover not only the administration of

difficulties in implementing arbitration agreements, using arbitration infrastructure and in the subsequent enforcement of arbitration awards. The international community is actively trying to adjust to this new reality to overcome the negative consequences of sanctions for international trade and dispute resolution. One such recent initiative is the so-called Anti-sanctions-arbitration-protocol (ASAP) proposed by the Russian Arbitration Association, which aims at assisting the parties to reinforce access to justice by choosing, in a transparent manner neutral to sanctions, arbitration rules, appointing authority, place of arbitration, place of hearing, arbitrators, currency of payment, and applicable law.[57]

Conclusion

Empirical studies demonstrate that UCMs are directly affecting access to justice both from a procedural and substantive point of law. Such restrictions imposed on private entities are irreconcilable with ideas of fair and equitable treatment and run counter the principle of non-discrimination and the prohibition of collective punishment mentioned in the Guiding Principles on Sanctions, Business and Human Rights.[58] Sanctioned persons are placed beyond the bounds of law and are often left without adequate and effective remedy to protect their fundamental rights in the sanctioning States.[59]

---

disputes by arbitral institutions, but also the use of the entire arbitration infrastructure. Otherwise, international arbitration involving sanctioned entities and individuals will face a serious threat to its very existence." V. Khvalei, "Impact of sanctions on International Arbitration," in G. Affaki, V. Khvalei (eds), *Overriding Mandatory Rules and Compliance in International Arbitration. International Chamber of Commerce* (2022), p. 150.

57 Protocol and its description can be found at https://arbitration.ru/en/events/conference/anti-sanctions-arbitration-protocol-asap-reinforcing-access-to-justice-in-the-era-of-economic-sancti/

58 Guiding Principles on Sanctions, Business and Human Rights (2024), The principle of non-discrimination. https://www.ohchr.org/en/documents/tools-and-resources/guiding-principles-sanctions-business-and-human-rights

59 As it is rightly stated in the Commentary to Guiding Principles on Sanctions, Business and Human Rights (2024), "unilateral sanctions, along with their enforcement and over-compliance, violate a number of international treaty provisions, provisions of private law contracts, and human rights. Despite the well-recognized right to access justice as a means of protecting violated rights, sanctioning countries usually provide very limited possibilities for access to justice," P. 95.

UCMs also have unavoidable implications for cross-border dispute resolution in civil and commercial matters because of the numerous jurisdictional links with sanctioning States (including place of arbitration, applicable law, or enforcement of awards) that allow them to control the result of dispute resolution; and the corresponding protective anti-sanctions measures taken by sanctioned jurisdictions, such as, for example, the extension of exclusive court jurisdiction to sanction related disputes in the case of Russia. This results in multiple parallel proceedings disregarding *lis pendens* and *res judicata* rules, frequent conflicting foreign and domestic decisions, and the termination of international cooperation in legal and judicial matters to the detriment of international comity and reciprocity.

The ongoing crisis of cross-border dispute resolution caused by the application of UCMs has led to the loss of trust both on inter-state and business to business levels. It also provoked tectonic changes, including the fragmentation of the dispute resolution market, the rise of neutral dispute resolution centers (such as Hong Kong,[60] Dubai,[61] Astana,[62] etc), a high demand for unbiased and neutral arbitrators and counsels, more frequent application to international commercial contracts of the governing law other than the law of sanctioning States, etc. It remains to be seen whether these changes would contribute to effective solutions of access to justice problems from a global perspective.

Our conclusions on the disruptive effects of UCMs for cross-border dispute resolution are in line with, and fully support, the findings and recommendations of the Special Rapporteur on the negative impact of unilateral coercive measures on the enjoyment of human rights made in her 2024 Report on Access to justice in the face of unilateral sanctions and over-compliance[63] and relevant parts of the

---

60 Hong Kong International Arbitration Center, https://www.hkiac.org/
61 Dubai International Arbitration Center, https://www.diac.com/en/home/
62 International Arbitration Center in Astana, https://iac.aifc.kz/en
63 Report of the Special Rapporteur on the negative impact of unilateral coercive measures on the enjoyment of human rights, Alena Douhan on Access to justice in the face of unilateral sanctions and over-compliance, A/79/183, 18 July 2024. The Special Rapporteur emphasized "the negative impact of unilateral sanctions on arbitration institutions and procedures" including *inter alia* "difficulties with the choice of legal regimes or arbitral institutions, the appointment of arbitrators, the increasing number of breaches of contracts with the reference to force-majeure, disputes regarding the jurisdiction of arbitral tribunals with reference to sanctions

2025 Guiding Principles on Sanctions, Business and Human Rights related to general principles and access to justice provisions.

---

regulations, […] the submission of disputes to several arbitration centres that results in parallel proceedings" and "the negative impact on the enforcement of arbitral awards.

CHAPTER 17

The Prohibition on Providing Legal Advice to the Russian State and Russian Legal Persons in Article 5n(2) of Regulation (EU) 833/2014

The Position of European Case Law

Lupicinio Rodríguez Jiménez,[1]
José Luis Ipiarte Ángel,[2]
Fátima Rodríguez González-Chaves[3]

Abstract

It is increasingly frequent in international sanctions regulations to introduce a restriction prohibiting the provision of legal services to a sanctioned State or to certain natural and legal persons of such State. This restriction usually applies in respect of advice in non-contentious situations. In light of this, the existence of this type of sanctions entails significant risks for the legal profession in the sense that it forces it to operate in a great deal of legal uncertainty.

For instance, European case law has already shown the difficulties for notaries public to determine the scope of the restriction. And in this line, lawyers also appear to be in a very uncertain situation when it comes to determining the possible pre-contentious nature of a legal work Furthermore, restrictions of this kind severely limit the

---

1 Managing Partner of Lupicinio International Law Firm

2 External Counsel of Lupicinio International Law Firm; Professor of Private International Law, Universidad Pública de Navarra.

3 International Sanctions Department Coordinator of Lupicinio International Law Firm

legal practitioners' right to exercise their profession and are also detrimental to their right to property in that they reduce their legal fees and so their professional income.

Introduction and Approach

Article 5n(2) of Regulation (EU) 833/2014 concerning restrictive measures motivated by actions of Russia destabilizing the situation in Ukraine prohibits providing legal advice to the Government of Russia or to legal persons, entities or bodies established in Russia, except for the provision of services which are strictly necessary to secure access to judicial, administrative or arbitral proceedings or for the recognition or enforcement of a judgment or arbitral award. This prohibition includes local lawyers of a Member State or those who provide their services from a Member State.

In a short period of time, this article has led to a judgment of the Court of Justice of the European Union ruling on a preliminary and three judgments of the General Court of the European Union (Grand Chamber) ruling on three actions for annulment. The purpose of this study is to analyze these judgments.

Judgment of the Court of Justice of September 5, 2024, in Case C-109/23

On September 5, 2024, the European Court of Justice issued an important ruling interpreting the prohibition on the provision of legal advice to Russian legal persons in connection with the notarial function.[4]

The legal and factual background to the said judgment were as follows: the German Civil Code stipulates that a sale and purchase agreement regarding real estate must be notarized and the Land Registration Act states that registration may only take place if the legal transactions necessary for registration are attested by official documents or authentic deeds. Within this legal framework, two Germans were about to purchase a flat in Berlin, which was registered in the name of a Russian company; the purchasers and the selling company asked a notary to execute a public deed of sale of the property. The

---

4 Case C-109/23 [Khemerak], ECLI:EU:C:2024:681. The Opinion of Advocate General Laila Medina: ECLI:EU:C:2024:307.

notary refused because the idea that the authentication of the agreement was in breach of the prohibition of Article 5n (2) could not discarded. In this sense, it should not be forgotten that the Commission in its Frequently Asked Questions[5] had said that the aforementioned Article was applicable to notarial services provided to legal persons established in Russia.

Facing the notary's refusal, an appeal was lodged at the Berlin Regional Civil and Criminal Court, which referred three questions to the European Court of Justice (Court of Justice) for a preliminary ruling, essentially addressing the following: Is the authentication by a notary of a sale and purchase agreement regarding a property owned by a Russian legal person prohibited? Are the acts of execution of that agreement carried out by the notary for the cancellation of charges on the property, registration, etc., prohibited? and are translation services provided by an interpreter regarding such authentication prohibited?

As regards the first question, the Court of Justice begins by providing two definitions which do not appear in positive law; it states that

> According to its ordinary meaning in everyday language, the term "legal advice" generally refers to an opinion on a question of law. The term "legal advice" used in combination with the term "services," expressed as "legal advisory services" in Article 5n(2) of Regulation No. 833/2014, refers to the pursuit of an activity of an economic nature, based on a relationship between a service provider and his or her client, the purpose of which is the provision of legal advice, and by which a provider delivers advice on questions of law to persons seeking that advice.

Having established these definitions, the Court of Justice points out several important aspects. Firstly, that the activities of legal advisory services are clearly different from those activities which public authorities may be obliged to perform in a general interest function and which have been endowed, for this purpose, with certain powers

---

5 FAQs on EU Sanctions Against Russia (Consolidated Version). https://finance. ec.europa.eu/document/download/66e8fd7d-8057-4b9b-96c2-5e54bf573cd1_ en?filename=faqs-sanctions-russia-consolidated_en.pdf

binding on citizens. In this regard, the Court considers that the function of the notary is limited to the authentication of the sale and purchase agreement and it does not seem like, in the context of this authentication, the notary acts in order to promote the specific interests of one or both of the parties, but impartially, with equidistance between the parties and their respective interests, solely in the interests of the law and legal certainty.

Secondly, the Court refers to the legislative context in which Article 5n(2) of Regulation No. 833/2014 is included and concludes that no provision provides for a general prohibition on intervening in a transaction with a legal person merely because it is established in Russia and that there is no general prohibition on transferring property located in the territory of the European Union and owned by such persons. In fact, not all Russian legal persons are subject to the European sanctions, so those that are not sanctioned can carry out transactions regarding property located in the Union, but such transactions could actually be hindered in some Member States, such as Germany, where notarial authentication of the sale and purchase agreement of a property is an essential condition for the disposal of that property. Moreover, if this were not the case, the different notarial systems in the various Member States would lead to different applications of Article 5n(2).

Finally, the Court recalls that, in accordance with the whereas clause 5 of Decision 2022/1909,[6] Article 5n(2) of Regulation 833/2014 pursues the objective of preventing the avoidance of European sanctions, but in so far as commercial transactions with Russian legal persons are not subject to a general prohibition, it is not possible to assess how the notarial authentication of a sale and purchase agreement regarding real estate owned by a Russian company could, *a priori* and in a generalized manner, contribute to the circumvention of European restrictive measures. All this resulted in the conclusion of the Court to as regards the first question: that notarization by a notary of a sale and purchase agreement regarding real estate owned by a Russian legal person is not prohibited.

As regards the second question, i.e. whether the tasks provided for in German law which the notary must perform in order to ensure

---

6 Council Decision (CFSP) 2022/1909, of 6 October 2022, amending Decision 2014/512/CFSP concerning restrictive measures in view of Russia's actions destabilising the situation in Ukraine. OJEU L 259I, 6 October 2022 p. 122.

the execution of the sale and purchase agreement of real estate (guaranteeing the safekeeping and payment of the price, cancelling encumbrances on the real estate, recording the transfer of ownership in the register, etc.) are permissible, the Court concludes that it is for the national court to assess whether they involve the provision by the notary of legal advice to the parties in accordance with the definition of legal advice set out above. However, the Court, despite the reference to the national court's assessment, states that such tasks do not seem to involve the provision of legal advice by the notary.

As regards the third question, i.e. whether the provision by an interpreter of translation services in connection with the authentication of a sale and purchase agreement of property is permissible, the Court concludes that, since the profession of interpreter does not have legal nature, the translation services provided by an interpreter do not have the characteristics of legal advice, so that activity is not prohibited.

Judgment of the General Court (Grand Chamber) of October 2, 2024, in Case T-797/22

On October 2, 2024, the General Court delivered three judgments ruling on three actions for annulment of Article 5n(2) of Regulation (EU) 833/2014. We will analyze the three judgments following the order of their numbering and, therefore, start with the judgment in case T-797/22.[7]

In this case the appellants sought the annulment of Article 1(12) of Council Regulation (EU) 2022/1904 of October 6, 2022, amending Regulation (EU) 833/2014 concerning restrictive measures given Russia's actions destabilizing the situation in Ukraine[8] and Article 1(13) of Council Regulation (EU) 2022/2474 of December 16, 2022, amending Regulation (EU) 833/2014, concerning restrictive measures given Russia's destabilizing the situation in Ukraine,[9] in so far as they replace and amend, respectively, Article 5n(2) and (4) to (12) and

---

7 Ordre néerlandais des avocats du barreau de Bruxelles and the other appellants supported by Bundesrechtsanwaltskammer and Ordre des avocats de Genevè v. Council of the European Union supported by Republic of Estonia, European Commission and High Representative of the Union for Foreign Affairs and Security Policy. ECLI:EU:T:2024:670.

8 OJEU L 259 I, 6 October 2022, p. 3.

9 OJEU L 322 I, 16 December 2022, p. 1.

Article 5n(2) and (4) to (11) of Regulation (EU) 833/2014 concerning restrictive measures given Russia's destabilizing the situation in Ukraine as regards legal advisory services. To support their claims, the appellants argued three grounds for annulment.

The first ground was built on infringement of the right to ask a lawyer for legal advice, as well as of the principle of respect for professional secrecy and the independence of the lawyer and also infringement of the right to an effective remedy, all of which are set forth in Articles 7, 47 and 52(1) of the Charter of Fundamental Rights of the European Union (hereinafter "the Charter").

The General Court rejected those arguments. First, it considers that the possibility of being advised, defended and represented by a lawyer, provided for in the context of the right to effective judicial protection and the right to a fair trial under Article 47 of the Charter, must be recognized only if there is a link with the legal proceedings. In that regard, it points out that the Court of Justice has recognized the fundamental role of lawyers in a State governed by the rule of law only in so far as they contribute to the proper functioning of justice and ensure the protection of their clients' interests in the context of legal proceedings.

Secondly, the General Court pointed out that the protection of professional secrecy set forth in Article 7 of the Charter is recognized in the absence of any connection with legal proceedings. However, that protection is not intended to guarantee a fundamental right to have access to a lawyer and to receive legal advice independently of any connection with legal proceedings, but is intended solely, in connection with the right to respect for private life, to preserve the confidentiality of correspondence between lawyer and client.

Consequently, the rights guaranteed by Articles 7 and 47 of the Charter, taken alone or as a whole, do not make it possible to establish the existence of a fundamental right of every person to have access to a lawyer and to receive advice from him or her outside the context of actual or likely litigation. As a result, the fundamental right to have access to a lawyer and to have his or her advice should only be recognized if there is a link with legal proceedings, whether these have already begun or whether they can be avoided or foreseen, on the basis of tangible elements, at the stage in which the lawyer is assessing his/her client's legal situation.

In this regard, the General Court made an important clarification which may have indisputable practical significance, since it states that Article 5n(5) and (6) of Regulation (EU) 833/2014 allow the lawyer to make a prior assessment of the legal situation of the legal persons, entities or bodies established in Russia which consult him or her, in order to determine whether the advice sought is strictly necessary to ensure access, in particular, to judicial proceedings, to prevent or anticipate such proceedings or to ensure their proper conduct if they have already begun.

The General Court literally stated the following:

> It is therefore clear from the wording of Article 5n(6) of Regulation No. 833/2014, in particular in so far as it refers to the legal advisory services "strictly necessary to ensure access to judicial, administrative or arbitral proceedings," that the prohibition at issue does not apply to the legal advisory services provided as soon as the lawyer is called upon for assistance in defending a client or in representing a client before the courts, or for advice as to the manner of instituting or avoiding judicial proceedings (see, to that effect and by analogy, judgment of 26 June 2007, Ordre des barreaux francophones et germanophone and Others, C305/05, EU:C:2007:383, paragraph 34). That provision therefore does not preclude the provision of legal advisory services which, at that preliminary stage, are intended only to assess the legal situation of the person concerned, with the sole aim of determining whether proceedings, including judicial proceedings, should be ruled out on the basis of that person's situation or whether, on the contrary, proceedings are probable or even inevitable. In the absence of such a preliminary assessment, it would in fact be impossible, as the applicants have noted, to ascertain the subject matter of the consultation and to determine whether or not the legal advice sought might have a link with judicial proceedings and, consequently, fall within the scope of the fundamental

right of access to a lawyer, as has been recalled in paragraph 51 of the present judgment.[10]

As regards the lawyer's professional secrecy, the General Court pointed out that disclosure by a lawyer to a third party other than his client, in particular of his identity or of the existence of a consultation for which he is responsible, where it is coerced and takes place without his client's consent, is considered an interference with the right to professional secrecy, as well as with his communications, guaranteed by Article 7 of the Charter. In that regard, the appellants argued that when the national authorities are asked for authorization to provide advice to Russian legal persons in cases where European law provides for an exemption, they would be obliged to communicate data, which would entail a breach of professional secrecy. However, the General Court rejected this argument, stating, on the one hand, that the European rules leave the competent national authorities a margin of discretion regarding the way in which such authorizations must be formulated, submitted and processed, and must, therefore, lay down legal rules about it which do not entail a breach of professional secrecy.

In addition, the General Court added that the contested provisions do not suggest that the lawyer is obliged to share with the competent authorities, without his client's consent, information covered by the professional secrecy guaranteed by Article 7 of the Charter. Regarding the necessary information to process the request for exemption referred to, the contested provisions do not mention the information which the competent authority must possess in order to carry out its

---

10 Paragraph 56. In paragraph 57 the same reasoning is projected as to the cases in which the prohibition operates, specifically stating: "By contrast, the prohibition at issue applies, in particular, where, in non-contentious matters, a lawyer assists a client or acts for and on behalf of a client in the preparation or conclusion of certain essentially financial and commercial transactions. As a rule, the nature of such activities is such that they take place in a context without any link with judicial proceedings and, consequently, fall outside the scope of the right to an effective remedy and the right to a fair trial guaranteed by Article 47 of the Charter. In that regard, where a lawyer provides a legal service at such an early stage and is not acting as the defense counsel for his or her client in a dispute, the mere fact that the lawyer's advice or the subject matter on which he or she was consulted may give rise to litigation at a later stage does not mean that the lawyer acted in the context or for the purposes of the rights of defense of his or her client (Judgment of 8 December 2022, Orde van Vlaamse Balies and Others, C694/20, EU:C:2022:963, paragraphs 63 and 64)."

examination and grant. However, when establishing the detailed rules for implementing the exemption procedures, the Member States are implementing European Union law in accordance with Article 51(1) of the Charter and are therefore required to ensure compliance with Article 7 of the Charter, in accordance with the conditions laid down in Article 52(1). Consequently, the General Court considered that the provisions governing the possible grant of exemptions do not involve, as such, any interference with the right guaranteed by Article 7 of the Charter.

The second ground for annulment argued by the appellants was infringement of the principle of proportionality. In particular, they claimed that the introduction of a general prohibition on the provision of legal advice to the Russian Government and to Russian legal persons is not an appropriate measure to achieve the legitimate objectives pursued by the European Union in the context of the conflict between Russia and Ukraine and goes beyond what is strictly necessary to achieve those objectives.

The General Court rejected this second ground arguing that, since the appellants have not demonstrated any interference with either the recognized independence of lawyers for the purposes of the right to an effective remedy or with the values of the rule of law, or that the prohibition at issue undermines the very essence of the task performed by lawyers in a State governed by the rule of law, the prohibition on the provision of legal advice to Russian legal persons is appropriate and consistent with the objective of further increasing pressure on Russia to cease its actions against Ukraine and cannot be considered manifestly inappropriate regarding that objective, and therefore concludes that there is no infringement of the principle of proportionality.

The ground for annulment was based on infringement of the principle of legal certainty. The appellants submitted that the general prohibition on the provision of legal advice introduced is unclear and imprecise and does not make it possible to foresee the circumstances in which it is to apply. The General Court rejected this ground for annulment arguing that there is legal certainty because of the wording of Article 5n of Regulation (EU) No. 833/2014 itself, in particular Article 5n(5) and (6), which allows the appellants to distinguish between the legal advice services which fall outside this controversial prohibition and those which are subject to it.

Judgment of the General Court (Grand Chamber) of October 2, 2024, in Case T-798/22

In this case[11] the appellants sought substantially the same as in Case T-797/22, that is, the cancellation of the same articles, and put forward two grounds for annulment.

The first ground for annulment was based on a breach of the obligation to state reasons laid down in Article 296 of the Treaty on the Functioning of the European Union. The appellants argued, in that regard, that the Council did not provide any explanation as to the reason for the general prohibition on the provision of legal advice in non-contentious matters to the Russian Government and to Russian legal persons. In fact, the only whereas clause related to that general prohibition (whereas clause 19 of Regulation 2022/1904) only consisted of a mere definition of the services concerned and in no way consisted of a "clear and unequivocal" explanation of the "reasoning followed by the institution which adopted the measure," as required by the Court of Justice and the General Court in their case law. In so far as that whereas clause does not contain any explanation for that prohibition and how it helps to achieve the objective pursued, it does not enable the appellants to know the reasons for the measure and does not enable the competent court to exercise its power.

The General Court rejected that ground of appeal, holding that, according to settled case law, the obligation to state reasons depends on the nature of the act. In the case of general application acts, it is enough to set out the general overall situation which led to their adoption and the general objectives which they are intended to achieve. The prohibition is therefore sufficiently reasoned as it aims to increase pressure on Russia to end its "war of aggression" against Ukraine. In particular, the ban aims to increase the difficulties for the Russian government and Russian companies to access goods, services or capital in the European Union by depriving them of essential legal and technical assistance for such operations.

The second ground relied on infringement of Articles 7 (breach of legal professional privilege), 47(2) (breach of the right to legal

---

11 Ordre des avocats à la Cour de Paris and Julie Couturier supported by Ordre de avocats de Genevè v. Council of the European Union supported by Republic of Estonia, by European Commission and by High Representative of the Union for Foreign Affairs and Security Policy. ECLI:EU:T:2024:671.

advice) and 52(1) (conditions under which rights may be restricted) of the Charter.

This ground was rejected by the General Court on the following arguments, which we shall set out in the same order as in the judgment under discussion.

Regarding the infringement of Article 47(2) of the Charter, i.e. the infringement of the right to legal advice, the appellants argued that, by depriving a person of their right to legal advice from a lawyer, Article 5n of Regulation (EU) No. 833/2014 prevents that person from being informed of the scope of their rights and from being able to decide to start proceedings in a competent court. The right to be advised must be duly protected in the context of the right to an effective remedy established in Article 47 of the Charter. Such an infringement of the right to be "advised" by a lawyer is neither appropriate to attain the objective pursued, nor strictly necessary for that objective.

However, the General Court rejected this argument, holding that the restrictions stemming from Article 5n of Regulation (EU) 833/2014 are justified and do not represent an excessive interference with these fundamental rights. The Court held that, while the right to a fair trial is essential, the measures at issue do not deny access to legal services but limit the types of services that can be provided to Russian entities in the context of these sanctions.

As regards the infringement of Article 7 of the Charter, to the effect that the professional secrecy of lawyers would be breached, the appellants argued that a lawyer wishing to advise a legal person or an entity established in Russia, considering that such legal advice would fall within the scope of the exceptions in Article 5n, paragraph 10 of Regulation (EU) No. 833/2014, would be required to ask for prior authorization from the competent national authority and, to that end, to disclose information relating not only to the content, but also to the very existence of the consultation which the lawyer is to provide and to the potential client, even if that information is of a strictly confidential nature. Such an interference with professional secrecy is neither appropriate for achieving the objective pursued nor strictly necessary for that objective.

However, the General Court dismissed this argument, holding that the above exemption provisions give the competent authorities discretion as to how an exemption request should be formulated, submitted and processed. It did not specify who has to submit the request, leaving it open for the applicant to be a lawyer, a third party, or even the Russian government or the legal person involved. The rules do not require a lawyer to share confidential client information without the client's consent. In addition, the competent authority must carefully assess the situation to ensure that the exemption meets the necessary objectives and conditions set out in the relevant Regulations.

Judgment of the General Court (Grand Chamber) of October 2, 2024, in Case T-828/22

In this case[12] the appellants sought the annulment of Article 1(12) of Regulation (EU) 2022/1904 in so far as it amends Article 5n(1), (2) and (5) of Regulation (EU) 833/2014. Four grounds for annulment were given.

The first ground of annulment was a breach of the obligation to state reasons. The appellants argued that the Council had failed to provide any explanation as to the reason for the general prohibition on the provision of legal advisory services in non-contentious matters to the Russian Government and Russian legal persons, and that vague and inadequate reasons which did not meet the standards of a proper statement of reasons were provided. The Council had failed to justify and demonstrate the necessary link between the prohibited services and the destabilization operations in Ukraine.

The General Court rejected this ground of appeal, reiterating the case law according to which the obligation to state reasons depends on the nature of the act. In the case of general application acts, it is enough to set out the general overall situation which led to their adoption and the general objectives which they are intended to achieve and, according to the Court, the contested rules set out the general situation in the context of which they were adopted and the objective which they were intended to achieve was clear, since the contested prohibition was intended to make it more difficult for the Russian Government and entities established in Russia to access goods and

---

12 ACE-Avocats, ensemble supported by Lupicinio Rodríguez Jiménez v. Council of the European Union supported by the Republic of Estonia and the European Commission. ECLI:EU:T:2024:672.

services or capital in the European Union by depriving them of the technical and legal assistance necessary for such operations.

The second ground of appeal relies on infringement of the right of lawyers to provide legal advice. The appellant, supported by his intervener, stated that legal advice is an essential part of the profession of lawyer, together with legal defense and representation, and relied in that regard on a number of provisions of EU law. More specifically, it stated that the contested prohibition constitutes an infringement, firstly, of primary EU law and of the "right to a fair hearing" and, secondly, of secondary EU law and the case law of the Court.

In addition, the intervener, Lupicinio Rodríguez Jiménez, argued that the contested prohibition constituted a violation of Article 15 of the Charter (professional freedom and the right to work) and implicitly a violation of the right to property (Article 17 of the Charter). The judgment, in a position which, as we shall see, is highly debatable, rejects these arguments of the intervener, stating that it must be kept in mind that the purpose of the intervention can only be to support, in whole or in part, the claims of one of the main parties (ACE-Avocats, in this case); however, the allegation of infringement of Articles 15 and 17 of the Charter constitutes, practically, new grounds which do not fall within the framework defined by the claims and grounds put forward by the appellant.

The General Court rejected the appellant's second ground for annulment, holding, firstly, that the general reference to EU primary law and the fundamental principle of the "right to effective judicial protection" does not make it possible to identify the provisions referred to or the scope and meaning of the provisions or principles supposedly infringed, and must therefore be considered inadmissible; and, secondly, that the various directives and case law cited cannot be used, since the whereas clauses are not legally binding; those directives have no relevance to the case, and the case law cited in support of the infringement of Article 56 TFEU is not shown in the demand, but in the reply.

The judgment deals both with the third and fourth grounds for annulment, arguing infringement of Articles 47 and 52(1) of the Charter and Article 6(1) of the European Convention on Human Rights (ECHR).

The appellant and the intervener argued that Article 47(2) of the Charter establishes the right of every person to be advised, defended and represented, while the case law of the Court has established the right to effective judicial protection as a general principle of Union law. The Council is bound by this when adopting secondary legislation. Furthermore, they pointed out that the right protected under Article 47(2) of the Charter must have the same meaning and scope as that conferred by Article 6(1) of the ECHR, which would reinforce the obligation of the EU institutions to respect it. In this respect, the distinction made between "legal advice which does not relate to a possible dispute," on one hand, and one that is "closely linked to the preparation of a contentious procedure," on the other hand, is artificial. This risky distinction may create legal uncertainty and cause damage to the rule of law. The lawyer has precisely a preventive function, i.e. dissuading a client, if necessary, from initiating legal proceedings.

However, the General Court did not accept these arguments and rejected them, stating that the fundamental right to be advised by a lawyer and to benefit therefrom is fully recognized in Article 47 of the Charter, but only if there is a link to legal proceedings, whether such proceedings have already begun or can be prevented or anticipated, on the basis of tangible elements, during the lawyer's assessment of his client's legal situation. Prohibited legal advice services do not include representation, advice, preparation of documents or verification of documents in the context of legal representation services, namely in cases or proceedings with administrative bodies, courts or other duly constituted official tribunals, or in arbitration and mediation proceedings.

Some Critical Considerations on the Analyzed Judgments

Some important conclusions can be drawn from these four rulings, although in our view most of their content is open to criticism.

The judgment of the Court of Justice of September 5, 2024 deserves a very positive assessment. Firstly, because it provides two very important definitions that do not appear in Positive Law; it states that "According to its ordinary meaning in everyday language, the term 'legal advice' generally refers to an opinion on a question of law. The term 'legal advice' used in combination with the term 'services,' expressed as 'legal advisory services' in Article 5n(2) of Regulation No. 833/2014, refers to the pursuit of an activity of an economic nature, based on a relationship between a service provider and his or her client, the purpose of which is the provision of legal advice, and by which a provider delivers advice on questions of law to persons seeking that advice." Having these two definitions is very useful and helps to introduce elements of legal certainty. Secondly, the judgment delimits very well and correctly the scope of the prohibition in Article 5n of Regulation (EU) 833/2014 with regard to the notarial function.

On the other hand, the three judgments of the General Court of October 2, 2024 deserve a negative review. However, before referring to some of these negative aspects, we would like to point out that the General Court's clarification in the judgment in Case T-797/22 is positive and of great practical significance, as Article 5n(5) and (6) of Regulation (EU) 833/2014 allow the lawyer to carry out a prior assessment of the legal status of legal persons, entities or bodies established in Russia which consult him, in order to determine whether the advice sought is strictly necessary to ensure access, in particular, to judicial proceedings, to prevent or anticipate such proceedings or to ensure the proper conduct of those proceedings if they have already begun.

However, having said that, we would like to highlight as particularly important, among other things, the following erroneous aspects of the above-mentioned judgments of the General Court. Firstly, the Court adopts a position that is too rigid and not aligned with the real needs of the practice of the legal profession when it considers that the possibility of being advised, defended and represented by a lawyer, provided for in the context of the right to an effective remedy and the right to a fair trial under Article 47 of the Charter, should only be recognized if there is a link with judicial or other type of proceedings.

Secondly, the General Court is also wrong when it states that the prohibition on the provision of legal advice to Russian legal entities is appropriate and consistent with the objective of further increasing pressure on Russia to cease its actions against Ukraine and cannot be regarded as manifestly inappropriate in relation to that objective, and therefore concludes that there is no infringement of the principle of proportionality. This position is clearly erroneous, since the prohibition in Article 5n of Regulation (EU) 833/2014 does nothing to put pressure on Russia, since Russian legal entities can seek legal advice outside the European Union, but instead, European lawyers, who are deprived of an important area of work and thus of financial income, are disadvantaged; it cannot therefore be claimed that there is a correlation between that prohibition and the achievement of the cease of Russia's actions in Ukraine.

Thirdly, the General Court's position, i.e. that the prohibition in Article 5n of Regulation (EU) 833/2014 does not undermine legal certainty, is not admissible. The reality is that the aforementioned provision creates a confusing situation in which lawyers are forced to act in a very uncertain legal framework, since the practical scope of the prohibition is not at all clear.

Fourthly, the General Court is seriously mistaken when, in the judgment in Case T-828/22, it rejects the intervener's argument that the contested prohibition represented an infringement of Article 15 of the Charter (freedom to choose an occupation and the right to work) and implicitly an infringement of the right to property (Article 17 of the Charter), stating that it must be kept in mind that the purpose of the intervention can only be to support, in whole or in part, the form of order sought by one of the main parties (ACE-Avocats, in the mentioned case); however, according to the Court, the allegation of infringement of Articles 15 and 17 of the Charter constitutes a new ground which does not fall within the framework defined by the form of order sought and the grounds relied on by the appellant. This is completely inadmissible since the main party had alleged as a ground of contestation the infringement of the right of lawyers to provide legal advice, coincident with Article 15 of the Charter as regards the right to exercise a profession.

Finally, we would like to recall that, recently, the three judgments of the General Court of October 2, 2024, have been appealed in cassation before the Court of Justice of the European Union, giving rise to cases C-865/24 P, C-866/24 P, C-867/24 P and C-868/24 P.

CHAPTER 18

Towards Fair Adjudication

Establishing Independent Mechanisms for the Review of Sanction Designations

Maryna Pogibko[1] | *Denys Nienov*[2]

Abstract

This chapter examines the practices and challenges of sanctions imposition and review across key jurisdictions, including the U.S., UK, EU, Canada and Australia. Highlighting issues of impartiality and due process, it notes how sanctions regimes often lack independent review, with the same executive body managing both designation and appeals. To address these concerns, the chapter proposes reforms at national and multilateral levels, including independent review bodies, clear access to designation information and standardized procedures. It further advocates for a multilateral convention and an international oversight body with binding authority to ensure fairness and human rights protections, aiming to create a balanced, credible, and globally consistent sanctions framework.

Introduction

Sanctions are tools in international relations, designed to influence the actions of States, organizations and individuals to address threats to international peace and security. While effective in addressing certain objectives, sanctions—particularly those applied unilaterally—can be perceived as lacking in fairness and transparency. Certain jurisdictions which regularly sanction third parties do not provide independent, impartial mechanisms for sanctioned parties to contest their designations. In many cases, the same authorities handle

---

1 Managing Partner, Amadeus Consultancy Limited, London, United Kingdom
2 Counsel, Amadeus Consultancy Limited, London, United Kingdom

both the imposition and review of sanctions, potentially affecting perceptions of due process and objectivity. This chapter, written from the perspective of practitioners dealing with challenges in specific cases and jurisdictions, focuses on the procedural aspects of existing sanctions mechanisms. It offers proposals for reforms at both national and multilateral levels, seeking to strengthen the legitimacy, fairness, and consistency of sanctions regimes. By considering these reforms, it is possible to establish a more balanced approach that ensures the protection of the rights of those impacted by sanctions.

Current Practices in Sanctions Imposition and Review: Proposals for Improvement

Sanctions regimes across jurisdictions such as the United States ("the U.S."), United Kingdom ("the UK"), European Union ("EU"), Canada and Australia[3] are primarily managed through executive agencies or governmental bodies for both imposition and review, thus limiting the transparency and impartiality of the review process.

U.S. Sanctions

In the U.S., individuals and legal entities designated under the Office of Foreign Assets Control (OFAC) lists can request removal by petitioning OFAC directly[4] and, if denied, may challenge the determination in federal court.[5] The timing of OFAC's review is not fixed and can vary significantly depending on factors such as inter-agency consultations and the specificity of the case. Meanwhile, designated parties have the option to bypass the administrative delisting process

---

3 These countries are the focus of this study because they have the largest number of unilateral sanctions that have the most global impact.

4 U.S. Department of Treasury, Office of Foreign Assets Control (OFAC), Filing a Petition for Removal from an OFAC List. https://ofac.treasury.gov/specially-designated-nationals-list-sdn-list/filing-a-petition-for-removal-from-an-ofac-list

5 Rakhimov, 2020 U.S. Dist. LEXIS 68764, at 5 (D.D.C., 20 April 2020) (citations omitted); *Al Haramain Islamic Foundation, Inc v. U.S. Dep't of Treasury,* 686 F.3d 965, 1027 (9th Cir., 2011) (noting the unsuccessful challenge to OFAC's "specially designated global terrorist" designation after no response from OFAC to a request for reconsideration); Rakhimov, No. 19-2554, at 5 (stating the plaintiff requested rescission, a temporary stay, and later sued, arguing that OFAC's failure to provide the record violated the APA [citations omitted]).

and seek direct judicial review.[6] However, designated parties that seek to delist through litigation should be aware that judicial review of OFAC's designation decisions is typically highly deferential.[7] Courts will "set aside OFAC's designation only if it is "arbitrary, capricious, an abuse of discretion, or otherwise not in accordance with law."[8] Thus, where the evidence "provides adequate basis to justify Treasury's determination,"[9] courts will deny the petitioner's application for delisting. Where OFAC refuses to provide reasons for the designation, however, if, for example, evidence is classified, courts have found a due process violation: "Without disclosure of the classified information, the designated entity cannot possibly know how to respond to OFAC's concerns." The court concluded that "the small burden on the agency of providing mitigation measures does not outweigh the potential value to AHIF-Oregon [a designated U.S. entity]. OFAC's failure to pursue mitigation measures violated AHIF-Oregon's due process rights."[10]

UK Sanctions

In the UK, multiple governmental departments enforce specific sanctions, such as the Department for Business and Trade ("DBT") for trade sanctions, HM Treasury through its Office of Financial Sanctions Implementation ("OFSI") for financial sanctions, the Department for Transport for aviation and maritime sanctions and the Home Office for

---

6 *Rakhimov v. Gacki,* 2020 U.S. Dist. LEXIS 68764, at 4.; *Olenga v. Gacki,* 507 F. Supp. 3d 260, 264 (D.D.C. 2020) (stating that the SDN-listed plaintiff filed a lawsuit while the administrative reconsideration process was ongoing); *Holy Land Foundation v. Ashcroft,* 333 F.3d 156, 160 (D.C. Cir. 2003), cert. denied, 540 U.S. ___ (2004) (stating that, soon after being designated as a Specially Designated Terrorist and as a Specially Designated Global Terrorist, an entity filed a lawsuit challenging its designations and the seizure of its assets, and alleging violations of, *inter alia,* its constitutional rights and its rights under the Administrative Procedure Act).

7 "A US lawyer's perspective on representing designated parties and those operating in sanctioned countries," *Global Investigations Review* (20 June 2024). https://globalinvestigationsreview.com/guide/the-guide-sanctions/fifth-edition/article/us-lawyers-perspective-representing-designated-parties-and-those-operating-in-sanctioned-countries

8 Al Haramain Islamic Foundation, 686 F.3d at 1029 (citing 5 USC §706(2)(A)).

9 *Zevallos v. Obama,* 793 F.3d at 114.

10 *Al Haramain Islamic Foundation, Inc v. U.S. Dep't of Treasury,* 686 F.3d at 1027.

immigration sanctions.[11] Designated persons may petition the relevant minister for variation or revocation.[12] "The Minister must make the decision on the request as soon as reasonably practicable after receiving the information needed for making the decision."[13] The Minister is required to promptly notify the applicant in writing of the decision and its rationale, but may withhold specific details if they pertain to national security, international relations, the prevention or detection of serious crime, or if it serves the interests of justice.[14] Furthermore, the designated persons may also apply to the High Court (or Court of Session in Scotland) to delist. However, "[. . .] no court can hear a delisting application until the ministerial review process [. . .] has been exhausted."[15] This requirement likely aims to give the Minister a chance to resolve issues administratively, thus reducing court burden. Unlike this approach, the U.S., EU, and Australia allow direct access to judicial review without requiring applicants to exhaust administrative options first [6, 19, 23].

Limiting direct judicial access in the UK can affect applicants by (i) potentially causing significant delays if the ministerial review is prolonged or if there are administrative backlogs, thus delaying any relief from judicial oversight, and (ii) causing individuals or entities to suffer continued reputational, financial, or operational harm while awaiting a judicial hearing. To create a balanced system, a potential improvement could be to set a specific timeframe within which the Minister must decide on delisting applications. If this timeframe is not

---

11 Foreign, Commonwealth & Development *Office, UK sanctions (10 October 2024). https://www.gov.uk/guidance/uk-sanctions.*

12 *Foreign, Commonwealth & Development Office, How to request variation or revocation of a sanctions designation or review of a UN listing (2 February 2023). https://www.gov.uk/government/publications/making-a-sanctions-challenge-how-to-seek-variation-or-revocation-of-a-sanctions-designation/making-a-sanctions-challenge-how-to-seek-a-variation-or-revocation-of-a-sanctions-designation.*

13 *The Sanctions Review Procedure (EU Exit) Regulations 2018, Regulation 7. https://www.legislation.gov.uk/uksi/2018/1269/regulation/7.*

14 *The Sanctions Review Procedure (EU Exit) Regulations 2018, Regulation 8. https://www.legislation.gov.uk/uksi/2018/1269/regulation/8.*

15 "A UK lawyer's perspective on representing designated persons," *Global Investigations Review* (14 August 2024). https://globalinvestigationsreview.com/guide/the-guide-sanctions/fifth-edition/article/uk-lawyers-perspective-representing-designated-persons.

met, applicants would then be allowed to seek judicial review directly without waiting for the Minister's determination.

EU Sanctions

Within the EU, the Council of the EU ("the Council") manages sanctions imposition. Designated parties may appeal directly to the Council with supporting documentation to reconsider their status.[16] "Individual requests [to the Council] for de-listing should be processed, as soon as they arrive [. . .]."[17] However, similar to the administrative procedures in the U.S. and the UK, the timing of the Council's review is also not fixed. The General Court has first-instance jurisdiction over challenges to sanctions measures,[18] with its decisions appealable to the Court of Justice of the EU. Annulment actions must be filed within two months from the measure's publication, notification, or if unnotified, the date the applicant became aware of it.[19] It is not mandatory to exhaust the administrative review process for delisting by the Council before seeking judicial redress. Applicants may proceed directly to the General Court to challenge their designation. Compared to the approach in the UK, this EU procedure is more favorable for upholding the right to a fair trial and the right to an effective remedy because it grants direct access to an independent judicial body without the requirement to complete potentially lengthy administrative steps. This ensures faster judicial oversight, reduces delays in cases where reputational or financial harm may be immediate, and aligns with international fair trial standards by allowing an independent court, rather than the designating authority to review the legality of sanctions.

---

16 The European Council, How the EU adopts and reviews sanctions (6 May 2024).   https://www.consilium.europa.eu/en/policies/sanctions-adoption-review-procedure.

17 The 2012 Council Sanctions Guidelines (4 May 2018). https://data.consilium.europa.eu/doc/document/ST-5664-2018-INIT/en/pdf

18 Treaty on the Functioning of the European Union, Article 256(1). https://eur-lex.europa.eu/legal-content/EN/TXT/?uri=celex%3A12012E%2FTXT.

19 Treaty on the Functioning of the European Union, Article 263(6). https://eur-lex.europa.eu/legal-content/EN/TXT/?uri=celex%3A12012E%2FTXT.

Canada Sanctions

Canada sanctions are imposed by the Minister of Foreign Affairs.[20] While designated persons can submit a delisting request to the Minister of Foreign Affairs with relevant supporting information, they often lack access to the specific reasoning behind their designation, complicating any appeal: "[. . .] when an individual wants to be delisted, they must submit a request to GAC [Global Affairs Canada] with the relevant information. Nevertheless, GAC does not provide any material or information providing support for the decision to list an individual or entity. The sanctioned person, therefore, has no access to the reasons of the Minister [of Foreign Affairs] relied on in including the person or entity on a sanctions list. This complicates any challenge to the listing – it is, obviously, difficult to challenge a decision when it is impossible to know why it was taken."[21]

In this regard, Canada's sanctions process is more restrictive than those of its allies. For instance, in the UK, the Minister issues a summary of reasons when sanctioning an individual, while in the U.S., authorities provide guidelines explaining the sanctions process and acceptable grounds for challenging a listing [21]. Furthermore, a sanctioned party may also apply to the federal court to delist. However, the problem of access to information on the reasons for the decision being challenged in the court remains. This leaves sanctioned individuals at a disadvantage when seeking judicial review, as they cannot adequately build a case. This restrictive approach contrasts with more transparent practices in comparable jurisdictions, highlighting a gap in procedural fairness within Canada's sanctions regime.

---

20 Special Economic Measures Act *(S.C. 1992, c. 17)*, Section 6(1). https://laws-lois.justice.gc.ca/eng/acts/S-14.5/page-2.html#h-434114; Justice for Victims of Corrupt Foreign Officials Act (Sergei Magnitsky Law*) (S.C. 2017, c. 21)*, Section 2.1(1). https://laws.justice.gc.ca/eng/acts/J-2.3/page-1.html#h-1416531.

21 "Complexities of international sanctions: Recent cases shed light on delisting applications in Canada," *Dentons Canada Regulatory Review* (7 June 2023). https://www.canadaregulatoryreview.com/complexities-of-international-sanctions-recent-cases-shed-light-on-delisting-applications-in-canada.

Australia Sanctions

Australia sanctions are imposed by the Australian Government as a matter of Australian foreign policy,[22] with the Minister for Foreign Affairs and Department of Foreign Affairs and Trade ("DFAT") responsible for implementation. Designated individuals or entities may challenge their sanctions status in two ways:[23] (i) they may apply to the Minister for Foreign Affairs in writing for revocation, which must be reviewed within a reasonable, unspecified timeframe (which will depend on the nature of the case, given that a specific timetable for a response is not provided for), or (ii) they may pursue judicial review of either the original designation or the Minister's refusal to revoke it. Applicants may directly approach the court to challenge their designation without first seeking a review by the Minister for Foreign Affairs. This approach aligns with practices in the U.S. and the EU but contrasts with the UK, where applicants must exhaust the administrative review process before seeking judicial intervention, thus delaying access to independent review.

Challenges in Sanctions Review Processes and the Need for Reform

As noted earlier, the executive agencies serve as both enforcers and reviewers of sanctions across the said jurisdictions, casting doubt on impartiality and underscoring the need for a standardized, independent review mechanism to ensure due process. In this context, it should be noted that the judgment of March 2, 2021 of the CJEU (Criminal proceedings against H.K.) in Case C-746/18 ("the CJEU judgment")[24] addresses judicial oversight in the context of access to personal data for criminal proceedings. In this case the CJEU was asked to determine whether and under what conditions access to telecommunications data by authorities is permissible, particularly

---

22 Department of Foreign Affairs and Trade, *About sanctions.* https://www.dfat.gov.au/international-relations/security/sanctions/about-sanctions#:~:text=Australian%20autonomous%20sanctions%20regimes%20are,or%20be%20separate%20from%20them

23 Carter-Ruck law firm, Australia Sanctions. https://www.carter-ruck.com/international-sanctions-guides/australian-sanctions-guide/

24 Court of Justice of the EU, Judgment of 2 March 2021, at para. 53. https://curia.europa.eu/juris/document/document.jsf?docid=238381&mode=req&pageIndex=1&dir=&occ=first&part=1&text=&doclang=EN&cid=9410193

concerning privacy rights under EU law. The CJEU emphasized that any body which is responsible for reviewing such sensitive access must be independent, objective, and impartial. To ensure impartiality, the CJEU stated that this body "must be a third party" [24, at para. 54], distinct from the investigative authority, to carry out its duties with objectivity. The CJEU judgment reiterated that adherence to independence standards protects fundamental rights and ensures fair, unbiased decisions.

The CJEU judgment is relevant to sanctions review processes because, similar to access to personal data, sanctions decisions can significantly impact individual rights, including reputation, financial status, and freedom of movement. In many jurisdictions, the same executive bodies that impose sanctions also handle reviews or appeals, raising concerns about impartiality and potential conflicts of interest. Applying the CJEU's standards for independence in this context underscores the need for a review mechanism that is free from the influence of sanction-imposing bodies. The CJEU underscored that, "[w]here that review is carried out not by a court but by an independent administrative body, that body must have a status enabling it to act objectively and impartially when carrying out its duties and must, for that purpose, be free from any external influence (see, to that effect, judgment of March 9, 2010, *Commission v. Germany,* C-518/07, EU:C:2010:125,[25] and Opinion 1/15 (EU-Canada PNR Agreement) of July 26, 2017, EU:C:2017:592[26])."

Applying these independence criteria to sanctions regimes, an administrative body reviewing sanctions must also maintain these characteristics. Specifically, it should: (i) be structurally and functionally distinct from the agency imposing the sanctions; (ii) have decision-making autonomy to avoid pressure or influence from sanction-imposing bodies; (iii) operate with a mandate to uphold impartiality in assessing cases on an objective basis, free from conflicts of interest.

---

25 Court of Justice of the EU, Judgment of 9 March 2010, *Commission v. Germany,* C-518/07, EU:C:2010:125, at para. 25. https://eur-lex.europa.eu/ legal-content/en/ TXT/HTML/?uri=ecli:ECLI%3AEU%3AC%3A2010%3A125&anchor=#point25

26 Opinion 1/15 (EU-Canada PNR Agreement) of 26 July 2017, EU:C:2017:592, at paras. 229–230. https://eur-lex.europa.eu/legal-content/en/TXT/ HTML/?uri=ecli:ECLI%3AEU%3AC%3A2017%3A592&anchor=#point229

In line with these principles, national frameworks could consider assigning this review role to institutions like the Ministry of Justice or the Office of the Attorney General, as they could meet the neutrality standards highlighted by the CJEU. This rationale also supports calls for establishing an independent review body at the international level with binding authority, similar to the European Court of Human Rights ("ECHR"), to enhance fairness and due process in sanctions decisions. This body would enhance human rights oversight in sanctions without serving as an appeals body for national courts or the CJEU. Its core role would be to ensure compliance with human rights standards across sanctions decisions, while leaving national and EU judicial authority intact. This mechanism would enable individuals to seek redress for potential human rights violations in different sanctions regimes, offering a dedicated layer of oversight that respects national jurisdictions and the CJEU's role.

The absence of clear international standards for the protection of fundamental rights in sanctions enforcement has led to disproportionate effects on persons, particularly vulnerable groups. The over-compliance phenomenon, in which businesses and financial institutions exceed the requirements of sanctions to avoid perceived risks, further restricts access to essential goods, financial services and humanitarian assistance.

The absence of specific deadlines in sanctions review processes across various countries also creates uncertainty for individuals and entities seeking removal from sanctions lists, potentially prolonging the reputational, financial and operational harms they face. This lack of deadlines can lead to significant delays, as reviews are completed within an undefined "reasonable" timeframe. To mitigate these delays and uphold fairness, setting specific timelines for reviewing decisions, with extensions allowed only for clearly justified reasons, could increase efficiency and reduce costs. This approach balances applicants' needs for resolution against the requirements of a comprehensive review process.

In Canada, sanctioned individuals and entities do not have access to information about the reasons for their sanctioning, making it difficult for them to challenge the listing. In contrast, the U.S. and UK take a more balanced approach by providing a summary of reasons for listing or general grounds for challenging sanctions. However, specific details may still be withheld to protect national security, international relations, or prevent serious crime. Judicial review of sanctions is generally limited to verifying whether the executive has followed formal procedures and specific grounds for designation, without assessing the substantive justification for imposing sanctions. This limitation is justified in order to prevent the judiciary from encroaching on the powers of the executive, particularly in areas of foreign policy and national security. In the interests of fairness, however, additional safeguards as described earlier should be provided for listed individuals and entities to compensate for this limitation.

There is a practice of sanctioning parties solely based on family connections rather than individual actions, which undermines both fairness and the credibility of sanctions. Sanctions should target the specific conduct of specific individuals rather than taking a scattergun approach. In one recent case an adult son of a prominent business and public person (who had no involvement whatsoever with the father's business affairs) was nevertheless sanctioned by OFAC, purely due to his family relationship. This case underscores the need for national policies that ensure sanctions are applied based on individual actions rather than mere associations, thus avoiding punitive measures against uninvolved family members.

Unfortunately, sanctions have at times been applied as tools to pressure individuals into cooperation or to pursue objectives beyond addressing direct security or policy concerns. As the experiences of our clients demonstrate, sanctions can be used as leverage, aiming to induce certain actions or alignments rather than to mitigate specific security threats. This approach can compromise the perceived legitimacy of sanctions as genuine diplomatic tools by blurring the line between enforcing security measures and pursuing coercive political aims. Cases such as this, where sanctions were seemingly applied to force cooperation, raise significant ethical concerns about the implementation of sanctions.

All of the issues outlined above should be addressed not only through the proposed reforms at the national level, but also through the harmonization of sanctions policies at the multilateral level, as discussed in more detail below.

Reforms at the multilateral level are essential for several key reasons:

Limitations of UN Sanctions: UN sanctions were created to support global peace and address issues such as nuclear proliferation and human rights abuses. However, Article 27(3) of the UN Charter[27] grants veto power to each permanent member of the Security Council, enabling any one of them to block sanction resolutions against any state. This setup allows a single permanent member to prevent the adoption of sanctions, underscoring a fundamental limitation in the Security Council's capacity to apply sanctions universally and consistently.

Lack of Unified Sanctions Standards: Even among closely allied nations, significant differences exist in their sanctions policies. This leads to varied legal outcomes, which impact compliance and the perceived fairness of sanctions regimes. OFAC has broad authority to impose a range of sanctions, including sanctions that restrict trade, finance, and other activities, as well as secondary sanctions, which penalize third-country entities conducting business with sanctioned entities, as seen in U.S. sanctions against Iran and Venezuela. By contrast, the EU generally avoids secondary sanctions and prioritizes human rights considerations, which has led to differences in enforcement and protections for designated individuals. The UK differs from the U.S. in its restrictions and criteria for designation. Australia's sanctions policies align with those of the U.S. and EU but maintain distinct criteria for humanitarian considerations. These variations complicate compliance for multinational businesses operating across borders, as entities must navigate different legal frameworks, which can lead to inconsistent application and challenges in maintaining uniform policies globally.

A more unified framework at the multilateral level could address these challenges by promoting consistency, fairness, and predictability, reinforcing sanctions as a legitimate tool of international diplomacy.

---

27 Charter of the United Nations, Article 27. https://legal.un.org/repertory/art27.shtml

Human Rights Considerations in Sanctions Adjudication

Under the Universal Declaration of Human Rights (UDHR)[28] and the International Covenant on Civil and Political Rights (ICCPR),[29] several key provisions impact sanctions by protecting fundamental rights directly related to fair adjudication.

Right to a Fair Hearing

The right to a fair and public hearing, as protected by Article 10 of the UDHR [28] and Article 14 of the ICCPR [29], is essential in the context of sanctions where individuals or entities need a meaningful opportunity to challenge their designation before an impartial tribunal. This right is compromised when executive bodies responsible for sanctions also manage reviews, creating a risk of bias within the process. Without independent oversight, procedural safeguards are weakened, and sanctioned individuals lack a genuine chance to present their case effectively.

Protection of Property

Article 17 of the UDHR [28] upholds the right to property, prohibiting arbitrary deprivation. Sanctions, particularly asset freezes, directly impact this right and those affected may lose control of essential financial resources, which jeopardizes their financial stability and livelihood. Independent review mechanisms are vital to prevent arbitrary or excessive restrictions, ensuring that any limitations on property rights are justified and fairly applied.

Right to an Effective Remedy

The right to an effective remedy, emphasized in Article 8 of the UDHR [28] and Article 2(3) of the ICCPR [29], requires that sanctioned individuals or entities can challenge sanctions before a neutral body. When executive agencies act as both enforcers and reviewers, the impartiality of the review process is inherently compromised,

---

28 Universal Declaration of Human Rights. https://www.un.org/en/about-us/universal-declaration-of-human-rights

29 International Covenant on Civil and Political Rights. https://www.ohchr.org/en/instruments-mechanisms/instruments/international-covenant-civil-and-political-rights

restricting available remedies and weakening the overall integrity of the system.

Right to Privacy

Articles 12 of the UDHR [28] and 17 of the ICCPR [29] protect individuals from arbitrary interference with their privacy, family, home, or correspondence. Sanctions often extend beyond a financial impact, affecting personal and social connections and intruding upon individuals' private lives. The absence of independent oversight increases the likelihood of unjust intrusions, compromising privacy rights and infringing on personal freedoms without due consideration.

This is well demonstrated by the high-profile case of the Venezuelan Special Envoy and humanitarian entrepreneur, Alex Saab. His case highlights significant concerns about the right to a fair hearing and the presumption of innocence where allegations blur the lines between administrative sanctions and criminal proceedings.

On July 25, 2019, OFAC imposed sanctions on Alex Saab,[30] alleging his involvement in a bribery scheme related to the Venezuelan food aid program known as CLAP.[31] This program was intended to address food shortages during Venezuela's economic blockade by the U.S. Notably, on the same day, the Florida Southern District Court indicted Saab on separate charges connected to a Venezuelan housing program.[32]

When sanctions are applied alongside criminal charges, they can create a presumption of guilt, swaying public opinion and potentially prejudicing legal proceedings. Furthermore, sanctioned persons face significant obstacles in mounting an effective defense, as both access to the necessary expertise and the financial resources to fund it are severely limited. These restrictions not only affect their ability to secure qualified legal representation, but also impede their access to other essential specialists, effectively undermining their right to a defense.

---

30 United States Department of Treasury, "Press Release SM-741" (2023). https://home.treasury.gov/news/press-releases/sm741

31 The Local Committees for Supply and Production [Spanish: Comité Local de Abastecimiento y Producción].

32 United States Department of Justice, "Alex Nain Saab Moran FCPA Case" (2023). https://www.justice.gov/criminal/criminal-fraud/fcpa/cases/alex-nain-saab-moran

Call for Reform

To enhance the protection of sanctioned persons' rights, fairness and alignment with international standards in sanctions regimes, improvements should be pursued at both national and multilateral levels. This involves addressing several critical issues that undermine the legitimacy and effectiveness of sanctions as a tool for diplomacy and security.

Measures to be Implemented on the National Level

States should establish frameworks that prioritize due process and impartiality in sanctions enforcement. Key measures include:

Independent Review Bodies. Each country could designate an independent body, such as the Ministry of Justice or the Office of the Attorney General, separate from the executive authorities responsible for imposing sanctions, to conduct unbiased reviews. This separation promotes impartial oversight.

Access to Reasons for Designation. National legislation should mandate that sanctioned individuals and entities be provided access to sufficient information about the grounds of their designation, including at least a summary of evidence. This transparency allows listed parties to understand the rationale behind sanctions and to prepare an informed delisting application.

Clear Procedures for Contesting Designations. Established procedures should include specific, transparent deadlines that allow sanctioned individuals to challenge designations and seek delisting within a defined timeframe, thereby reducing prolonged uncertainty.

Protection Against Abuse of Sanctions on Family Members. Sanctioning individuals solely because of family connections, rather than their own actions, undermines both fairness and the credibility of sanctions. National policies should establish clear guidelines to ensure that sanctions are based on a person's conduct, not merely on their associations.

Restrictions on Sanctions Use in Criminal Proceedings. Sanctions should not be excessively employed in criminal contexts in ways that undermine the presumption of innocence. Governments should ensure that sanctions are not prematurely applied to suspects in criminal cases, as such use can unfairly influence public perception and judicial impartiality.

Preventing Sanctions as a Tool of Coercion. Sanctions should not be used to coerce individuals into political cooperation or other objectives. Misusing sanctions in this manner erodes the credibility of sanctions as a legitimate foreign policy tool. National frameworks should implement ethical standards and oversight mechanisms to prevent coercive misuse of sanctions.

Measures to be Implemented on the Multilateral Level

A unified multilateral approach would enhance consistency, fairness, and legitimacy across sanctions regimes:

Adoption of a Multilateral Convention on Sanctions Standards. States could conclude an international convention to standardize criteria and procedural safeguards for the imposition, review, and removal of sanctions. This would align sanctions practices with international human rights standards, promoting consistency and adherence to due process. Such an approach aligns with the necessity of a human rights-based approach in sanctions enforcement, ensuring that sanctions do not disproportionately impact humanitarian access or the fundamental rights of affected persons.

Creation of an International Oversight Body. Such a convention could establish an independent international body, composed of representatives from each signatory State, to monitor compliance with the convention's standards. This body would act as an impartial arbiter, and its decisions should be binding on member States, similar to the ECHR. This binding authority would ensure uniform adherence to fair and due process standards across jurisdictions. This oversight body should ensure that affected individuals and businesses have access to effective legal remedies and are not obstructed from seeking redress due to sanctions-related restrictions.

Uniform Criteria for Imposition and Delisting. Setting consistent standards for designation, review, and delisting would minimize the risk of arbitrary sanctions.

Together, these reforms would establish a balanced framework that upholds the rule of law, human rights protections, and procedural fairness. Both national and multilateral measures would strengthen the legitimacy and effectiveness of sanctions regimes globally, ensuring they are applied in a just, consistent, and rights-respecting manner.

Conclusion

A balanced and consistent sanctions framework is essential to uphold human rights and reduce the negative effects of sanctions. The current structure of sanctions regimes in various jurisdictions, including the U.S., UK, EU, Canada and Australia, lacks independent review mechanisms, leading to concerns about impartiality, transparency, and due process. The absence of fixed timelines for delisting prolongs uncertainty, while limited access to designation reasoning prevents effective challenges. Judicial reviews often focus on procedural compliance rather than assessing the validity of sanctions imposition, reducing meaningful oversight. Sanctions are sometimes applied arbitrarily, including cases where individuals are targeted based on family ties rather than personal conduct. By adopting independent review mechanisms, ensuring transparent procedures, and establishing a multilateral convention on sanctions standards, States can foster a system that protects the rights of sanctioned persons during the application of sanctions.

Furthermore, it is crucial that States avoid shifting responsibility to non-governmental actors, including businesses and humanitarian organizations, and that all actors integrate a precautionary humanitarian approach into their decision-making processes when enforcing sanctions. The absence of standardized criteria across jurisdictions has led to discrepancies in enforcement. A unified convention would harmonize key principles governing sanctions, including clear criteria for imposition and delisting, protections against politically motivated designations, and safeguards against the misuse of sanctions for coercive purposes. National and international reforms—ranging from clear criteria for sanctions to binding oversight—can create a rights-respecting, fair, and effective sanctions regime. These improvements would establish a unified approach that supports due process, mitigates potential abuses, and promotes global stability.

CHAPTER 19

Lawfulness of Multiple Sanctioning Systems Under *Ne Bis in Idem*

Mykhailo Grydzhuk[1] | *Rafat Rizvi[2]*

Abstract

This chapter examines the intersection of unilateral coercive measures in the form of targeted sanctions and criminal prosecutions through the lens of Ne Bis in Idem, which prohibits double punishment for the same offense. It explores how sanctions, often framed as diplomatic tools, function as punitive measures akin to criminal penalties, blurring the line between administrative and criminal law. The chapter highlights the growing trend of States using sanctions alongside or prior to criminal charges, creating a presumption of guilt, restricting access to legal remedies, and undermining the right to a fair trial. Drawing on case studies and legal precedents, it analyzes jurisdictional inconsistencies in applying Ne Bis in Idem across international legal frameworks, particularly within the European Union and the United States. The study argues that sanctions, when quasi-criminal in nature, should be subject to the same legal protections as criminal prosecutions to prevent overlapping punitive actions. Ultimately, it calls for a harmonized international legal framework to regulate the concurrent use of sanctions and prosecutions, ensuring that individuals are not subjected to parallel punitive measures in violation of fundamental legal principles.

---

1 Counsel, Amadeus Consultancy Limited, London, United Kingdom
2 Senior Advisor. Amadeus Consultancy Limited, London, United Kingdom

Introduction

The principle of *Ne Bis in Idem*, which safeguards individuals from being punished or prosecuted multiple times for the same offense, faces new challenges in the context of modern international enforcement. Traditionally unilateral coercive measures were used as broad economic measures against States; however, the increasing reliance on smart or targeted sanctions aimed at specific individuals, companies and organizations has transformed their role.

These sanctions, often imposed through executive or administrative decisions, now function as quasi-criminal penalties, restricting financial access, freezing assets and limiting movement without due process. This shift raises critical concerns about whether such measures, when paired with formal criminal prosecutions, violate fundamental legal protections.

Unlike traditional criminal proceedings, which require judicial oversight and due process, smart sanctions are often applied preemptively and based on political or diplomatic considerations, leaving affected individuals with limited avenues for appeal. As states increasingly employ targeted sanctions as enforcement mechanisms alongside criminal charges, the boundaries between administrative measures and punitive actions become blurred.

Intersection of Sanctions and Criminal Prosecutions Under *Ne Bis in Idem*

Quasi-Criminal Nature of Sanctions

The last decade has been marked by an unprecedented surge in the use of unilateral coercive measures, predominantly in the form of targeted financial and economic restrictions. These measures, though framed as tools of diplomacy and accountability,[3] often overstep international law, raising questions about their legitimacy.

In certain cases, foreign governments, under the guise of upholding international order, exert jurisdictional overreach using unilateral restrictive measures, including targeted economic and financial restrictions. These measures, often referred to as sanctions or unilateral

---

3 European External Action Service (EEAS), European Union Sanctions (accessed 27 February 2025). https://www.eeas.europa.eu/eeas/european-union-sanctions_en

coercive measures, are imposed without international consensus and function as tools of economic pressure.

In this context, targeted sanctions carry consequences similar to criminal penalties, particularly those involving asset freezes, travel bans and financial restrictions. Once imposed, sanctions often create an aura of illegality, thus effectively laying the groundwork for subsequent criminal charges.

In this context, the principle of *Ne Bis in Idem*, which protects individuals from being tried or punished multiple times for the same offense, takes on a renewed significance. As governments continue to leverage sanctions in tandem with criminal proceedings, the question arises: should *Ne Bis in Idem* apply when sanctions are imposed, particularly given the quasi-criminal nature of these measures?

These measures are often pursued alongside or prior to formal criminal charges, exacerbating the burden on affected parties and undermining legal safeguards against double punishment. This also creates a perilous dynamic, where individuals find themselves ensnared in a legal quagmire: sanctioned by multiple jurisdictions and then subjected to a criminal prosecution which has emerged out of the shadow of sanctions.

This chapter seeks to explore the lawfulness of systems of parallel measures, analyzing whether international legal frameworks can be adapted to prevent overlapping punitive actions that violate the fundamental principles of justice.

At the international level, *Ne Bis In Idem* is articulated in several key legal documents which protect fundamental rights;[4] however, despite its widespread recognition, the principle is not considered customary international law.[5] Thus, no general rule obliges States to recognize the principle across borders.[6] As clarified in General

---

4 International Covenant on Civil and Political Rights (1966), Art. 14(7).; American Convention on Human Rights (1969), Art. 8(4).; European Convention on Human Rights (1984), Protocol No. 7, Art. 4.; Statute of the International Criminal Court (1998), Art. 20.; Statute of the International Criminal Court (1998), Art. 20. Charter of Fundamental Rights of the European Union (2000), Art. 50.

5 Schomburg W (2012) " Criminal matters: transnational ne bis in idem in Europe – conflict of jurisdictions – transfer of proceedings." *ERA Forum* 13(3): 311–324.

6 Vervaele JAE (2005) "The transnational ne bis in idem principle in the EU. Mutual recognition and equivalent protection of human rights," *Utrecht Law Rev* 1(2): 100–118.

Comment No. 32 of the UN Human Rights Committee, the protection provided under Article 14(7) of the International Covenant on Civil and Political Rights does not guarantee different States from prosecuting the same conduct under their respective legal systems.[7]

Furthermore, interpretations of the principle can vary significantly across different jurisdictions. For example, the Organization of American States' American Convention on Human Rights restricts the prohibition to retrials after acquittals, whilst in the United States, a final verdict is not a strict requirement to prevent a second prosecution for the same offense.[8] This protection is one of the least understood and the U.S. Supreme Court has done little to clarify its meaning,[9] struggling to maintain a consistent interpretation of the double jeopardy clause.[10]

While *Ne Bis In Idem* traditionally applies within the criminal law sphere, the quasi-criminal nature of sanctions, especially when coupled with criminal proceedings, warrants its extension. This interpretation emphasizes that the principle should be applied to prevent overlapping sanctions and prosecutions thus upholding fairness and legal certainty.

Challenges Faced by Individuals Subjected to Both Sanctions and Criminal Proceedings

Imposition of Sanctions and Parallel Criminal Prosecutions

Sanctions imposed unilaterally can disproportionately impact the targeted individuals or entities.

Furthermore, the application of targeted sanctions, especially those with extraterritorial effects, can often create a situation of legal uncertainty and over-compliance, where the boundaries between

---

7 UN Human Rights Committee (HRC), General Comment No. 32, Article 14, Right to Equality Before Courts and Tribunals and to Fair Trial, CCPR/C/GC/32, 23 August 2007, https://www.refworld.org/legal/general/hrc/2007/en/52583 [accessed 27 February 2025].

8 Supreme Court of the United States, *United States v. Scott*, 92 [1978]; *Green v. United States*, 188 [1957].

9 Supreme Court of the United States, *Whalen v. United States*, 699 (Rehnquist, J., dissenting) [1980].

10 George C. Thomas III, *Double Jeopardy: The History, The Law* (New York: University Press, 1998).

administrative sanctions and criminal penalties become blurred. This over-compliance, driven by the fear of inadvertently violating sanctions regulations, can significantly hamper the ability of affected individuals to access essential goods, services, and legal remedies. Therefore, States must take responsibility for ensuring that sanctions are designed and implemented in a way that avoids hindering the provision of critical infrastructure and humanitarian assistance.[11]

In European Union law, *Ne Bis in Idem* has been extended to certain administrative sanctions with punitive effects. This principle applies when a measure, despite being administrative, functions as a form of punishment akin to criminal penalties and thus should prevent parallel criminal prosecution for the same conduct.[12]

It follows from the decision of the Court of Justice of the European Union in the case of *Åklagaren v. Hans Åkerberg Fransson,* which dealt with the imposition of tax fines followed by criminal prosecution, that when an administrative sanction is criminal in nature *Ne Bis In Idem* would apply: "It is only if the tax penalty is criminal in nature for the purposes of Article 50 of the Charter [Charter of Fundamental Rights of the European Union] and has become final that that provision precludes criminal proceedings in respect of the same acts from being brought against the same person."[13] Moreover, it was further affirmed in *Åklagaren v. Hans Åkerberg Fransson* by the Court of Justice of the European Union that *Ne Bis in Idem* only applies to penalties and proceedings that are criminal in nature.

Sanctions in the form of asset freezes, travel bans and restrictions on economic activities, imposed without a criminal trial, have similar effects to criminal penalties. When these measures are imposed alongside or in addition to formal criminal prosecutions, they can create a situation where individuals face multiple forms of punishment for the same conduct, theoretically contravening the principle of *Ne Bis in Idem*.

---

11 Recommendations of the Participants of the International Conference on Sanctions, Business, and Human Rights, Geneva, 22 November 2024, https://www.ohchr.org/sites/default/files/documents/issues/ucm/events/international-conf-sanctions-business-hr/recommendations-nongovernmental-actors.pdf [accessed 27 February 2025].

12 Case C-617/10 *Åklagaren v. Hans Åkerberg Fransson* [2013] ECR I-0000

13 CJEU, *TN v. ENISA,* §103 [2019]; Menci, §25 [2018]; Garlsson Real Estate and Others, §27 [2018]; Spasic, §53 [2014].

In contrast, some countries, such as the United States, that rely on unilateral sanctions, have traditionally treated these measures as distinct from criminal prosecutions. This way they escape the constraints of double jeopardy protections, but their quasi-criminal nature makes them functionally equivalent to criminal penalties, in many respects raising significant questions about the lawfulness of such an approach.

One example of this overlap can be seen in the case of a businessman[14] engaged in international trade who was sanctioned by the United States Office of Foreign Assets Control (OFAC) for the alleged acts of bribery linked to his business. Due to confidentiality agreements, further details of the referenced cases cannot be disclosed, as noted in footnote 19. Subsequently, the United States brought criminal charges against him for the exact same conduct. According to the said indictment, the criminal proceedings also involve a substantial forfeiture of over US$1 billion.

Violation of Ne Bis in Idem *in the Above Case*

Ne Bis in Idem is widely recognized as a principle that protects individuals from facing multiple punitive actions for the same offense, ensuring that they are not tried or punished twice for the same conduct.

In this context, in the above case, *Ne Bis in Idem* appears to be violated by the initial imposition of sanctions by OFAC followed by a subsequent criminal prosecution for the same underlying conduct. The initial asset freeze restricted the businessman's access to financial resources, essentially functioning as a punitive measure. This was compounded by the inclusion of more than US$1 billion forfeiture request in the indictment, signalling the prosecution's intent to deprive the businessman of assets if convicted. The criminal case is currently ongoing and the presence of the forfeiture in the indictment amplifies the punitive effect of the combined measures, effectively subjecting the businessman to double punitive actions for the same conduct thereby undermining the essence of *Ne Bis in Idem*.

Such a compounded approach raises fundamental questions about fairness and proportionality. As noted earlier, when sanctions are applied before criminal charges, they create a presumption of

---

14 Due to confidentiality agreements, the authors cannot provide further details.

guilt, influencing public opinion and potentially prejudicing legal proceedings.

Limitations on Access to Fair Trial and Legal Remedies

The dual punitive actions taken against the businessman in the above case infringed upon his fundamental rights. Primarily, his right to a fair trial,[15] as the sanctions not only imply guilt but also restrict his access to financial resources required for his defense and/or to challenge the imposition of sanctions.

Moreover, the case highlights that, in order to prevent similar violations, an international framework is required to harmonize the imposition of sanctions and any related criminal prosecutions to avoid overlapping actions.

Conclusion

The growing convergence of sanctions and criminal prosecutions presents a significant challenge to the rule of law, particularly in situations where individuals are subjected to both measures simultaneously. This overlap undermines fundamental legal principles, including *Ne Bis in Idem*.

There is a clear and urgent need for reform in this area to harmonize the imposition of sanctions and criminal prosecutions. It should be agreed on the multilateral level that States will, on the best-efforts basis:

(a) Avoid the imposition of sanctions followed by criminal prosecutions for the same conduct.

(b) Apply the principle of *Ne Bis In Idem* as sanctions are administrative in nature but result in punitive measures.

(c) Sanctions often target a conduct which is outside of the jurisdiction of the sanctioning State. Prosecution for the same conduct would not only violate the principle of *Ne Bis In Idem* but would also risk resulting in extraterritorial judicial overreach, which is a trend that should be monitored and discouraged.

---

15 Universal Declaration of Human Rights (1948), Art. 10. International Covenant on Civil and Political Rights (1966), Art. 14(1).

In conclusion, as the international legal landscape continues to evolve, it is crucial that legal frameworks adapt to prevent individuals from being caught in overlapping punitive measures. A harmonized approach is essential to safeguard the rights of individuals and preserve the integrity of international law, ensuring that punitive actions do not violate fundamental principles of justice.

CHAPTER 20

Sanctions as a Ground to Refuse Contractual Performance or to Escape from Liability for Failure to Perform

Alexey Anischenko[1] | *Vitali Vabishchevich*[2]

Abstract

   This research attempts to reveal the impact of sanctions on the normal course of foreign trade with references to the real practical cases of the authors, available judicial and arbitration practice in Belarus, including the experience of the Belarusian Chamber of Commerce and Industry. The authors consider the typical situations provoked by sanctions, based on the subjective attitude of the parties affected by them, e.g. the problem of over-compliance, breach of the contract, withdrawal from it, qualification of sanctions as force majeure etc.

Introduction

   Are sanctions a proper legal instrument or are unilateral economic, financial and trade measures not in accordance with the principles of international law or provisions of the UN Charter sanctions or "self-sanctioning"?[3] Regardless of the correct answer, sanctions have

---

1 Partner at Anischenko Laptev, Board member of Chamber of Arbitrators in Minsk, Belarus and member of Public Advisory Board at the State Customs Committee of the Republic of Belarus and VIAC International Advisory Board, senior lecturer at the Belarusian State University, arbitrator, mediator

2 PhD, Head of the Department of Legal Support and Digital Technologies of the Belarusian Chamber of Commerce and Industry (BelCCI), Member of the Presidium of the International Arbitration Court at the BelCCI, Advisory Committee on Entrepreneurship at the Eurasian Economic Commission, arbitrator, mediator

3 Situation where a company makes a voluntary decision to limit its own

already had a significant and probably irreversible impact on international trade, which will always be based on a foreign trade contract between the parties to a foreign economic transaction. Conscientious participants of foreign economic activity almost without notice found themselves in a situation where sanctions at one moment "paralyzed" the performance of obligations under concluded foreign trade contracts. And in many cases, a way out of this situation has not yet been found, and courts and arbitration institutions around the world will have to seek a fair solution to international commercial disputes provoked by sanctions for a long time to come.

The "struggle of jurisdictions," i.e. determination of the legal status of sanctions in different legal systems, has led to ambiguous approaches to assessing their impact on the performance of contracts, the legality of refusal of obligations, and the recognition of force majeure. Sanctions restrictions have become a real obstacle to obtaining qualified legal assistance and access to fair and independent resolution of disputes by means of international commercial arbitration, traditionally perceived as a truly neutral forum. Business entities are forced to "navigate" in conditions of legal uncertainty, to always be on alert when carrying out of their foreign economic activity, promptly respond to emerging risks and try to foresee future ones.

In this paper, the authors tried to reflect on the impact of sanctions on the normal course of foreign trade, based on the analysis of available judicial and arbitration practice in the Republic of Belarus,[4] including the accumulated experience of the Belarusian Chamber of Commerce and Industry (BelCCI) in considering applications of business entities on certifying the events of force majeure prompted by sanctions, as well as to recommend on possible mitigation of the negative impact of sanctions on the conclusion and fulfilment of foreign trade contracts in the context of the Guiding Principles on Sanctions, Business and Human Rights prepared by the Special Rapporteur (Guiding Principles).

---

activities in response to potential sanctions, even if those sanctions are not yet legally imposed or directly applicable.

4 Authors would like to express sincere appreciation of the contribution to this part of research by Ms. Darya Korsak, 4th year international law student at the Faculty of International Law of the Belarusian State University.

Sanctions in Local Legal Context and Their Negative Impact on Foreign Trade Contracts

As already mentioned, the cornerstone of international trade and its lawful implementation is a foreign trade contract. The foundation of a foreign trade contract is the agreement of the parties on its subject matter and other terms, based on party autonomy.[5] Nowadays such party autonomy is, however, greatly limited by sanctions, as will be shown below with practical examples of performance (or rather non-performance) of foreign trade contracts involving Belarusian parties.

Each State is primarily oriented towards protecting its own interests and building its sovereign economic and political system. States pursue these fundamental goals in various ways, including by creating unique legal frameworks that shape their public order and national imperatives. To build common approaches in the international arena, States, based on mutual benefit, conclude interstate agreements, as well as enter or become founders of interstate associations, empowering them to create uniform rules that take into account diverse social, economic and legal systems, aimed at eliminating barriers and obstacles.[6]

The Preamble to the Charter of the United Nations Organization (UN Charter) affirms the necessity to establish conditions under which justice and respect for the obligations arising from treaties and other sources of international law can be maintained.[7]

Restrictions of all kinds at the State level are not and cannot be considered as violations when their adoption is dictated by the defense of national interests and is not aimed at damaging third parties. Such measures can include various kinds of tariff and non-tariff measures,

---

5 V. Vabishchevich, *Applicable Law Governing the Foreign Economic Transaction: Based On The Agreement Of The Parties.* Available at: https://ilex-private.ilex.by/

6 For example, States conclude bilateral or multilateral assistance treaties on mutual legal assistance, investment protection, avoidance of double taxation, etc. As to interstate associations, Belarus actively participates in the Eurasian Economic Union (EAEU), the Commonwealth of Independent States (CIS), Shanghai Cooperation Organization (SCO) and other organizations.

7 UNCIO XV, 335; amendments by General Assembly Resolution in UNTS 557, 143/638, 308/892, 119.

licensing of exports of "sensitive" goods, export restrictions in order to safeguard, e.g. one's own food security, etc.

Any restrictive measures at the international level should be based on legal norms and can only be adopted in accordance with an established procedure. For instance, Article 41 of the UN Charter authorizes the UN Security Council to decide "what measures not involving the use of armed force are to be employed to give effect to its decisions ... [t]hese may include complete or partial interruption of economic relations and of rail, sea, air, postal, telegraphic, radio, and other means of communication, and the severance of diplomatic relations."

Hence, it seems logical and reasonable that unilateral restrictions of an economic nature imposed on Belarus by other states are referred to as "unilateral sanctions," "restrictions," etc. Nevertheless, there is a pattern of "avoiding" the use of the term "sanctions" in the domestic legal environment as well. Firstly, the "avoidance" of direct reference to the word "sanctions" may be related to a negative attitude to sanctions as a legal phenomenon since they are usually considered illegitimate and contrary to international law.[8] Secondly, the term "sanctions" is habitually interpreted in the domestic legal environment as a measure of punishment, i.e. to impose a "sanction" means to "punish."[9]

While individual States and interstate associations represented by public authorities are constantly updating "sanctions packages," business entities in a "shock mode" are trying to carry on their foreign economic activities within the permitted limits.

This "shock mode" always affects the interests of all parties involved in a foreign economic transaction. Let's take one of the cases we faced as an illustration. An Italian seller received a partial pre-payment from a Belarusian buyer for the production and delivery of wood processing equipment, engaged subcontractors, and eventually produced a state-of-the-art machine. However, due to certain sectoral sanctions affecting the banking industry, the whole deal broke apart

---

8 Constitutional Court of the Republic of Belarus, Decision No. P-1286/2021 dated December 15, 2021, On the compliance with generally recognized principles and norms of international law of documents adopted (issued) by the European Union, some foreign States and their bodies, providing for the introduction of restrictive measures in relation to the Republic of Belarus, resolutive part.

9 V. Vabishchevich, *Sanctions against Belarus: Terminology, their Legal Nature and Characteristics, Sanction Compliance.* Available at: https://ilex-private.ilex.by/

even though neither the buyer, who was the end user, nor the seller, nor any of the subcontractors were individually targeted by sanctions. They had over 20 years of thriving business relationships and genuinely wanted to continue. But in the end the Italian company could not receive the second part of payment, could not deliver the goods, and moreover, could not even return the prepayment and got stuck with not even being able to resell the machine, which was tailor made for this unique technological project. On the other hand, the Belarusian buyer could not pay the price and get the ordered equipment, put it into operation and start generating revenues to pay loans and salaries to several thousands of people, who need to feed their families.[10]

In such situations, even if the partnership relations are eventually maintained, it is extremely difficult to find a mutually beneficial solution, as sanctions affect not only payments and logistics, but also settlement of disputes, recognition and enforcement of judgment and even risks of criminal prosecution if there is a suspicion of circumvention of sanctions by national controlling authorities.

There are many such examples, and in practice the issue of the possibility and legality of using "sanctions" as ground for refusal to perform a contract or for exemption from liability for its breach at some point in time becomes relevant.

Refusal or termination of a foreign trade contract is based on its terms and rules of applicable law, as well as the potentially peremptory norms of other relevant jurisdictions, *inter alia* the countries of domicile (registration) of the parties. Imperative and public policy considerations may also play a role, as sanctions are imposed and implemented by normative legal acts belonging to the legal system of the States that enacted them. At the same time, in several countries, including Belarus, sanctions are recognized at the constitutional level as illegal and contrary to the norms of international law.[10]

This is of particular importance when the law of the Republic of Belarus is applied to a foreign trade contract between a Belarusian resident and a resident of an "unfriendly" jurisdiction (i.e. one that imposes or recognizes the legality of sanctions). It should be taken into account that Belarus is a party to the United Nations Convention on Contracts for the International Sale of Goods (Vienna Convention),[11]

---

10 The source of this information is protected by confidentiality obligations.

11 United Nations, Convention on Contracts for the International Sale of Goods

and the norms of the Vienna Convention are the part of the Belarusian legislation and as a rule are applied by courts and arbitration institutions located in the Belarusian territory as the main statute, while the norms of national law are applied subsidiarily.

The range of possible grounds and reasons for refusal to perform a foreign trade contract is wide, ranging from reciprocal, and sometimes mutually beneficial, when the parties themselves agree to terminate the foreign trade contract without mutual claims, up to bad faith deliberate avoidance (apparently, hoping that such a breach of a foreign trade contract will not entail negative consequences for the party in breach or even create some financial or other benefits).

Contract Termination due to Sanctions: Possible Scenarios

The authors' research and practice in recent years allowed them to identify the following typical situations provoked by sanctions, based on the subjective attitude of the parties affected by them.

Agreement between the Parties

The contracting parties are free to stipulate grounds for unilateral refusal to perform contractual obligations, including inclusion of a party into the sanctions list of a particular jurisdiction, or the indirect impact of sanctions on a party to the contract, like imposition of a sanction against the "domestic" jurisdiction of one of the parties.[12]

For instance, a contract between a Belarusian resident and an Italian resident provides that the imposition of any sanctions against the Republic of Belarus by the United States or the European Union is a stand-alone ground for unilateral withdrawal from the contract, including in the absence of any breaches or culpable actions on the part of the Belarusian resident.

The practice of recent years shows that such conditions are regularly included in the so-called "sanctions clauses" ("clauses on compliance with sanctions restrictions"), not only in contracts with counterparties from jurisdictions "unfriendly" to Belarus, but also in foreign trade contracts with counterparties in neutral jurisdictions

---

(Vienna, 11.04.1980).

12 V. Vabishchevich, *Sanctions as a ground for unilateral refusal to perform the contract.* Available at: https://ilex-private.ilex.by/

(for example, sales contracts between residents of Belarus and Kazakhstan).[13]

However, even in such a case, it is problematic to avoid the negative impact of sanctions on normal economic turnover. The Belarusian exporter or importer must bear in mind that the consequence of such a lawful refusal of a foreign trade contract may be the failure to fulfill other related deals (for example, a Belarusian resident, due to the introduction of sanctions and the refusal of a foreign supplier from the concluded contract, was unable to purchase a component product that was intended for use in the production of the final multi-component product for supply to a State customer), in relation to which sanctions can no longer be recognized as force majeure, since there is no formal obstacle in the form of a sanction prohibition for the performance of that related deal.

Impossibility to Perform the Contract in the Future

If the parties are performing their contractual obligations in good faith at the time the sanctions are imposed, the performance of the obligation affected by the sanctions is usually not yet due (e.g., the sanctions are imposed on March 2, 2022, while the contractual delivery date is December 10, 2023).

In such a situation, the parties may use legal mechanisms allowing them to withdraw from the contract in the event that the other party declares that it is impossible to perform the contract due to sanctions, although there is no formal breach of the contract yet (for example, if a Swedish supplier informs a Belarusian buyer that it will not be able to fulfill warranty obligations in the future with respect to the supplied equipment, the Belarusian buyer, in turn, may lawfully withdraw from the contract, notifying the Swedish counterparty of this, and attempt to obtain warranty service from an alternative provider not affected by sanctions).

As legal justification, the parties may use the provisions of Article 73 of the Vienna Convention or similar provisions of applicable national law.

---

13 The conclusion is based on the authors' practice over the recent years.

Non-performance of Contractual Obligations

One of the main remedies in the event of a material breach of obligations under a contract is the right to withdraw from it. The reasons for the breach of obligations vary and may include bad faith, objective circumstances, actions of third parties, etc. Sanctions, which have become a headache for participants of foreign economic activities, can definitely serve as such a reason and complying with the requirements and terms of the applicable law, giving a party the right to avoid the contract (for example, a contract with a German supplier provides that a breach of obligations to supply goods for more than 50 calendar days entitles the Belarusian buyer to unilaterally withdraw from the contract).

In the absence of special terms in the contract, the parties in those situations typically refer to the provisions of Articles 25, 49(1), 64(1) of the Vienna Convention and similar provisions of national law (e.g. Article 420 of the Civil Code of the Republic of Belarus[14] (hereinafter – the Civil Code)).

Under the Vienna Convention, only a fundamental breach triggers the right of the parties to avoid the contract. Therefore, parties bear the risk that a court / arbitration institution will classify a breach of obligation as merely minor.[15] Hence, while drafting the contract, parties can set forth provisions stating fundamental breaches to directly establish or exclude sanctions as an exemption for non-performance.

It is essential to realize that, unlike the previously discussed scenarios, the likelihood of a direct conflict between the parties and subsequent referral of the dispute to court or arbitration institution is much higher in such a scenario.

For instance, the Polish party failed to fulfil its obligations to deliver the goods due to sanctions, while there were no special conditions for unilateral withdrawal in the contract and the Vienna Convention was applicable. The Belarusian buyer withdrew from the contract with reference to the fundamental breach (i.e. the length of the delay). The Polish resident, while not denying the breach and

---

14 Civil Code of the Republic of Belarus dated 07.12.1998 No. 218-3, last amendments by the Law of the Republic of Belarus dated 22.04.2024 No. 365-3.

15 I. Schwenzer (ed.), P. Schlechtriem and I. Schwenzer, *Commentary on the UN Convention on the International Sale of Goods (CISG)*, (Oxford, 4th ed., 2016), p. 776, para. 2.

duration of the delay, tried to question its fundamental nature under Article 25 of the Vienna Convention, arguing, though unsuccessfully, that the default was related to sanctions restrictions, the imposition of which at the time of contract conclusion it could not and should not have considered.[12]

Sanctions as a Circumstance Beyond One's Control (Force Majeure)

When refusing to perform a foreign trade contract or justifying the reason for the impossibility of its proper fulfilment, the parties often try to qualify the sanctions as force majeure. Article 372 of the Civil Code defines force majeure in the following way: "unless otherwise provided for by the legislation or contract, a person who has failed to fulfill an obligation or has fulfilled it improperly in the course of entrepreneurial activity shall be liable unless he proves that the proper fulfillment of the obligation is impossible due to **force majeure**, i.e. extraordinary and unavoidable circumstances under the given conditions."

Foreign trade contracts, even if not governed by Belarusian law, often stipulate that proven force majeure is indeed considered as a legitimate ground both for exemption from civil liability for breach of contract as well as for unilateral termination of the contract, typically if such force majeure lasts long enough.[16]

Issues related to exemption from liability are governed by Article 79 of the Vienna Convention, although the words "circumstances beyond one's reasonable control" or "force majeure" do not appear in the literal wording of this article. The following prerequisites are necessary for its successful application:

- there must be a party that fails to fulfil any of its obligations;
- the default must be caused by an impediment beyond that party's control;
- the party could not reasonably have been expected to take the impediment into account when entering into the contract or to avoid or overcome the impediment or its consequences.

---

16 Usually not less than 60 days.

State interventions (*faits du prince*) preventing performance generally lie outside of the parties' sphere of control. Nevertheless, in various jurisdictions the approach to this issue differentiates and often depends on the foreseeability at the time of the foreign trade contract conclusion. Therefore, such state regulatory measures as quotas, export or import bans, rationing of goods, exchange controls, and trade bans will not always qualify for the exemption under Article 79 of the Vienna Convention.[17]

It is important to note that Article 79 of the Vienna Convention does not refer to the termination of a contract as a consequence of force majeure. Nevertheless, contracting parties in the so called "force majeure clause" can determine more flexible legal consequences than Article 79 does.[18] The contract may provide for a wide variety of grounds and consequences for termination of the contract due to the occurrence of force majeure circumstances, their duration, confirmation procedure, etc. (e.g. the right to unilaterally terminate the contract arises for the party not under the influence of force majeure circumstances).

For example, a contract between a Belarusian supplier and a French buyer may include a condition that "if force majeure continues for more than 3 months, each Party is entitled to unilaterally terminate this contract with written notice to the other Party. Neither Party shall have the right to claim damages in such case. "

Special attention should be paid to the legal grounds for the termination of obligations due to force majeure.

For example, under Article 387(1) of the Civil Code "if because of the issuance of an act of a state body the performance of an obligation becomes impossible wholly or partially, the obligation shall terminate wholly or in respective part. The parties which have incurred losses as a result thereof shall have the right to demand compensation in accordance with the legislation."

The concept of *force majeure* must also be distinguished from the concept of termination of a contract due to a *material change of circumstances*.

---

17 I. Schwenzer (ed.), P. Schlechtriem and I. Schwenzer, *Commentary on the UN Convention on the International Sale of Goods (CISG)*, (Oxford, 4th ed., 2016), p. 1137, para. 18.

18 Ibid., p. 1152, para. 58.

Neither the term "hardship" nor "change of circumstances" is used in the Vienna Convention. The parties may expressly or impliedly agree upon the allocation of the risk of events leading to hardship, relevant threshold of hardship, and remedies to which the aggrieved party may be entitled.[19]

In accordance with the Advisory Council Opinion No. 20 to the Vienna Convention, hardship situations are governed by Article 79, as well as general principles underlying the Vienna Convention, such as reasonableness and duty to cooperate (e.g., Articles 39, 46, 48 and 54), which may be taken into account in the context of hardship.[20]

Under Article 421(1) of the Civil Code "a material change of circumstances from which the parties proceeded when concluding a contract shall be a ground for the change or termination thereof unless otherwise provided by the contract or it arises from the essence thereof. A change of circumstances shall be deemed to be material when they have changed such that if the parties could reasonably foresee this, the contract would not have been concluded at all by them or it would have been concluded on significantly differing conditions."

In simple words we speak of force majeure when the fulfilment of obligations is impossible, and of a material change of circumstances when it is still possible, but extremely unfavorable and inconvenient for the performing party.

For instance, a ban on the sale of metal can be considered as force majeure if it arose after the conclusion of the contract and made it impossible for the manufacturer to produce goods without the metal that was banned from purchase. However, if such metal can nevertheless be purchased, but at much higher (say twenty times) cost due to introduction of sanctions, then this is not an event of force majeure (the contract is enforceable, the metal can still be purchased). However, it can be potentially qualified as a material change in circumstances if

---

19 S. Kröll, L. Mistelis, P. Perales Viscasillas (eds.), UN Convention on Contracts for the International Sale of Goods (CISG). Commentary, (C.H. Beck, Hart, Nomos, 2011), p. 1088, para. 78; CISG-AC Opinion No. 20, Hardship under the CISG, Rapporteur: Prof. Dr. Edgardo Muñoz, adopted by the CISG Advisory Council following its 27th meeting, in Puerto Vallarta, Mexico on 2–5 February 2020, para. 1.1.

20 CISG-AC Opinion No. 20, Hardship under the CISG, Rapporteur: Prof. Dr. Edgardo Muñoz, adopted by the CISG Advisory Council following its 27th meeting, in Puerto Vallarta, Mexico on 2–5 February 2020, para. 2.2.

the parties could not reasonably foresee this and the interested party could not overcome it (purchase the metal elsewhere at a reasonable [which he expected when concluding the contract] price).[12]

Neither the Vienna Convention nor the Civil Code stipulates that a party is obliged to apply to competent authorities for confirmation of force majeure circumstances, except in cases where this is expressly provided for in legislation or an agreement. At the same time, the parties themselves have the right to specify the procedure for confirming force majeure, and the conclusions of competent authorities are in any case subject to assessment within the framework of judicial and arbitration proceedings.

In Belarus, the authorized organization for certification of force majeure circumstances is the Belarusian Chamber of Commerce (BelCCI). The competence of the BelCCI is defined by a number of regulatory legal acts, the Charter of the BelCCI, as well as its internal local legal acts.[21]

It seems that the tradition of specifying in contracts that the party referring to force majeure must apply to the competent body (usually the national chamber of commerce and industry) is related to the complexity of this issue, the importance of eliminating any abuse and misrepresentation regarding the real reasons for non-fulfillment of obligations, and the serious consequences of force majeure (release from civil liability, the possibility of initiating the procedure for termination of the contract, unilateral refusal of obligations), etc.

Likely for similar reasons, in practice, Belarusian companies usually strive to obtain from a foreign counterparty referring to force majeure, including sanctions, a certificate from the competent authority at the place where the force majeure circumstances arose.

For example, if a Belarusian company fails to fulfill its obligations towards a Russian counterparty and if this failure was caused by force majeure that arose in Poland for the Polish supplier of a Belarusian company, it is essential for the latter to get from its Polish contract partner an official confirmation (certificate) issued by the competent authority in Poland to verify the event of a force majeure to be later used in settling matters with an unhappy Russian buyer.

---

21 Official website of the Belarusian Chamber of Commerce and Industry. https://www.cci.by/en/ .

A significant number of problematic issues arise in practice when the parties face the need to get documentary prove certifying force majeure circumstances:

A. *Applicable law*

When applying to the BelCCI for a certificate of force majeure, applicants often mistakenly believe that since the BelCCI is competent to issue such certificates, the law of the Republic of Belarus should be applicable to both procedural and substantive matters.

For example, the Belarusian resident, applying to the BelCCI and proving force majeure, refers to the norms of the Belarusian Civil Code, while in the contract the parties agreed to apply Austrian law and expressly excluded the application of the Vienna Convention.

The practice of reviewing force majeure certificates issued by foreign authorities also shows that such authorities often ignore the law applicable to a foreign trade contract (for example, an authorized body in one of European Union's countries issued a force majeure conclusion to an EU resident, referring to the regulations of the relevant EU country, although in the contract the parties defined the legislation of the Republic of Belarus as the applicable law).

Paragraph 3 of Article 401 of the Civil Code of the Russian Federation (hereinafter – Civil Code of Russia) is almost identical to paragraph 3 of Article 372 of the Belarusian Civil Code, with the exception of one important addition, namely: "... Such circumstances [force majeure] shall not be referred, in particular, the breaches of obligations on the part of the debtor's counterparties, or the absence on the market of commodities, indispensable for the discharge, or the absence of the monetary funds at the debtor's disposal."[22]

That is of particular importance for regular cases when "a breach of obligations by the debtor's counterparties" is directly related to sanctions restrictions and has direct impact down the whole international "chain" up to the ultimate victim.

Thus, the approaches laid down in the national legislation and the Vienna Convention in relation to the termination of a contract and release from liability are similar, but not identical and may have

---

22 Civil Code of the Russian Federation dated 30.11.1994 No. 51-ФЗ, last amendments by the Federal Law of the Russian Federation dated 08.08.2024 No. 237-ФЗ.

important, even fundamental differences. Business entities must keep that in mind, both at the stage of concluding foreign trade contracts (taking into account the optionality of force majeure as a legal institution) and at the stage of proving the force majeure circumstances, including those related to sanctions restrictions.

B. Burden of proof

The party in breach must prove the occurrence of the obstacle, as well as a direct causal relationship. However, frequently applicants, referring to sanctions and asking for their confirmation as force majeure, claim that these circumstances are well known and need no proof.

However, sanctions are not usually plain and straightforward; they are often vaguely formulated and rather comprehensive, have subject regulation, scope of application and effect, as well as a significant number of reservations, including those establishing legal mechanisms for overcoming them (for example, obtaining special licenses or permits), which is extremely important when proving force majeure. The party that refers to force majeure must prove the absence of legal opportunities to overcome it, including constructive attempts to do so (for example, an application for a special permit was submitted, but the authorized body refused to satisfy such an application).

In addition, the direct impact of sanctions on the fulfillment of obligations under the contract must be proven, for example, that "a certain named product" is actually included in the sanctions list or is a dual-use product, etc.

C. Third parties

This issue is directly connected to the burden of proof and very often is absolutely crucial in proving force majeure.

The sanctions restrictions have undoubtedly affected the ability of Belarusian entities to fulfil their obligations under contracts, both foreign and domestic, and can potentially be qualified as force majeure. However, although from the factual point of view such impact is usually obvious, in the legal sense the impossibility or difficulty of fulfilling obligations under a "domestic" contract is often caused by non-fulfilment of obligations under an "external" one, most often by foreign counterparties invoking the sanctions restrictions.

For example, a Belarusian company has entered a supply contract with another Belarusian company and undertaken to supply certain goods. To produce these goods, the Belarusian manufacturer ordered components from a German supplier under a separate foreign trade contract. However, the sanctions imposed by the EU prevented the German supplier from delivery of the goods to the Belarusian buyer. The latter, in turn, was unable to produce the goods and deliver them under the original supply contract.

Thus, force majeure arose for the German company (as the German supplier was prohibited from fulfilling its obligations to the Belarusian buyer) under the foreign trade contract. At the same time, it is important for the Belarusian company to confirm force majeure under a domestic deal – the original supply contract, under which there are no formal prohibitions to perform obligations in the territory of Belarus.

Such a situation may be considered as a breach of obligations by the debtor's counterparty and not recognized as force majeure, since it formally falls under the concept of entrepreneurial risk. In other words, any business entity that establishes various interdependent business relationships assumes obligations to supply goods that are not in its warehouse, but must be produced, including using foreign components, must bear in mind the risks of non-fulfillment of obligations by third parties and the impact of this on the chains of interdependent contracts.

As noted above, Russian law, for example, explicitly provides that force majeure circumstances do not include breach of duty on the part of the debtor's counterparties. Under such a straightforward interpretation and approach, in most "domestic" contracts sanctions may not be regarded as force majeure and create a paradox, when foreign entities that have failed to fulfil a "foreign" trade contract to the detriment of the "domestic" one will be able to invoke sanctions as force majeure and excuse themselves from due performance upon presentation of the force majeure certificate issued by competent foreign authority.

In the authors' opinion, it would be more equitable to allow a debtor to refer to the failure of its counterparty to meet its obligations when such counterparty failed to fulfil the contract due to a confirmed force majeure and the debtor had no reasonable opportunity to overcome encountered challenges (e.g., a German supplier was unable to fulfil its obligations due to force majeure, but a Belarusian buyer-manufacturer had an objective opportunity to purchase component parts from another entity, albeit at a higher but reasonable price). In this case, the circumstance exempting from liability is not the breach of obligations of the debtor's counterparty itself, but force majeure that arose in the territory of a foreign state and had an insurmountable impact on the fulfilment of both "external" and "internal" contracts.

That approach, in our opinion, would be more in line with the purpose of force majeure and the principles of the Vienna Convention. Thus, according to Article 79(2) of the Vienna Convention, if the party's failure is due to the failure by a third person whom he has engaged to perform the whole or a part of the contract, that party is exempt from liability only if:

(a) he is exempt from the liability under Article 79(1); and

(b) the person whom he has so engaged would be so exempt if the provisions of Article 79(1) were applied to him.

The validity of the proposed approach is indirectly indicated by the established practice of confirming force majeure by the competent authorities of the countries where the force majeure circumstances arose, and not the countries where the parties themselves are located.

Over-compliance

A separate problem of foreign trade contracts fulfilment in the sanction context is the so-called *over-compliance*. The Guiding Principles define this phenomenon as "going beyond compliance with sanctions, often to minimize the risk of penalties for inadvertent violations, and/or to avoid reputational risks that can arise from dealing, or having any other nexus, with a State, entity or individual under sanctions, or because the complexity and uncertainty of sanctions, and/or high penalties as a form of sanctions enforcement, make effective compliance too costly or risky."

Even the most prudent participants in foreign economic activity must reckon with the fact that even unfounded suspicions and unmotivated claims for non-compliance with sanctions by national regulators, media or even ordinary laymen can have a highly negative impact on business reputation and financial performance, including shareholder value.

As a result, even when sanctions are objectively absent or legally inapplicable to a particular foreign trade contract, other parties involved, primarily banks, might still be triggered and implement so-called zero-risk or derisking policies, which will create a paradoxical, perverse situation from a legal state point, when "punishment" precedes "violation," which is in fact presumed and may well not exist.

For example, in one of the researched cases, the foreign principal holding a well-known western brand suspected circumvention of sanctions by a Belarusian distributor and immediately terminated the contract and all deliveries of goods, even though they had been pre-paid. Eventually, after several months of investigations and proceedings, all charges were dropped, but it was now too late to resume previously successful commercial relations and deliveries. The former partners were left to deal with the financial consequences and share losses rather than profits. For obvious reasons, the customers of the Belarusian distributor did not rely on luck and the goodwill of the "unfriendly" brand, but quickly and irrevocably switched to its eastern competitors, who were not overcompliant.[12]

As the Guiding Principles emphasize "businesses shall undertake due diligence procedures and methods in interpreting and implementing all requirements, exemptions, exceptions and derogations," the authors agree that such a proactive and informed approach, if indeed implemented by businesses, can help to minimize over-compliance and consequently reduce sanctions pressure.

Bad faith

From the authors' perspective the worst manifestation of sanction interference in the normal course of foreign economic turnover is the deliberate use of a sanction "pretext" by one of the parties to avoid or breach the contract yet not become responsible for its avoidance or non-performance.

Unfortunately, Belarusian practice comes across many cases when, having no legal obstacle to the fulfilment of their contractual obligations (delivery of goods, performance of work, rendering of services or their payment), dishonest contractors refused to do so solely for mercenary reasons (e.g. when there was an opportunity for a more profitable resale or in pursuit of anti-competitive goals) and then attempted to justify themselves, often successfully, by compliance concerns.

The most unpleasant thing in that situation for the affected party is that even having all the legal grounds for bringing the unfair counterparty to justice or forcing them to perform the contract, it may be impossible to exercise and enforce the relevant legal rights in practice, again due to sanctions. Thus, having found itself in a similar situation, a large Belarusian manufacturer tried to apply to a foreign arbitration institution in accordance with the terms of the arbitration clause contained in the contract. However, even after competent and well-known foreign arbitration lawyers with the strictest internal rules were found and agreed to represent the Belarusian claimant, it turned out to be impossible to even apply to the arbitration institution, since, firstly, foreign lawyers were unable to receive their retainer even after the money reached their account in a foreign bank and, secondly, it turned out to be almost impossible to pay the arbitration fee to the account of the international arbitration institution, located in a third state, also "unfriendly" to Belarus.[12]

Conclusion

Summing up, our modest piece of research clearly shows *three main dimensions* of the negative impact of sanctions on the conclusion and execution of foreign trade contracts.

Firstly, even in cases where the parties comply with the terms of the concluded contract, the rules of the applicable law and try to follow in good faith the imperative sanction requirements of national regulators, they have to bear a complex and costly burden of verifying and proving their correctness both at the national and international levels. At a minimum, as a result of this, both parties experience a time-consuming and costly process, which results in an increase in the transaction's cost, to the point where it becomes impractical or irrelevant.

Secondly, a separate problem, duly noted by the Special Rapporteur in the Guiding Principles on Sanctions, Business and

Human Rights (2025), is massive over-compliance, which multiplies the above-mentioned problems many times over, and at each of the numerous layers of practical implementation of a foreign economic transaction, including money transfers, logistics and dispute resolution.

Finally, and this is the saddest, sanctions may provoke and encourage unfair behaviors by contractual parties, which hardly match the declared objectives of sanctions. As for the possible medicines or preventives, while the practice of unilateral introduction of restrictive measures remains, in the authors' opinion, it is impossible to completely neutralize the negative consequences of their introduction. In this case, one can only sympathize with conscientious participants in foreign economic activity and advise them to pay maximum attention to the contract drafting and attempt to forecast "black swans" or at least to set up clear and unambiguous but at the same time flexible algorithms for the events of force majeure provoked by sanctions.

CONTRIBUTORS

ALENA DOUHAN

Professor Alena Douhan (Belarus), Dr. Dr. hab., UN Special Rapporteur on the negative impact of unilateral coercive measures on the enjoyment of human rights (2020–until now), a professor of International Law Department at the Belarusian State University (Belarus). Her teaching and research interests are in the fields of international law, sanctions and human rights law, international security law, law of international organizations, international dispute settlement, and international environmental law. She has authored over 190 publications on various aspects of international law.

JOY GORDON

Joy Gordon is the Ignacio Ellacuría, S.J. Professor of Social Ethics in the Loyola Philosophy Department at Loyola University-Chicago. She teaches and publishes in the areas of social and political philosophy, human rights, international law and global governance, and ethical issues in international relations. She has published extensively on legal and ethical aspects of economic sanctions, including *Invisible War: The United States and the Iraq Sanctions* (Harvard University Press). She has published articles in academic journals including *Ethics and International Affairs, Georgetown Journal of International Law, Le Monde Diplomatique, Yale Journal of International Law, Journal of International Development, Philosophy and Public Policy Quarterly, Yale Journal of International Affairs, Global Governance, Arab Studies Quarterly, Philosophy and Social Criticism, Foreign Policy, Chicago Journal of International Law,* and *Yale Human Rights and Development Law Journal.*

POURIA ASKARY

Ph.D., Associate Professor of International Law, Allameh Tabataba'i University (Iran). Associate Professor of International Law, Allameh Tabataba'i University (ATU). Member of the Executive Council of the Asian Society of International Law (ASIANSIL). Board Member & Secretary General of the Iranian Association for UN Studies (IAUNS). Scientific and Executive Manager of the Iranian Review for UN Studies (IRUNS). Editorial Board Member of the International Law Review Journal (ILR). Lawyer at the Iranian Central Bar Association. Dr. Pouria Askary currently holds the position of Associate Professor of International Law at the Law School of ATU, in addition to his role as Visiting Professor of Law at Islamic Azad University and Tarbiat Modarres University. Mr. Askary's primary interests lie in the fields of International Human Rights Law (IHRL), International Humanitarian Law (IHL), and the International Law of Foreign Investment. He is a prolific author and has published numerous books and articles in these areas. Dr. Askary is also an attorney at law and an arbitrator at the Iran Chamber of Commerce. From 2005 to 2015, he served as a legal advisor for the International Committee of the Red Cross in Iran.

ROBERT WALKER

Robert Walker moved to China in 2018, under China's "High Level Foreign Talents" program, where he is now a Professor in the Jingxi Academy, Beijing Normal University. He was the 2021–2 Joan Shorenstein Fellow, Harvard University and is Professor Emeritus at the University of Oxford where he is also Emeritus Fellow of Green Templeton College. He is a Fellow of the UK Royal Society of Arts and of the Academy of Social Sciences. His research interests include poverty, social security, children's studies, media presentation, policy evaluation and research methodology. He has authored 23 books including *Poverty and the World Order* (Agenda, 2023), *The Shame of Poverty* (OUP, 2014) and *Social policy in a Developing World* (with Rebecca Surender, Edward Elgar, 2013) and over 250 academic articles, research reports and contributions.

RAÚL RODRÍGUEZ RODRIGUEZ

Raúl Rodríguez Rodriguez is a full professor of North American History and International Relations and currently the Director of the Center for Hemispheric and United States Studies at the University of Havana. Mr. Rodríguez heads the National Social Sciences and Humanities Program of Cuba. His research interests include the history of North America, U.S. and Canadian foreign policy, and triangular relations between Canada, United States, and Cuba, and more specifically, the U.S. system of economic sanctions on Cuba. His recent publications on that last topic include: "The U.S. Economic Sanctions on Cuba in the context of the Pandemic COVID-19," in *Ethics and International Affairs,* Carnegie Council for Ethics and International Affairs, December 2020; "Las sanciones económicas de Estados Unidos contra Cuba en la era Trump (2017–2021) en El Legado de Trump en un mundo en crisis," CLACSO siglo XXI editores Buenos Aires 2021; "Las sanciones económicas como pilar de la política de Estados Unidos hacia Cuba a partir de 1959," *Études Caribéennes,* 54, April 2023; and *The Political Economy of Sanctions: The case of Cuba* in *The Routledge Handbook of the Political Economy of Sanctions,* Ksenia Kirkham (Ed.) Routledge 2024.

ALFRED DE ZAYAS

U.S. and Switzerland, Professor at the Geneva School of Diplomacy, former UN Independent Expert on International Order (2012–18), former Secretary of the UN Human Rights Committee, former Chief of the Petitions Section at OHCHR, author of 12 books including *Building a Just World Order* (Clarity Press, 2021) and *The Human Rights Industry* (Clarity, 2023).

NICHOLAS TURNER

Nick Turner is an American lawyer residing in Hong Kong. He advises multinational financial institutions and corporations on all aspects of economic sanctions, anti-money laundering, and anti-bribery and corruption compliance and investigations. His experience includes acting as Managing Associate General Counsel for Financial Crime Legal Advisory at a leading UK-headquartered financial institution and as an attorney in the Hong Kong office of a U.S.-based law firm specializing in advising clients on economic sanctions and related matters at the height of the U.S. government's sanctions targeting Hong Kong. Earlier in his career, he served as a regional sanctions compliance officer for the Asia Pacific region at a U.S.-based bank. In addition to his legal practice, Mr. Turner co-developed and taught, with Dr. John Lee, a course on Sanctions Law and Practice at Hong Kong University, in which students explore the application of complex and sometimes contradictory sanctions laws and regulations to corporate actors.

ATTIYA WARIS

Professor Attiya Waris is the only known Professor of Fiscal Law on the African continent and Kenya's second female full law professor. Her pioneering scholarly work has focused on linking finance and development through taxation, debt, illicit financial flows, and the promotion of human rights and living standards. She currently serves as Chair of the Supervisory Board of the Capabuild Foundation (Netherlands), Managing Editor of the *Journal on Financing for Development* (University of Nairobi), and a member of the Working Group on Debt at the Madrid Club. Professor Waris also holds the UN mandate as Independent Expert on foreign debt and human rights. She has been a founding member of several influential initiatives, including the African Tax Researcher's Network, Tax Justice Network Africa, and the House of Fiscal Wisdom, a Nairobi-based think tank focused on international fiscal architecture.

WEI ZHANG

Dr. Wei Zhang is a Professor of Human Rights Law and Co-Director of the Institute for Human Rights at the China University of Political Science and Law (CUPL). The majority of his publications relate to the rule of law, human rights education, national human rights institutions, business and human rights. Dr. Zhang is the Editor-in-Chief of the *Chinese Journal of Human Rights* (in Chinese language), the Acting Editor-in-Chief of the *Journal of Human Rights* (in English language). He is also the Editor-in-Chief of the English Book Series on *Good Governance and Human Rights*, and Co-Editor-in-Chief of the *Chinese Yearbook on Human Rights* published by the Brill.

XIAOFAN HU

Xiaofan Hu holds a Juris Doctor (J.D.) degree from Vanderbilt Law School. She is currently a Ph.D. candidate at China University of Political Science and Law, focusing on the research of business and human rights. Her scholarly work includes published articles on diplomatic immunity, foreign state immunity and countermeasures against unilateral sanctions. Xiaofan Hu has interned with the Office of Legal Counsel at UN Headquarters in New York, and the Office of the Prosecutor of the UN International Residual Mechanism for Criminal Tribunals in The Hague.

TATSIANA MIKHALIOVA

Dr. Tatsiana N. Mikhaliova is Associate Professor at the Belarusian State University, Faculty of International Relations. Dr. Mikhaliova is author of more than 130 publications and tutorials in International Public Law, and Law of Regional Integration. She was a Visiting Lecturer to the Russian University of Peoples' Friendship, ELGS/RANEPA double degree program contributor. She took part in drafting the Treaty of the EAEU, and is a general councillor to the CIS Economic Court, the Court of the EAEU. Dr. Mikhaliova was an external evaluator to the EACEA, UNDP projects, a consultant to the OHCHR and other UN projects.

GILLES-EMMANUEL JACQUET

Gilles-Emmanuel Jacquet holds a License in Political Science from the University of Geneva and a D.E.A. in European Studies from the European institute of the University of Geneva. G.E. Jacquet worked as an intern for the UNHCR and then for the French Ministry of Justice, the French Embassy to the Republic of Moldova, the Alliance Française de Moldavie, and foreign press agencies at the United Nations in Geneva. He is a lecturer in International Relations in various private universities in Geneva and abroad (Afghanistan, Algeria, Congo, Ivory Coast, Niger), and the Vice-President of the Geneva International Peace Research Institute. He is the author and co-author of various publications, including his book *Histoire du conflit moldo-transnistrien* (Éd. Connaissances & Savoirs, 2017).

MICHAEL SWAINSTON KC

Michael Swainston KC is a barrister at Brick Court Chambers in London and a Bencher at Lincoln's Inn. He is a specialist in international litigation and arbitration, including inter-State cases dealing with human rights in the context of conflict, and bilateral investment cases raising inconsistencies between sanctions and investment protection. Mr. Swainston has an extensive practice in inter-State litigation, international commercial arbitration, investment treaty cases, and substantial domestic litigation. He has particular experience in disputes connected with Russia and former CIS countries and has acted for the Russian Federation in a range of International Courts and Tribunals. Called to the Bar in 1985; Lincoln's Inn (Hardwicke and Denning scholarships); called to the California Bar in 1988 (inactive); KC, 2002. Bencher of Lincoln's Inn. Expert on sanctions and human rights working with the UN Special Rapporteur on Unilateral Coercive Measures. Former Chairman of the International Relations Committee of the Bar of England & Wales. UK delegate to the European Commission "Common Frame of Reference" project.

ALI RASTBEEN

Professor Ali Rastbeen is a geopolitical expert specializing in Iran and Middle Eastern strategic and energy issues. He is the founder and president of the Académie de Géopolitique de Paris and editor-in-chief of the journal *Géostratégiques*. He also serves as President of Horizons University, a private higher education institution in Paris. Professor Rastbeen holds degrees in electrical engineering and biomedical analysis, and he earned doctorates in law and administrative sciences, as well as in information and communication sciences from the University of Paris. He has authored numerous books and articles on geopolitics and regularly organizes international conferences. His teaching and research focus on geopolitical developments, with particular attention to strategic affairs in the Middle East.

AMAL YAZJI-YAKOUB

Professor Amal Yazji-Yakoub, PhD in International Law from Paris Nanterre University (La Sorbonne), is a professor at the Faculty of Law, Department of International Law, Damascus University. She served as Head of the Department of International Law during the periods 2009–2013, 2016–2020, and 2021–2024. Her academic work focuses on international humanitarian law, migration law, and human rights. She is the author of several books in French, including *Introduction aux droits de l'homme* (2014), *La nationalité, droit multidisciplinaire* (2016), and *Droit international humanitaire* (2023). Professor Yazji-Yakoub has also published numerous articles on international legal issues, including gender and migration, Security Council powers, and principles of non-intervention.

FLORIANA POLITO

Floriana Polito currently serves as the Humanitarian and Human Rights Advocacy Officer for Caritas Internationalis in the Geneva delegation to the United Nations. She has extensive professional experience in international human rights law and advocacy, as well as humanitarian policy at the multilateral level. Throughout her career, she has had the privilege of working with a diverse range of stakeholders, including governments, UN agencies, civil society organizations and faith-based partners. She holds a degree from the Geneva Graduate Institute with a focus on international relations and international law and an advanced master of the University of Geneva in European Studies, European Institutions and European Law.

PETER PROVE

Peter Prove is Director of International Affairs at the World Council of Churches (WCC), where he has led the Commission of the Churches on International Affairs (CCIA) since 2014. In this role, he is responsible for WCC's work in peacebuilding, disarmament, human rights, and relations with the United Nations system. Prior to this, he served over 12 years as Assistant General Secretary for International Affairs and Human Rights at the Lutheran World Federation (LWF) and four years as Executive Director of the Ecumenical Advocacy Alliance (EAA). He has held several advisory and leadership positions, including President of the NGO Special Committee on Human Rights (Geneva, 2000–2008), member of the UNCTAD Expert Advisory Group on Sovereign Lending and Borrowing

(2009), member of the UNAIDS International Advisory Group on Universal Access (2011), the World Economic Forum Global Agenda Councils (2012–2014), and the Steering Board of the International Partnership on Religion and Sustainable Development (PaRD) since 2018.

EMMANUEL TRONC

HEKS/EPER Syria Country Office Director. Chemistry engineer with twenty years' experience in the humanitarian & development fields in the Middle East and Latin America, specialized in anti-fraud and anti-corruption interventions. He is currently focal point for the Damascus INGOs forum for sanctions and UCMs related issues, and advisor for local and international organizations, United Nation agencies and researchers. Emmanuel spent nine years in Syria, addressing the negative and counterproductive impact of unilateral coercive measures on the population and the delivery of humanitarian aid through research and publications, as a speaker in international events and briefings, based on mappings, systematic and systemic analyses and conceptual modeling.

VLADISLAV STARZHENETSKIY

Vladislav Starzhenetskiy is an Associate Professor at the Faculty of Law of the National Research University "Higher School of Economics" (HSE), the Academic Director of the HSE Master Program "Law of International Trade and Dispute Resolution" and as the Head of the HSE Laboratory of International Justice. He teaches courses on Economic sanctions, International Economic Law, Regulation of International Trade, Protection of Intellectual Property, etc. His main fields of research interest include private and public international law, the impact of economic sanctions on business relations, jurisdiction of courts, enforcement of foreign court judgments and arbitration awards, intellectual property, State immunity, etc. He is the author of more than 60 articles, chapters, and monographs.

LUPICINIO RODRÍGUEZ

Lupicinio Rodríguez is an international lawyer and legal innovator, known for pioneering the co-branding model in the legal profession during the 1980s. He founded and led the firm Denton Lupicinio, which has played a key role in energy, corporate, and international transactions. He contributed to the liberalization of Spain's energy and industrial sectors, co-authoring 12 foundational studies that shaped legislation on privatization and regulatory reform. His academic contributions include works on corporate governance and financial regulation, including *Las Cajas de Ahorros: Modelo de Negocio, Estructura de Propiedad y Gobierno Corporativo*. He serves as President of SCEVOLA, an association promoting legal ethics, and is a member of the Spanish Chapter of the ICC and the Advisory Board of IOC. With a global network of legal professionals, he continues to advance a "neo-law" model that emphasizes mature talent and local expertise in international legal practice.

JOSÉ LUIS IRIARTE

Professor José Luis Iriarte is a Professor of Private International Law and Jean Monnet Chair on European Union Law. He holds a Doctorate in Private International Law from the Universidad Autónoma de Madrid (1984, *cum laude*), and degrees in Law and Legal-Economic Studies from the University of Deusto. He has lectured widely on international and European law in universities and institutions across Europe, the Americas, and Asia. His research has resulted in numerous monographs, legal commentaries—including co-authored work with judges of the Spanish Supreme Court—and dozens of academic articles. Professor Iriarte has served as legal counsel in major cases before the General Court of the European Union, including representation of the Iranian Offshore Engineering and Construction Company and Dmitry Ovsyannikov. He has also advised international companies such as INECO, Unilever, and Chemo. He is a recognized media commentator on litigation related to Cuban nationalizations and serves as the Spanish Representative of the International Union of Lawyers.

FÁTIMA RODRÍGUEZ

Dr. Fátima Rodríguez is Head of the Criminal Law Department at Lupicinio International Law Firm, where she specializes in high-profile criminal litigation and corporate compliance. She has worked on prominent cases such as *Black Cards*, *Púnica*, *Vitaldent*, and *Isabel II Canal*. In addition to criminal law, she advises companies on the design and implementation of crime prevention systems, including risk mapping, codes of ethics, and anti-corruption policies. Dr. Rodríguez combines her legal practice with academic work: she lectures in the Master's Program in Legal Practice at Garrigues and teaches Legal Theory of Crime at Villanueva University. She holds a PhD in Criminal Law from the Complutense University of Madrid and has a background in clinical psychology, enhancing her specialization in crimes against individuals. She is also an active member of the "What is Law?" Foundation, promoting transparency and the rule of law through advocacy and public engagement.

MARYNA POGIBKO

Maryna Pogibko is an advocate and public international law specialist. Trained as an economist in Ukraine, she later obtained a law degree from BPP University (UK) and passed the UK Bar exams with distinction. She is a member of Lincoln's Inn, the Defence Extradition Lawyers' Forum, the European Criminal Bar Association, and the Odesa Bar Association. Her legal practice at Amadeus Consultancy Limited (London) focuses on defending against state overreach, protecting human rights, and navigating complex cross-border investigations, including those involving INTERPOL. She has represented shipping companies from Eastern Europe and the Middle East in sanctions-related cases. Notably, she served as principal legal advisor in the high-profile case of a Venezuelan Special Envoy, resulting in a presidential pardon by U.S. President Joe Biden in 2023.

DENYS NIENOV

Denys Nienov is an attorney-at-law based in Kyiv and Counsel at Amadeus Consultancy Limited. He holds LL.B. and LL.M. (magna cum laude) degrees in Criminal Law from Taras Shevchenko National University of Kyiv. Since 2013, he has specialized in criminal proceedings in Ukraine and internationally, with a focus on extradition, INTERPOL matters, and legal defence in economic and professional misconduct cases. Mr. Nienov has extensive experience handling pre-trial and trial proceedings, including detention, bail, and asset seizures, as well as representing victims in fraud recovery. His current work includes strategic litigation in complex cross-border matters.

MYKHAILO GRYDZHUK

Mykhailo Grydzhuk is Counsel at Amadeus Consultancy Limited and a specialist in civil law and multi-jurisdictional litigation. He holds LL.B. and LL.M. (magna cum laude) degrees in Civil Law from Taras Shevchenko National University of Kyiv. His career began in the banking sector, where he led high-stakes litigation and debt restructuring. He later advised major IT firms and startups on regulatory and transactional matters. Currently based in London, he provides strategic legal support in complex cross-border disputes for a diverse international clientele.

RAFAT RIZVI

Rafat Rizvi is an investment banking and ESG specialist with over four decades of international experience. He began his career in London in 1982 and has since worked across Singapore, the United States, Switzerland, and Saudi Arabia. His expertise covers global compliance, financial regulation, and sanctions. He is a member of the Association of Certified Sanctions Specialists and the Swiss Chapter of the Association of Certified Fraud Examiners. Rafat is the Founder and Managing Partner of Serendib Capital Limited, a leading London-based firm focused on Blue Carbon and marine ecosystem preservation.

ALEXEY ANISCHENKO

Alexey Anischenko is Partner at Anischenko Laptev, Board member of Chamber of Arbitrators in Minsk, Belarus and VIAC International Advisory Board, Public Advisory Board at the State Customs Committee of the Republic of Belarus, arbitrator, mediator, a senior lecturer at the Belarusian State University. Mr. Anischenko has over twenty years of legal practice with a particular focus on complex international disputes involving state and private companies in such sectors as infrastructure, machinery, TMT, banking, insurance and construction. Acting as counsel and arbitrator, Mr. Anischenko has dealt with major international arbitration rules, including ICC, ICSID, LCIA, RAC, SCC, SIAC, UNCITRAL, VIAC as well as many regional ones, like IAC at the BelCCI and TIAC.

VITALI VABISHCHEVICH

Vitali Vabishchevich, PhD, is Head of the Department of Legal Support and Digital Technology of the Belarusian Chamber of Commerce and Industry (BelCCI), Member of the Presidium of the International Arbitration Court at the BelCCI, Advisory Committee on Entrepreneurship at the Eurasian Economic Commission, Arbitrator, mediator. For the last four years Vitaly was directly responsible for reviewing applications for force majeure in the Republic of Belarus, as well as for sanctions compliance assessment at the BelCCI. He actively speaks and publishes in Belarus and abroad on variety of topics related to international trade and dispute resolution.

INDEX